Business and Human Rights

Between Obligation and Responsibility

Die Veröffentlichung dieses Werkes beruht auf einer Dissertation in der Abteilung Rechtswissenschaft an der Universität Mannheim.

Business and Human Rights

Between Obligation and Responsibility

First Published on 29, August 2025

Written by Jong-Gil Woo

Published by Sechang Publishing Co.
Address Room 602, Kyonggi Building, Kyonggidae-ro 58, Seodaemun-gu, Seoul, 03736, Republic of Korea
Tel 82-2-723-8660 Fax 82-2-720-4579 Email edit@sechangpub.co.kr
Website http://www.sechangpub.co.kr SNS @sechang_official

ISBN 979-11-6684-448-5 93360

Business and Human Rights

Between Obligation and Responsibility

Jong-Gil Woo*
Masters of Law (Korea University)
LL.M. (Harvard Law School)

* Jong-Gil WOO holds an LL.B. and a Master of Law from Korea University in the Republic of Korea, obtained in 1992 and 1994 respectively, as well as an LL.M. from Harvard Law School in 1995. He was called to the NY State Bar in 2006. The thesis makes extensive use of official UN publications, including public resolutions, reports, general comments, and other guidance documents, such as those from treaty bodies, the Human Rights Council, and the UN Guiding Principles on Business and Human Rights. However, the views expressed herein are those of the author and do not necessarily reflect the views of the United Nations.

Sechang Publishing Co.

Preface

This study was accepted as a dissertation by the University of Mannheim's School of Law and Economics in September 2024. This book owes a primary debt to Professor Dr. Eibe Riedel whose enthusiastic and meticulous supervision, advice and encouragement were an essential element and a firm support from beginning to end. He served as an inspirational, passionate and caring mentor all throughout the years of research and writing. Without his unwavering support, the book would not have seen the light of the day. I should also like to express my deep gratitude to Professor Dr. Hans-Joachim Cremer for his expeditious and critical evaluation of this dissertation. Moreover, I should like to express my appreciation to Mr. Anthony Donnarumma from the OHCHR Library of his unsurpassed research support.

Throughout the time of writing this study I was incredibly lucky to receive continuing moral support from various people, including my beloved friend, Mr. Carlo Dorer, my beloved adoptive nephew, Mr. Marc Adolf who has kindly allowed me to use his photography as the cover of this book, and all my family members. Their boundless love and support were a constant source of inspiration whenever I was in doubt. This work is dedicated to my father and to the loving memory of my mother.

Geneva, August 2025

Table of Contents

List of Abbreviations

ATCA	US Alien Tort Claims Act
BDA	Confederation of German Employers' Associations
BHR	Business and Human Rights
BMAS	German Federal Ministry for Labour and Social Affairs
BMZ	German Federal Ministry for Economic Cooperation and Development
CAT	Convention against Torture and other Cruel, Inhuman or Degrading Treatment or Punishment
CCPR-Committee	Human Rights Committee
CEDAW	Convention on the Elimination of All Forms of Discrimination against Women
CEDAW-Committee	Committee on the Elimination of Discrimination against Women
CERD-Committee	Committee on the Elimination of Racial Discrimination
CESCR-Committee	Committee on Economic, Social and Cultural Rights
CoE	Council of Europe
CRC	Convention on the Rights of the Child
CRC-Committee	Committee on the Rights of the Child
CRPD	Convention on the Rights of Persons with Disabilities
CSOs	Civil Society Organizations
EC	European Commission
ECOSOC	United Nations Economic and Social Council
ED-Committee	Committee on Enforced Disappearances
EJIL	European Journal of International Law
EITI	Extractive Industries Transparency Initiative
EU	European Union
FAO	Food and Agriculture Organization
FIDH	International Federation of Human Rights
GPIL	General principles of international law
GPL	General principles of law
GYIL	German Yearbook of International Law
G7	The Group of Seven
G20	The Group of Twenty

HRC	United Nations Human Rights Council
IAIA	International Association for Impact Assessment
ICCPR	International Covenant on Civil and Political Rights
ICCPR-OP1	Optional Protocol to the International Covenant on Civil and Political Rights
ICCPR-OP2	Optional Protocol to the International Covenant on Civil and Political Rights aiming at the abolition of the death penalty
ICERD	International Convention on the Elimination of All Forms of Racial Discrimination
ICESCR	International Covenant on Economic, Social and Cultural Rights
ICJ	International Court of Justice
ICPPED	International Convention for the Protection of All Persons from Enforced Disappearance
ICRMW	International Convention on the Protection of the Rights of All Migrant Workers and Members of Their Families
ICS	Investment Court System
IFC	International Finance Corporation
ILO	International Labour Organization
ISDS	Investor-State Dispute Settlement
LkSG	Lieferkettensorgfaltspflichtengesetz
MEPs	Members of the European Parliament
MNEs	Multinational Enterprises
MPEPIL	Max Planck Encyclopaedia of Public International Law
NCPs	National Contact Points
NFPs	National Focal Points
NGOs	Non-governmental Organizations
OECD	Organization for Economic Cooperation and Development
OEIGWG	United Nations Human Rights Council Open-ended Intergovernmental Working Group on transnational corporations and other business enterprises with respect to human rights
OHCHR	Office of the United Nations High Commissioner for Human Rights
OP-CAT	Optional Protocol to the Convention against Torture
OP-CEDAW	Optional Protocol to the Convention on the Elimination of All Forms of Discrimination against Women
OP-CRC-AC	Optional Protocol to the Convention on the Rights of the Child on the involvement of children in armed conflict
OP-CRC-IC	Optional Protocol to the Convention on the Rights of the Child

	on a communications procedure
OP-CRC-SC	Optional Protocol to the Convention on the Rights of the Child on the sale of children, child prostitution and child pornography
OP-CRPD	Optional Protocol to the Convention on the Rights of Persons with Disabilities
OP-ICESCR	Optional Protocol to the International Covenant on Economic, Social and Cultural Rights
PANTHER	Principles of participation, accountability, non-discrimination, transparency, human dignity, empowerment of discriminated persons and the rule of law and redress of grievances
SDGs	Sustainable Development Goals
SOEs	State-Owned Enterprises
TNCs	Transnational Corporations
UDHR	Universal Declaration of Human Rights
UK	United Kingdom of Great Britain and Northern Ireland
US	United States of America
UN	United Nations
UNCTC	United Nations Centre for Transnational Corporations
UNCTAD	United Nations Conference on Trade and Development
UNESCO	United Nations Educational, Scientific, Cultural Organization
UNICEF	United Nations Children's Fund
UN Sub-Commission	United Nations Sub-Commission on the Promotion and Protection of Human Rights
UPR	Universal Periodic Review
VDPA	Vienna Declaration and Programme of Action
WTO	World Trade Organization

Introduction

As the process of globalization has accelerated in the 1990s, the international community has increasingly preoccupied itself with the negative impacts that those fast-paced globalizing processes have had on the enjoyment of human rights. Considering that one distinctive feature of globalization is the exponential growth of corporate power that has far-reaching implications for human rights, it has every reason to pay increased attention to the need to address the impacts of corporate activities on the enjoyment of human rights, in particular those negative ones. As such, the international community has responded to such a need by focusing its attention on how not only to clarify the *State obligations* to respect, protect and fulfil human rights in relation to business activities, but also to clarify the content of the *Corporate responsibility* and/or to establish the *Corporate obligation* to respect human rights at the international level, notably that of transnational corporations that have been increasingly implicated in human rights violations.[1]

Against this background, the past decades have seen a proliferation of international human rights standards on business and human rights,

---

1 Susan Marks and Andrew Clapham, International Human Rights Lexicon (Oxford University Press, 2005); Stéphanie Bijlmakers, Corporate Social Responsibility, Human Rights, and the Law (Routledge, 2009), in particular Chapter 1.

which aims at addressing the negative impacts of business activities on the enjoyment of human rights. Of the most prominent is the UN Guiding Principles on Business and Human Rights (the United Nations Protect, Respect and Remedy Framework), which constitutes "*Combination/zebra* standards"[2] on business and human rights, as it lays out the existing *State obligation* to protect from corporate human rights abuse, as well as the *Corporate responsibility* to respect human rights as an emerging international human rights standard. In parallel, the international community, in particular through the work of treaty monitoring bodies, has continued with its efforts to provide a clearer understanding and clarification of the *State obligations* to respect, protect and fulfil human rights in relation to business activities under the existing international human rights law regime. Other international protection mechanisms, including the Special Procedures and the Universal Periodic Review of the United Nations Human Rights Council have also addressed issues related to business and human rights within the *modus operandi* of the respective mechanisms.

The thesis has the triple purposes: firstly, it seeks to examine and identify the existing international human rights norms and standards that could serve as the normative bases for the *State obligations* to respect, protect and fulfil human rights in relation to business activities under the current international human rights law regime, which will, in turn, help clarify the specific content of such *State obligations* with the aim of assisting States in meeting those international obligations by effectively addressing the negative impacts[3] of business activities on the enjoyment of human rights. Considering

---

2 Eibe Riedel, 'Standards as Sources,' German Yearbook of International Law (GYIL) vol. 63 (220), 369-417.

3 Negative impacts of business activities such as environmental pollution, forced evictions, violations of the right to personal security in the extractive industries, obstruction of justice through bribing judicial officials, allegations of encroachments on the lands and territories of Indigenous Peoples without obtaining their prior, free and informed consent, human rights violations of human rights defenders, including environmental defenders have been on the rise and widely reported. For the details of some human rights cases, see, Human Rights Translated 2.0: A Business Reference Guide (HR/PUB/17/1 (UN), 2017). It can be accessed at the following

that the international human rights protection system, in particular the United Nations treaty bodies have played a critically important role in clarifying the content of the *State obligations* to respect, protect and fulfil human rights in relation to business activities through issuing interpretative guidance on relevant treaty provisions, which are called "General Comments" or "General Recommendations", the thesis also seeks to make an analysis of those General Comments with a view to further clarifying the normative contours of the *State obligations* to respect, protect and fulfil human rights in relation to business activities; secondly, it seeks to provide an overview of ongoing efforts to clarify the content of the *Corporate responsibility* to respect human rights as part of an emerging international "*Combination/zebra* standard" on business and human rights, as well as those efforts to establish it as an obligation on the international law plane either through interpretation of the existing international human rights law regime or through codifying it in a treaty as a treaty norm. A host of the existing international standards aimed at strengthening responsible business conduct by affirming the *Corporate responsibility* to respect human rights such as the OECD Guidelines for Multinational Enterprises and the ILO Tripartite Declaration of Principles Concerning Multinational Enterprises and Social Policy will also be analyzed in order to demonstrate that these existing standards have now been brought into convergence with the currently most authoritative international standards on the *Corporate responsibility* to respect human rights elaborated in the UN Guiding Principles on Business and Human Rights. The study will seek to further analyze the ongoing trajectory of the United Nations Human Rights Council treaty-making process on business and human rights, whose aim is to establish an internationally legally binding instrument to regulate, in international law, the activities of transnational corporations and other business enterprises; and thirdly, the thesis seeks to examine an array of national measures that "*must*" and "*should*" be taken by States in order to

---

OHCHR webpage: https://www.ohchr.org/sites/default/files/Documents/Publications/HRT_2_0_EN.pdf (Accessed as of 12 August 2024).

meet their international obligations to respect, protect and fulfil human rights in relation to business activities, including legislative, administrative, policy and judicial measures with an argument being made that the strengthened national human rights protection system is the key not only to meeting their international obligations to respect, protect and fulfil human rights in relation to business activities, but also to ensuring that the international-level *Corporate responsibility* to respect human rights is translated into a concrete national-level legal obligation ensuring accountability for corporate human rights abuse. In so doing, the study focuses its attention on examining legislative measures that have already been taken or are being contemplated at the country and regional levels, in particular mandatory human rights/environmental due diligence law. The essence of such mandatory human rights/environmental due diligence law is to obligate business enterprises to conduct human rights and environmental due diligence in their operations and in the supply chain to identify, prevent and mitigate potential adverse human rights impacts, as well as to redress any actual human rights harms caused by their operations or those that they contributed to, or that are directly linked to their operations, products or services by business relationships. The study concludes that these legislative developments have significantly contributed to clarifying the core content of the *Corporate responsibility* to respect human rights, both in law and in practice, as a national-level legal obligation at a minimum, largely in line with the most authoritative international human rights standards (*Combination/zebra* standards) on business and human rights (the United Nations Guiding Principles on Business and Human Rights).[4]

Whereas the study is anchored in the clear distinction between the *State obligations* to respect, protect and fulfil human rights in relation to

---

4 Guiding Principles on Business and Human Rights: Implementing the United Nations Protect, Respect and Remedy Framework, Office of the United Nations High Commissioner for Human Rights, UN Publication, HR/PUB/11/04. It can be accessed at the following webpage: https://www.ohchr.org/en/publications/reference-publications/guiding-principles-business-and-human-rights. (Accessed as of 8 September 2024).

business activities and the *Corporate responsibility* to respect human rights under the current international human rights law regime, it also concludes that the existing international human rights standards on business and human rights (*Combination/zebra* standards on business and human rights)[5] as one of the sources of international law[6] serve multiple purposes. These include interpretative aide for clarifying the content of the *State obligations* to respect, protect and fulfil human rights in relation to business activities, in particular the State duty/obligation to protect and recommendations and/or policy options to be taken, as well as for clarifying the content of the emerging international standards on the *Corporate responsibility* to respect human rights on the international law plane. In particular, the current most authoritative and comprehensive international standards on business and human rights, namely the UN Guiding Principles on Business and Human Rights (*Combination/zebra* standards on business and human rights) provide for benchmarks/yardsticks, against which it can be measured as to whether States and business enterprises meet their respective *State obligation* to protect from corporate human rights abuse, and the *Corporate responsibility* to respect human rights.

The study also identifies the content of human rights due diligence as one of the main components of the *Corporate responsibility* to respect human rights, *i.e.,* business enterprises should conduct human rights due diligence in their own operations and in the supply chain. As such, it is concluded that mandating human rights due diligence in the context of the *Corporate responsibility* to respect human rights is an essential means for business enterprises "*to proactively manage potential and actual adverse human rights impacts with which they are involved.*"[7] Human rights due diligence

---

5 Ibid.

6 For a general exposition on sources of international law, see Rüdiger Wolfrum, 'General International Law, Principles, Rules, and Standards', Max Planck Encyclopedia for Public International Law (2010).

7 The United Nations Working Group on Business and Human Rights, 'Corporate human rights due diligence – identifying and leveraging merging practices,' (Accessible at: Corporate human

comprises four core elements: firstly, it aims to identify and assess actual or potential adverse human rights impacts (human rights impacts assessment) that the business enterprise may directly cause or contribute to through its own activities, or which may be linked to its operations, products or services by its business relationships; secondly, the business enterprise should integrate findings from such human rights impact assessments across relevant company processes and take action appropriate to its involvement in the particular impact; thirdly, the business enterprise should track the effectiveness of measures and processes to address adverse human rights impacts in order to *know* if they are working; and fourthly, the business enterprise should communicate on how impacts are being addressed and *show* stakeholders that there are adequate policies and processes in place (the *know and show* doctrine).[8]

The study further concludes that despite the fact that there is limited added-value in concluding an international treaty on business and human rights unless the direct obligation is imposed on business enterprises to respect human rights on the international law plane, these currently existing international "*Combination/zebra* standards" on business and human rights can provide an inspiration for codifying the international standard on the *Corporate responsibility* to respect human rights into a treaty norm, which is currently being deliberated under the auspices of the United Nations Human Rights Council.

---

rights due diligence – identifying and leveraging emerging practices | OHCHR). (Accessed as of 21 February 2025). See also John Ruggie, 'Protect, Respect and Remedy: a Framework for Business and Human Rights,' Report of the Special Representative of the Secretary-General on the issue of human rights and transnational corporations and other business enterprises, UN Doc., A/HRC/8/5, para. 25. It can be accessed at the following webpage: https://documents.un.org/doc/undoc/gen/g08/128/61/pdf/g0812861.pdf. (Accessed as of 21 February 2025). Due diligence is defined as "*the diligence reasonably expected from, and ordinarily exercised by, a person who seeks to satisfy a legal requirement or discharge an obligation*". Black's Law Dictionary, 8th edition (2006).

8 Ibid. See also supra note 4, Guiding Principles on Business and Human Rights: Implementing the United Nations Protect, Respect and Remedy Framework, Office of the United Nations High Commissioner for Human Rights, UN Publication, HR/PUB/11/04. Principles 11-24.

Part 1

Fundamentals of the "State Obligation" to Respect, Protect and Fulfil Human Rights in Relation to Business Activities and the "Corporate Responsibility" to Respect Human Rights

Chapter 1: Legal Bases

While States have the primary obligations/duties to respect, protect and fulfil the human rights of the people under their territory and/or jurisdiction, non-state actors such as business enterprises also bear the responsibility to respect human rights.[9] Regard must therefore be had to the clear distinction between the "*State obligation/duty*" to respect, protect and fulfil human rights in relation to business activities and the "*Corporate responsibility*" to respect human rights under the current international human rights law regime.[10] The State *obligations/duties* to respect, protect and fulfil

9 For the argument that business enterprises have the international obligation to respect human rights, see David Weissbrodt and Muria Kruger, 'Norms on the Responsibilities of Transnational Corporations and Other Business Enterprises with Regard to Human Rights,' 97 Am. J. Int'l L. 901 (2003), available at: https://scholarship.law.umn.edu/cgi/viewcontent.cgi?article=1247&context=faculty_articles (Accessed as of 12 August 2024); Andrew Clapham, Human Rights Obligations of Non-State Actors, Oxford University Press (2006), 59-107.

10 For a thorough exposition of sources of international law, supra note 2, Eibe Riedel, 'Standards as Sources,' German Yearbook of International Law (GYIL) vol. 63 (220), 369-417. Some academicians argue that non-state actors, including armed non-state groups and business enterprises, are also subject to international law obligation under customary international law. See also supra note 9, Andrew Clapham, Human Rights Obligations of Non-State Actors, Oxford University Press (2006), pp. 59-107.

human rights in relation to business activities is firmly established as treaty norms under various international human rights treaties, which serves as a source of international law. On the contrary, the precise meaning and content of the *Corporate responsibility* to respect human rights is still being shaped up and understood through the development of *Combination/zebra* standards on business and human rights such as the United Nations Guiding Principles on Business and Human Rights.[11]

Before identifying the legal bases for the *State obligations* to respect, protect and fulfil human rights in relation to business activities, as well as the *Corporate responsibility* to respect human rights as an international standard, the situation of the individual, including juridical persons such as business enterprises in public international law deserves a brief overview. The varying scholarly positions/understandings on how to posit the status and the legal position of the individual in public international law have closely linked to the interpretative evolution of what is public international law. Traditionally, international law scholars understood that international law was the legal system that governed the relations among nations, which assumed that States/nations were the only subjects of international law.[12]

However, in the twentieth century, particularly after World War II, the understandings and positions on the situation/status/role of the individual in public international law have significantly changed, mainly due to the increased importance of humanitarian values in the process of development and creation of international legal rules.[13] As such, a multitude of international human rights treaties have been concluded that had created the international

11 Supra note 2, Eibe Riedel, 'Standards as Sources,' German Yearbook of International Law (GYIL) vol. 63 (220), 369-417.

12 Carl A. Norgaard, The Position of the Individual in International Law 11 (1962). (Requoted from note 10 of infra note 13, Alexander Orakhelashvili, 'The Position of the Individual in International Law,' California Western International Law Journal vol. 31, 241-276, p. 3.

13 Alexander Orakhelashvili, 'The Position of the Individual in International Law,' California Western International Law Journal vol. 31, 241-276, p. 1.

rules on human rights protection of individuals, starting from the Charter of the United Nations.[14] In addition to these treaty obligations to protect human rights of individuals under international human rights treaties, it has been argued that the rights of the individual in international law are recognized as part of customary international law, and some of which constitute part of *ius cogens*.[15]

When it comes to the status of the corporation under public international law, the debate has occurred, mainly due to the conceptual uncertainty caused by the doctrine of international legal personality.[16] Corporations were not initially treated as "subjects" of international law. Contrastingly, a more policy oriented approach has developed that allows for certain rights and obligations of corporations under international law along with the acceptance of the criminal liability of corporations for international crimes such as war crimes or crimes against humanity, despite the fact that corporations have been excluded from the jurisdiction of the International Criminal Court.

The recent policy oriented approach argues that transnational corporations have the legal personality under public international law as participants in the process of international law. As such, they can "*make*

---

14 Relevant provisions on protection of human rights can be found in Articles 1(3) and 56 of the Charter of the United Nations.

15 See supra note 13, Alexander Orakhelashvili, 'The Position of the Individual in International Law,' California Western International Law Journal vol. 31, 241-276, pp. 1-2. See also Theodor Meron, Human Rights and Humanitarian Norms as Customary Law 48 (1989); Lauri Hannikainen, Peremtory Norms (Jus Cogens) in International Law: Historical Development, Criteria, Present Status 425-521 (1988). (Requoted from note 5 of Alexander Orakhelashvili, 'The Position of the Individual in International Law,' California Western International Law Journal vol. 31, 241-276, p. 2).

16 Peter T Muchlinski, 'Corporation sin International Law,' Max Planck Encyclopedia of Public International Law in R Wolfrum (ed.) (2010), para. 6. It can be accessed at the following webpage: https://opil.ouplaw.com/display/10.1093/law:epil/9780199231690/law-9780199231690-e1513. (Accessed as of 5 March 2025). See also R Portmann, *Legal Personality in international Law* (CUP Cambridge 2010), pp. 280-81; J Alvarez, 'Are Corporations "Subjects" of International Law?' (2011) 9 Santa Clara Journal of International Law 1-35.

claims across State lines with the aim of maximizing certain values such as, for example, fairness and predictability in international business transactions."[17] One scholar of international law has argued that the formal legal status of the corporation is irrelevant as the actions of corporations result in legal consequences at the international level.[18] The thesis subscribes to this policy-oriented approach as there is a strong need to recognize that corporations are important participants in the process of international law that have certain claims and responsibilities on the international law plane.

As emphasized at the outset of this chapter, a clear distinction must be made between *the State obligation* to protect from corporate human rights abuse and *the Corporate responsibility* to respect human rights under international human rights law. "Obligation/duty" and/or "accountability" are being interchangeably used with "responsibility" in some human rights documents, including UN documents. In the present thesis, "obligation/duty/accountability" is restrictedly being used to refer to the legal obligation owed to "duty-bearers" under international human rights law, the main of which is States(Governments), whereas "responsibility" refers to the expectations that society has of business enterprises, not as a legal obligation, where their activities can have the negative impacts on the enjoyment of human rights by various stakeholders, including their own workers, sub-contractors, and more widely consumers, and the general population, in particular those populations such as Indigenous Peoples, whose rights can be affected by corporate activities, for instance, those in the mining and extractive industry.

As such, the *State obligation/duty* to protect from corporate human rights abuse is an essential part of the *State obligations* to respect, protect and fulfil the human rights of people under their territories and/or jurisdictions.

---

17 Ibid., para. 8. See also R Higgins, *Problems and Process: International Law and How We Use It*, (Clarendon Oxford 1994), at p. 50.

18 Supra note 9, Andrew Clapham, Human Rights Obligations of Non-State Actors, Oxford University Press (2006), at p. 80.

Such *State obligation/duty* to protect requires States to protect people from their human rights' being infringed by third parties, including business enterprises, as explained below in the duty typology.[19] On the contrary, except for some cases of international crimes such as war crimes, crimes of genocide, and crimes against humanity, business enterprises bear no direct legal obligation to respect human rights on the international law plane. Accordingly, business enterprises are merely expected to respect human rights as an organ of society having specialized functions, i.e., *the Corporate responsibility* to respect human rights.

Under international human rights law, States have the following duties/obligations (the typology of duty): the duty to respect; the duty to protect; and the duty to fulfil.[20] The duty to respect requires that States as primary duty-bearers not infringe on the enjoyment of human rights by rights-holders. The duty to protect requires that States take the necessary legislative, administrative, policy and judicial measures to protect rights-holders under their territory and/or jurisdiction from human rights abuses by third parties, including both natural and juridical persons such as business enterprises. This duty to protect can be extended to apply to corporate human rights harms caused by business enterprises extraterritorially (in host States) beyond the territory where business enterprises are registered as their Headquarters (home States).[21] The duty to fulfil requires that States take the necessary actions to facilitate, promote and provide for human rights: the duty to facilitate requires that States take positive measures to assist rights-holders to enjoy their human

---

19 See infra note 20.

20 For a general exposition of the duty typology, see Chapter 3 of Walter Kälin and Jörg Künzli (Eds.), The Legal Nature of Human Rights Obligations, Oxford University Press (2009), pp. 77-120.

21 With respect to the extraterritorial obligation under the State duty to protect, the United Nations treaty bodies generally posit that the State duty to protect extends its scope of application beyond the State border as it applies to areas within their power or effective control. See John Ruggie, 'Report of the Special Representative of the Secretary-General on the issue of human rights and transnational corporations and other business enterprises,' UN Doc., A/HRC/4/35, para. 15.

rights; the duty to promote obliges States to take steps to ensure that there is appropriate education and public awareness concerning their rights; and the duty to provide obliges States to provide for rights when rights-holders are unable to realize the rights themselves on grounds reasonably considered to be beyond their control.[22]

Per contra, considerable theoretical debates exist as to whether business enterprises have the obligation/duty to respect human rights on the international law plane. While some scholars advocate for the concept of the *Corporate obligation* to respect human rights on the international law plane,[23] the prevailing view is that currently under international human rights law, business enterprises have only the responsibility, not the obligation/duty, to respect human rights. More precisely, non-state actors such as business enterprises are not subject to legal obligation under international human rights law (public international law) except for the fact that they are also subject to legal obligation under customary international law and *ius cogens*. For instance, non-state actors are subject not to inflict torture, freedom from which is an integral part of a peremptory norm (*ius cogens*).

However, some scholars have interpreted that the Preamble[24] of the

---

22 Henry Shue, Basic Rights: Subsistence, Affluence and U.S. Foreign Policy, Princeton University Press, 2nd ed., (1996). See also Asbjørn Eide, 'Realization of Social and Economic Rights and the Minimum Threshold Approach,' Human Rights Law Journal, 1989 Vol. 10, No. 1–2, pp. 36–51; Asbjørn Eide, 'The Right to Food as a Human Right,' UN Doc. E/CN.4/Sub.2/1987/23, in particular paras. 66-70; and supra note 16, Chapter 3 of Walter Kälin and Jörg Künzli (Eds.), The Legal Nature of Human Rights Obligations, Oxford University Press (2009), pp. 77-120.

23 Supra note 9, Andrew Clapham, Human Rights Obligations of Non-State Actors, Oxford University Press (2006), pp. 59-107.

24 Preamble of the Universal Declaration of Human Rights, adopted and proclaimed by General Assembly resolution 217 A (III) of 10 December 1948. The General Assembly, "Proclaims this Universal Declaration of Human Rights as a common standard of achievement for all peoples and all nations, to the end that every individual and *every organ of society* (emphasis added), keeping this Declaration constantly in mind, shall strive by teaching and education to promote respect for these rights and freedoms and by progressive measures, national and international, to secure their universal and effective recognition and observance, both among the peoples of

Universal Declaration of Human Rights implies that not only States have the legal obligation to promote and protect the human rights of the people under their territory and/or jurisdiction, but also business enterprises, as an organ of society, have the international obligation to respect human rights, which led to the theory/interpretation that the "*Corporate responsibility*" to respect human rights actually means the obligation/duty to respect human rights on the international law plane.[25] In this vein, Professor Andrew Clapham has also promoted the idea of individuals' having certain "*international civil law obligations*" as follows:

> "*If we do not want the development of international law to stagnate we should perhaps admit the progressive idea that individuals have, in addition to these rights and criminal law obligations, certain international civil law obligations; this step could help to build an international community which properly recognizes the role of the individual in international law.*"[26]

It is submitted that while private persons (both natural persons (individuals) and juridical persons such as business enterprises) have some capacities that can be considered to be the participants (subjects) of international law, including by holding human rights and being subject to international criminal obligations (under exceptional circumstances based on customary international law, *ius cogens*, and general principles of international law), business enterprises do not have the international law obligation to respect human rights on the international law plane unlike States have the international obligations to

---

Member States themselves and among the peoples of territories under their jurisdiction."

25 Supra note 9, David Weissbrodt and Muria Kruger, 'Norms on the Responsibilities of Transnational Corporations and Other Business Enterprises with Regard to Human Rights,' 97 Am. J. Int'l L. 901 (2003), available at: https://scholarship.law.umn.edu/cgi/viewcontent.cgi?article=1247&context=faculty_articles (Accessed as of 12 August 2024); Andrew Clapham, Human Rights Obligations of Non-State Actors, Oxford University Press (2006), 59-107.

26 Andrew Clapham, 'The Role of the Individual in International Law,' The European Journal of International Law (EJIL) (2010), Vol.21 No. 1, pp. 25-30, at p. 30.

respect, protect and fulfil human rights in relation to business activities.

The *Corporate responsibility* to respect human rights means that business enterprises *should* have in place policies and processes appropriate to their size and circumstances, including a policy commitment to meeting their *Corporate responsibility* to respect human rights; a human rights due diligence process aimed at identifying, preventing, mitigating and accounting for how they address human rights impacts; and processes enabling remediation of any adverse human rights impacts caused by or contributed to, and those that are directly linked to their operations, products or services by their business relationships. This *Corporate responsibility* refers to all internationally recognized human rights, and to all business enterprises, regardless of their size, sector, operational context, ownership and structure.[27]

There have been two contrasting approaches when it comes to the identification of the scope of application of the *Corporate responsibility* to respect human rights at the international level. "The Norms on the Responsibilities of Transnational Corporations and Other Business Enterprises With Regard to Human Rights" (hereinafter referred to as "the Norms") developed by the former UN Sub-Commission on the Promotion and Protection of Human Rights have listed a limited set of rights that can be impacted by the activities of business enterprises with attaching corresponding *duties* on business enterprises at the international level while using such undefined concepts as "*primary obligations*" of States versus "*secondary obligations*" of business enterprises and "corporate sphere of influence."[28] Accordingly, the Norms established that business enterprises

---

27 Supra note 4, Guiding Principles on Business and Human Rights: Implementing the United Nations Protect, Respect and Remedy Framework, Office of the United Nations High Commissioner for Human Rights, UN Publication, HR/PUB/11/04, Principles 11-24.

28 Supra note 7, John Ruggie, 'Protect, Respect and Remedy: a Framework for Business and Human Rights,' Report of the Special Representative of the Secretary-General on the issue of human rights and transnational corporations and other business enterprises, UN Doc., A/HRC/8/5, paras. 51-53. Para. 51 provides for a detailed explanation with regard to these

also bear the *international obligation* to respect human rights (a limited set of human rights listed in the Norms), which had sparked intense debates and eventually led to the result that the then UN Commission on Human Rights did not endorse the Norms. Contrary to this approach, the late Special Representative of the Secretary-General on the issue of human rights and transnational corporations and other business enterprises, Mr. John Ruggie, advocated for the approach that should acknowledge that the activities of business enterprises have impact on the enjoyment of all human rights thus necessitating to define the specific *responsibilities* of companies with regard to all human rights.[29]

In addition, there already exist an array of international human rights norms and standards, including *Combination/zebra* standards on business and human rights relevant to addressing the impacts of the activities of business enterprises, in particular transnational corporations (multinational enterprises), on the enjoyment of human rights, which can serve as legal bases for the *State obligation/duty* to respect, protect and fulfil human rights in relation to business activities, but also for the *Corporate responsibility* to respect human rights by business enterprises.

A. Legal Bases

I. International Human Rights Norms and Standards

There currently exist 9 core international human rights treaties: the International Convention on the Elimination of All Forms of Racial Discrimination (ICERD); the International Covenant on Economic, Social and Cultural Rights (ICESCR) and the Optional Protocol to ICESCR (OP-

---

attempts and debates, particularly in regard to the Norms on Business and Human Rights by the then UN Sub-Commission on the Promotion and Protection of Human Rights.

29 Ibid.

ICESCR); the International Covenant on Civil and Political Rights (ICCPR) and the Optional Protocol to ICCPR (ICCPR-OP1) and the Second Optional Protocol to ICCPR, aiming at the abolition of the death penalty (ICCPR-OP2); the Convention on the Elimination of All Forms of Discrimination against Women (CEDAW) and the Optional Protocol to CEDAW (OP-CEDAW); the Convention against Torture and Other Cruel, Inhuman or Degrading Treatment or Punishment (CAT) and the Optional Protocol to CAT (OP-CAT); the Convention on the Rights of the Child (CRC) and the Optional Protocol to CRC on the involvement of children in armed conflict (OP-CRC-AC), the Optional Protocol to CRC on the sale of children, child prostitution and child pornography (OP-CRC-SC) and the Optional Protocol to CRC on a communications procedure (OP-CRC-IC); the International Convention on the Protection of the Rights of All Migrant Workers and Members of Their Families (ICRMW); the Convention on the Rights of Persons with Disabilities (CRPD) and the Optional Protocol to CRPD (OP-CRPD); and the International Convention for the Protection of All Persons from Enforced Disappearance (ICPPED). There also exist a body of international human rights standards, including the Universal Declaration of Human Rights on human rights, as well as those on a vast range of specific thematic human rights issues.[30]

30 For the text of these instruments, see United Nations, Human Rights: A Compilation of International Instruments (2002) (New York/Geneva). See also Gudmundur Alfredsson/Asbjørn EIDE (Eds.), The Universal Declaration of Human Rights – A Common Standard of Achievement (1999) (The Hague); Philip ALSTON (Ed.), The United Nations and Human Rights: A Critical Appraisal (1992) (Oxford); Philip ALSTON/James CRAWFORD (Eds.), The Future of UN Human Rights Treaty Monitoring (2000) (Cambridge); Eibe Riedel, The Universality of Human Rights (original title: *Die Universalität der Menschenrechte)* Christian Koenig/Ralph Alexander Lorz (Eds.), Veröffentlichungen des Walther-Schücking-Instituts für Internationales Recht an der Universität Kiel, Bd. 143, Duncker & Humboldt, Berlin, 2003; Matthew Craven, The International Covenant on Economic, Social and Cultural Rights (1999) (Turku/Abo); Manfred Nowak (2nd revised Ed.), UN Covenant on Civil and Political Rights: CCPR Commentary (2005) (N.P. Engel Verlag); Christof Heyens/Frans Viljoen, The Impact of the United Nations Human Rights Treaties on the Domestic Level (2002) (The Hague); Manfred Nowak, Introduction to the International Human Rights Regime (2003) (Leiden/Boston) 73 ff.; Bertrand Ramcharan, The United Nations High Commissioner for Human Rights: The Challenges of International Protection (2002) (The Hague); Henry J. Steiner/Philip Alston (Eds.),

In addition, regarding the *Corporate responsibility* to respect human rights on the international law plane, the UN Guiding Principles on Business and Human Rights constitutes the primary international standards (*Combination/zebra standards*). In the process of preparing the UN Guiding Principles on Business and Human Rights, the then Special Representative of the Secretary-General on the issue of human rights and transnational corporations and other business enterprises provided a comprehensive mapping of international standards of responsibility and accountability for corporate acts. As such, he suggested "*five clusters of standards and practices governing corporate "responsibility" (the legal, social or moral obligations imposed on companies) and "accountability" (the mechanisms holding them to those obligations).*" They are: *State duty* to protect; *Corporate responsibility* and accountability for international crimes; *Corporate responsibility* for other human rights violations under international law; soft law mechanisms; and self-regulation.[31]

1. The Universal Declaration of Human Rights

At the 1945 San Francisco Conference held to draft the United Nations Charter, a proposal was put forward to prepare a "Declaration on the Essential Rights of Man." However, the proposal was not examined on the grounds that it was not possible to give adequate consideration thereto. The United Nations Charter included the promotion of human rights as one of its purposes. Article 1, paragraph 3 of the UN Charter sets out its objectives as "*to achieve international co-operation in solving international problems of an economic, social, cultural, or humanitarian character, and in promoting and encouraging respect for human rights and for fundamental freedoms for*

International Human Rights in Context: Law, Politics, Morals, Oxford University Press (1996).

31 See supra note 18, John Ruggie, 'Business and human rights: mapping international standards of responsibility and accountability for corporate acts', Report of the Special Representative of the Secretary-General on the issue of human rights and transnational corporations and other business enterprises, UN Doc., A/HRC/4/35, para. 6.

all without distinction as to race, sex, language, or religion." Article 55 (c) of the United Nations Charter also provides that "*with a view to the creation of conditions of stability and well-being which are necessary for peaceful and friendly relations among nations based on respect for the principle of equal rights and self-determination of peoples, the United Nations shall promote universal respect for, and observance of, human rights and fundamental freedoms for all without distinction as to race, sex, language, or religion.*"[32] Furthermore, the United Nations Charter provides the Economic and Social Council (ECOSOC) with the power to "*make recommendations for the purpose of promoting respect for, and observance of, human rights and fundamental freedoms for all.*"[33] In the light of these United Nations Charter provisions, ECOSOC was empowered to set up a commission for the promotion of human rights,[34] which was established in 1946 as the Commission on Human Rights.

The General Assembly, at its first session in 1946, considered a draft Declaration on Fundamental Human Rights and Freedoms, which was transmitted to ECOSOC for reference to the Commission on Human Rights for consideration in its preparation of an international bill of rights.[35] In 1947, the Commission on Human Rights authorized its officers to prepare "*a preliminary draft International Bill of Rights*", whose work was later taken over by a formal drafting committee consisting of 8 members of the Commission on Human Rights. There were different views regarding the form of the bill of rights. The drafting committee decided to prepare two documents: one in the form of a declaration and the other in the form of a

---

32 Eibe Riedel, 'Commentary to Art.55(c) UN-Charter, in Simma (Ed.): The Charter of the United Nations – A Commentary,' (2nd ed.), Oxford University Press, 2002, 34pp.

33 Article 62 (2) of the United Nations Charter.

34 Article 68 of the United Nations Charter: "*The Economic and Social Council shall set up commissions in economic and social fields and for the promotion of human rights, and such other commissions as may be required for the performance of its functions.*"

35 United Nations General Assembly "*Resolution adopted on the Report of the Joint First and Third committee*" UN Doc., A/RES/43(I).

convention. The drafting committee then transmitted draft articles of an international declaration and an international convention on human rights to the Commission on Human Rights. In its second session also in 1947, the Commission on Human Rights established three working groups: one on the declaration, one on the convention, renamed as covenant afterward; and one on implementation.[36] In its third session in 1948, the Commission on Human Rights revised the draft declaration taking the comments received from Governments into account. It however did not have time to consider either the covenant or the measures of implementation. Hence, only the draft declaration was submitted through ECOSOC to the General Assembly meeting in Paris.[37]

On 10 December 1948, the General Assembly adopted the Universal Declaration of Human Rights (UDHR) "*as a common standard of achievement for all peoples and all nations, to the end that every individual and every organ of society, keeping this Declaration constantly in mind, shall strive by teaching and education to promote respect for these rights and freedoms and by progressive measures, national and international, to secure their universal and effective recognition and observance, both among the peoples of Member States themselves and among the peoples of territories under their jurisdiction*," i.e., not as a truly binding treaty.[38]

The UDHR provides for the whole spectrum of human rights, both economic, social and cultural rights, as well as civil and political rights in a single document. It provides for not only the so-called first-generation rights, which are understood to comprise civil and political rights, but also the second-generation rights, namely economic, social and cultural rights. The

---

36 Chapter 1 of Ed Bates, History in International Human Rights Law, (Daniel Moeckli et al eds), Oxford University Press, 2010, pp. 35-37.

37 For the detailed drafting history of UDHR, see Mary Ann Glendon, A World Made New, Random House Trade (First Edition), 2002 and OHCHR Fact Sheet No. 2 (Rev.1), The International Bill of Human Rights.

38 See supra note 21.

main characteristics of the first-generation rights impose obligation on duty-bearers (mostly Governments) to respect such rights, in other words, not to infringe upon the enjoyment of such rights by rights-holders (individuals under the territory and/or under the jurisdiction of States), while the so-called second-generation rights mainly impose positive legal obligation on the Government to promote and fulfil. In this regard, Professor Riedel argued that considering that civil and political rights and economic, social and cultural rights have both dimensions (negative obligation and positive obligation), and that they are inter-dependent, indivisible and inter-related, such a categorization of the first- and second-generation rights may be misleading. Hence, he proposed the use of the term "dimension" instead of "generation" when it comes to referring to the catalogue of all inalienable human rights belonging to all individuals, which ultimately stems from human dignity.[39]

As for the *State duty* to protect from corporate human rights abuse, the UDHR provides a catalogue of the most comprehensive and important standards on international human rights. Most of the rights spelled out in the UDHR, if not in its entirety, are said to have the status of customary international law while some of them have the status of *ius cogens*.[40] In this regard, it is worth noting that there are some debates continuing as to what rights contained in the Universal Declaration of Human Rights have obtained the status of customary international law thus becoming a legally binding source of international law.[41]

When it comes to the *Corporate responsibility* to respect human rights, it is particularly worth noting that the UDHR specifically mentions in its

---

39 Eibe Riedel, 'Reflections on the UN Human Rights Covenants at Fifty,' Archiv des Völkerrechts (AVR) 2016.

40 For a detailed exposition on the status of human rights norms and standards as customary international law or *ius cogens*, see particularly, pp. 68-71 of Chapter 3 of Walter Kälin and Jörg Künzli (Eds.), The Legal Nature of Human Rights Obligations, Oxford University Press, 2009, pp. 77-120.

41 Ibid., Chapter 1.A.I.3-5.

Preamble that "*every organ of society*" shall strive to promote respect for the rights and freedoms contained therein. This provision has led to some scholars' arguing that the Universal Declaration of Human Rights, in effect, provides for a direct legal obligation on business enterprises as "*organ of society*" to respect human rights on the international law plane.[42] However, as noted above, the prevailing view is that only States have the international obligations to respect, protect and fulfil human rights in relation to business activities while business enterprises have only the *Corporate responsibility* to respect human rights under the current international human rights law regime.[43] As a result, it can be said that the UDHR provides for international human rights standards both on the *State obligations* to respect, protect and fulfil human rights in relation to business activities and on the *Corporate responsibility* to respect human rights.

Since its adoption in 1948, the UDHR has continued serving as an inspiration for a large number of subsequent human rights instruments (treaties) both within the United Nations system and other regional systems. It also had a powerful impact for the elaboration of many national constitutions and laws.[44]

2. International Treaties

The beginnings of the Cold War and the prevailing East-West ideological divide led to the failure of States to agree on a legally binding

---

42 See supra note 9. See also 'Norms on Business and Human Rights, the then Sub-Commission on the Promotion and Protection of Human Rights,' UN Doc., E/CN.4/Sub.2/2003/12/Rev.2. It can be accessed at the following webpage: https://documents.un.org/doc/undoc/gen/g03/160/08/pdf/g0316008.pdf. (Accessed as of 12 September 2024); UN Doc., E/CN.4/Sub.2/RES/2003/16. It can be accessed at the following webpage: https://ap.ohchr.org/documents/dpage_e.aspx?si=E/CN.4/Sub.2/RES/2003/16. (Accessed as of 12 September 2024).

43 CESCR-Committee General Comment No. 24 (2017) on State obligations under the International Covenant on Economic, Social and Cultural Rights in the context of business activities, UN Doc., E/C.12/GC/24.

44 See OHCHR Fact Sheet No. 2 (Rev.1), The International Bill of Human Rights.

treaty on international human rights.[45] The group of Western States held the view that civil and political rights were only human rights that were capable of implementation whereas economic, social and cultural rights were not legally enforceable human rights but merely those for policy consideration and programming. On the contrary, the Soviet bloc subscribed to the view that economic, social and cultural rights were equally capable of legal enforcement like civil and political rights. One extreme view argued that economic, social and cultural rights were superior to civil and political rights in terms of an appropriate value hierarchy and in chronological terms.[46] Due to this ideological divide, the Commission on Human Rights only managed to agree on a legally non-binding declaration that encompassed the whole spectrum of human rights, namely the Universal Declaration of Human Rights (UDHR).

The UDHR was subsequently supplemented by two separate legally binding treaties on economic, social and cultural rights (International Covenant on Economic, Social and Cultural Rights-ICESCR) and on civil and political rights (International Covenant on Civil and Political Rights-ICCPR). Even though the UDHR was adopted as a legally non-binding standard (declaration), some scholars argued that most of its provisions obtained the status of customary international law thereby being considered legally binding.[47] It took nearly two

---

45 Professor Eibe Riedel remarked this failure as follows: "*The drafters of the [United Nations] Charter left it to the newly established Commission on Human Rights (CHR) to work out the text of a planned treaty on human rights. By 1948 it became obvious though that rapid agreement on such a treaty was illusory. The beginnings of the Cold War and East-West ideological disputes prevented that*", Supra note 36, Eibe Riedel, 'Reflections on the UN Human Rights Covenants at Fifty,' Archiv des Völkerrechts (AVR) 2016.

46 Supra note 27, see, Chapter 5 of Henry J. Steiner/Philip Alston (Eds.), International Human Rights in Context: Law, Politics, Morals, Oxford University Press (1996), pp. 256-328.

47 See supra note 37; Olivier de Schutter, International Human Rights Law: Cases, Materials, Commentary (2nd edition), Cambridge University Press (2014), p. 63. See also L. Henkin, The age of Rights (New York: Columbia University, 1990), p. 19; N.S. Rodley, 'Human Rights and Humanitarian Intervention: the Case Law of the World Court', International and Comparative Law Quarterly, 38 (1989), at 321, especially. 333; T. Meron, Human Rights and Humanitarian Norms as Customary Law (Oxford: Clarendon Press, 1989); L.B Sohn, 'The Human Rights Law of the Charter', Texas International Law Journal, 12 (1977), 129 at 132-4; H. Hannum, 'The Status of the Universal Declaration of Human Rights in National and International Law', Georgia

further decades for the two international Covenants to be concluded in 1966. The UDHR along with the ICESCR and ICCPR is made up of the Bill of International Human Rights, the bedrock of international normative regime in relation to human rights.

a. International Covenant on Economic, Social and Cultural Rights

The International Covenant on Economic, Social and Cultural Rights provides for a comprehensive list of economic, social and cultural rights, including workers' rights, the right to social security and social protection, the rights related to protection of and assistance to the family, the right to an adequate standard of living, including the rights to food, adequate housing, water and sanitation, the right to health, the right to education, and cultural rights.[48]

When it comes to the *State obligation* to protect from corporate human rights abuse, the International Covenant on Economic, Social and Cultural Rights provides for a fundamental legal basis regarding economic, social and cultural rights. The *State duty* to protect from corporate human rights abuse obligates States to take all necessary legislative, administrative, policy and judicial measures to prevent, mitigate and redress human rights violations by third parties, including juridical persons such as business enterprises from being committed.

Journal of International and Comparative Law, 25 (1995-1996), 287 (Requoted from Olivier de Schutter, International Human Rights Law: Cases, Materials, Commentary (2nd edition), Cambridge University Press (2014), p. 63.)

48 See Part III (Articles 6-25) of the International Covenant on Economic, Social and Cultural Rights, adopted and opened for signature, ratification and accession by General Assembly resolution 2200 A(XXI) of 16 December 1966. The Covenant entered into force on 3 January 1976 in accordance with Article 27. It is important to bear in mind that economic, social and cultural rights like civil and political rights contain dual freedoms. In other words, they can be realized by "freedom from the State and freedom through the State". See OHCHR Fact Sheet No. 3, 'Frequently Asked Questions on Economic, Social and Cultural Rights'.

The Committee on Economic, Social and Cultural Rights specifies what constitutes a violation of this *State duty* to protect in relation to the right to health in its General Comments: "*Violations of the obligation to protect follow from the failure of a State to take all necessary measures to safeguard persons within their jurisdiction from infringements of the right to health by third parties. This category includes such omissions as the failure to regulate the activities of individuals, groups or* ***corporations*** (emphasis added) *so as to prevent them from violating the right to health of others.*"[49]

While the International Covenant on Economic, Social and Cultural Rights provides for a clear legal basis to regulate corporate human rights abuses regarding economic, social and cultural rights through the framework of the *State obligation* to protect, it does not necessarily set out explicitly any direct legal obligation for business enterprises to respect human rights. Despite the fact that currently there contains no treaty obligation on business enterprises to respect human rights in the International Covenant on Economic, Social and Cultural Rights, it is important to recognize that the International Covenant on Economic, Social and Cultural Rights provides a comprehensive list of economic, social and cultural rights, which should be considered when business enterprises conduct human rights due diligence as an essential component of the *Corporate responsibility* to respect human rights, in order to identify what impacts the activities of business enterprises can have on the enjoyment of economic, social and cultural rights by rights-holders.

The enjoyment of a whole range of the economic, social and cultural rights contained in the International Covenant on Economic, Social and Cultural Rights can indeed be impacted by the activities of business enterprises. The rights to work and to the enjoyment of just and favourable

---

49 The United Nations Committee on Economic, Social and Cultural Rights, General Comment No.14, The right to the highest attainable standard of health (Twenty-second session, 2000), U.N. Doc. E/C.12/2000/4 (2000), para 51.

conditions of work can be directly impacted by business activities. As such, exploitative labour practices can lead to breaching the rights to just conditions of work and to form trade unions, and poor occupational and health and safety standards can also harm the rights to health of workers. In addition, by exposing consumers to dangerous products and through poor environmental practices, the rights to health and food can also negatively be impacted. Privatization of basic public services such as water can lead to a breach of the right to water and sanitation. Allowing companies to hold the patent rights to life-saving medicines and vital necessities such as anti-retroviral drug to combat HIV/AIDS and the patent right to the seeds of agricultural items, including grains and vegetable plants, can also lead to violations of the rights to health and food, thus eventually leading to a violation of the right to life.[50] In this regard, it is important to emphasize that under the ICESCR, only States have the obligations to respect, protect and fulfil human rights in relation to such business activities that are having the negative impacts on the enjoyment of economic, social and cultural rights. Business enterprises themselves have only the *Corporate responsibility* to respect economic, social and cultural rights on the international law plane.

The prominent feature of the International Covenant on Economic, Social and Cultural Rights as compared to the International Covenant on Civil and Political Rights lies in the fact that the States parties to the former Covenant are obligated to implement the rights recognized thereunder progressively to the maximum of their available resources, the so-called progressive realization principle.[51] Under this principle, States are required to

---

50 For a more detailed analysis of negative impacts of transnational corporations' activities on the enjoyment of economic, social and cultural rights, see Sarah Joseph, 'Liability of Multinational Corporations,' pp. 613-627 in Malcolm Langford (Ed.), Social Rights Jurisprudence – Emerging Trends in International and Comparative Law, Cambridge University Press (2008, 2010 and 2011 reprinted).

51 Article 2(1) of the International Covenant on Economic, Social and Cultural Rights. For a detailed exposition of the progressive realization of economic, social and cultural rights, See Eibe Riedel, 'Core Obligations in Social Rights and Human Dignity,' pp. 79-91 in Max-Emanuel Geis, Markus Winkler, Christian Bickenbach (Eds.), Von der Kultur der Verfassung,

take steps to the maximum of their available resources to achieve progressively the full realization of economic, social and cultural rights. On the other hand, like the requirements under the International Covenant on Civil and Political Rights, the International Covenant on Economic, Social and Cultural Rights also enshrines the principle of non-discrimination requiring States parties to guarantee without discrimination to all people under their territory and/ or jurisdiction the enjoyment of economic, social and cultural rights, which constitutes immediate obligation of implementation.[52]

Despite this unique characteristic of economic, social and cultural rights in terms of its full realization, i.e., the principle of progressive realization to the maximum available resources in a given country, it is indisputably established that all human rights, economic, social and cultural, or civil and political rights are indivisible, inter-related, inter-connected and inter-dependent for their full realization, which has been resoundingly reaffirmed by the Vienna Declaration and Programme of Action, declared during the second World Conference on Human Rights in 1993.[53]

Festschrift Für Friedhelm Hufen Zum 70. Geburtstag, C.H.Beck (2015, special print); Eibe Riedel, 'International Covenant on Economic, Social and Cultural Rights (1966),' in R. Wolfrum (Ed.), Max Planck Encyclopedia of Public International Law (MPEPIL), Oxford University Press (2010), No. 836, paras. 7-9. See also Eibe Riedel, 'International Law Shaping constitutional Law – Realization of Economic, Social and Cultural Rights – ,' in Eibe Riedel (Ed.), Constitutionalism – Old Concepts, New Worlds, German Contributions to the VI.th World Congress of the International Association of Constitutional Law (IACL), Berliner Wissenschaftsverlag (Berlin 2005), pp. 105-121; CESCR-Committee General Comment No. 3. On the nature of States parties' obligations (art. 2, para. 1 of the Covenant), UN Doc. E/1991/23 of 14 December 1990 – E/C.12/1990/8 and corr. 1, annex III.

52 Supra note 48, Eibe Riedel, 'Core Obligations in Social Rights and Human Dignity,' in Max-Emanuel Geis, Markus Winkler, Christian Bickenbach (Eds.), Von der Kultur der Verfassung, Festschrift Für Friedhelm Hufen Zum 70. Geburtstag, C.H.Beck (2015, special print), pp. 79-91. See also CESCR-Committee General Comment No. 20 on non-discrimination in economic, social and cultural rights (art.2, para. 2 of the Covenant), UN Doc. E/2010/22-E/C.12/2009/3, annex VI.

53 Ibid., at 79 et seq. See also paragraph 5 of the Vienna Declaration and Programme of Action, adopted by the World Conference on Human Rights in Vienna on 25 June 1993, which stated that *"All human rights are universal, indivisible and interdependent and interrelated. The international community must treat human rights globally in a fair and equal manner, on the same footing, and with the same emphasis. While the significance of national and regional*

b. International Covenant on Civil and Political Rights

The International Covenant on Civil and Political Rights (ICCPR) is a twin covenant to the ICESCR that codifies the civil and political rights enshrined in the Universal Declaration of Human Rights. It lists all civil and political rights ranging from the rights to life, security of the person, freedom from torture, freedom from slavery and servitude, freedom of religion, expression, association, and peaceful assembly to fair trial rights.

With respect to the *State obligation* to protect from corporate human rights abuse, the International Covenant on Civil and Political Rights also explicitly enunciates such obligation to protect, along with the obligations to respect and fulfil, as the International Covenant on Economic, Social and Cultural Rights. Article 2 of the ICCPR provides that a State party must respect and ensure the rights of the Covenant to all persons within its jurisdiction, which means that State parties must take all necessary legislative, administrative and, judicial other measures to properly guarantee these rights. It is also crucial that States parties provide remedies to persons whose rights under the Covenant are violated. Specifically, the *State obligation* to protect requires that State parties must not only refrain from violating an individual's rights itself (the obligation to respect), but also protect an individual from a violation of his or her rights by third parties, including private individuals, corporations, or other non-State actors.[54]

---

particularities and various historical, cultural and religious backgrounds must be borne in mind, it is the duty of States, regardless of their political, economic and cultural systems, to promote and protect all human rights and fundamental freedoms." It can be accessed at the following OHCHR webpage: https://www.ohchr.org/sites/default/files/vienna.pdf. (Accessed as of 02 October 2023).

54 Article 2 of the International Covenant on Civil and Political Rights. For a greater detail, see OHCHR Fact Sheet No. 15 (Rev.1): Civil and Political Rights: The Human Rights Committee, p.5. "It states that "this [the State obligation to protect] may well require positive action by the State party, for example by establishing an appropriate legislative and policy framework and devoting sufficient resources to their effective implementation." See also Manfred Nowak (2nd revised Ed.), UN Covenant on Civil and Political Rights: CCPR Commentary (2005) (N.P. Engel Verlag), paras. 3-6; Sarah Joseph, Jenny Schultz, Melissa Castan (Eds.), The International

The Human Rights Committee (CCPR-Committee), which is a monitoring body of the implementation of the rights by States Parties to the ICCPR, further elaborates upon this *State duty* to protect from corporate human rights abuse in its General Comment No. 31: "*the positive obligations on State parties to ensure Covenant rights will only be fully discharged if individuals are protected by the State, not just against violations of Covenant rights by its agents, but also against acts committed by private persons or entities.*" States are deemed violating Covenant rights where they permit or fail "*to take appropriate measures or to exercise due diligence to prevent, punish, investigate or redress the harm caused by such acts by private persons or entities.*"[55]

With respect to the *Corporate responsibility* to respect human rights, the following rights may be particularly impacted by the activities of business activities, depending on the various operational contexts where business activities are involved. In the extractive industry, business enterprises are often alleged to be complicit in human rights violations committed by local security apparatus while protecting company facilities. In this connection, the rights to life, security of the person, association and peaceful assembly can be negatively affected through business enterprises' benefiting either knowingly or unwittingly from such human rights violations committed by state security authorities. Indigenous Peoples have also reportedly been subjected to corporate human rights abuses, in particular in the contexts of the right to personal security, the right to prior, informed consent to development on their lands and territories, which is recognized under the ILO Convention No. 169 on Indigenous and Tribal Peoples,[56] as well as international human

---

Covenant on Civil and Political Rights – Cases, Materials, and Commentary, Oxford University Press (2000), paras. [1.59]-[1.62].

55 The Human Rights Committee General Comment No. 31, para 8, UN Doc., CCPR/C/21/Rev.1/Add. 13.

56 It can be accessed at the following ILO webpage: https://normlex.ilo.org/dyn/normlex/en/f?p=NORMLEXPUB:12100:0::NO:12100:P12100_INSTRUMENT_ID:312314:NO (Accessed as of 28 August 2024).

rights standards such as the Declaration on the Rights of Indigenous Peoples.[57] Environmental human rights defenders are also increasingly faced with corporate human rights abuses in the context of their advocacy work for protecting the environment, on which economic development activities have deleterious impact, for instance in the extractive and agri-business sectors. Moreover, increasingly with the advent of the digital age, the right to privacy has come to the fore as an emerging major concern in the context of the *Corporate responsibility* to respect human rights.[58]

It is worth noting that the debate has been focusing on the identification of the human rights that companies bear the obligation to respect. Towards this end, fluid concepts and notions such as "*sphere of influence*"[59] have been used by legal scholars to establish a set of human rights that can be negatively impacted by the activities of business enterprises. However, it is widely acknowledged that the activities of business activities can impact the whole range of human rights, including economic, social and cultural rights, as well as civil and political rights.[60]

c. Other Conventions

As seen above, the two International Covenants (ICESCR and ICCPR)

---

57 United Nations Declaration on the Rights of Indigenous Peoples adopted by the General Assembly on 13 September 2017. It can be accessed at the following OHCHR webpage: https://www.ohchr.org/sites/default/files/Documents/Publications/Declaration_indigenous_en.pdf (Accessed as of 28 August 2024).

58 For further detail on the impacts of new technology on human rights, including the rights to privacy and peaceful assemblies, see OHCHR 'The right to privacy in the digital age: Report of the United Nations High Commissioner for Human Rights,' UN Doc., A/HRC/48/31 (right to privacy); OHCHR, 'Impact of new technologies on the promotion and protection of human rights in the context of assemblies, including peaceful protests: Report of the United Nations High Commissioner for Human Rights,' UN Doc., A/HRC/44/24 (right to peaceful assemblies).

59 See supra note 7, John Ruggie, 'Protect, Respect and Remedy: A Framework for Business and Human Rights', Report of the Special Representative of the Secretary-General on the issue of human rights and transnational corporations and other business enterprises, UN Doc, A/HRC/8/5, paras. 65-72.

60 Ibid., para. 52.

impose generalized obligations to ensure the enjoyment of rights and prevent human rights abuse by non-State actors, including corporate human rights abuse, under the *State duty* to protect. In addition to these two Covenants, there exist 7 additional international human rights treaties that constitute core international human rights treaties: the International Convention on the Elimination of All Forms of Racial Discrimination (1965) – (ICERD); the Convention on the Elimination of All Forms of Discrimination against Women (1979) – (CEDAW); the Convention against Torture and Other Cruel, Inhuman or Degrading Treatment or Punishment (1984) – (CAT); the Convention on the Rights of the Child (1989) – (CRC); and the International Convention on the Protection of the Rights of All Migrant Workers and Members of Their Families (1990) – (ICRMW); the International Convention on the Rights of Persons with Disabilities (2006) – (CRPD); and the International Convention for the Protection of All Persons from Enforced Disappearance (2006) – (ICPPED).

These core international human rights treaties also provide for the *State duty* to protect from corporate human rights abuse. For instance, Article 2.1(d) of ICERD specifically requires that each State party prohibit racial discrimination by "*any persons, group or organization.*" (emphasis added) On the other hand, CEDAW, CRC and CRPD address business enterprises in a more direct language. For instance, article 2(e) of CEDAW requires that States parties take all appropriate measures to eliminate discrimination against women by any enterprise. Further, Article 13(b) specifies this *State duty* to protect in the context of "*bank loans, mortgages and other forms of financial credit*" (emphasis added). In its Preamble, CRPD also recognizes the general responsibility of the individual towards other individuals and toward communities "*to strive for the promotion and observance of the rights recognized in the International Bill of Human Rights.*"(emphasis added). Article 4 (e) of CRPD further specifically requires States "*to take all appropriate measures to eliminate discrimination on the basis of disability by any person, organization or* ***private enterprise***"(emphasis added).

Accordingly, it can be said that these provisions provide for specific legal bases under international human rights law to impose the *Corporate obligation* to respect human rights on the municipal law plane as part of States' treaty obligations.

3. Customary International Law

The classic doctrine of customary law[61] is reflected in the *North Sea Continental Shelf* judgment[62] of the International Court of Justice (ICJ).[63] For a rule to be considered to be customary international law, there should be a general recognition among States of a certain practice as obligatory *(opinio iuris)*. Article 38 of the Statute of the International Court of Justice (ICJ) makes it explicit that customary international law constitutes one of the sources of international law. It refers to *"international custom, as evidence of a general practice accepted as law"*[64] The ICJ judgment in the North Sea Continental Shelf case has intimated that in order for a rule to be customary international law, "*various factors have cumulatively evidenced or been creative of the opinio juris sive necessitatis, requisite for the formation of new rules of customary international law.*"[65]

It has been argued that, from state practice, "*it cannot be easily identified rules in the field of human rights*" for the following reason that it is hard to observe the way, in which states behave *vis-à-vis* their own citizens

---

61 Christian Tomuschat, Human Rights Between Idealism and Realism (2nd Ed.), Oxford University Press (2008), p. 37.

62 International Court of Justice *North Sea Continental Shelf Cases* (Federal Republic of Germany/ Denmark; Federal Republic of Germany/Netherlands) ICJ Reports (1969) 3, at 43-4.

63 Supra notes 37, 44 and 58. See also supra note 2, Eibe Riedel, 'Standards as Sources,' German Yearbook of International Law (GYIL) vol. 63 (220), 369-417.

64 For a detailed exposition on sources of international law, see supra note 2, Eibe Riedel, 'Standards as Sources,' German Yearbook of International Law (GYIL) vol. 63 (220), 369-417. See also Ian Brownlie, Principles of Public International Law, (4th Ed.), Oxford University Press (1990), pp. 4-11.

65 Supra note 59.

and people under their jurisdictions through empirical means.[66] The difficulty of identifying state practice on the *Corporate responsibility* to respect human rights has also been highlighted by the then Special Representative of the UN Secretary-General on the issue of human rights and transnational corporations and other business enterprises, John Ruggie: "*preliminary research has not identified the emergence of uniform and consistent State practice establishing corporate responsibilities under customary international law.*"[67] It is therefore essential that an emphasis be placed on official acts and statements, in order to grasp the relevant practice and *opinio iuris*, for which the methodology used by the International Court of Justice in its *Nicaragua* judgement[68] is of great value. Namely, it must be closely verified to what extent States' practices fully correspond to the international rule of law or simply they deny charges of human rights violations brought against them.

In the area of international human rights law, Professor Riedel argues that "*the rapidly increasing ratification practice of specific human rights treaties and the behaviour of States inside and outside of the UN was taken as evidence of State practice, and the UDHR itself as proof of an accepted opinio iuris.*" In this regard, it is worth noting the broad agreement that the majority of the rights enshrined in the UDHR has now become part of customary international law, in particular the rights to life, freedom from torture, security of the person, as well as the prohibition of discrimination on

---

66 Supra note 58, Christian Tomuschat, Human Rights Between Idealism and Realism (2nd Ed.), Oxford University Press(2008), p. 37.

67 Supra note 18, John Ruggie, 'Business and human rights: mapping international standards of responsibility and accountability for corporate acts: Report of the Special Representative of the Secretary-General on the issue of human rights and transnational corporations and other business enterprises,' UN Doc., A/HRC/4/35, para. 34. See also A. Zerk, Multinationals and Corporate Social Responsibility, Cambridge University Press (2006) and John Ruggie,'Report of the Special Representative of the Secretary-General on the issue of human rights and transnational corporations and other business enterprises, Addendum: Human Rights Policies and Management Practices: Results from questionnaire surveys of Governments and Fortune Global 500 firms,' UN Doc., A/HRC/4/35/Add.3.

68 *Military and Paramilitary Activities in and against Nicaragua (Nicaragua v United States of America), Merits* (1986) ICJ Reports 14 at 106-109.

racial grounds.[69]

Additionally, the *Corporate responsibility* to respect human rights can be established on the international law plane, for instance through the interpretation of treaty norms by the concerned treaty bodies in the form of General Comments, which can potentially ripen into sources of international law, "by recourse to general principles of law."[70] Furthermore, the United Nations Human Rights Council and the General Assembly can develop, through their acts (resolutions), a range of new rules of customary international law, in particular regarding specific areas or groups of persons, in spite of the fact that to determine with caution that the acts (resolutions) of these UN bodies and organs serve as proof of *opinio iuris*. These acts not only can have a tremendous influence on the development of treaty law, but also could serve

---

69 See supra note 2, Eibe Riedel, 'Standards as Sources,' German Yearbook of International Law (GYIL) vol. 63 (220), 369-417, at 380-381. See also supra note 62, Christian Tomuschat, Human Rights Between Idealism and Realism (2nd Ed.), Oxford University Press (2008), p. 37; the judgement in *Barcelona Traction, Light and Power Company* (1970) ICJ Reports 3 at 32, para 34, which mentions the prohibition of genocide and protection from slavery and racial discrimination. The American Law Institute, 2 *Restatement of the Law Third. The Foreign Relations Law of the United States* (St Paul, Minn, American Law Institute, 1987) 161, para. 702, which mentions prohibitions of genocide, slavery or slave trade, the murder or causing the disappearance of individuals, torture, prolonged arbitrary detention, systematic racial discrimination, or a consistent pattern of gross violations of internationally recognized human rights. Tomuschat has employed another interesting methodology to discern which rights under the UDHR have acquired the status of customary international law. For instance, he identified the three rights from the UDHR, which did not make it in the ICCPR, namely the rights to asylum, to a nationality, as well as the right of ownership/property, which he concludes do not qualify as having acquired the status of customary international law. See also Hurst Hannum, 'The Status of the Universal Declaration of Human Rights in National and International Law,' 25 Georgia Journal of International and Comparative Law (1995/1996) 287; John P. Humphrey, 'The Universal Declaration of Human Rights: its History, Impact and Judicial Character,' in Bertrand G. Ramcharan (Ed.), Human Rights, Thirty Years after the Universal Declaration (1979) 21; Eibe Riedel, *Die Universalität der Menschenrechte* (2003), at 15; Henry J. Steiner, Philip Alston, and Ryan Goodman, International Human Rights in Context (3rd ed. 2008), at 136 et seq.; von Arnauld, *Völkerrecht* (4th ed., 2019) at marginal note 278, 611 et seq., 751.

70 See supra note 2, Eibe Riedel, 'Standards as Sources,' German Yearbook of International Law (GYIL) vol. 63 (220), 369-417, at 380-381. See also supra note 59, Christian Tomuschat, Human Rights Between Idealism and Realism(2nd Ed.), Oxford University Press (2008). Tomuschat emphasizes the importance of looking at the deliberations of relevant treaty monitoring bodies (treaty bodies) to see what has been crystalized into customary law in the field of human rights.

as guiding principles or standards for State actions once they have ripened into rules of customary international law.[71]

4. *Ius cogens*

Ius cogens is understood as "*certain overriding principles of international law.*" "*They are rules of customary law which cannot be set aside by treaty or acquiescence but only by the formation of a subsequent customary rule of contrary effect.*"[72] Chapter 2.B of the Vienna Convention on the Law of Treaties terms it "peremptory norm" and defines as follows: "*A treaty is void if, at the time of its conclusion, it conflicts with a peremptory norm of general international law. For the purposes of the present Convention, a peremptory norm of general international law is a norm accepted and recognized by the international community of states as a whole as a norm from which no derogation is permitted and which can be modified only by a subsequent norm of general international law having the same character.*"[73]

When it comes to human rights, it has been argued that the core rights that are directly related to human existence are classified as *ius cogens*. For instance, regarding the right to life, only specific forms of interference with human life may fall within the scope of *ius cogens* such as genocide.[74] The International Court of Justice, in the *Barcelona Traction* case, also clarifies that certain particularly serious forms of human rights violation infringe on obligations *erga omnes*.[75] Accordingly, *ius cogens norms* in particular public

---

71 Supra note 59, Christian Tomuschat, Human Rights Between Idealism and Realism(2nd Ed.), Oxford University Press (2008).

72 Supra note 62, Ian Brownlie, Principles of Public International Law(4th Ed.), Oxford University Press (1990), pp. 509-517. See also Mark W. Janis, An Introduction to International Law (2nd Ed.), Little, Brown and Company (1993), pp. 62-66.

73 UN Doc., A/CONF.39/27 (1969).

74 Supra note 59, Christian Tomuschat, Human Rights Between Idealism and Realism(2nd Ed.), Oxford University Press (2008)., at p. 38.

75 For the list of *ius cogens* human rights norms, see L. Hannikainen, Peremptory Norms (Jus Cogens) in International Law, Finnish Lawyers' Publishing Company (1988), pp.425-520. See

interest norms such as prohibition of piracy, slavery and genocide as part of general principles of international law apply not only to States but to juridical persons such as business enterprises on the international law plane.

5. General Principles of International Law

The general principles of law, a broad category of law encompassing "*different levels and spheres of norms*",[76] are part of the triad sources of international law, listed under Article 38(1) of the International Court of Justice Statute. Professor Riedel has identified the five distinct purposes of general principles of law, namely: (1) premises, preconditions of any legal order; (2) Article 38 (1) ICJ-Statute; (3) principles of legal logic; (4) general principles at the level of international relations (general principles of international law-GPIL); and (5) principles of inter-relation between different treaties or treaty systems.[77]

When it comes to identifying as to whether there exist general principles of law regarding the *State duty* to protect from corporate human rights abuses and the *Corporate responsibility* to respect human rights, it is worth paying close attention to the above second and fourth purposes. First, the general principles of law under Article 38 (1)(c) of the Statute of the International Court of Justice requires a mere "*assessment of general principles found at the domestic law level, capable of being transposed to the international level, and being established by comparative law methods.*"[78]

In addition, substantive general principles of law can be generated at

---

also supra note 73, Mark W. Janis, An Introduction to International Law (2nd Ed.), Little, Brown and Company (1993), at p. 64. Robledo, Le *jus cogens* international: sa génese, sa nature, ses fonctions, 172 *Hague Recuueil* 9, 167-187 (1981).

76 See supra note 2, Eibe Riedel, 'Standards as Sources,' German Yearbook of International Law (GYIL) vol. 63 (220), at pp. 381-387.

77 Ibid.

78 Ibid., at p. 382.

the international level. These principles "*embrace elementary humanitarian concerns*", including rules applied in armed conflicts and during peacetime, as well as principles such as the right to self-determination of peoples, and freedom of the seas. The core principle of human rights obligations under international human rights law, namely the minimum standards of human rights, can also be said part of general principles of law.[79] Furthermore, further examples of substantive general principles of law (GPL) as general principles of international law (GPIL) have been identified, for instance, the so-called PANTHER-principles: the principles of participation, accountability, non-discrimination, transparency, human dignity, empowerment of discriminated persons, and the rule of law and redress of grievances.[80]

When it is applied to the *Corporate responsibility* to respect human rights, it can be said that the *Corporate responsibility* to respect human rights is currently in the process of becoming a general principle of law. In fact, the *Corporate responsibility* to respect human rights, whose main component is to require business enterprises to conduct human rights due diligence in their own operations and in their supply chains, is increasingly being legislated in many countries, in particular in European countries.[81] Considering that Article 38(1)(c) requires a mere "*assessment of general principles found at the domestic law level, capable of being transposed to the international level, and being established by comparative law methods,*"[82] it can be said that the *Corporate responsibility* to respect human rights can be transposed at the international level as general principles of international law, once a critical number of countries make the *Corporate responsibility* to respect human rights at the domestic level a legal obligation, which will be eventually considered as an autonomous source of international law under the purview of Article 38(1)(c) of the Statute of the ICJ. Once it becomes general principles

79 Ibid., at 383.
80 Ibid., at 384-386.
81 See infra Ch. 8.
82 Supra note 76.

of international law, the *Corporate responsibility* to respect human rights will serve as an international law obligation binding on business enterprises, independently of the *State duty* to protect from corporate human rights abuse on the international law plane. This process of the *Corporate responsibility* to respect human rights at the domestic level developing into a general principle of international law will further be precipitated, once an international treaty on business and human rights, currently being elaborated under the auspices of the United Nations Human Rights Council, will have been concluded.

6. Standards (Combination/zebra Standards) on Business and Human Rights

There exist some international standards and mechanisms[83] in relation to the *Corporate responsibility* to respect human rights. Such international standards and mechanisms are used to chart possible future directions and to fill the gaps in the international legal order. They are also useful in a situation where it is deemed that legally binding norms and mechanisms are not the best tools to address corporate human rights abuses.

Types of international standards and mechanisms in this area include: standards set by inter-governmental organizations; the enhanced

---

83 It is worth noting that HRC resolutions related to the issue of business and human rights have consistently emphasized that business enterprises have a responsibility to respect human rights. This is an indication that States increasingly acknowledge the *Corporate responsibility* to respect human rights could be potentially ripened into customary international law, even though one should be careful not to rush into concluding that such resolutions of the UN Human Rights Council constitute *opinio iuris*, the requirement for becoming customary international law. See, United Nations Human Rights Council *"Resolution adopted by the Human Rights Council: Human rights and transnational corporations and other business enterprises"* UN Doc., A/HRC/RES/17/4, United Nations Human Rights Council *"Resolution adopted by the Human Rights Council: Human rights and transnational corporations and other business enterprises"* UN Doc., A/HRC/RES/26/22 and United Nations Human Rights Council *"Resolution adopted by the Human Rights Council: Business and human rights: mandate of the Working Group on the issue of human rights and transnational corporations and other business enterprises,"* UN Doc., A/HRC/RES/35/7.

accountability mechanisms of inter-governmental organizations; and multi-stakeholder format that addresses and redresses sources of corporate human rights abuse, directly involving corporations with States and civil society organizations. For instance, the ILO Tripartite Declaration of Principles Concerning Multinational Enterprises and Social Policy proclaims that all parties, including multinational enterprises (MNEs) "*should respect the Universal Declaration of Human Rights and the corresponding national Covenants.*" The OECD Guidelines for Multinational Enterprises also recommends that firms "*respect the human rights of those affected by their activities consistent with the host Government's obligations and commitments.*" Both standards[84] could be ripened into both customary international law, general principles of international law and treaty norms. Therefore, such standards play an essential role in elaborating and further developing norms and standards of corporate accountability.

Inter-governmental organizations have also adopted enhanced accountability mechanisms in this regard. For instance, under the OECD Guidelines for Multinational Enterprises, anyone can bring a complaint against a multinational firm to the attention of a National Contact Point (NCP), which is a non-judicial review procedure. The International Finance Corporation (IFC) has also performance standards that companies are required to meet in return for IFC investment funds, which includes 8 performance standards on: assessment and management of environmental and social risks and impacts; labour and working conditions; resource efficiency and pollution prevention; community health, safety, and security; land acquisition and involuntary resettlement; biodiversity conservation and sustainable management of living natural resources; Indigenous Peoples; and cultural heritage. Client compliance is subject to review by an ombudsman. This mechanism has accountability spill-over effects, for these are tracked by banks adhering to the Equator Principles, which account for some two thirds

84 Both ILO Declaration and OCED Guidelines will be examined in detail in Chapter 5.

of global commercial project lending.[85]

Another form of international standards on the *Corporate responsibility* to respect human rights adopts a multi-stakeholder format: the Voluntary Principles on Security and Human Rights, for instance, promote corporate human rights risk assessments and training of security providers in the extractive sector; the Kimberley Process Certification Scheme (Kimberley) aims to stem the flow of conflict diamonds; and the Extractive Industries Transparency Initiative (EITI) also establishes a degree of revenue transparency in the taxes, royalties and fees that companies pay to host Governments. These initiatives seek to "*close regulatory gaps that contribute to human rights abuses*" in specific operational contexts. They also seek to "*allocate shared responsibilities and establish mutual accountability mechanisms within complex collaborative networks*." They go often hand in hand with governmental regulatory action. For instance, under the Kimberley process, a global certification scheme is implemented through domestic law.[86]

It is critical to ensure the effectiveness of these voluntary initiatives. There exist some criteria to judge the effectiveness of these voluntary initiatives, including the perceived credibility of their governance structures and their effectiveness.[87] The credibility of governance structures hinges on three factors: participation, transparency, and ongoing status reviews. The effectiveness can also be measured in two ways: their operational impact on the ground: and whether they serve as examples for others. Once companies accept IFC financing or loans from Equator banks, certain performance

---

85 UN Doc., A/HRC/4/35; "Performance Standards on Environmental and Social Sustainability", International Finance Corporation (IFC), which can be accessed at the following website: https://www.ifc.org/content/dam/ifc/doc/2010/2012-ifc-performance-standards-en.pdf. (Accessed as of 31 August 2024).

86 Ibid.

87 Nico Krisch and Benedict Kingsbury, 'Global Governance and Global Administrative Law in the International Legal Order,' European Journal of International Law, vol. 17, No. 1 (February, 2006).

criteria are required for continued funding. States are free to join the EITI, but if they do, extractive companies are required to issue public reports of their payments to Governments. Suspension or expulsion from the Kimberley process has also a direct economic impact on countries and companies. The Voluntary Principles on Security and Human Rights language has also been incorporated into legal agreements between Governments and companies. Once the Voluntary Principles on Security and Human Rights adopt participation criteria, non-compliance could lead to expulsion.[88]

The most recent and authoritative international standards in this regard is the United Nations Guiding Principles on Business and Human Rights, which is unique in the sense that they contain both the treaty norms of the *State duty* to protect from corporate human rights abuse and international standards on the *Corporate responsibility* to respect human rights. Professor Eibe Riedel has called it as "*Combination/zebra standards*."[89]

B. Interim Conclusions

There currently exists the international legal framework that provides a legal basis for the *State obligation* to protect from corporate human rights abuse. The Bill of International Human Rights made up of the Universal Declaration of Human Rights, the International Covenant on Economic, Social and Cultural Rights and the International Covenant on Civil and Political Rights is the most prominent international human rights legal framework in this regard. In addition to this, there are 7 other international human rights treaties, which forms part of the 9 core international human rights treaties. They also serve as the important legal bases for the *State obligation* to protect from corporate human rights abuse. A wide range of

---

88 For detailed explanations on these mechanisms, see UN Doc., A/HRC/4/35, paras. 45-62.

89 Supra note 2, Eibe Riedel, 'Standards as Sources,' German Yearbook of International Law (GYIL) vol. 63 (220).

customary international law, *ius cogens*, general principles of law, as well as other relevant international standards, in particular the UN Guiding Principles on Business and Human Rights, can also serve as the important legal bases for the *State obligation* to protect from corporate human rights abuse.

On the contrary, when it comes to the *Corporate responsibility* to respect human rights, currently under international human rights law, there exist no firm legal basis to impose direct obligation on business enterprises to respect human rights (corporate accountability) on the international law plane. The exception to this is *ius cogens* as part of general principles of international law in particular public interest norms[90] such as prohibition of piracy, slavery and genocide, which applies not only to States but also to juridical persons such as business enterprises. At the same time, there has been emerging international standards on the *Corporate responsibility* to respect human rights, the most recent and authoritative of which is the United Nations Guiding Principles on Business and Human Rights. The UN Guiding Principles on Business and Human Rights is unique in that it constitutes *Combination/zebra* standards whereby both the treaty norms on the *State duty* to protect from corporate human rights abuse and the international standards on the *Corporate responsibility* to respect human rights are included.

As such, the traditional view holds that international human rights instruments impose only indirect obligations on corporations, i.e. obligations under domestic law in accordance with States' international obligations. Others argue that these instruments already impose direct legal obligations on corporations but they merely lack direct accountability mechanisms.[91]

---

90 Ibid., Eibe Riedel, 'Standards as Sources,' German Yearbook of International Law (GYIL) vol. 63 (220), at pp. 385-386.

91 Supra note 18, John Ruggie, 'Business and human rights: mapping international standards of responsibility and accountability for corporate acts: Report of the Special Representative of

For instance, the UN Sub-Commission Norms on the Responsibilities of Transnational Corporations and Other Business Enterprises with Regard to Human Rights clearly state that the Norms "*reflect and restate existing international law, attributed the entire spectrum of State duties under the treaties – to respect, protect, promote and fulfil rights – to corporations within their spheres of influence.*"[92] It is submitted that while the *State duty* to protect from corporate human rights abuse is a well-established norm under international human rights law, the *Corporate responsibility* to respect human rights on the international law plane still needs to be matured into hard norms, either as treaty norms or as part of customary international law and/or general principles of international law. However, considering the emerging international standards as part of the so-called *Combination/zebra* standards on the *Corporate responsibility* to respect human rights, whose main component is to require business enterprises to conduct human rights due diligence in their own operations and in their supply chains, are being further concretized through national-level legislative action, they could be used as important "*yardsticks or signposts of legal development*"[93] in this regard at the international level.

Moreover, under the system of international criminal law, individuals can be held accountable for certain categories of international crimes such as genocide and crimes against humanity. However, there exist longstanding doctrinal arguments as to whether legal persons such as business enterprises can be held accountable for international crimes as subjects of international law. It suffices to conclude *ad interim* that currently under international criminal law, only natural persons (individuals), not legal persons, are within the jurisdiction of international criminal tribunals that are mandated to have

---

the Secretary-General on the issue of human rights and transnational corporations and other business enterprises,' UN Doc., A/HRC/4/35, para. 35.

92 'Norms on the Responsibilities of Transnational Corporations and Other Business Enterprises with Regard to Human Rights,' UN Doc, E/CN.4/Sub.2/2003/12/Rev.2 of 26 August 2003.

93 Supra note 2, Eibe Riedel, 'Standards as Sources,' German Yearbook of International Law (GYIL) vol. 63 (220), at p. 388.

jurisdiction over certain crimes such as war crimes, genocide, crimes against humanity and the crime of aggression. It is submitted that individuals are subject to direct obligation for the international crimes of piracy and slavery as part of *ius cogens*. Accordingly, in the absence of international accountability mechanisms for these international crimes, business enterprises could be held liable only by national legal systems.[94]

It is worth noting that corporations are increasingly recognized as "participants" on the international law plane with the capacity to bear some rights and duties: corporations have certain rights under bilateral investment treaties; they are subject to duties under several civil liability conventions dealing with environmental pollution. It is further established that even where a corporation does not intend for the crime to occur, it will not be absolved of liability if it knew or should have known that it was providing assistance, and that the assistance would contribute to the commission of a crime.[95]

In this regard, it should be noted that some efforts have been made to impose direct legal obligations on business enterprises on the international law plane. The United Nations Human Rights Council is currently in the process of deliberating on the elaboration of a legally binding treaty for business enterprises. It remains to be seen as to whether this future treaty will actually be concluded.[96] However, it can be said that the current discussions in the context of the Human Rights Council serve as an additional impetus for States to make further efforts to strengthen the *State obligation* to protect from corporate human rights abuse, including enactment of mandatory

---

94 Supra note 18, John Ruggie, 'Business and human rights: mapping international standards of responsibility and accountability for corporate acts: Report of the Special Representative of the Secretary-General on the issue of human rights and transnational corporations and other business enterprises,' UN Doc., A/HRC/4/35, para. 19.

95 For further details, see UN Doc., A/HRC/4/35.

96 For a further detailed exposition on the work of the UN Human Rights Council open-ended working group to elaborate a legally binding instrument in international human rights law to regulate the activities of transnational corporations and other business enterprises, see infra Chapter 7.

human rights due diligence law.

Moreover, there exist a number of international standards in the field of business and human rights, which sets out the clear expectation that business enterprises as a social organ having specialized functions in society should respect human rights throughout their entire operations and in their supply chains. These take various forms of voluntary initiatives and standards. Ironically on the international law plane, these voluntary standards and/or codes of conduct in various business sectors provide currently the most realistic opportunity to improve corporate behaviour *vis-à-vis* respect for human rights. Through long years of best corporate practices of these voluntary initiatives, potential rules of international law either in the form of customary international law or as part of general principles of international law can be formed, which will, in turn, provide the legal basis for corporate accountability for human rights violations on the international law plane. However, it is submitted that there is a firm legal basis yet to be established for the direct legal obligation for business enterprises to respect human rights under international human rights law.

Chapter 2: Dichotomy Between *Obligation* and *Responsibility*

A clear distinction can be made between *the State obligation* to protect from corporate human rights abuse and *the Corporate responsibility* to respect human rights under international human rights law. As noted in the above Chapter 1, "Obligation/duty" and/or "accountability" are being interchangeably used with "responsibility" in some human rights documents, including UN documents. In this thesis, "obligation/duty/accountability" is restrictedly being used to refer to the legal obligation owed to "duty-bearers" under international human rights law, the main of which are Governments, whereas "responsibility" refers to the expectations that society has of business enterprises, not as a legal duty/obligation, when their actions lead to violations of human rights of various stakeholders, including their own workers, sub-contractors, and more widely consumers, and the general population, in particular those populations such as Indigenous Peoples whose rights are particularly affected, for instance, in the mining and extractive industry.

As such, the *State obligation/duty* to protect from corporate human rights abuse is an essential part of the *State obligations* to respect, protect and fulfil the human rights of people under their territories and/or jurisdictions. Such *State obligation/duty* to protect requires States to protect people from their human rights' being infringed by third parties, including business enterprises. On the contrary, except for some cases of international crimes such as war crimes, crimes of genocide, and crimes against humanity, as well as exceptions under customary international law and general principles of international law, business enterprises bear no direct legal obligation to respect human rights on the international law plane. Business enterprises are thus merely expected to respect human rights as an organ of society having specialized functions in society on the international law plane, i.e., they have *the Corporate responsibility* to respect human rights.

A. The *State Obligation* to Protect

Under international human rights law, there exist three duties (legal obligations), namely the duty to respect, the duty to protect, and the duty to fulfil. The duty to fulfil can be further divided into the duty to promote and the duty to provide.[97] The duty to respect is characterized by its negative dimension of obligation. In other words, the duty to respect requires that the Governments (duty-bearers) must refrain from taking any action that will impede or infringe upon realization of the human rights of the people under their territories and/or jurisdictions. The duty to protect requires positive action on the part of duty bearers. Along with the duty to fulfil, this duty is a classic example of positive obligation. Under both the duty to protect and fulfil, Governments must take all necessary measures, whether they may be legislative, administrative, policy and judicial, to ensure that the human rights of the people under their territories and/or jurisdictions are protected and fulfilled. The duty to protect obliges States to take all necessary measures to protect the rights of the people under their territories and/or jurisdictions from being violated by third parties, including business enterprises. Under the duty to fulfil, the Governments (duty-bearers) must not only promote awareness-raising of human rights (the right to promote) through a variety of actions such as human rights education and training, but also they must provide adequate social services, particularly for the populations in vulnerable situations such as access to healthcare, adequate housing, food, water, and sanitation, which will allow them to live a dignified life (the duty to provide).

In relation to this duty typology of respect, protect and fulfil, one

---

97 Supra note 19, Henry Shue, Basic Rights: Subsistence, Affluence and U.S. Foreign Policy, Princeton University Press, 2nd ed., (1996). See also Asbjørn Eide, 'Realization of Social and Economic Rights and the Minimum Threshold Approach,' Human Rights Law Journal, 1989 Vol. 10, No. 1–2, pp. 36–51; Asbjørn Eide, 'The Right to Food as a Human Right,' UN Doc. E/CN.4/Sub.2/1987/23, in particular paras. 66-70; and Chapter 3 of Walter Kälin and Jörg Künzli (Eds.), The Legal Nature of Human Rights Obligations, Oxford University Press (2009), pp. 77-120.

school of thought has argued that civil and political rights are only negative freedoms, while economic, social and cultural rights require positive action to realize them. However, civil, cultural, economic, political and social rights have all three dimensions, the duty to respect, protect and fulfil, which represents the fact that civil and political rights and economic, social and cultural rights are universal, indivisible, inter-dependent and inter-related.[98] It can be said that among these State obligations under international human rights law, the duty/obligation to protect from human rights abuses is the most relevant obligation for States, when it comes to corporate human rights abuse. The main purpose of this chapter is therefore to examine provisions contained in international human rights treaties, which provides for the legal basis for the *State obligation/duty* to protect from corporate human rights abuse. It also aims to ascertain the core content of this *State obligation/duty* to protect from corporate human rights abuse. It further seeks to identify the main elements that can serve as inspirations for clarifying the content of the *Corporate responsibility to respect* human rights building upon treaty norms on the *State obligations/duties* to respect, protect and fulfil human rights in relation to business activities.

The interpretative guidance on the scope and nature of the *State duty* to protect from corporate human rights abuse has been clarified and

---

98 Para. 5 of the Vienna Declaration and Programme of Action adopted by the World Conference on Human Rights in Vienna on 25 June 1993. See also Supra note 51, Eibe Riedel, 'International Covenant on Economic, Social and Cultural Rights (1966),' in R. Wolfrum (Ed.), Max Planck Encyclopedia of Public International Law (MPEPIL), Oxford University Press (2010), No. 836, paras. 7-9. See also supra note 37, Eibe Riedel, 'International Law Shaping constitutional Law – Realization of Economic, Social and Cultural Rights – ,' in Eibe Riedel (Ed.), Constitutionalism – Old Concepts, New Worlds, German Contributions to the VI.th World Congress of the International Association of Constitutional Law (IACL), Berliner Wissenschaftsverlag (Berlin 2005), at 107-113; Eibe Riedel, 'Core Obligations in Social Rights and Human Dignity,' pp. 79-91 in Max-Emanuel Geis, Markus Winkler, Christian Bickenbach (Eds.), Von der Kultur der Verfassung, Festschrift Für Friedhelm Hufen Zum 70. Geburtstag, C.H.Beck (2015, special print); P. Alston/G Quinn, 'The Nature and Scope of State Parties' Obligations under the International Covenant on Economic, Social and Cultural Rights,' Human Rights Quarterly, vol.9, 1987, 156 et seq., at 172.

elaborated by various treaty bodies both in the form of General Comments/ General Recommendations and/or through Concluding Observations issued through review of States parties' periodic reporting to the treaty bodies. An in-depth analysis of such interpretative guidance by treaty bodies regarding the *State duty* to protect from corporate human rights abuse shall be examined in Chapter 3. A specific interpretative guidance (General Comments) on the content of the States parties' obligations in the context of business activities and the enjoyment of economic, social and cultural rights was adopted in 2017, which will be dealt with in Chapter 4, as it deserves separate detailed treatment.

I. Treaty Provisions

International human rights treaties provide for the general obligations imposed on States parties, from which the *State duty* to protect from corporate human rights abuse can be established. For instance, Article 2(1)(d) of the International Convention on the Elimination of All Forms of Racial Discrimination (ICERD)[99] obliges States parties to "*prohibit and bring to an end, by all appropriate means, including legislation as required by circumstances, racial discrimination by any persons, group or organization.*" "Any organization" in this Article includes business enterprises. Under this Article, the States parties to the ICERD are therefore obligated to take all necessary measures, including legislative action to ensure that third parties, including business enterprises, do not commit racial discrimination. Article 3(4) of the Optional Protocol to the Convention on the Rights of the Child on the Sale of Children, Child Prostitution and Child Pornography (OP-CRC-SC)[100] also specifically requires that States parties prohibit practices

---

99 It was adopted and opened for signature, ratification and accession on 21 December 1965 by the United Nations General Assembly resolution 2106(XX) and entered into force on 4 January 1969.

100 It was adopted and opened for signature, ratification and accession by the United Nations General Assembly resolution, A/RES/54/263 of 25 May 2000 entered into force on 18 January 2002.

such as sale of children, child prostitution and child pornography, including through taking action against legal persons, where appropriate, by establishing legal liability of such legal persons. "Legal persons" encompass business enterprises. Hence, the States parties to the OP-CRC-SC are obligated to ensure that business enterprises committing offences of sale of children, child prostitution and child pornography are legally held accountable for such corporate human rights abuses.

As such, the *State duty* to protect from corporate human rights abuse is established as a legal obligation under these treaty provisions that provide for the generalized obligations of the States parties. It is worth noting that although these treaty provisions in question do not make specific reference to "business enterprises", but generally to "legal persons,", it clearly contemplates the legal obligation/liability of business enterprises for corporate human rights harms. While the States parties have the legal obligation/duty under these treaties as part of their generalized international human rights obligations to protect from corporate human rights abuse, it is important to make it clear that business enterprises only have the responsibility to respect human rights on the international law plane.

Similarly, Article 16(2) of the International Convention on the Protection of the Rights of Migrant Workers and Members of Their Families (ICRMW) refer to the *State duty* to protect from human rights abuses by third parties. It provides that "*migrant workers and members of their families shall be entitled to effective protection by the State against violence, physical injury, threats and intimidation, whether by public officials or by private individuals, groups or institutions.*" "Private institutions" here include business enterprises. [101]

Moreover, some international human rights treaties contain provisions that both explicitly and implicitly make reference to the *State obligation*

101 It was adopted on 18 December 1990 by the United Nations General Assembly A/RES/45/158.

to protect from corporate human rights abuse, including those relevant to particular sectors or industries.[102] Article 2 (e) of the International Convention on the Elimination of All Forms of Discrimination against Women (CEDAW)[103] makes explicit reference to business by requiring that States parties "*take all appropriate measures to eliminate discrimination against women by any person, organization or enterprise.*" Article 13 (b) of CEDAW also makes specific reference to the particular business sector, namely the financial sector, by requiring that "*States parties shall take all appropriate measures to eliminate discrimination against women in other areas of economic and social life in order to ensure, on a basis of equality of men and women, the same rights, in particular the right to bank loans, mortgages and other forms of financial credit.*" While both provisions are aimed at specifying the States parties' duty to take all necessary actions to eliminate discrimination against women, they make it clear that the *State duty* to protect from corporate human rights abuse is an integral part of that generalized States parties' obligation to protect from corporate human rights abuse by making specific reference both to "enterprise" generally and to the particular business sector – the banking and finance sector – specifically as one of the objects for regulation. Article 14(2)(g) of CEDAW similarly requires that States parties take appropriate measures for rural women for them to access agricultural credit and loans, marketing facilities, appropriate technology and equal treatment in land and agrarian reform, as well as in land resettlement schemes with a view to ensuring equal rights and eliminating discrimination against them.

The Convention on the Rights of Persons with Disabilities (CRPD)[104]

---

102 Such references to business enterprises in the treaties are not common. Instead, the treaties tend to refer to particular sectors rather than making references to private business. See para. 12, UN Doc., A/HRC/4/35/Add.1.

103 It was adopted on 18 December 1978 by the United Nations General Assembly in New York. It entered into force as an international treaty on 3 September 1981 after the twentieth ratification.

104 It was adopted on 13 December 2006 by the United Nations General Assembly resolution A/RES/61/106 and opened for signature on 30 March 2007. It entered into force on 3 May 2008

has a similar provision, which makes explicit reference to businesses when it comes to the States parties' specific obligation to protect from corporate human rights abuse. For instance, Article 2(e) of CRPD requires that States parties "*take all appropriate measures to eliminate discrimination on the basis of disability by any person, organization or private entities*". Article 9(2)(b) of CRPD also specifically mentions "private entities" by requiring States parties to ensure that "*private entities that offer facilities and services which are open or provided to the public take into account all aspects of accessibility for persons with disabilities.*"

As in CEDAW referring to the particular business sector, other treaties also refer to the particular business sector in the implicit recognition of the need by States parties to regulate the activities of business enterprises. For instance, Article 5(f) of the International Convention on the Elimination of All Forms of Racial Discrimination (ICERD)[105] obliges States parties to take measures to prohibit and eliminate racial discrimination in relation to the right of access to any place or service intended for use by the general public such as transport, hotels, restaurants, cafes, theatres and parks. Article 17(a) of the Convention on the Rights of the Child (CRC)[106] also obligates States parties to encourage the mass media to disseminate information of social and cultural benefit to children. Furthermore, the Preamble of OP-CRC-SC expresses concern about sex tourism and the availability of child pornography on the Internet. Thus, these latter two Conventions address the *State obligation* to protect from corporate human rights abuse, in particular in the media and IT sectors, in addition to imposing the generalized *State obligation/duty* to protect from corporate human rights abuse.

---

after the twentieth ratification.

105 It was adopted and opened for signature and ratification by the United Nations General Assembly resolution 2016 (XX) on 21 December 1965. It entered into force on 4 January 1969.

106 It was adopted and opened for signature, ratification and accession on 20 December 1990 by the United Nations General Assembly resolution A/RES/44/25 and entered into force on 2 September 1990.

II. Required Measures

A wide array of possible actions can be taken under the *State duty* to protect from corporate human rights abuse. These actions are designed to prevent, address and mitigate, and redress human rights harms to be caused by corporate human rights abuses. Under this *State duty* to protect from corporate human rights abuse, States must and should take various legislative, policy, administrative and judicial measures such as enacting the general mandatory human rights due diligence law and/or special laws that require business enterprises to conduct human rights due diligence in their own operations and in their supply chains, adoption of national action plans on business and human rights, etc. In addition, as part of the *State obligations* to respect, protect and fulfil human rights in relation to business activities, they should take some promotional measures with a view to preventing corporate human rights abuses from being committed by business enterprises.

1. Monitoring

To prevent corporate human rights abuse, all necessary actions, including legislative action, must be put in place. For instance, corporate human rights abuse must be prohibited by law. Towards this end, it is critically important that States conduct an ongoing, consistent, independent monitoring of compliance by business enterprises even before corporate human rights abuse is alleged. In this regard, the Human Rights Committee emphasizes the importance of monitoring of compliance, particularly in relation to legislative measures, as part of States parties' obligation to provide effective remedy under the International Covenant on Civil and Political Rights (ICCPR). Accordingly, the Human Rights Committee, in its General Comment 31, highlights that to prevent a violation of Covenant rights, States parties must take measures "*beyond a victim-specific remedy*," which may require changes in the laws and practices of States parties.[107]

Also in recognition of the importance of such monitoring, the

Committee on Economic, Social and Cultural Rights (CESCR-Committee) clarifies that States parties should have in place effective monitoring mechanisms in the labour context and in relation to privatized social services.[108] The Committee on the Elimination of Discrimination against Women (CEDAW-Committee) also clarifies that States parties should report on how public and private healthcare providers meet their duties and/or responsibilities to respect women's rights to have access to healthcare.[109] This implies that States parties must conduct an ongoing monitoring of private healthcare providers' compliance regarding women's rights to have access to healthcare.

In relation to private service providers, the Committee on the Rights of the Child (CRC-Committee) also reminds States parties that "*they have an obligation to monitor and regulate the quality of provision to ensure that children's rights are protected and their best interests served.*"[110] Similarly, the Committee on the Elimination of Racial Discrimination (CERD-Committee) issued Concluding Observations in reviewing Suriname's periodic report in 2004 recommending that "*independent monitoring bodies be set up to conduct environmental impact assessment before any operating license is issued, as well as health and safety checks on the sites of gold mining activities.*"[111] In the context of the rights of Indigenous Peoples, treaty bodies

---

107 See para. 17, CCPR-Committee General Comment No. 31 [80] on *"The Nature of the General Legal Obligation Imposed on States Parties to the Covenant"*, UN DOC, CCPR/C/21/Rev.1/Add.13.

108 CESCR-Committee General Comment No. 16 on *"The equal right of men and women to the enjoyment of all economic, social and cultural rights."*

109 CEDAW-Committee General Recommendation No. 24.

110 CRC-Committee General Comment No. 7.

111 CERD-Committee Concluding observations, Suriname, UN Doc. CERD/C/64/CO/9, para. 15. See also John Ruggie, 'Report of the Special Representative of the Secretary-General on the issue of human rights and transnational corporations and other business enterprises, Addendum, 'State responsibilities to regulate and adjudicate corporate activities under the United Nations core human rights treaties: an overview of treaty body commentaries,' UN Doc. A/HRC/4/35/Add.1, para. 40.

also highlight the importance of monitoring.[112] As such, States must monitor whether business enterprises are consulting with indigenous communities in order to ensure their effective participation in any development decisions affecting them. Treaty bodies have also emphasized that an important role can be played by national human rights institutions in monitoring third party compliance by encouraging such institutions to consider complaints in relation to private actors and entities, including business enterprises.[113]

2. Regulation

Under the *State obligation* to protect from corporate human rights abuse, States must adopt appropriate legislation to prevent and address third party human rights abuse.[114] The role of legislation in regulating corporate activities that may cause human rights harm is most frequently considered in the employment context. Treaty bodies emphasize that States parties must adopt legislation to prohibit discrimination, forced labour, child labour and unsafe working conditions. Treaty bodies also highlight the key role of legislation in regulating discriminatory practices in access to services and protection against industrial accidents.[115] For instance, the CESCR-Committee underscores that legislation may be indispensable for protection against discrimination, as well as in relation to the rights to health and water. The CESCR-Committee specifically refers to the need to regulate third party actions, including business enterprises, in relation to the right to water by highlighting that States parties' failure to "*enact or enforce laws to prevent the contamination and inequitable extraction of water*" amount to a violation of

---

112 CCPR-Committee General Comment No. 23 and CERD-Committee General Recommendation No. 23.

113 CESCR-Committee General Comment Nos. 15 and 16.

114 It is worth noting that treaty bodies do not necessarily specify what would be required in terms of legislation content or other forms of regulation. They instead refer to the State obligation to take legislative measures to prevent such abuse in general terms. This gives States parties some latitude when it comes to deciding how to implement treaty provisions.

115 CCPR-Committee General Comment No. 3, CCPR-Committee General Comment No. 5, CESCR-Committee General Comment No. 7.

the *State obligation* to protect from human rights abuses by third parties.[116]

The CERD-Committee also emphasizes the importance of regulation by highlighting that States parties must take legislative or administrative measures to protect local communities and prevent abuses by business enterprises in relation to large infrastructure or mining projects, particularly those affecting Indigenous Peoples.[117] Treaty bodies have also recommended various measures such as adoption of a legislative framework that clearly sets forth the broad principles governing exploitation of land, including the obligation to abide by strict environmental standards and equitable revenue distribution;[118] information gathering and monitoring on the possible environmental effects of large development or mining projects before its launching;[119] and putting in place rules and procedures aimed at ensuring for the right of affected communities, especially Indigenous Peoples to participate in decisions related to these projects, in particular their right to a prior, free and informed consent.[120]

3. Adjudication

To fulfil the *State obligation* to protect from corporate human rights abuse, States must put in place judicial mechanisms aimed at providing

---

116 CESCR-Committee General Comment No. 15. See also Eibe Riedel, 'The Human Right to Water,' in Veröffentlichungen des Walther-Schücking-Instituts für Internationales Recht an der Universität Kiel, Festschrift Delbrück, Bd. 155, Duncker & Humblot, Berlin 2006, pp. 585-606.

117 See CERD-Committee Concluding Observations for Suriname, UN Doc., CERD/C/64/CO/9, para. 15, in which the CERD-Committee emphasized that "Development objectives are no justification for encroachments on human rights, and that along with the right to exploit natural resources there are specific, concomitant obligations toward the local population."

118 CERD-Committee Concluding Observations for Suriname (UN Doc., CERD/C/64/CO/9) and for Nigeria (UN Doc., CERD/C/NGA/CO/18).

119 CESCR-Committee Concluding Observations for China (UN Doc., E/C.12/1/Add.107) and CERD-Committee Concluding Observations for Suriname (UN Doc., CERD/C/64/CO/9) and for Guyana (UN Doc., CERD/C/GUY/CO/14).

120 CERD-Committee Concluding Observations for Guatemala (UN Doc., CERD/C/GTM/CO/11).

corporate human rights abuse victims with access to remedies. As such, the *State obligation* to protect from corporate human rights abuse requires States to take a range of judicial actions, in particular investigation, sanction by government authorities, and remediation of violations by third parties. In this regard, the Human Rights Committee specifies that it "*attaches importance to States Parties' establishing appropriate judicial (emphasis added) and administrative mechanisms for addressing claims of rights violations under domestic law.*"[121]

a. Investigation

Treaty bodies are of the opinion that States parties' failure to adequately investigate and redress violations by third parties, including business enterprises, is deemed to be a violation of the *State duty* to protect from corporate human rights abuse under international human rights law. In its General Comment No. 31, the Human Rights Committee highlights that a failure to investigate violations by private actors or entities amounts to a breach of the ICCPR. It also emphasizes that States parties must conduct prompt, thorough and effective investigations through independent and impartial bodies.[122]

b. Prosecution

The *State duty* to protect from corporate human rights abuse also obligates States to ensure that third party abuse, including corporate human rights abuse, is punished and perpetrators of such abuse are brought to justice. The importance of such sanctions is highlighted by some treaty bodies. For

---

121 Supra note 92, CCPR-Committee General Comment No. 31 [80] on "*The Nature of the General Legal Obligation Imposed on States Parties to the Covenant*", UN DOC, CCPR/C/21/Rev.1/Add.13, para. 15.

122 Ibid. The CESCR-Committee and the CERD-Committee also highlight the importance of investigation as part of the *State duty* to protect from corporate human rights abuse.

instance, the Human Rights Committee opines that a States parties' failure to bring perpetrators to justice for *"recognized breaches of domestic or international law"* amounts to a violation of the ICCPR.[123] In addition, the CESCR-Committee clarifies that States parties must support sanctions, including penalties in relation to employers' violations regarding non-discrimination, the right to work, including working conditions, slave labour, child labour, and trafficking.[124]

c. The right to remedy

Some international human rights treaties contain specific requirements to provide remedy to victims of human rights violations/abuses.[125] Even in the absence of such specific provisions on the right to remedy, the obligation to provide remedies is implied.[126] As part of provision of a remedy, the importance of equal access to justice has been highlighted by some treaty bodies.[127] Further, the need of taking protective measures is considered to be an essential element of the right to remedy. As such, the CEDAW-Committee emphasizes the need to take protective measures such as rehabilitation,

---

123 CCPR Supra note 92, CCPR-Committee General Comment No. 31 [80] on *"The Nature of the General Legal Obligation Imposed on States Parties to the Covenant"*, UN DOC, CCPR/C/21/Rev.1/Add.13, para. 18.

124 CESCR-Committee Concluding Observations for China, UN Doc., E/C.12/1/Add.107; for Russian Federation, UN Doc., E/C.12/1/Add.94; for Mexico, UN Doc., E/C.12/MEX/CO/4. See also CEDAW-Committee Concluding Observations for Ecuador, UN Doc., A/58/38 (SUPP), 18 July 2003, at paras. 311-312.

125 See Article. 2(3) of the ICCPR and Article 6 of the ICERD.

126 In its General Comment No. 4, the CESCR-Committee provides some examples of remedies in relation to the right to adequate housing as follows: "(a) legal appeals aimed at preventing planned evictions or demolitions through the issuance of court-ordered injunctions; (b) legal procedures seeking compensation following an illegal eviction; (c) complaints against illegal actions carried out or supported by landlords (whether public or private) in relation to rent levels, dwelling maintenance, and racial or other forms of discrimination; (d) allegations of any form of discrimination in the allocation and availability of access to housing; and (e) complaints against landlords concerning unhealthy or inadequate housing conditions."

127 See CERD-Committee Concluding Observations for Guatemala, UN Doc., CERD/C/GTM/CO/11 and for Guyana, UN Doc., CERD/C/GUY/CO/14.

counselling and support for victims.[128]

d. Reparation

Under the right to remedy, some form of reparation is required. It can take various forms such as compensation, restitution, guarantees of non-repetition, changes in relevant laws, and public apologies. In general, compensatory measures are recommended to redress corporate human rights abuses. As such, in its General Comment No. 31, the Human Rights Committee notes that, "*where appropriate, reparation can involve restitution, rehabilitation and measures of satisfaction, such as public apologies, public memorials, guarantees of non-repetition and changes in relevant laws and practices, as well as bringing to justice the perpetrators of human rights violations.*"[129]

4. Promotional measures

States must also take promotional measures such as awareness-raising, human rights education and training for private actors. In General Comment No. 5 on "Persons with Disabilities", the CESCR-Committee stresses the importance of raising the awareness of the rights of persons with disabilities while recognizing that there is the absence of an explicit, disability-related provision in the ICESCR. As such, the CESCR-Committee highlights the wide acceptance that "*the human rights of persons with disabilities must be protected and promoted through general, as well as specifically designed,*

---

128 See CEDAW-Committee General Recommendation No. 19.

129 Supra note 108, CCPR-Committee General Comment No. 31 [80] on *"The Nature of the General Legal Obligation Imposed on States Parties to the Covenant"*, UN DOC, CCPR/C/21/Rev.1/Add.13, para. 16.
See also Eibe Riedel, 'Commentary to Art. 55 (c), UN-Charter,' in Simma (Ed.): The Charter of the United Nations, A Commentary, (2002) (2nd ed.), Oxford University Press, 24 pp; 'Commentary to Art.68, UN-Charter,' in Simma (Ed.): The Charter of the United Nations, A Commentary, (2002) (2nd ed.), Oxford University Press, 34 pp.

laws, policies and programmes."[130] Further, the CESCR-Committee notes the emphasis laid on the need for States parties "*to take action to raise awareness in society about persons with disabilities, their rights, their needs, their potential and their contribution*" contained in the Standard Rules on the Equalization of Opportunities with Disabilities.[131] In addition, the Committee on the Rights of Persons with Disabilities (CRPD-Committee) also stresses the importance of awareness-raising.[132] The CESCR-Committee, in its Concluding Observations[133] for Iceland, further notes that it is particularly common to see directions to raise awareness among the media, the IT industry, as well as the need to eliminate stereotypes and dissemination of harmful material.

The *State duty* to protect also includes encouragement for private entities to develop or amend codes of conduct and institutional charters that would include the respect and promotion of human rights therein. In its General Comment No. 12 on the right to food, the CESCR-Committee specifically states that "*the State should provide an environment that facilitates implementation of these responsibilities. The private business sector – national and transnational – should pursue its activities within the framework of a code of conduct conducive to respect of the right to adequate food, agreed upon jointly with the Government and civil society.*"[134]

B. The *Corporate Responsibility* to Respect

As noted above in Chapter 1, business enterprises are held accountable only for certain international crimes under the international criminal law

130 CESCR-Committee General Comment No.5: Persons with Disabilities, UN Doc., E/1995/22.
131 Ibid.
132 Art. 8(2)(a)(iii) and 2(c) of CRPD.
133 UN Doc., E/C.12/1/Add.89.
134 UN Doc., E/C.12/1999/5.

regime and/or under customary international law and *ius cogens* norms on the international law plane. In terms of how to establish such corporate accountability at the national level, there is currently no uniform and consistent state practice establishing it.

As seen above, the traditional view of international human rights law holds that indirect legal obligation can only be imposed on corporations, *i.e.*, business enterprises have only the responsibility to respect human rights, whereas States have the direct international legal obligations to respect, protect and fulfil human rights in relation to business activities.[135] Treaty bodies also tend to confirm that corporations have only this indirect responsibility to respect human rights, when it comes to corporate human rights abuse. As such, they reaffirm that the treaty obligations only extend to States parties, not to other social actors such as corporations. For instance, the CESCR-Committee, in General Comment No. 8, paragraph 52, clarifies that corporations are not bound by the ICSCER while they "*have a particular role to play in job creation, hiring policies and non-discriminatory access to work*."[136] The CRC-Committee General Comment No. 5,[137] paragraph 56 however suggests, if not explicitly, that the direct obligation can be extended to corporations in practice. It states that the *State duty* to respect "extends in practice" to non-State organizations without clearly specifying what this entails. The Human Rights Committee, in General Comment No. 31,[138] paragraph 8, also concludes that the treaty obligations "*do not… have direct horizontal effect as a matter of international law*," which means that they take effect between non-State actors only on the domestic law plane.

---

135 Some observers argue that international human rights instruments "*already impose direct legal obligation on corporations but merely lack direct accountability mechanisms*." See para. 35 of UN Doc., A/HRC/4/35.

136 UN Doc., E/C.12/1997/8.

137 UN Doc., CRC/GC/2003/5.

138 UN Doc., CCPR/C/21/Rev.1/Add. 13.

I. The Definition

As repeatedly been argued, the present thesis is premised on the theory that there is a clear distinction between the *State obligation* to protect from corporate human rights abuse and the *Corporate responsibility* to respect human rights. Some commentators have argued that corporations as part of "organs of society" are also legally obliged to respect human rights on the international law plane. However, a more common view holds that corporations are "specialized economic organs", not "democratic public interest institutions". Hence, their responsibilities are different from the duties of States.[139] Hence, unlike the *State obligation* to protect from corporate human rights abuse, there is no direct legal obligation on companies under international human rights law, apart from a few exceptions under international criminal law, customary international law and *ius cogens*. Accordingly, corporations, as special organs of society, *should* simply meet the expectations placed on them by society to respect human rights. The *Corporate responsibility* to respect human rights is "*a basic expectation that society has of business*."[140] This responsibility, however, is not merely a negative responsibility of "*doing no harm,*" but it entails taking positive steps, for instance, adopting specific recruitment and training programmes in the framework of a workplace non-discrimination policy. Such societal expectations placed on business enterprises point to a range of important actions that corporations *should* take, which constitutes the core elements of such *Corporate responsibility* to respect human rights. It is therefore crucial to identify those core elements of the *Corporate responsibility* to respect

---

139 Supra note 9, David Weissbrodt and Muria Kruger, 'Norms on the Responsibilities of Transnational Corporations and Other Business Enterprises with Regard to Human Rights,' 97 Am. J. Int'l L. 901 (2003), available at: https://scholarship.law.umn.edu/cgi/viewcontent.cgi?article=1247&context=faculty_articles (Accessed as of 01 September 2024); Andrew Clapham, Human Rights Obligations of Non-State Actors, Oxford University Press (2006), 59-107.

140 Supra note 7, John Ruggie, 'Protect, Respect and Remedy: A Framework for Business and Human Rights', Report of the Special Representative of the Secretary-General on the issue of human rights and transnational corporations and other business enterprises UN Doc, A/HRC/8/5, para. 9.

human rights under the current existing international standards (*Combination/zebra* standards),[141] which should become part and parcel of the distinctive responsibilities of business enterprises in relation to human rights.

II. Human Rights Due Diligence

To fulfil the responsibility to respect human rights, companies should conduct human rights due diligence in their own operations and in their supply chains, which constitutes a core element of the *Corporate responsibility* to respect human rights. As such, human rights due diligence lies at the heart of the *Corporate responsibility* to respect human rights under the most recent and authoritative *Combination/zebra* standards, namely the UN Guiding Principles on Business and Human Rights.

Human rights due diligence under the UN Guiding Principles on Business and Human Rights is understood as "*the processes that all business enterprises should undertake to identify, prevent, mitigate and account for how they address potential and actual impacts on human rights caused by or contributed to through their own activities, or directly linked to their operations, products or services by their business relationships.*"[142] In this regard, it is worth noting that due diligence encompasses two different concepts: firstly, due diligence as the process of managing business risks; and secondly, due diligence as the standard of conduct required to discharge an obligation.[143] Both concepts were employed in the UN Guiding Principles on Business and Human Rights. The latter concept of due diligence as a

---

141 See supra notes 2 and 90.

142 Supra note 4, Guiding Principles on Business and Human Rights: Implementing the United Nations Protect, Respect and Remedy Framework, Office of the United Nations High Commissioner for Human Rights, UN Publication, HR/PUB/11/04, Principles 17-24. See also 'The report of the Working Group on the issue of human rights and transnational corporations and other business enterprises to the UN General Assembly,' UN Doc. A/73/163, para. 2.

143 Jonathan Bonnitcha and Robert McCorquodale, "The Concept of 'Due Diligence' in the UN Guiding Principles on Business and Human Rights," European Journal of International Law (EJIL) (2017) Vol. 28 No. 3, pp. 899-919.

standard of conduct required to discharge an obligation traces its origin in Roman law, under which, a person who has caused accidental harm to others must be liable if the harm caused resulted from the person's failure to meet the standard conduct expected of a *diligens paterfamilias*. It was an objective standard in that a defendant's conduct was to be assessed against an external standard of expected conduct, not against his/her intentions and motivations. It was also a fact-specific standard in that the expected standard of conduct by a prudent person was dependent on the circumstances of the specific case.[144]

The concept of due diligence as a standard of conduct required to discharge an obligation has been introduced into international law in the 17th century. Due diligence in international law serves to function primarily as "*a standard of conduct that defines and circumscribes the responsibility of a state in relation to the conduct of third parties*."[145] This concept of due diligence plays an important role in defining the State obligation to prevent, punish, investigate, or redress the harm caused by private persons or entities, including business enterprises under international human rights law. In other words, as long as the conduct of private actors is not attributable to the State, the State is under an obligation to meet a certain standard of conduct (due diligence) in preventing and responding to the conduct of such third private actors.[146] This concept of due diligence has important implications on interpreting the requirements of the human rights due diligence to be conducted by companies in their own operations and in their supply chains under the UN Guiding Principles on Business and Human Rights. Under the *Corporate responsibility* to respect human rights laid out in the UN Guiding

---

144 Supra note 143, Jonathan Bonnitcha and Robert McCorquodale, "The Concept of 'Due Diligence' in the UN Guiding Principles on Business and Human Rights," European Journal of International Law (EJIL) (2017) Vol. 28 No. 3, 899-919, at p. 902; R. Zimmerman, The Law of Obligations: Roman Foundations of the Civilian Tradition (1996), at 1008; Justinian, The Digest of Roman Law: Theft, Rapine, Damage and Insult, translated by Colin Kolbert (1979), at 91.

145 Supra note 143, Jonathan Bonnitcha and Robert McCorquodale, "The Concept of 'Due Diligence' in the UN Guiding Principles on Business and Human Rights," European Journal of International Law (EJIL) (2017) Vol. 28 No. 3, 899-919, at p. 903.

146 Ibid., at pp.904-906.

Principles on Business and Human Rights, business enterprises are expected to conduct human rights due diligence in order to identify, prevent, mitigate and account for how they address their adverse human rights impacts. Human rights due diligence should cover adverse human rights impacts caused or contributed to by the enterprise through its own activities, or those adverse human rights impacts which may be directly linked to its operations, products or services by its business relationships. As such, particularly when it comes to determining what is required of business enterprise as part of them conducting human rights due diligence in relation to those adverse human rights impacts, which may be directly linked to the business enterprise's operations, products or services by its business relationships, the concept of due diligence as a standard of conduct to discharge an obligation applied to States in the framework of the *State duty* to protect from corporate human rights abuse can also be applied to business enterprises in the context of the *Corporate responsibility* to respect human rights.

There currently exist a host of regulatory schemes linking due diligence as a standard conduct with the process of investigation as part of the due diligence conducted aimed at assessing business risks. These regulatory schemes can provide some inspirations for interpreting the concept of human rights due diligence under the *Corporate responsibility* to respect human rights under the UN Guiding Principles on Business and Human Rights. For instance, section 11 of the US Federal Securities Act 1933[147] imposes a legal liability on the directors of a company for incorrect statements and omissions of material facts in the documentation accompanying a securities offering. It also recognizes a 'due diligence' defence to liability. Under this law, the directors of the company must meet the two requirements: the first requirement is that the defendant must show that he or she has carried out a process of reasonable investigation to establish that the statements are

---

147 Securities Act of 1933, 15 U.S.C. §§ 77a-77aa. It can be accessed at: https://www.govinfo.gov/content/pkg/COMPS-1884/pdf/COMPS-1884.pdf. (Accessed as of 1 September 2024).

true and complete. The second requirement is that the defendant must have reasonably believed that the statements are true and complete.[148] On the other hand, in spite of the fact that two concepts of due diligence are incorporated therein, the UK Modern Slavery Act 2015,[149] which requires companies to publish an annual statement documenting the steps taken to eradicate slavery and human trafficking in their own operations and in their supply chains simply encourages companies to establish due diligence processes in relation to slavery and human trafficking without incurring any legal liability for slavery and human trafficking within their supply chains thus the concept of due diligence as a standard of expected conduct required to discharge an obligation playing no role.[150]

Under the UN Guiding Principles on Business and Human Rights, the two concepts of due diligence have been confusingly used with the result that it makes it difficult to identify when it can be said that business enterprises have breached the *Corporate responsibility* to respect human rights, for which they have a responsibility to provide remedy. If human rights due diligence as a standard of expected conduct to discharge an obligation applies, business enterprises are only responsible for adverse human rights impacts that result from their failure to act with reasonable diligence. In contrast, if business enterprises are deemed to breach the responsibility to respect human rights whenever there are adverse human rights impacts, they are responsible for all adverse human rights impacts regardless of whether those adverse impacts were unexpected or costly to prevent.[151]

---

148 Supra note 146, Jonathan Bonnitcha and Robert McCorquodale, "The Concept of 'Due Diligence' in the UN Guiding Principles on Business and Human Rights," European Journal of International Law (EJIL) (2017) Vol. 28 No. 3, 899-919, at p. 906.

149 Modern Slavery Act 2015, 2015 CHAPTER 30. It can be accessed at the following webpage: https://www.legislation.gov.uk/ukpga/2015/30/contents/enacted. (Accessed as of 1 September 2024).

150 Supra note 146, Jonathan Bonnitcha and Robert McCorquodale, "The Concept of 'Due Diligence' in the UN Guiding Principles on Business and Human Rights," European Journal of International Law (EJIL) (2017) Vol. 28 No. 3, 899-919, at p. 908.

151 Ibid., at pp. 908-911.

An interpretation more consistent with international human rights law appears that the *Corporate responsibility* to respect human rights under the UN Guiding Principles on Business and Human Rights comprises two elements: the first element is the responsibility for their own adverse human rights impacts; and the second is their responsibility for the human rights impacts of third parties, with which they have business relationships. The former responsibility is a no-fault strict responsibility, and the latter responsibility requires that business enterprises meet a due diligence standard of conduct. Accordingly, business enterprises have a correlative responsibility to provide remedy to all their own adverse human rights impacts, regardless as to whether those adverse human rights impacts have resulted from their failure to act with reasonable diligence or not. On the other hand, business enterprises are only required to take reasonable steps to prevent and mitigate the adverse human rights impacts of third parties, with which they have business relationships.[152] In contrast, it has been argued that the responsibility to respect human rights entails a due diligence standard of conduct, which suggests that the same standard of due diligence conduct applies both to the responsibility of business enterprises for their own adverse impacts and for the adverse impacts of third parties, with which they have business relationships.[153]

This thesis subscribes to the interpretation that while business enterprises have the responsibility and its correlative responsibility to provide a remedy (strict responsibility) for their own adverse human rights impacts, they have the responsibility and its correlative responsibility to provide remedy only for the adverse human rights impacts caused by third parties, with which they have business relationships that have resulted from their failure to act with reasonable diligence to prevent and mitigate such adverse human rights

152 Ibid., at pp. 912-919.

153 Sanders, 'The Impact of the "Ruggie Framework" and the United Nations Guiding Principles on Business and Human Rights on Transnational Human Rights Litigation', LSE Law, Society and Economy Working Papers 18/2014 (2014), at pp. 15-17.

impacts. This interpretation provides necessary clarity about the standard of conduct (due diligence) that business enterprises are expected to satisfy in avoiding their own adverse human rights impacts. It can also provide much-needed clarity for corporate human rights victims regarding what corporate human rights harm they can claim the responsibility to provide a remedy against. Further, it can be relevant to any future domestic and international norms and standards on the *Corporate responsibility* to respect human rights, in particular the content of the required human rights due diligence, as the *Corporate responsibility* to respect human rights cannot be implemented in law, unless it is clarified whether the standard of conduct to discharge an obligation applies to the adverse human rights impacts caused by third parties or also to their own adverse human rights impacts.[154]

When conducting human rights due diligence, corporations should consider the following main three factors: firstly, the country contexts in which their business activities take place, which will enable corporations to highlight any specific human rights challenges that their business activities may pose; secondly, what human rights impacts their own activities may have within that context; and thirdly, whether their business activities might contribute to human rights abuses through the relationships connected to their activities such as with business partners, suppliers, State agencies and other non-State actors.[155]

More concretely, there exist three principal pillars of action to be taken by corporations to fulfil their responsibility to respect human rights, the human rights due diligence component of which is considered to be essential. These include: firstly, adoption of a human rights policy and its

---

154 Supra note 146, Jonathan Bonnitcha and Robert McCorquodale, "The Concept of 'Due Diligence' in the UN Guiding Principles on Business and Human Rights," European Journal of International Law (EJIL) (2017) Vol. 28 No. 3, 899-919, at p. 919.

155 Supra note 145, The report of the Working Group on the issue of human rights and transnational corporations and other business enterprises to the UN General Assembly, UN Doc. A/73/163, para. 57.

embedding in the entire business operations, including in the context of partnership relationships with suppliers and other stakeholders. In this regard, it is also critical to design detailed guidance in specific functional areas to give meaning to the policy. In terms of embedding/integration of human rights policies, leadership and commitment from the top is essential to the respect of human rights throughout the business enterprise; secondly, conducting human rights impact assessments before a proposed business activity starts; and thirdly, monitoring and auditing performance aimed at tracking ongoing developments, which allows for regular updates on human rights impacts and performance. Here, it is worth recalling that confidential means to report non-compliance may serve as useful feedback regarding tracking performance.[156]

Other important additional element to consider as regards defining the core elements of human rights due diligence is the concept of "sphere of influence."[157] In this regard, the then Special Representative of the Secretary General on the issue of human rights and transnational corporations and other business enterprises argued that the sphere of influence was too broad and ambiguous a concept to define the scope of due diligence as part of the *Corporate responsibility* to respect. He, instead, proposed to use an alternative approach, namely, to use the concept of avoiding complicity or being implicated in human rights violations. As such, avoiding complicity is viewed as an integral part of the human rights due diligence that business enterprises are required to conduct, as it describes a sub-set of the indirect ways, in which

---

156 Ibid., paras. 56-64. The Special Representative identified the four principal actions as follows: human rights policies; human rights impact assessments; integration; and tracking performance. On the other hand, the present thesis subsumes integration (embedding) under the category of human rights policies in order to highlight the fact that embedding human rights policies in the company's entire operations is a real sign of commitment on the part of the enterprise to respect human rights, not as a mere public relations exercise or as a lip-service to the growing demand that society places on companies to respect human rights.

157 Supra note 9, David Weissbrodt and Muria Kruger, 'Norms on the Responsibilities of Transnational Corporations and Other Business Enterprises with Regard to Human Rights,' 97 Am. J. Int'l L. 901 (2003), available at: https://scholarship.law.umn.edu/cgi/viewcontent.cgi?article=1247&context=faculty_articles (Accessed as of 1 September 2024).

business enterprises can have adverse human rights impacts through their relationships.[158]

Out of these three principal elements of human rights due diligence for business enterprises to meet the *Corporate responsibility* to respect human rights, conducting human rights impact assessments lies at the heart of such human rights due diligence exercise. As such, conducting human rights impact assessments has been gaining growing importance. Despite such growing importance, human rights impact assessments are a relatively recent emerging trend, as compared to the established practice of environmental and social impact assessments. Hence, many business enterprises conduct human rights impact assessments building upon the methodological principles and characteristics of environmental and social impact assessments, which offer some similarities for human rights impact assessments. Furthermore, human rights impact assessments have their own distinctive characteristics from those of environmental and social impact assessments.

Impact assessment can simply be defined as "*the process of identifying the future consequences of a current or proposed action*".[159] To apply this simple definition to the context of human rights impact assessments, one should ask a range of questions. The primordial question to ask is how

---

158 John Ruggie, 'Report of the Special Representative of the Secretary-General on the Issue of Human Rights and Transnational Corporations and other Business Enterprises: Clarifying the Concepts of "Sphere of influence" and "Complicity",' UN Doc., A/HRC/8/16. It can be accessed at the following webpage: https://documents.un.org/doc/undoc/gen/g08/134/78/pdf/g0813478.pdf. (Accessed as of 10 February 2025).

159 International Association for Impact Assessment (IAIA), Social Impact Assessment: International principles. Special Publication Series No. 2, May 2003. International Principles for Social Impact Assessment defines it as "the processes of analysing, monitoring and managing the intended and unintended social consequences, both positive and negative, of planned interventions (policies, programs, plans, projects) and any social change processes invoked by those interventions." International Association for Impact Association, Social Impact Assessment: Guidance for assessing and managing the social impacts of projects, April 2015. It can be accessed at the following webpage: https://www.iaia.org/uploads/pdf/SIA_Guidance_Document_IAIA.pdf. (Accessed as of 1 September 2024).

business activity will impact human rights. In this way, human rights impact assessments can identify those who are most directly involved and affected by such a business activity. These include both rights-holders and duty-bearers and other stakeholders, including local communities, Governments, and employees. Through identification of those people who are most directly involved and affected, interventions can be designed, aimed at enhancing positive effects, as well as preventing/avoiding or mitigating any negative impacts and adverse risks that the proposed business activity can pose. It is critical to take such interventions prior to rather than in response to changes brought out by that business activity.[160]

Similar to environmental and social impact assessment, human rights impact assessments contain the following basic conditions: firstly, human rights impact assessments should describe the proposed business activity considering its full business life cycle; secondly, they should map out the legal, regulatory and administrative standards, to which the concerned business activity shall be subjected, including the relevant national and local laws and regulations of the home and host states, requirements of project financiers, and internal company policies; thirdly, they should contain the description of human rights conditions in the area surrounding the business activity. Herein, engagement of human rights experts and local stakeholders is critical; fourthly, they should be able to put forth a view of what is likely to change because of the business activity; fifthly, it is critical that human rights impact assessments prioritize the human rights risks to be presented by the proposed business activity, and suggest practical recommendations aimed at addressing those risks; sixthly, those recommendations of human rights impact assessments should be incorporated into a management plan that includes provisions for monitoring the baseline indicators as well as regular consultation with affected parties; seventhly, human rights impact assessments should include

---

160 John Ruggie, 'Report of the Special Representative of the Secretary-General on the issue of human rights and transnational corporations and other business enterprises: Human rights impact assessments – resolving key methodological questions,' UN Doc., A/HRC/4/74, para. 2.

a discussion of applicable good practices; eighthly, from a perspective of process, it is critical to involve experts in the industry, local context and human rights. As such, the human rights impact assessments process can serve as an important convening mechanism to bring representatives of the company, community, and government into a dialogue; and ninthly, once human rights impact assessments are finalized, their results should be fully published, bearing in mind reasonable potential risks that may force a partial or summary publication.[161]

The distinctiveness of human rights impact assessments *vis-à-vis* environmental and social impact assessments lies in the fact that: firstly, human rights impact assessment should be framed by the International Bill of Human Rights at a minimum; secondly, human rights impact assessments should also map out the relevant human rights standards and other standards such as indigenous customary laws and traditions, and international humanitarian law; thirdly, if there exist associated investment treaty obligations, human rights impact assessments should examine whether human rights protections have been adequately built therein; fourthly, human rights impact assessments require a careful and detailed consideration of how the proposed activity could possibly interact with each and every right; fifthly, human rights impact assessments could draw upon the principles of the human rights-based approach to programming, in particular such principles as empowerment, participation, non-discrimination, accountability and prioritization of vulnerable groups; and sixthly, drawing upon the methodological tools of the human rights-based approach to programming, human rights impact assessments could include an assessment of the causes of the non-realization of rights and the capacity of the rights holders to claim their rights and the duty-bearers to fulfil their obligations. As such, where weak governance is present in a country, such an analysis may conclude that

161 Ibid., paras. 11-21.

the company finds itself assuming the role of the duty-bearer.[162]

For human rights impact assessments to be effective, a collaborative approach to human rights impact assessments should be employed. Collaborative human rights impact assessments could: improve information sharing thereby leading to deeper understandings of impacts; facilitate stakeholders' efforts to engage in dialogue, identify shared priorities and reach agreement on key issues; reduce the risk of social conflicts and associated financial and reputational costs; improve the company's human rights capacities, engagement strategies and decision-making, including for future projects; provide a new avenue for direct communication for project-affected people with the company thereby helping them to more effectively influence the company's decision-making regarding the design or implementation of a project or operation that stands to affect them. When governments participate in such collaborative human rights impact assessments, their involvement could send an important signal to companies regarding the importance of rights-compliant investments. It could also increase the potential that governments will engage meaningfully with the recommendations flowing from such collaborative human rights impacts assessments.[163]

C. Interim Conclusions

A clear distinction can be made under the current international human rights law regime between the *State obligation* to protect from corporate human rights abuse and the *Corporate responsibility* to respect human rights. The former is a well-established legal obligation as part of the *State obligations*

162 Ibid., paras. 22-29.

163 Columbia Center on Sustainable Investment, Danish Institute for Human Rights, and Sciences Po Law School Clinic, A Collaborative Approach to Human Rights Impact Assessments, March 2017, at pp.7-12. It can be accessed at the following webpage: https://ccsi.columbia.edu/sites/default/files/content/A-Collaborative-Approach-to-HRIAs_Web.pdf. (Accessed as of 1 September 2024).

to respect, protect and fulfil (promote and provide) under international human rights law. On the other hand, the *Corporate responsibility* to respect human rights is not a legal obligation *per se*. However, it is a basic expectation that society has of business as a social organ carrying out specialized functions in society. It should be noted that under certain special circumstances, business enterprises are also directly held to legal accountability/obligation. For instance, in the case of international crimes such as genocide, crimes against humanity and war crimes, individuals, including legal persons such as business enterprises can be legally liable for committing such international crimes. Individuals, including legal persons, are also subject to customary international law, *ius cogens* norms and general principles of international law. However, the *Corporate responsibility* to respect human rights has yet to be established as a legal obligation through being ripened into customary international law and/or general principles of international law on the international law plane.

When it comes to the *State obligation* to protect from corporate human rights abuse, international human rights treaties impose such an obligation on States parties in many ways: firstly, the generalized obligations under various international human rights treaties are imposed on States parties to take all necessary measures to protect from human rights abuses by third parties, including business enterprises. As such, the *State obligation* to protect from corporate human rights abuse can be established from these generalized obligations imposed on States parties when they voluntarily agree to become a State party to such international human rights treaties; and secondly, some international human rights treaties make specific references to the obligation of States parties in relation to business enterprises and/or specific industries or sectors such as banking and finance, agricultural or media sectors.

What constitutes the main elements of this *State obligation* to protect from corporate human rights abuse is a question of interpretation. The Human Rights Committee has employed the concept of "due diligence" to prevent, punish, investigate, adjudicate, and eventually provide remedies to victims of corporate human rights abuses. The concept of due diligence as a standard of conduct to discharge an obligation applied to States in the framework of the *State duty* to protect from corporate human rights abuse can also equally be applied to business enterprises in the context of the *Corporate responsibility* to respect human rights. It can be particularly applied, when it comes to determining what is required of business enterprises' conducting human rights due diligence as part of meeting their *Corporate responsibility* to respect human rights in relation to adverse human rights impacts, which may be directly linked to the business enterprise's operations, products or services by its business relationships. It is submitted that States parties must and should take an array of legislative, administrative, policy and judicial measures necessary to meet their international obligation to protect from human rights abuse by third parties, including business enterprises. Broadly categorized, these measures, include monitoring, regulation, adjudication, reparation, as well as promotional measures.

The *Corporate responsibility* to respect human rights is societal expectations placed on business enterprises to respect human rights in relation to their business operations that could impact on the enjoyment of the rights of the people. The concept of 'sphere of influence' could serve a useful purpose in determining the degree and extent of such impacts on the enjoyment of the human rights of the people affected by business operations. This will further help identify corresponding responsibilities of companies to individual situations. The more proximate the sphere of influence of a company's operations is to the human rights impacts caused by company's operations, the more direct responsibility the company should bear. For instance, a company has a more direct responsibility to make sure that company workers' rights are respected. In most cases, such a direct responsibility is part of a legal obligation under domestic labour law. However, when it comes to protecting the rights of its suppliers or the rights of wider consumers, the *Corporate responsibility* to respect human rights becomes less strong, even though this does not necessarily mean that the *Corporate responsibility* ceases to exist in these cases. There is an alternative approach to using the concept of 'complicity' when it comes to identifying the *Corporate responsibility* to respect human rights, in particular the scope of "due diligence." This approach requires that companies should avoid complicity in human rights violations, for which they should act with "due diligence" to avoid knowingly contributing to human rights violations/abuses, regardless of a potential risk of legal liability. As such, "due diligence" will help companies to identify and act upon risks in a way that companies can ensure that they do not knowingly contribute to such human rights violations/abuses or knowingly benefit from them.[164]

The core elements of the *Corporate responsibility* to respect human rights has the three principal components: a policy commitment to meet the responsibility to respect human rights; a human rights due diligence process to identify, prevent, mitigate and account for how a business enterprise addresses its adverse human rights impacts; and the remediation processes of adverse human rights impacts that it has caused or contributed to. Human rights due diligence is a core element of the *Corporate responsibility* to respect human rights. Conducting human rights due diligence under the *Corporate responsibility* to respect human rights requires business enterprises to: carry out human rights impact assessments before initiating any business activity; adopting human rights policies whereby business enterprises commit themselves to the imperative of respecting human rights throughout their entire operations and beyond; and tracking human rights performance in order to not only adjust human rights policies to the changing business contexts but also to ensure for mechanisms that allow victims of corporate human rights abuses to have access to adequate remedies. Such human rights due diligence should not only be conducted in the context of companies'

---

164 Supra note 161, John Ruggie, 'Report of the Special Representative of the Secretary-General on the Issue of Human Rights and Transnational Corporations and other Business Enterprises: Clarifying the Concepts of "Sphere of influence" and "Complicity",' UN Doc., A/HRC/8/16, para. 71. It can be accessed at the following webpage: https://documents.un.org/doc/undoc/gen/g08/134/78/pdf/g0813478.pdf. (Accessed as of 10 February 2025).

own operations, but also in the framework of the relationships associated with such company operations with a view to ensuring that companies are not complicit or implicated in human rights harms caused by third parties such as in the supply chain.[165] In this connection, it is also important to make a clear distinction that business enterprises hold the responsibility for their own adverse human rights impacts (human rights harms caused by their own operations) regardless of whether they have taken reasonable steps to prevent and mitigate such adverse human rights impacts, while they hold the responsibility and its correlative responsibility to provide a remedy to the adverse human rights impacts (human rights harms) of third parties that resulted from their failure to act with reasonable due diligence, with which they have business relationships.

Human rights impact assessments to be conducted under the framework of human rights due diligence should be done ideally in a collaborative manner in collaboration with stakeholders, including the affected people by the company's projects or operations and governments.

165 Ibid., para. 72.

Part 2

Interpretative Guidance by UN Treaty Bodies

Chapter 3: Interpretative Guidance of Various Treaty Bodies

A. Main Functions of Treaty Bodies

The United Nations Treaty Bodies is a system of expert monitoring bodies created under the relevant international human rights treaties or by the relevant UN inter-governmental bodies such as the United Nations Economic and Social Council (ECOSOC), particularly in the case of the United Nations Committee on Economic, Social and Cultural Rights (hereinafter referred to as the CESCR-Committee).

The main functions of treaty bodies are largely threefold: firstly, monitoring the level of implementation by States parties of treaty provisions under the concerned treaty. This monitoring takes place in the form of a periodic review of the state report through constructive dialogue with the States party concerned.[166] It is worth noting here that there needs clarifying

166 For a general exposition of the monitoring by the CESCR-Committee, see Eibe Riedel, 'The Committee on Economic, Social and Cultural Rights,' in Max Planck Encyclopedia of Public International Law (MPEPIL), Oxford University Press (2010), No. 765; Eibe Riedel,

that the concept of "constructive dialogue" is employed by treaty bodies not to obfuscate the international obligations of States parties to respect, protect and fulfil human rights but rather to "*entice the country concerned to do everything in its power to improve the human rights situation for its population*"[167] This approach has limitations. Hence, once treaty bodies conclude that there are violations of the obligations to respect, protect and fulfil human rights by States parties, they clearly point that out. Treaty bodies use this constructive dialogue approach as it is felt to be better to suggest and recommend remedial action, instead of insisting on the fact that violations have occurred.[168] The outcome of the review is normally called "Concluding Observations." The Concluding Observations can serve as "*a catalyst to state action in developing national benchmarks and devising appropriate mechanisms for establishing accountability*," and provide for means of remedy for victims of human rights violations. They further seek to hold the States

---

'Monitoring the International Covenant on Economic, Social and Cultural Rights (1966)," in: Politakis, George P. (Ed.): Protecting Labour Rights as Human Rights: Present and Future of International Supervision, International Colloquium on the 80th anniversary of the ILO Committee of Experts,' Geneva, pp. 24-25 November 2006, ILO Geneva 2007, pp. 3-13. Cf B. Simma, 'The Examination of State Reports,' in E. Klein (ed.), The Monitoring System of Human Rights Treaty Obligations, Berlin, 1998, pp.31-48; Eibe Riedel, 'The Examination of State Reports,' *ibid.*, pp. 95-105.

167 Supra note 166, Eibe Riedel, 'Monitoring the International Covenant on Economic, Social and Cultural Rights (1966)," in: Politakis, George P. (Ed.): Protecting Labour Rights as Human Rights: Present and Future of International Supervision, International Colloquium on the 80th anniversary of the ILO Committee of Experts,' Geneva, pp. 24-25 November 2006, ILO Geneva 2007, pp. 3-13, at 10-11.

168 Ibid. See also Eibe Riedel, 'Core Obligations in Social Rights and Human Dignity,' pp. 79-91 at pp. 82-83, and 89-90 in 'Von der Kultur der Verfassung' (Max-Emanuel Geis, Markus Winkler, Christian Bickenbach Eds.), Festschrift Für Friedhelm Hufen Zum 70. Geburtstag, C.H.Beck (2015, special print); For a critical analysis of the "constructive dialogue" approach, Supra note 49, Christian Tomuschat, Human Rights Between Idealism and Realism(2nd Ed.), Oxford University Press (2008), p. 38 et seq. Contra, see A. Eide, "Economic and Social Rights" in J. Symonides (Ed.), Human Rights. Concept and Standards, Aldershot, 2000, reprinted 2005, pp.109-174; M. Craven, The International Covenant on Economic, Social and Cultural Rights – A Perspective on its Development, Oxford, 1995, p. 106 et seq.; E. Riedel, 'International Law Shaping Constitutional Law – Realization of Economic, Social and Cultural Rights,' in Eibe Riedel (Ed.), Constitutionalism – Old Concepts, New Worlds, Berlin, 2005, pp. 109-126, p. 109 et seq.

parties accountable at the national level[169]; secondly, issuing interpretative guidance on the content of the treaty provisions contained in each concerned treaty in the form of "General Comments" or "General Recommendations." These General Comments seek to clarify the normative content of the rights recognized in respective treaties thus providing authoritative interpretation of the rights, which can, in turn, serve as a source of interpretation at national-level adjudication processes.[170] These General Comments are legally non-binding on States parties. They rather serve as authoritative guidance/ standards, in particular as interpretation aids regarding the scope of the substantive treaty provisions. However, once adopted, they are frequently invoked by States parties in formulating their periodic reports to the concerned treaty bodies. They are also increasingly invoked by national courts in their judicial decisions, which points, according to Professor Riedel, to the possibility that they could be transformed into customary international law, "first as expressions of an established *opinio iuris*, and later as contributory – but not exclusive – evidence of state practice"[171]; and thirdly, processing individual complaints/petitions.[172]

In addition, some treaty bodies, based on the provisions of the relevant

---

169 Supra note 27, Henry J. Steiner/Philip Alston (Eds.), International Human Rights in Context: Law, Politics, Morals, Oxford University Press (1996), p. 316.

170 Jane Connors, 'United Nations,' International Human Rights Law (Daniel Moeckli, Sangeeta Shah & Sandesh Sivakumaran Eds.), Oxford University Press (2014), pp.369-410 at pp. 391-392.

171 Eibe Riedel, 'The Development of International Law: Alternatives to Treaty-Making? International Organizations and Non-State-Actors, Developments of International Law in Treaty Making, Rüdiger Wolfrum/Volker Röben (Eds.), Heidelberg (2005), pp. 301-318, at p. 315.

172 Any individual who claims that her or his rights under the treaty have been violated may bring a complaint called "communication" before the relevant committee, provided that the States party has recognized the competence of the committee to receive such complaints or they are a State party to optional protocols that establish such an individual complaint system such as the first optional protocol to the International Covenant on Civil and Political Rights (ICCPR-OP1), the Optional Protocol to the International Covenant on Economic, Social and Cultural Rights, the Optional Protocol to the Convention on the Rights of the Child on a communications procedure, the Optional Protocol to the Convention on the Elimination of All Forms of Discrimination against Women, and the Optional Protocol to the Convention on the Rights of Persons with Disabilities.

treaties can conduct inquiries if they receive reliable information that contains well-founded indications of serious, grave, or systematic violations of the conventions in a State party. Upon receipt of such reliable information, treaty bodies, on their own initiatives, can initiate inquires, which can be conducted with respect to the State parties that have recognized the competence of the relevant committee. Inquiries procedure is provided in the Convention against Torture (Article 20), the OP-CEDAW (Article 8), the OP-CRPD (Article 6), the ICPPED (Article 33), the OP-ICESCR (Article 11) and the OP-CRC on a communications procedure (Article. 13). As an exception, under the ICPPED (Article 3), the Committee on Enforced Disappearances (ED-Committee) can conduct inquiries without the acceptance of the competence of the Committee by States Parties.

The process of inquiries is as follows: firstly, upon receipt of reliable information containing well-founded indications of serious, grave, or systematic violations of the concerned convention in a State party, the relevant committee invites the concerned State party to cooperate in the examination of the information through submitting its own observations; secondly, on the basis of the State party's observations and other information available to it, the Committee may decide to designate one or more of its members to conduct an inquiry and report urgently to the Committee. If warranted and with the consent of the concerned State party, an inquiry may include a visit to the country; thirdly, the findings of the inquiry member/s will be examined by the Committee and transmitted to the concerned State party with any other comments and recommendations; and fourthly, the concerned State party will be invited to submit its own observations on the findings, comments and recommendations of the Committee within a specific timeframe (usually 6 months), and if invited by the Committee, the concerned State party is also invited to inform the Committee of the measures taken in response to the inquiry. The inquiry procedure is confidential, and the cooperation of the concerned State party is sought at all stages of proceedings.[173] Furthermore, the Subcommittee on Prevention of Torture and Other Cruel, Inhuman or Degrading Treatment or Punishment established under the Optional Protocol to the Convention against Torture (OP-CAT) can visit places of detention to prevent torture and other cruel, inhuman or degrading treatment or punishment.[174]

B. General Comments

As elaborated in Chapter 2, treaty bodies have clarified both through General Comments/General Recommendations and Concluding Observations what the *State duty* to protect entails in general terms. It is crucial to note that General Comments mainly focus on providing interpretative guidance on the legal obligations of States parties regarding the scope of substantive provisions of the concerned treaties and/or the general obligations imposed on States parties under those treaties. Professor Eibe Riedel referred to these General Comments as "*the most important interpretation aids for the rights enshrined in the ICESCR.*"[175]

On the other hand, Concluding Observations mainly focus on measures, including legislative, administrative and policy, judicial as well as promotional measures, to be taken by States parties to fully respect, protect and fulfil the human rights provided for in the concerned treaties.[176]

---

173 For further details, see the following OHCHR webpage: https://www.ohchr.org/en/treaty-bodies/complaints-about-human-rights-violations#inquiries (Accessed as of 29 November 2023). See also supra note 173, Jane Connors, 'United Nations,' International Human Rights Law (Daniel Moeckli, Sangeeta Shah & Sandesh Sivakumaran Eds.), Oxford University Press (2014), pp.369-410 at pp. 392-393.

174 Article 11 of the Optional Protocol to the Convention against Torture and Other Cruel, Inhuman or Degrading Treatment or Punishment, adopted on 18 December 2002 at the fifty-seventh session of the General Assembly of the United Nations by resolution A/RES/57/199 and entered into force on 22 June 2006.

175 Supra note 169, Eibe Riedel, 'The Committee on Economic, Social and Cultural Rights,' in Max Planck Encyclopedia of Public International Law (MPEPIL), Oxford University Press (2010), No. 765.

176 See supra note 173, Jane Connors, 'United Nations,' International Human Rights Law (Daniel Moeckli, Sangeeta Shah & Sandesh Sivakumaran Eds.), Oxford University Press (2014), pp.369-410 at pp. 389-391.

Increasingly, some treaty bodies have also specifically addressed the *State obligation* to protect from corporate human rights abuse through Concluding Observations, as well as General Comments in relation to certain specific rights. Furthermore, the CESCR and CRC-Committees have issued comprehensive General Comments regarding the *State obligations* in the context of business and human rights.[177]

This chapter attempts to provide a general overview of interpretative guidance of treaty bodies on the *State obligation* to protect from corporate human rights abuse through an examination of both General Comments and Concluding Observations, as well as any relevant statements issued by them thereon. Considering that in 2017, the CESCR-Committee issued the most recent and comprehensive General Comments on the *State obligations* in the context of business activities and economic, social and cultural rights, its content will be separately examined in Chapter 4.

In providing interpretative guidance on the nature of the general obligations imposed on the States parties to the International Covenant on Civil and Political Rights, the Human Rights Committee (CCPR-Committee) emphasizes that the legal obligations under article 2 of the ICCPR have both negative and positive dimensions. As an integral part of the positive dimension of the general obligations of the States parties to the ICCPR, the Human Rights Committee makes it clear that the positive obligations can only be fully discharged if "*individuals are protected by the State, not just against violations of Covenant rights by its agents, but also against acts committed by private persons or entities that would impair the enjoyment of Covenant rights in so far as they are amenable to application between private*

---

177 CESCR-Committee General Comment No. 24 (2017) on "*State obligations under the International Covenant on Economic, Social and Cultural Rights in the context of business activities*," UN Doc., E/C.12/GC/24; CRC-Committee General Comment No. 16 (2013) on "*State obligations regarding the impact of the business sector on children's rights*," UN Doc., C/CRC/GC/16.

persons or entities."[178] It further highlighted that if the States parties to the ICCPR permitted or failed to take appropriate measures or to exercise due diligence to prevent, punish, investigate or redress the harm caused by acts by private persons or entities, it would give rise to violations by the States parties of the rights set forth in the ICCPR. In this regard, the Human Rights Committee reminded States parties of "*the interrelationship between the positive obligations imposed under article 2 and the need to provide effective remedies in the event of breach under article 2, paragraph 3*."[179]

The Human Rights Committee further provided examples of areas where there existed positive obligations on States parties to address the activities of private persons or entities under the ICCPR. These areas included the privacy-related guarantees of article 17; the obligation to take positive measures to ensure that private persons or entities do not inflict torture or cruel, inhuman or degrading treatment or punishment on others, prohibited under article 7; and the obligation under article 26 to protect individuals from discrimination in fields such as work or housing.[180]

The Human Rights Committee also speaks of the *State obligation* to protect from corporate human rights abuse in the general framework of the State obligations to respect, protect and fulfil the rights recognized under the ICCPR. In so doing, the Human Rights Committee establishes the States parties' obligation to conduct due diligence to prevent, punish, investigate or redress the harm caused by acts of private persons or entities.[181]

When it comes to the *Corporate responsibility* to respect human

---

178 CCPR-Committee General Comment No. 31, "*The Nature of the General Legal Obligation Imposed on States Parties to the Covenant*", UN Doc., CCPR/C/21/Rev.1/Add.13, para. 8. Available at the following webpage: https://documents.un.org/doc/undoc/gen/g04/419/56/pdf/g0441956.pdf. (Accessed as of 2 September 2024).

179 Ibid.

180 Ibid.

181 Ibid.

rights, the Human Rights Committee has not elaborated what entails such *Corporate responsibility* to respect human rights in the framework of the ICCPR. Such *Corporate responsibility* to respect human rights is in a way implicitly affirmed by the Human Rights Committee by referring to "private entities." The obligation to exercise due diligence on the part of the States parties established by the Human Rights Committee in the context of their generalized obligations to respect, protect and fulfil the rights under the ICCPR, in particular the obligation to protect from corporate human rights abuse can be inferred when it comes to establishing what are the core elements of human rights due diligence to be conducted under the *Corporate responsibility* to respect human rights. As seen above in Chapter 2, more specifically, the concept of due diligence as a standard of conduct to discharge an obligation applied to States in the framework of the *State duty* to protect from corporate human rights abuse can also equally be applied to business enterprises in the context of the *Corporate responsibility* to respect human rights. It can be applied, in particular when it comes to determining what is required of business enterprises' conducting human rights due diligence as part of meeting their *Corporate responsibility* to respect human rights in relation to adverse human rights impacts, which may be directly linked to the business enterprise's operations, products or services by its business relationships. Hence, as an integral and critical element of the *Corporate responsibility* to respect human rights, business enterprises should exercise human rights due diligence to prevent, identify and redress the human rights harms caused by their own operations and/or they may have contributed to in the supply chain.[182]

The Human Rights Committee has also been making specific recommendations in its Concluding Observations regarding the States parties' obligation to protect from corporate human rights abuse under the ICCPR. Those recommendations address the extraterritorial obligation of the

---

182 Supra Chapter 2.B.II: Human Rights Due Diligence and Interim Conclusions.

States parties to prevent, identify and redress corporate human rights abuses committed abroad by business enterprises under their jurisdiction, including the establishment of a mechanism to investigate the human rights abuses committed.[183] These Concluding Observations also emphasize the need to remove barriers to legal remedies, including judicial remedies for corporate human rights abuse victims, as part of meeting their international obligations under article 2 (the right to an effective remedy) of the ICCPR.[184]

The CESCR-Committee has also addressed such State obligations in relation to business activities, in particular, regarding some of the specific rights contained in the International Covenant on Economic, Social and Cultural Rights (ICESCR). For instance, the CESCR-Committee General Comment No. 19 on the right to social security[185] clarifies that States parties have the obligation to protect from the violation of the right to social security by third parties, including "*individuals, groups, corporations and other*

---

183 For instance, see CCPR-Committee Concluding Observations for Germany, UN Doc., CCPR/C/DEU/CO/7, para. 7(a)-(b). See also CCPR-Committee Concluding Observations for the Republic of Korea, UN Doc., CCPR/C/KOR/CO/4, para. 12.

184 Ibid., para. 7(c), and para. 12 of UN Doc., CCPR/C/KOR/CO/4. Article 2(3) of the ICCPR provides that " *Each State Party to the present Covenant undertakes: (a) To ensure that any person whose rights or freedoms as herein recognized are violated shall have an effective remedy, notwithstanding that the violation has been committed by persons acting in an official capacity; (b) To ensure that any person claiming such a remedy shall have his right thereto determined by competent judicial, administrative or legislative authorities, or by any other competent authority provided for by the legal system of the State, and to develop the possibilities of judicial remedy; (c) To ensure that the competent authorities shall enforce such remedies when granted*." See also M. Scheinin, 'The Right to Social Security,' in A. Eide, C. Krause, A. Rosas (eds.), Economic, Social and Cultural Rights – A Textbook, (2001) (2nd ed.), (Dordrecht), pp. 211-222; L. Lamarche, 'The Right to Social Security in the International Covenant on Economic, Social and Cultural Rights,' in A. Chapman and S. Russell (Eds.), Core Obligations: Building a Framework for Economic, Social and Cultural Rights, (2002) (Antwerp), pp.87-114.

185 CESCR-Committee General Comment No. 19 on the right to social security, UN Doc., E/C.12/GC/19. See also Eibe Riedel, 'The Human Right to Social Security: Some Challenges,' in Eibe Riedel (Ed.), Social Security as a Human Right, (2007) (Berlin/Heidelberg), pp.17-28; E. Renaud, 'The Right to Social Security – Current Challenges in International Perspective,' *ibid*., pp.1-16; M. Langford, 'The Right to Social Security and Implications for Law, Policy and Practice,' *ibid*., pp.29-53; A. Nussberger, 'Evaluating the ILO's Approach to Standard-Setting and Monitoring in the Field of Social Security,' *ibid*., pp.103-116.

entities, as well as agents acting under their authority." As such, under the duty to protect, States parties are required to take a wide range of measures, including adoption of the necessary and effective legislative and other measures. States parties should adopt measures that restrain third parties from denying equal access to social security schemes and imposing unreasonable eligibility condition. Furthermore, States parties must ensure that private actors, including business enterprises do not compromise "*equal, adequate, affordable and accessible social security.*"[186]

As an essential part of the *State obligation* to protect from third-party violations of the right to social security, the CESCR-Committee also emphasizes the need to create a climate conducive to the realization of the right to social security by taking "*appropriate steps to ensure that the private business sector* (emphasis added) *and civil society are aware of and consider its importance in pursuing their activities*".[187] It is important to clarify that States parties must adopt certain legislative, administrative, judicial measures aimed at realizing the right to social security recognized in the ICESCR as part of meeting their international obligations under the Covenant. This is to say that States parties have the legal obligations to adopt all necessary measures to provide the core minimum essential levels of protection for the rights recognized in the relevant treaties. At the same time, States parties have the discretion to adopt appropriate policy and other measures to fully realize the right to social security. Hence, it is critically important to distinguish what must be done and what could/should be done when it comes to States parties' fulling their international obligations to respect, protect and fulfil the right to social security recognized under the ICESCR. A clear identification of the content of the legal obligations and recommendations and suggestions of policy options for States parties should be provided by the Committee on Economic, Social and Cultural Rights through General Comments, which

---

186 Supra note 185, CESCR-Committee General Comment No. 19 on the right to social security, UN Doc., E/C.12/GC/19, para. 46.

187 Ibid., para. 71.

can further clarify the contours of the normative contents of the rights recognized in the ICESCR.[188]

In its General Comment on the right to health, the CESCR-Committee also recognizes the responsibility of business enterprises regarding the realization of the right to health.[189] As such, the Committee on Economic, Social and Cultural Rights through this General Comment, specified that the *State obligation* to protect in relation to the right to health included the duties of States parties to adopt legislation or other measures aimed at ensuring equal access to healthcare and health-related services provided by third parties, including business enterprises. States parties also hold the duty to ensure that privatization of the health sector does not pose a threat to the availability, accessibility, acceptability and quality of health facilities, goods and services. They also must take measures aimed at controlling the marketing of medical equipment and medicines by third parties, including business enterprises, and ensuring that medical practitioners and other health professionals meet appropriate standards of education, skill, and ethical codes of conduct; and that harmful social or traditional practices do not interfere with access to pre- and post-natal care and family planning. Furthermore, States parties have the duty to adopt necessary measures aimed at preventing third parties, including business enterprises, from coercing women to undergo traditional practices, e.g. female genital mutilation, as well as protecting all vulnerable or marginalized groups of society, in particular women, children, adolescents, and older persons in the light of gender-based expressions of violence. States parties must also take measures aimed at ensuring that third parties, including

---

188 Supra note 169, Eibe Riedel, 'Monitoring the International Covenant on Economic, Social and Cultural Rights (1966)," in: Politakis, George P. (Ed.): Protecting Labour Rights as Human Rights: Present and Future of International Supervision, International Colloquium on the 80th anniversary of the ILO Committee of Experts,' Geneva, pp. 24-25 November 2006, ILO Geneva 2007, pp. 3-13, at pp. 9-10. For the legal nature of General Comments on the international law plane, see supra note 174.

189 CESCR-Committee General Comment No. 14 on the right to health, UN Doc., E/C.12/GC/14. It can be accessed at the following webpage: https://documents.un.org/doc/undoc/gen/g00/439/34/pdf/g0043934.pdf. (Accessed as of 2 September 2024).

business enterprise and private entities such as private hospitals, do not limit people's access to health-related information and services."[190]

In addition, with respect to national-level implementation of the right to health, the General Comment made explicit reference to the need for State parties to take appropriate steps to ensure that the private business sector and civil society are aware of and consider the importance of the right to health in pursuing their activities in order for States parties to create a favourable climate for the realization of the right. It further emphasized the importance of adopting a framework law, in which the means by which right to health benchmarks could be achieved and the intended collaboration with civil society, including health experts, the private sector and international organizations, among others, should be spelled out.[191]

The CESCR-Committee also indicated its intention to consider the role of health professional associations and other non-governmental organizations in relation to the States' obligations under article 12 of the ICESCR without specifying the private business sector, when it comes to addressing the responsibilities of actors other than States parties.[192] The General Comment also reaffirmed the need to ensure that not only the public health sector but also private providers of health services and facilities should comply with the principle of non-discrimination in relation to persons with disabilities.[193]

It further referred to the extraterritorial obligation to protect in relation to the right to health: "*States parties have to respect the enjoyment of the right to health in other countries and to prevent third parties from violating the right in other countries, if they are able to influence these third parties by*

---

190 Ibid., para. 35.

191 Ibid., para. 56.

192 Ibid., para. 64.

193 Ibid., para. 26. See also CESCR-Committee General Comment No.5: Persons with Disabilities, contained in UN Doc, E/1995/22, paras. 11 and 12.

way of legal or political means, in accordance with the Charter of the United Nations and applicable international law."[194] Third parties here include business enterprises.

Based on the above interpretation of the international legal obligations of the States parties to the ICESCR in relation to the right to health, it can be inferred that the CESCR-Committee is of the view that while States parties must adopt necessary legislative, administrative, policy, judicial and other measures aimed at providing the core minimum essential levels of protection to realize the right to health with them having a certain level of discretion to decide on what concrete measures they should take, the private business sector does not necessarily bear the direct legal obligation to realize the right to health, but can play an important role in realizing it through meeting their *Corporate responsibility* to respect the right to health.[195]

With respect to the extraterritorial obligation to protect in relation to the right to health, the CESCR-Committee is of the opinion that as part of meeting the obligation to protect, States parties must take measures to regulate the actions of business enterprises in countries other than the home state by invoking extraterritorial obligation, as far as such measures are not contrary to the principles of the United Nations Charter and applicable

194 Ibid., para. 39. For the issue of the extraterritorial obligation, see also supra note 169, Eibe Riedel, 'Monitoring the International Covenant on Economic, Social and Cultural Rights (1966)," in: Politakis, George P. (Ed.): Protecting Labour Rights as Human Rights: Present and Future of International Supervision, International Colloquium on the 80th anniversary of the ILO Committee of Experts,' Geneva, pp. 24-25 November 2006, ILO Geneva 2007, pp. 3-13, at 9; C. Scott, 'Multinational Enterprises and Emergent Jurisprudence on Violations of Economic, Social and Cultural Rights,' in Eide, Krause, Rosas (Eds.), Economic, Social and Cultural Rights – A Textbook, (2001) (2nd ed.) (Dordrecht), pp. 563-595, at 580. See also supra note 9, Supra note 9, Andrew Clapham, Human Rights Obligations of Non-State Actors, Oxford University Press (2006), p.195 et seq.

195 For a detailed exposition on core obligations in social rights, see Supra note 48, Eibe Riedel, 'Core Obligations in Social Rights and Human Dignity,' in Max-Emanuel Geis, Markus Winkler, Christian Bickenbach (Eds.), Von der Kultur der Verfassung, Festschrift Für Friedhelm Hufen Zum 70. Geburtstag, C.H.Beck (2015, special print), pp. 79-91.

international law.

As such, while recognizing the primary responsibility for States parties to comply with the obligations under the Covenant, the General Comment on the right to health also highlights the responsibilities of all members of society, including business enterprises, regarding the realization of the right to health. As a result, States parties have the obligation to provide an environment which facilitates the discharge of the responsibilities of these actors, including the private business sector.[196]

The General Comment on the right to health exemplifies examples of violations of the obligation to respect in the context of the right to health, including: the denial of access to health facilities, goods and services to particular individuals or groups as a result of *de jure* or *de facto* discrimination; the deliberate withholding or misrepresentation of information vital to health protection or treatment; the suspension of legislation or the adoption of laws or policies that interfere with the enjoyment of any of the components of the right to health; and the failure of the State to take into account its legal obligations regarding the right to health when entering into bilateral or multilateral agreements with other States, international organizations and other entities such as *multinational corporations* (emphasis added).[197]

The General Comment also exemplifies violations of the obligation to protect, including: the failure to regulate the activities of individuals, groups or *corporations* (emphasis added) so as to prevent them from violating the right to health of others; the failure to protect consumers and workers from practices

---

196 Supra note 193, CESCR-Committee General Comment No. 14 on the right to the highest attainable standard of health, UN Doc., E/C.12/2000/4, para. 42.

197 Ibid., para. 50. See also Eibe Riedel, 'The Human Rights to Health, Conceptual Foundations,' in Andrew Clapham/Mary Robinson, et al. (Eds.): Realizing the Right to Health, Rüffer & Rub. Zürich (2009), pp. 23-41.

detrimental to health, e.g., by employers and manufacturers of medicines or food; the failure to discourage production, marketing and consumption of tobacco, narcotics and other harmful substances; the failure to protect women against violence or to prosecute perpetrators; the failure to discourage the continued observance of harmful traditional medical or cultural practices; and the failure to enact or enforce laws to prevent the pollution of water, air and soil by extractive and manufacturing industries.[198]

Moreover, the CESCR-Committee through the General Comment on the right to health emphasizes the importance of international assistance and cooperation, which is set forth in the context of States parties' obligation to take steps, individually and through international assistance and cooperation, especially economic and technical towards the full realization of the right to health, which is called "international obligation." This international obligation exists in the spirit of the UN Charter Article 56, the specific provisions of the ICESCR (articles 2 (1), 12 and 21-23) and the Alma-Ata Declaration on primary health care.[199]

With respect to this international obligation, the CESCR-Committee draws attention to the fact that under article 2 (1), the States parties to the ICESCR is "*to take steps, individually and through international assistance and cooperation* (emphasis added), *especially economic and technical to the maximum of its available resources* ···," highlighting that the intention of the drafters of the Covenant to refer both the resources existing within a State party and those available from international assistance and cooperation. As such, considering the essential role to be played by international assistance and cooperation in progressively realizing the rights recognized in the ICESCR, the CESCR-Committee is of the opinion that "*in accordance with Articles 55 and 56 of the Charter of the United Nations, with wellestablished principles of*

198 Ibid., para. 51.

199 See Article 56 of the UN Charter; Articles 12, 21, 22 and 23 of the ICESCR; The Alma-Ata Declaration on Primary Health Care.

international law, and with the provisions of the Covenant itself, international cooperation for development and thus for the realization of economic, social and cultural rights is an obligation of all States."[200]

The Committee on the Rights of the Child (CRC-Committee) issued a General Comment elaborating on the State obligations regarding the impact of the business sector on children's rights in 2013.[201] In it, the CRC-Committee clarifies the general obligations of the States parties to the Convention on the Rights of the Child (CRC) and its protocols, and specifies the State obligations to respect, protect and fulfil children's rights in relation to business activities. In relation to the general obligations of the States Parties to the CRC and its protocols, the CRC-Committee referred to Article 4 of the CRC that "*sets out the obligation for States to undertake all appropriate legislative, administrative and other measures for the implementation of the rights in the Convention and devote the maximum amount of available resources to the realization of economic, social and cultural rights of the child.*"[202]

The CRC-Committee specifically elaborates on the State obligations to respect, protect, and fulfil children's rights in relation to business activities. The obligation to respect children's rights in relation to business activities requires that "*States should not directly or indirectly facilitate, aid and abet any infringement of children's rights,*"[203] including the obligation to ensure that "*all actors respect children's rights, including in the context of business activities and operations.*"[204] In this regard, States must ensure that "*all*

---

200 See CESCR-Committee General Comment No. 3: The Nature of States parties obligations (Art.2, par 1), 14 December 1990, paras. 13-14. It can be accessed at the following webpage: https://tbinternet.ohchr.org/_layouts/15/treatybodyexternal/Download.aspx?symbolno=INT%2FCESCR%2FGEC%2F4758&Lang=en) (Accessed as of 2 September 2024).

201 UN Doc., CRC/C/GC/16.

202 Ibid., para. 24.

203 Ibid., para. 26.

204 Ibid.

business-related policy, legislation or administrative acts and decision-making should be transparent, informed and include full and continuous consideration of the impact on the rights of the child."[205] The obligation to respect also requires that "*a State should not engage in, support or condone abuses of children's rights when it has a business role itself or conducts business with private enterprises.*"[206] As such, as part of meeting this obligation to respect, "*States must take steps to ensure that public procurement contracts are awarded to bidders that are committed to respecting children's rights. State agencies and institutions, including security forces, should not collaborate with or condone the infringement of the rights of the child by third parties. Furthermore, States should not invest public finances and other resources in business activities that violate children's rights.*"[207]

While emphasizing that the obligation to protect is of primary importance when considering the State obligations with respect to business activities and children's rights, the CRC-Committee clarifies that under the obligation to protect, States parties must take all necessary preventive measures aimed at preventing business enterprises from causing or contributing to abuses of children's rights, including the passing of law and regulation, their monitoring and enforcement, as well as investigation, adjudication and redress of violations of children's rights caused or contributed to by business enterprises. States parties are therefore in a breach of the obligation to protect where they failed to undertake necessary, appropriate and reasonable measures to prevent and remedy or collaborated with or tolerated such corporate human rights infringements/abuses.[208]

Under the obligation to fulfil, the CRC-Committee clarifies that States parties are required to implement legislative, administrative, budgetary,

---

205 Ibid.
206 Ibid., para. 27.
207 Ibid.
208 Ibid., para. 28.

judicial, promotional, and other measures regarding business activities impacting adversely on children's rights. These measures include: ensuring the best environment for full realization of the CRC; providing stable and predictable legal and regulatory environments for business enterprises to respect children's rights such as clear and well-enforced law and standards on labour, employment, health and safety, environment, anti-corruption, land use and taxation, as well as law and policies designed to create equality of opportunity and treatment in employment, measures aimed at promoting vocational training and decent work and raising living standards, and policies conducive to the promotion of small and medium enterprises; and putting in place measures to promote knowledge and understanding of the CRC within government departments, agencies and other State-based institutions that shape business practices.[209]

Moreover, as an integral part of meeting the State obligations to respect, protect and fulfil children's rights in relation to business activities, the CRC-Committee emphasizes the importance of ensuring remedies against and reparations for corporate children's rights abuses, including "*having in place child-sensitive mechanisms – criminal, civil or administrative – that are known by children and their representatives, that are prompt, genuinely available and accessible and that provide adequate reparation for harm suffered.*"[210] It also emphasizes the role to be played by agencies with oversight powers relevant to children's rights, including labour, education and health and safety inspectorates, environmental tribunals, taxation authorities, national human rights institutions in the provision of remedies.[211] Accordingly, it is key to ensuring that corporate human rights abuses are proactively investigated and monitored with the power of imposing administrative sanctions on businesses that violate children's rights. It is also critically important that children have recourse to independent and impartial

209 Ibid., para. 29.
210 Ibid., para. 30.
211 Ibid.

judicial remedies.[212]

The CEDAW-Committee has also specified the States obligations under the Convention on the Elimination of All Forms of Discrimination against Women (CEDAW). In its General Recommendation No. 28, the CEDAW-Committee specifies that under the obligation to respect, States parties must refrain from making laws, policies, regulations, programmes, administrative procedures, and institutional structures that directly or indirectly result in the denial of the equal enjoyment by women of their civil, political, economic, social and cultural rights. Under the obligation to protect, States parties must protect women from discrimination by private actors, including business enterprises and take measures aimed at eliminating customary and all other discriminatory practices. Under the obligation to fulfil, States parties must take a wide variety of steps to ensure that women and men enjoy equal rights *de jure* and *de facto*, including, where appropriate, the adoption of temporary special measures.[213]

The CEDAW-Committee also emphasizes that State parties have an obligation not to cause and to react actively against discrimination against women regardless of whether acts of discrimination or omissions amount to acts of discrimination are perpetrated by the State or by private actors, including business enterprises.[214] It also highlights the importance of exercising extraterritorial jurisdiction as "*States parties are responsible for all their actions affecting human rights, regardless of whether the affected persons are in their territory.*"[215] It further highlights "*a due diligence*

212 Ibid.

213 CEDAW-Committee, General recommendation No. 28 on the core obligations of States parties under article 2 of the Convention on the Elimination of All Forms of Discrimination against Women, UN Doc., CEDAW/C/GC/28, para. 9. It can be accessed at the following webpage: https://documents.un.org/doc/undoc/gen/g10/472/60/pdf/g1047260.pdf. (Accessed as of 2 September 2024).

214 Ibid., para. 10.

215 Ibid., para. 12.

obligation on States parties to prevent discrimination by private actors."[216] To meet this obligation, States parties must take appropriate measures, for instance, to regulate "*the activities of private actors with regard to education, employment and health policies and practices, working conditions and work standards, and other areas, in which private actors provide services or facilities such as banking and housing.*" As such, the CEDAW-Committee highlights that the States parties' obligations to establish legal protection of the rights of women, ensure the effective protection of women against any act of discrimination and take all appropriate measures aimed at eliminating discrimination against women by business enterprises "*also extend to acts of national corporations operating extraterritorially.*"[217]

C. Concluding Observations

Treaty bodies have also been addressing the impacts of business activities on the enjoyment of human rights through reviews of States parties' periodic reporting to respective treaty bodies. The outcome of these reviews called Concluding Observations is the assessment and evaluation by the concerned treaty body of the State party's progress in implementing the rights contained in the concerned treaty. These Concluding Observations usually not only point out positive developments but also express criticism on negligence and retrogression in terms of protection of the rights recognized under the concerned treaty. They also offer recommendations and suggestions for better implementation of the rights recognized under the concerned treaty, which serve as, in most cases, options for legislative, administrative, policy and judicial and other necessary action to be taken by the concerned State party, aimed at fully meeting the obligations to respect, protect and fulfil the human rights in relation to business activities.[218]

---

216 Ibid., para. 13.
217 Ibid., para. 32.
218 For a general explanation on the nature of Concluding Observations, see Supra note 169,

As such, the Concluding Observations point to the need to establish a legislative framework to make the international-level *Corporate responsibility* to respect human rights a legal obligation on the domestic law plane. Since the endorsement of the UN Guiding Principles on Business and Human Rights by the UN Human Rights Council in 2011, the main recommendations of treaty bodies have been formulated, based on the guidance contained therein. Emphasis in those recommendations has been placed on the States parties' obligation to protect from corporate human rights abuse in particular through the enactment of mandatory human rights due diligence law. For instance, to Germany, the Committee on Economic, Social and Cultural Rights, in its Concluding Observations, specifically recommended that Germany "*adopt a regulatory framework that ensures that all companies domiciled in the State party or under its jurisdiction identify, prevent and address human rights abuses in their operations not only in Germany but also abroad and that such companies can be held liable for violations.*"[219] It can be said that follow-up to and implementation of this recommendation by the CESCR-Committee has led to Germany enacting the Corporate Due Diligence Obligations in Supply Chains (*Lieferkettensorgfaltspflichtengesetz – LkSG*) in 2021, which came into force on 1 January 2023.[220]

The CESCR-Committee also made recommendations to a number of States parties, through its Concluding Observations, that they must establish effective legislative frameworks that legally obligate business enterprises to conduct human rights due diligence in order to identify, prevent and mitigate the adverse impacts of their activities on the enjoyment of economic, social

---

Eibe Riedel, 'The Committee on Economic, Social and Cultural Rights,' in Max Planck Encyclopedia of Public International Law (MPEPIL), Oxford University Press (2010), No. 765, para. 10.

219 See paras. 7-15 of the CESCR-Committee's 'Concluding observations on the sixth periodic report of Germany', UN Doc., E/C.12/DEU/CO/6.

220 Gesetz über die unternehmerischen Sorgfaltspflichten zur Vermeidung von Menschenrechtsverletzungen in Lieferketten (Lieferkettensorgfaltspflichtengesetz – LkSG). It can be accessed at the following webpage: https://www.gesetze-im-internet.de/lksg/LkSG.pdf. (Accessed as of 2 September 2024). For the details of the law, see infra Chapter 8.II.

and cultural rights, as well as to prevent abuses of such rights in their supply chains and by business partners, as well as mechanisms to ensure that business enterprises exercise human rights due diligence.[221]

The CESCR-Committee has also made recommendations regarding the extraterritorial obligation of States parties to protect economic, social and cultural rights. For instance, the CESCR-Committee specifically recommended to Azerbaijan that the latter must "*ensure that businesses entities operating in the State party and those domiciled under its jurisdiction and acting abroad, irrespective of whether they are privately or State-owned, are held accountable for economic, social and cultural rights violations for which they are responsible.*"[222]

As for Germany, the CESCR-Committee also expressed concerns about: the practical obstacles impeding access to justice in Germany by non-nationals who alleged human rights abuses committed by German companies abroad; the absence of collective redress mechanisms in the Code of Civil

---

221 Para. 11 of the CESCR-Committee's 'Concluding observations on the fourth periodic report of Switzerland', UN Doc., E/C.12/CHE/CO/4. See also 'Concluding observations on the fourth periodic report of Azerbaijan', UN Doc., E/C.12/AZE/CO/4; 'Concluding observations on the third periodic report of Kuwait', UN Doc., E/C.12/KWT/CO/3; 'Concluding observations on the seventh periodic report of Finland', UN Doc., E/C.12/FIN/CO/7; 'Concluding observations on the sixth periodic report of Norway', UN Doc., E/C.12/NOR/CO/6; 'Concluding observations on the fifth periodic report of Belgium', UN Doc., E/C.12/BEL/CO/5; 'Concluding observations on sixth periodic report of Denmark, UN Doc., E/C.12/DNK/CO/6; 'Concluding observations on the second periodic report of Kazakhstan' (E/C.12/KAZ/CO/2); 'Concluding observations on the fifth periodic report of Mauritius, UN Doc., E/C.12/MUS/CO/5; 'Concluding observations on the fourth periodic report of Argentina', UN Doc., E/C.12/ARG/CO/4; 'Concluding observations on the combined fifth and sixth periodic reports of Mexico', UN Doc., E/C.12/MEX/CO/5-6; 'Concluding observations on the sixth periodic report of Colombia', UN Doc., E/C.12/COL/CO/6; 'Concluding observations on the fourth periodic report of the Republic of Korea', UN Doc., E/C.12/KOR/CO/4; 'Concluding observations on the sixth periodic report of the Russian Federation', UN Doc., E/C.12/RUS/CO/6; 'Concluding observations on the fifth periodic report of Australia', UN Doc., E/C.12/AUS/CO/5; and 'Concluding observations on the sixth periodic report of the United Kingdom of Great Britain and Northern Ireland', UN Doc., E/C.12/GBR/CO/6.

222 Para 15 (b) of the CESCR-Committee's 'Concluding observations on the fourth periodic report of Azerbaijan', UN Doc., E/C.12/AZE/CO/4.

Procedure, except for consumers' claims; the lack of the criminal liability of corporations under German law; and the lack of disclosure procedures, which makes it extremely difficult for claimants to prove corporate human rights abuse committed by a company,[223] thus recommending that Germany must establish the extraterritorial obligation by ensuring affective remedies against corporate human rights abuses committed by German companies abroad through taking various measures, including "*the provision of enhanced legal assistance for victims and the introduction of collective redress mechanisms in civil proceedings, criminal liability of corporations and disclosure procedures, to guarantee that the victims of human rights abuses by companies domiciled in Germany or under the country's jurisdiction have access to effective remedies and compensation in Germany.*"[224]

Moreover, the CESCR-Committee highlights the importance of ensuring effective remedies against corporate human rights abuse as an integral part of the States parties' obligations to respect, protect and fulfil the economic, social and cultural rights provided for in the International Covenant on Economic Social and Cultural Rights in relation to business activities.[225]

The CESCR-Committee has also addressed the nexus between the

---

223 Para. 9 of the CESCR-Committee's 'Concluding observations on the sixth periodic report of Germany', UN Doc., E/C.12/DEU/CO/6.

224 Ibid., para. 10.

225 Para. 13 (c) of the CESCR-Committee's 'Concluding observations on the sixth periodic report of Colombia', UN Doc., E/C.12/COL/CO/6; Para. 13 of the CESCR-Committee's 'Concluding observations on the third periodic report of Kuwait', UN Doc., E/C.12/KWT/CO/3; Para. 7 of the CESCR-Committee's 'Concluding observations on the seventh periodic report of Finland', UN Doc., E/C.12/FIN/CO/7; Paras. 8-9 of the CESCR-Committee's 'Concluding observations on the sixth periodic report of Norway', UN Doc., E/C.12/NOR/CO/6; Para. 12(c) of the CESCR-Committee's 'Concluding observations on the fifth periodic report of Belgium', UN Doc., E/C.12/BEL/CO/5; Para. 11 of the CESCR-Committee's 'Concluding observations on the fourth periodic report of Switzerland', UN Doc., E/C.12/CHE/CO/4; Para. 19 (c) of the CESCR-Committee's 'Concluding observations on sixth periodic report of Denmark, UN Doc., E/C.12/DNK/CO/6.

States parties' obligation to protect from corporate human rights abuse and the conclusion of bilateral and/or multilateral trade and investment agreements, the latter of which can have negative impacts on the enjoyment of economic, social and cultural rights in the concerned States parties.[226]

D. Interim Conclusions

It is evident from the interpretative guidance of various treaty bodies that States have the primary obligations to respect, protect and fulfil human rights in relation to business activities. These State obligations are explicitly affirmed in the treaties and the treaty bodies have clearly established these obligations through monitoring of national implementation of the treaty provisions contained in the respective treaties. The *Corporate responsibility* to respect human rights is however not explicitly established in these treaties. Nevertheless, through the interpretation of the *State obligation* to protect from corporate human rights abuse, treaty bodies have established the important principle of conducting due diligence on the part of States parties to prevent, identify, investigate, punish or redress the harm caused by the acts of private persons and entities, including business enterprises. This State obligation to exercise due diligence, as part of the *State duty* to protect from corporate human rights abuse can serve as an inspiration for clarifying what can constitute core elements of human rights due diligence to be conducted by business enterprises as part of their *Corporate responsibility* to respect human rights, which is a legal obligation at least within the national legislative framework, if exists such a mandatory human rights due diligence law in a given State party. More specifically, the concept of due diligence as a standard of conduct to discharge an obligation applied to States in the framework of the *State duty* to protect from corporate human rights abuse can also

226 Paras. 12-15 of the CESCR-Committee's 'Concluding observations on the sixth periodic report of Germany', UN Doc., E/C.12/DEU/CO/6.

equally be applied to business enterprises in the context of the *Corporate responsibility* to respect human rights. It can be applied, in particular when it comes to determining what is required of business enterprises' conducting human rights due diligence as part of meeting their *Corporate responsibility* to respect human rights in relation to adverse human rights impacts, which may be directly linked to the business enterprise's operations, products or services by its business relationships. As such, to take legislative measures such as enacting mandatory human rights due diligence law is an essential action that States parties must take as part of meeting their international obligation to protect from corporate human rights abuse under the international human rights treaties.

Treaty bodies issue General Comments/General Recommendation to clarify the content of the substantive rights provided for in the treaties. Although these General Comments are legally non-binding on States parties, they serve as authoritative guidance/standards, particularly as interpretation aids regarding the scope of these substantive treaty provisions. However, once adopted, they are frequently invoked by States parties in formulating their periodic reports to the concerned treaty bodies. They are also increasingly invoked by national courts in their judicial decisions, which indicates the possibility that they can be transformed into customary international law, "first as expressions of an established *opinio iuris*, and later as contributory – but not exclusive – evidence of state practice."[227] The General Comments also commonly emphasize the importance of Stares parties' exercising their extraterritorial obligations, as well as providing remedies against corporate human rights abuses, when it comes to ensuring that the *State obligation* to protect from corporate human rights abuse is fully met.

Through Concluding Observations, treaty bodies have identified the State obligations to respect, protect and fulfil human rights in relation

---

227 Supra note 174.

to business activities. It is worth noting that the recommendations given through these Concluding Observations have increasingly become more specific since the endorsement of the UN Guiding Principles on Business and Human Rights by the United Nations Human Rights Council in 2011. Along the lines of the interpretative guidance regarding States parties' obligations to respect, protect and fulfil human rights in relation to business activities (General Comments), these Concluding Observations have recommended that States parties must establish effective legislative frameworks that legally obligate business enterprises to conduct human rights due diligence in order to identify, prevent and mitigate the adverse impacts of the activities of business enterprises and in their supply chains on the enjoyment of human rights, as part of meeting the *State duty* to protect. Similar to the interpretative guidance provided in General Comments, these Concluding Observations have also emphasized the importance of providing remedies against corporate human rights abuses, as well as that of States parties' exercising the extraterritorial obligation in order to regulate the activities of corporations abroad.

Chapter 4: General Comment on State Obligations under the International Covenant on Economic, Social and Cultural Rights in the Context of Business Activities

The Committee on Economic, Social and Cultural Rights has been in the forefront of clarifying the *State obligations* to respect, protect and fulfil the economic, social and cultural rights provided for in the International Covenant on Economic, Social and Cultural Rights in relation to business activities. As such, the CESCR-Committee has been focusing its attention on clarifying the *State obligations* regarding corporate human rights abuse in a number of Concluding Observations and General Comments related to some specific substantive rights.[228]

In 2011, the CESCR-Committee adopted a statement specifically addressing the obligations of the States parties to the ICESCR, regarding the corporate sector and economic, social and cultural rights, in which it clarified the *State obligations* to respect, protect and fulfil the Covenant rights in the context of business activities. More specifically, in relation to the *State obligation* to Respect, the CESCR-Committee highlighted the *State duty* to ensure that companies demonstrate due diligence with a view to making it certain that their business activities would not impede the enjoyment of the Covenant rights by those who were negatively affected by such business activities. It also highlighted the importance of establishing appropriate laws and regulations along with monitoring, investigation and accountability procedures aimed at enforcing standards for the performance of corporations. Under this *State duty* to protect, it also emphasized the importance of providing effective remedies for victims of corporate human rights abuses. Furthermore, it stressed that the *State obligation* to protect from corporate human rights abuse extended extraterritorially for States parties shall take

228 For further details, see supra Chapter 3.B. (General Comments) and 3.C. (Concluding Observations).

steps to "*prevent human rights contraventions abroad by corporations which have their main offices under their jurisdiction, without infringing the sovereignty or diminishing the obligations of the host States under the Covenant.*" The CESCR-Committee couched the *State duty* to fulfil in terms of undertakings to obtain the corporate sector's support for the realization of economic, social and cultural rights. From an extraterritorial perspective, it also emphasized the need for companies to help host States to build the needed capacity to meet the *Corporate responsibility* to respect the Covenant rights, as appropriate, including in armed conflicts and natural disasters. [229]

In addition, the CESCR-Committee addressed the negative impacts of business activities on the enjoyment of specific Covenant rights (the right to an adequate housing) in its first decision on an individual communication in 2015 under the OP-ICESCR.[230] Complaints can be submitted by or on behalf of a person or a group of individuals, under the jurisdiction of a State party to the OP-ICESCR, claiming to be victims of violation of any of the Covenant rights recognized in the ICESCR.[231]

These series of General Comments, Concluding Observations, statements, and the emerging "jurisprudence" have culminated in the CESCR-Committee's adopting, in 2017, a comprehensive General Comment No. 24 on the *State obligations* under the ICESCR in the context of business activities, which aimed at providing the States parties to the ICESCR with detailed interpretative guidance on their international obligations to respect, protect, and fulfil the economic, social and cultural rights set forth in the

---

229 The CESCR-Committee, "*Statement on the obligations of States parties regarding the corporate sector and economic, social and cultural rights*", UN Doc., E/C.12/2011/1.

230 Communication No. 2 /2014, *I.D.G. v. Spain*, decision was adopted in 2015. It can be accessed at the following webpage: https://juris.ohchr.org/casedetails/2010/en-US. (Accessed as of 3 September 2024).

231 For the details, see the following OHCHR webpage: https://www.ohchr.org/en/treaty-bodies/cescr/individual-communications (Accessed as of 3 September 2024).

ICESCR in the context of business activities.[232] This General Comment considered the UN Guiding Principles on Business and Human Rights endorsed by the UN Human Rights Council in 2011. Accordingly, some parts of this interpretative guidance on the *State obligations* to respect, protect and fulfil economic, social and cultural rights in relation to business activities were relied upon the UN Guiding Principles on Business and Human Rights, in particular with respect to the *State duty* to protect economic, social and cultural rights that requires States parties to take legislative, administrative, policy, judicial and other necessary measures to ensure that the third parties, including business enterprises do not abuse the economic, social and cultural rights of the people under their territory and/or jurisdiction, for instance, adoption of mandatory human rights due diligence law that requires business enterprises to conduct human rights due diligence in their operations and in their supply chains.[233]

This General Comment serves an important purpose as it seeks to clarify comprehensively the content of the *State obligations* regarding how to address the negative impacts of business activities on the enjoyment of economic, social and cultural rights. It is particularly significant since while business activities can impact on the whole spectrum of human rights, including both civil and political rights, as well as economic, social and cultural rights, they tend to have stronger impact on the enjoyment of economic, social and cultural rights. For instance, the CESCR-Committee exemplifies some corporate sector-related economic, social and cultural rights problems ranging from "*child labour and unsafe working conditions through*

---

232 CESCR-Committee General Comment No. 24 (2017) on State obligations under the International Covenant on Economic, Social and Cultural Rights in the context of business activities, UN Doc., E/C.12/GC/24.

233 Ibid., paras. 2, 17, 15-16, 33, 38 and 55. See supra note 4, Guiding Principles on Business and Human Rights: Implementing the United Nations Protect, Respect and Remedy Framework, Office of the United Nations High Commissioner for Human Rights, UN Publication, HR/PUB/11/04: it can be accessed at: https://www.ohchr.org/en/publications/reference-publications/guiding-principles-business-and-human-rights. (Accessed as of 6 September 2024).

restrictions on trade union rights and discrimination against female workers to harmful impact on the right to health, standard of living, including of indigenous peoples, and the natural environment, to the destructive role of corruption."[234]

This General Comment is anchored in the CESCR-Committee's traditionally-held opinion that, while States parties have direct human rights *obligations,* business enterprises should also assume human rights *responsibilities* under international human rights law. As examined in Chapter 1, business enterprises only have the *obligation* not to commit international crimes such as genocide, war crimes, and crimes against humanity under customary international law and *ius cogens* norms, despite the fact that there exists a lack of clarity as to whether corporations themselves shall be held to account for these crimes or as to whether individuals in the concerned corporations shall be held to account for such international crimes.

In relation to the *Corporate responsibility* to respect human rights, this General Comment clarifies at the outset that it addresses the conduct of private actors (business enterprises in the present case) indirectly within the broad framework of clarifying the *State obligations* to respect, protect and fulfil economic, social, and cultural rights provided for in the International Covenant on Economic, Social and Cultural Rights in relation to business activities. However, the General Comment also specifies that States parties may be directly held responsible for the action or inaction of business enterprises when such action or inaction can be attributable to States parties themselves under the following circumstances[235]: firstly, as affirmed in the Draft articles on responsibility of States for internationally wrongful acts by the International Law Commission, the conduct of private actors shall be considered an act of a State under international law if those private actors

---

234 Ibid.
235 Ibid., para. 11.

are in fact acting on the instructions of, or under the direction or control of, that State in carrying out the conduct.[236] For the action of private actors to be attributable to the State, it is essential to determine the degree of control in a particular case. Hence, the Commentary to article 8 cites the existing jurisprudence in this regard. In particular, it refers to the International Court of Justice case of *Military and Paramilitary Activities in and against Nicaragua*,[237] in which the International Court of Justice (ICJ) used the notion of control to decide as to whether the actions of the contras in Nicaragua could be attributable to the United States of America accused of directing and controlling the contras who were alleged to have committed breaches of international humanitarian law. The Commentary also refers to the *Tadi´c* case[238] of the International Tribunal for the Former Yugoslavia (ITFY), in which the majority of the Appeals Chamber of the ITFY disapproved the ICJ approach in the *Military and Paramilitary Activities in and against Nicaragua* case, when it comes to determining the degree of control. The Commentary to article 8 further emphasizes that when it comes to determining the degree of control in order for the action of private actors to be attributable to a State, it is "*a matter for appreciation in each case whether particular conduct was or was not carried out under the control of a State, to such an extent that the conduct controlled should be attributed to it*"[239]; secondly, when private actors which are not an organ of the State are empowered by the law of the State to exercise elements of the governmental authority, the conduct of those

---

236 See article 8 of Draft articles on responsibility of States for internationally wrongful acts, with commentaries adopted by the International Law Commission, UN Doc., A/56/10. It can be accessed at the following webpage: https://legal.un.org/ilc/documentation/english/reports/a_56_10.pdf. (Accessed as of 4 September 2024).

237 Military and Paramilitary Activities in and against Nicaragua (Nicaragua v. United States of America), Merits, Judgment, I.C.J. Reports 1986, p. 14.

238 *Prosecutor v. Duško Tadi´c*, International Tribunal for the Former Yugoslavia, Case IT-94-1-A (1999), International Legal Materials (Washington D.C.) (ILM), vol. 38, No. 6 (November 1999), p. 1518. For the judgment of the Trial Chamber (Case IT-94-1-T (1997)), see International Law Reports (ILR), vol. 112, p. 1.

239 See Commentary to article 8 of Draft articles on responsibility of States for internationally wrongful acts, with commentaries adopted by the International Law Commission, UN Doc., A/56/10, at p. 48.

private actors shall be considered an act of the State under international law, provided those private actors are acting in that capacity in the particular instance[240]; thirdly, the conduct of private actors shall be considered an act of a State under international law if those private actors are in fact exercising elements of the governmental authority in the absence or default of the official authorities and in circumstances such as to call for the exercise of those elements of authority[241]; and fourthly, the conduct of private actors shall be attributable to the State under international law if the conduct in question is acknowledged and adopted by the State as its own.[242]

The aims of this General Comment not only seek to clarify the *State obligations* to respect, protect and fulfil economic, social and cultural rights in relation to business activities, but also to assist the business sector in discharging their human rights *obligations* on the domestic law plane, as well as in assuming their *responsibilities* whereby they can identify, prevent, mitigate and redress any human rights harm that their activities have directly caused or contributed to, as well as those human rights harms that are directly linked to their operations, products or services by their business relationships on the international law plane. Accordingly, the General Comment highlights the existence of many domestic laws that protect specific economic, social and cultural rights, which apply directly to business entities, including in the areas of non-discrimination, healthcare provision, education, the environment, employment relations and consumer safety.[243]

In terms of the scope of its application, the CESCR-Committee makes clear that the *State obligations* clarified under this General Comment apply to

---

240 Ibid. See article 5 of Draft articles on responsibility of States for internationally wrongful acts, with commentaries adopted by the International Law Commission, UN Doc., A/56/10.

241 Ibid. See article 9 of Draft articles on responsibility of States for internationally wrongful acts, with commentaries adopted by the International Law Commission, UN Doc., A/56/10.

242 Ibid. See article 11 of Draft articles on responsibility of States for internationally wrongful acts, with commentaries adopted by the International Law Commission, UN Doc., A/56/10.

243 Ibid., para. 4.

all business activities, whether they are those of transnational, domestic, state-owned, or purely private corporations.[244]

A. State Obligations

I. Obligations of Non-discrimination

The States parties to the ICESCR have the obligation to guarantee all Covenant rights without discrimination, which is an overarching obligation that applies in relation to the realization of all Covenant rights flowing from part II of the Covenant and its articles, 2(1)-2(2) and 3. The States parties are therefore obligated to eliminate all forms of discrimination both formal and substantive forms of discrimination, including prohibition of discrimination by non-State actors such as business enterprises, in the enjoyment of economic, social and cultural rights. In this regard, the CESCR-Committee has previously underlined the fact that "*discrimination in the exercise of economic, social and cultural rights is frequently found in private spheres, including in workplaces and the labour market and in the housing and lending sectors.*"[245]

The CESCR-Committee identifies the following groups in this General Comment that are at a particular risk of being affected by the adverse impacts of business activities: women, children, Indigenous Peoples, peasants, fisher-folk and other people working in rural areas, persons with disabilities, asylum seekers and undocumented workers, as well as politically disempowered ethnic or religious minorities. In addition, the General Comment emphasizes the situation of certain segments of the population faced with a greater risk of suffering inter-sectional and multiple discrimination. For instance, women and

---

244 Ibid., para. 3.
245 Ibid., para. 7.

girls suffered from physical and sexual violence in the context of investment-linked evictions and displacements. It notes that Indigenous women and girls faced multiple discrimination, due to their gender and their identification as Indigenous People. Along these lines, the CESCR-Committee highlights the importance of the *State obligation* to address the specific impacts of business activities on women and girls, including Indigenous women and girls. As such, it suggests policy measures such as integration of a gender perspective into all regulation measures of business activities and adoption of temporary special measures aimed at improving women's representation in the labour market.[246] However, it is submitted that the General Comment falls short of specifying what the *State obligations* are in this regard. For instance, adoption of temporary special measures (affirmative action) aimed at improving women's representation should have been clearly identified as part of the *State obligations*, instead of clustering them together with some policy suggestions and recommendations such as adopting a gender perspective into regulation measures of business activities, which are considered to fall within the discretion of States parties.

The General Comment also highlights the negative impacts that business activities can have on the enjoyment of the rights of Indigenous Peoples, particularly in the extractive industry.[247] In recognition of "*the special relationship existing between indigenous peoples and their traditional territories, which form the basis of their distinct identities and cultures*,"[248] the General Comment specifically refers to the *State duty* to obtain the free,

---

246 "*States parties address the specific impacts of business activities on women and girls, including indigenous women and girls, and incorporate a gender perspective into all measures to regulate business activities that may adversely affect economic, social and cultural rights, including by consulting the Guidance on National Action Plans on Business and Human Rights. States parties should also take appropriate steps, including through temporary special measures, to improve women's representation in the labour market, including at the upper echelons of the corporate hierarchy.*" Ibid., para. 9.

247 Ibid., para. 17.

248 James Anaya, 'Report of the Special Rapporteur on the Rights of indigenous peoples,' UN Doc., A/66/288, para. 97.

prior, informed consent of Indigenous Peoples (the duty to consult) with regard to decisions affecting the enjoyment of the rights of Indigenous Peoples, in particular those decisions affecting the right to traditional territories, lands and resources.[249] It should be critiqued that the General Comment has confusingly mixed the *State obligation* and the *Corporate responsibility* to respect in this regard. As such, the General Comment does not clearly spell out as to whether States parties *must* consult Indigenous Peoples and obtain the free, prior, and informed consent before it permits business enterprises to extract natural resources on the traditional lands and territories of Indigenous Peoples. Instead, it simply recommends that "*States parties* ***should*** (emphasis added) *ensure that, where appropriate, the impacts of business activities on indigenous peoples specifically (in particular, actual or potential adverse impacts on indigenous peoples' rights to land, resources, territories, cultural heritage, traditional knowledge and culture) are incorporated into human rights impact assessments.*"[250]

II. Specific Obligations Linked to Business Activities, Including Extraterritorial Obligation

The General Comment elaborates upon the States parties' obligations linked to business activities along the lines of the duty typology, namely the duty to respect, protect and fulfil human rights. Therein, the States parties'

249 Article 19 of the United Nations Declaration on the Rights of Indigenous Peoples provides that "*States shall consult and cooperate in good faith with the indigenous peoples concerned through their own representative institutions in order to obtain their free, prior and informed consent before adopting and implementing legislative or administrative measures that may affect them.*" UN Doc., A/RES/61/295. It can be accessed at the following webpage: https://documents.un.org/doc/undoc/gen/n06/512/07/pdf/n0651207.pdf. (Accessed as of 6 September 2024). For a detailed explanation on the duty of States to consult, see supra note 252, James Anaya, 'Report of the Special Rapporteur on the Rights of indigenous peoples,' UN Doc., A/66/288, paras. 77-111. See also James Anaya, 'Report of the Special Rapporteur on the Rights of indigenous peoples,' UN Doc., A/HRC/15/37.

250 Supra note 236, CESCR-Committee General Comment No. 24 (2017) on State obligations under the International Covenant on Economic, Social and Cultural Rights in the context of business activities, UN Doc., E/C.12/GC/24, para. 17.

specific obligations regarding the extraterritorial obligations have also been clarified. As such, the General Comment makes it explicit that these States parties' obligations related to business activities apply "*both with respect to situations on the State's national territory, and outside the national territory in situations over which States parties may exercise control*".[251]

The extraterritorial obligations of the States parties to the ICESCR to regulate the activities overseas of business enterprises under their territories and/or under their jurisdictions flow from the fact that "*the obligations of the Covenant are expressed without any restriction linked to territory or jurisdiction.*"[252] Based on Article 2(1) which refers to international assistance and cooperation for the purpose of fully realizing Covenant rights progressively within the existing resources, the General Comment interprets that it is contradictory for the States parties to the Covenant to remain passive where private actors domiciled in their territories or under their jurisdictions violate the economic, social and cultural rights in other States parties. The General Comment also anchors these extraterritorial obligations in public international law: the General Comment opines that the duty of the Member States of the United Nations "*to take joint and separate action in cooperation with the Organization*" to achieve the purposes set forth in article 55 of the Charter of the United Nations, including "*universal respect for, and observance of, human rights and fundamental freedoms for all without distinction as to race, sex, language, or religion*"[253] is expressed without any territorial limitation. Furthermore, the General Comment highlights the acknowledgment of the extraterritorial scope of core human rights treaties by the International Court of Justice.[254] In addition, the General Comment emphasizes that the UN Human Rights Council has extended the application

---

251 Ibid., para. 10.

252 Ibid., para. 27.

253 See article 55 of the Charter of the United Nations. It can be accessed at the following webpage: https://www.un.org/en/about-us/un-charter. (Accessed as of 6 September 2024).

254 Supra note 250. See also *Legal Consequences of the Construction of a Wall in the Occupied Palestinian Territory, Advisory Opinion, I.C.J. Reports (2004)*, paras. 109-112.

of the customary international law rules prohibiting a State from allowing its territory to be used to cause damage on the territory of another State under international environmental law[255] to international human rights law, when it endorsed the UN Guiding Principles on Extreme Poverty and Human Rights in 2012.[256]

1. Obligation to respect

The General Comment specifies that the obligation to respect economic, social and cultural rights in the context of business activities is violated when States parties prioritize the interests of business entities over the Covenant rights without adequate justification or when they pursue policies that negatively affect economic, social and cultural rights. For instance, violations of Indigenous cultural values and rights associated with their ancestral lands constitute a violation of the *State obligation* to respect, in the case of forced evictions in the context of investment projects.[257]

---

255 *Trail Smelter* case *(United States of America v. Canada)*, *Reports of International Arbitral Awards*, vol. 3 (1941), p. 1965; International Court of Justice, *Corfu Channel* case *(United Kingdom of Great Britain and Northern Ireland v. Albania) (Merits)*, *I.C.J. Reports*, vol. 4 (9 April 1949), para. 22; and International Court of Justice, *Legality of the Threat or Use of Nuclear Weapons, Advisory Opinion, I.C.J. Reports* (8 July 1996), para. 29. See also UN Doc., A/61/10, Principle 4 of 'Draft principles on the allocation of loss in the case of transboundary harm arising out of hazardous activities, adopted at the fifty-eighth session of the International Law Commission, in 2006,' which stipulates that "*each State should take all necessary measures to ensure that prompt and adequate compensation is available for victims of transboundary damage caused by hazardous activities located within its territory or otherwise under its jurisdiction or control*"). See further 'The Maastricht Principles on Extraterritorial Obligations of States in the Area of Economic, Social and Cultural Rights,' which provides a restatement of the current state of international human rights law on this topic (accessible at the following webpage: https://www.fidh.org/IMG/pdf/maastricht-eto-principles-uk_web.pdf. (Accessed as of 6 September 2024). (Requoted from footnote 71 of supra note 236, CESCR-Committee General Comment No. 24 (2017) on State obligations under the International Covenant on Economic, Social and Cultural Rights in the context of business activities, UN Doc., E/C.12/GC/24, para. 27.

256 See Principle 92 of the UN Guiding Principles on Extreme Poverty and Human Rights. It can be accessed at the following webpage: https://www.ohchr.org/sites/default/files/Documents/Publications/OHCHR_ExtremePovertyandHumanRights_EN.pdf. (Accessed as of 6 September 2024).

257 Ibid., para. 12. In this regard, the CESCR-Committee highlights the importance of both States

As an integral part of the *State obligation* to respect, the General Comment explicitly recognizes the primacy of the human rights obligations under the ICESCR over the obligations flowing from trade or investment treaties. As such, the General Comment highlights the need by States parties to identify any potential conflict between their obligations under the Covenant and under trade or investment treaties. The General Comment establishes that under the *State obligation* to respect, States parties should refrain from concluding such trade or investment treaties that would potentially conflict with the provisions of the Covenant, while emphasizing the need for States parties to undertake human rights impact assessments that consider both the positive and negative human rights impacts of trade and investment treaties, prior to concluding such treaties. It further underscores that these human rights impact assessments should be conducted on a regular basis in the course of implementation of such trade and investment treaties whereby corrective measures are allowed to be adopted, when required. The General Comment clarifies that consistent with Article 103 of the Charter of the United Nations and the specific nature of human rights obligations, the interpretation of trade and investment treaties should take into account the human rights obligations of State parties.[258] Further, the General Comment emphasizes that "*States parties cannot derogate from the obligations under the Covenant in trade and investment treaties that they may conclude.*"[259] The General Comment in this regard recommends that State parties insert, in future such trade and investment treaties, a provision explicitly referring to their human rights obligations, and ensure that investor-State dispute settlement mechanisms take human rights into account in interpreting such

---

Parties' and business enterprises' respecting the principle of free, prior and informed consent of Indigenous Peoples when it comes to matters that could affect the rights of Indigenous Peoples, including their rights to lands, territories and resources.

258 Ibid., para. 13. See also Inter-American Court of Human Rights, *Sawhoyamaxa Indigenous Community v. Paraguay* (judgment of 29 March 2006, Series C No. 146), para. 140. It can be accessed at the following webpage: https://www.corteidh.or.cr/docs/casos/articulos/seriec_146_ing.pdf. (Accessed as of 6 September 2024).

259 Ibid.

treaties.[260]

It can be critiqued that the General Comment is ambiguous as to whether as an integral part of the *State obligation* to respect the Covenant rights in the context of business activities, States parties *must* undertake human rights impact assessments with a view to upholding the primacy of international human rights obligations under the Covenant when the provisions of trade or investment treaties/agreements conflict with the Covenant provisions or simply whether States parties *should* consider taking measures such as undertaking human rights impact assessments and explicitly integrating human rights obligations in such trade and investment treaties as part of meeting their *State obligation* to respect the Covenant rights in the context of business activities. It is imperative that the General Comment distinguish between "what must be done" and "what should be done" in this regard. It is, therefore, submitted that considering the primacy of human rights obligations under the Covenant over the obligations flowing from trade or investment agreements, State parties, under the ICESCR, are *obligated* not to conclude trade and/or investment treaties that could potentially conflict with Covenant provisions. When concluding such trade and/or investment treaties, States parties *should* consider taking measures such as undertaking human rights impact assessments, as well as explicitly referring to human rights obligations therein.

The General Comment emphasizes that States parties have the extraterritorial obligation to respect, which obliges them to refrain from interfering directly or indirectly with the enjoyment of the Covenant rights by persons, including juridical persons such as business enterprises outside their territories. This extraterritorial obligation to respect also requires States parties not to obstruct another State from complying with the human rights obligations under the Covenant, which is particularly relevant when States

---

260 Ibid.

parties negotiate and conclude trade and/or investment agreements or financial and tax treaties, as well as judicial cooperation.[261]

2. Obligation to protect

The *State obligation* to protect requires States parties to "*prevent effectively infringements of economic, social and cultural rights in the context of business activities.*"[262] To realize this *State obligation* to protect, States parties must take a wide range of legislative, administrative, policy and judicial measures, as well as other appropriate measures with a view to effectively protecting against violations of economic, social and cultural rights linked to business activities. These measures are further aimed at providing corporate human rights abuse victims with access to effective remedies. It is important to define the effectiveness of remedies at this stage: the UN Guiding Principles on Business and Human Rights set out effectiveness criteria when it comes to non-judicial grievance mechanisms in its Principle 31. On the other hand, the UN Guiding Principles on Business and Human Rights do not explicitly set out effectiveness criteria for judicial mechanisms. Instead, Principle 26 of the UN Guiding Principles on Business and Human Rights provides that "*States should take appropriate steps to ensure the effectiveness of domestic judicial mechanisms when addressing business-related human rights abuses, including considering ways to reduce legal, practical and other relevant barriers that could lead to a denial of access to remedy.*"[263] The current international standards regarding access to an effective remedy is that States should provide for "*adequate, effective prompt reparation for harm*

---

261 Ibid., paras. 13 and 25-29.

262 Ibid., para. 14.

263 Supra note 4, Guiding Principles on Business and Human Rights: Implementing the United Nations Protect, Respect and Remedy Framework, Office of the United Nations High Commissioner for Human Rights, UN Publication, HR/PUB/11/04: it can be accessed at: https://www.ohchr.org/en/publications/reference-publications/guiding-principles-business-and-human-rights. (Accessed as of 1 September 2024).

suffered."[264]

Regarding effective remedies, the General Comment suggests that States parties should impose criminal or administrative sanctions and penalties, as appropriate, when business enterprises fail to act with due diligence to mitigate risks. Such remedial measures could include allowing civil suits and other effective means of claiming reparations by victims, particularly by: lowering the costs to victims and allowing collective redress; revoking business licences and subsidies; revising tax codes, public procurement contracts, export credits and other forms of State support to businesses; and reviewing the adequacy of laws and identifying and addressing compliance and information gaps on a regular basis.[265] It is worth noting that it is of significance to victims of corporate human rights abuses that full and effective reparation should be provided for corporate human rights abuse. In this regard, civil remedies in the forms of restitution, compensation, rehabilitation, satisfaction and guarantees of non-repetition[266] serve an important function, when it comes to taking necessary judicial measures as part of meeting the *State obligation* to protect the Covenant rights in the context of business activities.

---

264 See, article I.2 (b) and Chapter VII, 'Basic Principles and Guidelines on the Right to a Remedy and Reparation for Victims of Gross Violations of International Human Rights Law and Serious Violations of International Humanitarian Law,' General Assembly resolution 60/147, annex), UN Doc., A/RES/60/147, annex. It can be accessed at the following OHCHR webpage: https://www.ohchr.org/en/instruments-mechanisms/instruments/basic-principles-and-guidelines-right-remedy-and-reparation. (Accessed as of 6 September 2024). See also infra Chapter 8.C: Judicial Measures.

265 Supra note 236, CESCR-Committee General Comment No. 24 (2017) on State obligations under the International Covenant on Economic, Social and Cultural Rights in the context of business activities, UN Doc., E/C.12/GC/24, para. 15.

266 Supra note 264, Chapters VII-X of 'Basic Principles and Guidelines on the Right to a Remedy and Reparation for Victims of Gross Violations of International Human Rights Law and Serious Violations of International Humanitarian Law,' General Assembly resolution 60/147, annex), UN Doc., A/RES/60/147, annex. It can be accessed at the following OHCHR webpage: https://www.ohchr.org/en/instruments-mechanisms/instruments/basic-principles-and-guidelines-right-remedy-and-reparation. (Accessed as of 6 September 2024).

Under *the State obligation* to protect, the General Comment clearly identifies a duty to adopt a legal framework that obligates business enterprises to exercise human rights due diligence to identify, prevent and mitigate corporate abuse of economic, social and cultural rights and hold the perpetrators of such corporate human rights abuses to account for the human rights harms caused or contributed to by their own operations and by those entities under their control. The General Comment in this regard also recommends imposing human rights due diligence requirements on business enterprises aimed at preventing abuses of Covenant rights in their supply chains. [267] This clarification has been informed by the *Combination/zebra* standards of the UN Guiding Principles on Business and Human Rights, particularly regarding the *Corporate responsibility* to respect human rights. The core element of the *Corporate responsibility* to respect human rights (*the white stripe*) contained in the UN Guiding Principles on Business and Human Rights[268] is that business enterprises should conduct human rights due diligence to identify, prevent, mitigate and account for how they address their adverse human rights impacts.[269] However, it should be noted that the General Comment confuses the content of the UN Guiding Principles on Business and Human Rights: under the *State duty* to protect contained therein (*the black stripe*), States parties *must* adopt all necessary legislative,

---

267 Supra note 236, CESCR-Committee General Comment No. 24 (2017) on State obligations under the International Covenant on Economic, Social and Cultural Rights in the context of business activities, UN Doc., E/C.12/GC/24, para. 15., para. 16.

268 Supra note 4, Guiding Principles on Business and Human Rights: Implementing the United Nations Protect, Respect and Remedy Framework, Office of the United Nations High Commissioner for Human Rights, UN Publication, HR/PUB/11/04: it can be accessed at: https://www.ohchr.org/en/publications/reference-publications/guiding-principles-business-and-human-rights. (Accessed as of 7 September 2024). The UN Guiding Principles on Business and Human Rights (Combination/zebra Standards) contains the *State duty* to protect (*the black stripe*), the *Corporate responsibility* to respect human rights (*the white stripe*), and access to remedy (this can be said both as the black stripe (when it refers to the State obligation to ensure that victims of corporate human rights abuse have access to remedy against it) and the white stripe (when it refers to the responsibility of business enterprises to remedy human rights abuses caused by business enterprises in their own operations, and those that are directly linked to their operations, products or services by their business relationships).

269 Ibid., Principle 17.

administrative, policy and judicial measures to ensure that corporate human rights abuses do not occur, and remedy corporate human rights harms if they occur. Under the *Corporate responsibility* to respect human rights (*the white stripe*) requires business enterprises to conduct human rights due diligence not only in their own operations but also in their supply chains, which constitutes a core element of the *Corporate responsibility* to respect human rights.[270] Instead, the General Comment obligates the States parties to the ICESCR to adopt a specific legal framework mandating business enterprises to conduct human rights due diligence only in their own operations, and recommends the imposition of such human rights due diligence requirements on business enterprises to conduct in their supply chains. It is submitted in this regard that while the States parties *must* adopt legislative measures, including mandatory human rights due diligence law under the *State duty* to protect, the specific nature of such legislative measures should be left to the discretion of the States parties. Accordingly, the States parties to the ICESCR are recommended to adopt law mandating business enterprises to carry out human rights due diligence in their own operations and in their supply chains.

The General Comment also makes it clear that this *State obligation* to protect can be breached if States parties fail "*to prevent or to counter conduct by businesses that leads to such rights being abused or that has the foreseeable effect of leading to such rights being abused*."[271] Such violations could occur when States parties: lower the criteria for approving new medicines; fail to incorporate a requirement linked to reasonable accommodation of persons with disabilities in public contracts; grant exploration and exploitation permits for natural resources without having due consideration of the potential negative impacts; exempt certain projects or certain geographical areas from the application of laws protecting Covenant rights; and fail to regulate the real estate market and the financial actors so as to ensure access to affordable and

---

270 Supra note 236.
271 Ibid., para. 18.

adequate housing for all.

As part of meeting this *State obligation* to protect, the General Comment highlights the importance of direct regulation and intervention, including: restrictions on marketing and advertising of certain goods and services in order to protect public health such as tobacco products and breast-milk substitutes; combating gender role stereotyping and discrimination; introducing rent control in the private housing market; establishing a minimum wage; and regulating other business activities that will impact on the substantive rights to education, employment and reproductive health, etc.[272]

Considering the negative impacts of corruption on the enjoyment of Covenant rights, the General Comment clarifies that States parties should establish specialized mechanisms against corruption ensuring their independence, as well as providing sufficient resources for their proper functioning, as corruption could lead to discriminatory access to public services favouring those who are in a position to influence authorities, including through bribery and political pressure.[273]

As part of the *State obligation* to protect, the General Comment specifies that privatization of public services such as health services and education *must* be subjected to strict regulations. As such, it exemplifies that in the provision of water or electricity by private providers, States parties *must* include requirements concerning universal coverage and continuity of service, pricing policies, quality requirements and user participation. States parties also must ensure that private health-care providers do not deny certain segments of society of access to affordable and adequate services, treatments or information. As such, the General Comment emphasizes that States parties

272 Ibid., para. 19.
273 Ibid., para. 20.

must regulate private actors to ensure that such privatized public services are accessible, adequate, affordable, regularly assessed to meet the changing needs of the public and adapted to those needs. States parties *must* also adopt accountability measures to ensure the right of individuals to participate in assessing the adequacy of such privatized goods and services.[274]

Regarding the States parties' extraterritorial obligation to protect, the General Comment emphasizes that States parties *must* extend this extraterritorial obligation to protect to business entities, over which they may exercise control, in accordance with the Charter of the United Nations and applicable international law. States parties therefore *must* regulate corporations domiciled in their territory and/or jurisdiction as long as such regulation is "*consistent with the admissible scope of jurisdiction under general international law*".[275]

The *State obligation* to protect also requires States parties to ensure that business entities deploy their best efforts to ensure that their subsidiaries and business partners such as suppliers, franchisees, and sub-contractors respect Covenant rights. As such, corporations domiciled in the territory and/or jurisdiction of Sates parties should be required to exercise due diligence to identify, prevent and address abuses of Covenant rights by such subsidiaries and business partners, no matter where they may be located. In this regard, the General Comment underlines that even though the imposition of due diligence obligations might have impacts on situations outside the State parties' national territories, States parties *must* put in place appropriate accountability and monitoring procedures to ensure effective prevention and enforcement, as part of exercising the extraterritorial obligation to regulate the activities of business enterprises under their jurisdiction.[276]

---

274 Ibid., para. 21.

275 Ibid., para. 31. See also supra notes, 256-260.

276 Ibid., para. 33.

Considering that international cooperation is crucial when it comes to ensuring effective accountability and access to remedy in transnational cases, the General Comment stresses that States parties *should* take steps "*to improve the effectiveness of cross-border cooperation between State agencies and judicial bodies, with respect to both public and private law enforcement of domestic legal regimes.*" In this regard, the General Comment encourages States parties to use direct communication between law enforcement agencies for mutual assistance, as improved international cooperation can reduce the risks of positive and negative conflicts of jurisdiction, which may lead to legal uncertainty in forum-shopping or to an inability for victims to access an effective remedy.[277]

3. Obligation to fulfil

Under the *State obligation* to fulfil Covenant rights in relation to business activities, States parties *must* take necessary steps, to the maximum of available resources, to facilitate and promote the enjoyment of Covenant rights , including direct provision of goods and services in certain cases. Toward this end, the General Comment insinuates that States parties have the obligation to seek "*business cooperation and support for implementing Covenant rights and comply with other human rights standards and principles.*"[278]

The General Comment also specifies that under the *State obligation* to fulfil, States parties are required to direct the efforts of business entities towards the fulfilment of Covenant rights, including: designing of intellectual property rights in such a way that protection of intellectual property rights would not lead to denial or restriction on everyone's access to essential medicines or productive resources such as seeds; and protecting the right of

277 Ibid., para. 34. See also UN Doc., A/HRC/39/19 and its annex.
278 Ibid., para. 23.

Indigenous Peoples to control the intellectual property over their cultural heritage, traditional knowledge and traditional cultural expressions.[279]

Under the extraterritorial obligation to fulfil, States parties must contribute to the creation of an international environment conducive to the fulfilment of Covenant rights in compliance with Article 2 (1) of the ICESCR, which specifically provides that States parties should take collective action through international cooperation to help fulfil the rights contained in the Covenant. Accordingly, State parties must take necessary legislative and policy measures, including diplomatic and foreign relations measures, in order to promote and help create such an environment, including such measures as combating abusive tax practices by transnational corporations, and avoiding the lowering of the corporate tax rate solely for the purpose of attracting investors.[280]

B. Remedies

With respect to the need for corporate human rights abuse victims to have access to effective remedies, the General Comment emphasizss that as part of discharging the *State duty* to protect, States parties must create appropriate and necessary regulatory and policy frameworks. The General Comment considers it legally obligatory for States parties to establish effective monitoring, investigation and accountability mechanisms aimed at ensuring accountability for violations of Covenant rights, as well as providing victims of such violations with access to effective remedies. State parties should also inform the rights-holders of their rights and the available remedies in the context of corporate human rights abuses of Covenant rights through ensuring that information and guidance, including human rights impact

279 Ibid., para. 24.
280 Ibid., paras. 36-37.

assessments are accessible to them, in particular Indigenous Peoples, as well as through providing relevant information, training and support for business actors.[281]

I. General Principles

As part of meeting the *State obligations* to respect, protect and fulfil in relation to business activities, States parties must provide appropriate means of redress for corporate human rights abuses. Access to independent and impartial judicial bodies (judicial remedies) should be the preferred means of redress as other means of accountability could be rendered ineffective, if they are not reinforced or complemented by judicial remedies.[282] Such judicial remedies should be effective, available and accessible to victims of violations of Covenant rights.[283]

When it comes to defining what constitutes effective remedies, the General Comment has drawn inspiration from the Guidelines on remedies for victims of gross violations of international human rights law and serious violations of international humanitarian law.[284] As such, States

---

281 Ibid., para. 38.

282 Ibid., para. 39.

283 CESCR-Committee General Comment No. 9: The domestic application of the Covenant, para.9: General Comment No. 14: The right to the highest attainable standard of health, para. 59; General Comment No. 15: The right to water, para. 55; General Comment No. 17: The right of everyone to benefit from the protection of the moral and material interests resulting from any scientific, literary, or artistic production of which he or she is the author, para. 18; and General Comment No. 19: The right to social security, paras.77-80. See also Amnesty International's Comment on the draft General Comment on State Obligations under the International Covenant on Economic, Social and Cultural Rights in the Context of Business Activities. It can be accessed at the following webpage: https://www.amnesty.org/en/documents/ior40/5491/2017/en/. (Accessed as of 7 September 2024); CESCR-Committee General Comment No. 24 (2017) on State obligations under the International Covenant on Economic, Social and Cultural Rights in the context of business activities, UN Doc. E/C.12/GC/24, para. 41 clearly articulates this principle.

284 Supra note 269, article 3(a)-(d) of 'Basic Principles and Guidelines on the Right to a Remedy and Reparation for Victims of Gross Violations of International Human Rights Law and Serious Violations of International Humanitarian Law,' General Assembly resolution 60/147, annex),

parties should "*take all measures necessary to prevent rights violations; where such preventive measures fail, thoroughly investigate violations and take appropriate actions against alleged offenders; provide victims with effective access to justice, irrespective of who may ultimately be the bearer of responsibility for the violation; and provide effective remedies to victims, including reparation.*"[285] It is therefore important that States parties ensure that victims must have prompt access to an independent public authority to provide effective remedies, including reparation. Reparation can take the forms of restitution, compensation, rehabilitation, satisfaction and guarantee of non-repetition.[286]

While noting that there exist a number of barriers for corporate human rights victims to access justice, the General Comment recommends that States parties should remove these barriers to ensure for access to effective remedies, including through establishing the piercing the corporate veil principle in order to hold the parent company accountable for human rights abuses committed by the acts of its subsidiaries of transnational corporations. States parties should also ensure that victims are able to access the information and evidence held by the defendant companies to substantiate claims. States parties should also address the unavailability of collective redress mechanisms and the lack of legal and other funding arrangements, with a view to helping

---

UN Doc., A/RES/60/147, annex. It can be accessed at the following OHCHR webpage: https://www.ohchr.org/en/instruments-mechanisms/instruments/basic-principles-and-guidelines-right-remedy-and-reparation. (Accessed as of 6 September 2024).

285 Supra note 236, CESCR-Committee General Comment No. 24 (2017) on State obligations under the International Covenant on Economic, Social and Cultural Rights in the context of business activities, UN Doc., E/C.12/GC/24, para. 40. See also supra notes 270-271.

286 Ibid., paras. 41 and 49. See also CESCR-Committee General Comment No. 19: The right to social security (art.9), para. 77; UN Doc., A/HRC/32/19, Annex, for the guidance to improve corporate accountability and access to judicial remedy for business-related human rights abuse; and the Corporate Crimes Principles, developed in October 2016 by the Independent Commission of Experts established by the International Corporate Accountability Roundtable and Amnesty International. It can be accessed at the following webpage: https://www.commercecrimehumanrights.org/wp-content/uploads/2016/10/CCHR-0929-Final.pdf. (Accessed as of 7 September 2024).

make claims by corporate human rights abuse victims financially viable.

There also exist a host of specific obstacles to access to effective remedies in transnational corporate human rights abuse cases. These include: the prohibitively expensive litigation costs; the difficulty to prove damage or to establish the causal link between the corporate conduct in one jurisdiction and a resulting violation in another jurisdiction; and the absence of mechanisms for mutual legal assistance, the collection of evidence and the execution of judgements, all of which would hinder corporate human rights abuse victims from accessing remedies. In some jurisdictions, the *forum non conveniens* doctrine constitutes a barrier to the ability of corporate human rights abuse victims in one jurisdiction to seek remedies in the courts of the country where the corporate defendant is domiciled.

In addition to removing these substantive, procedural and practical barriers to access to effective remedies, States parties should facilitate access to relevant information, for instance, through mandatory disclosure laws and other procedural laws that allow corporate human rights abuse victims to obtain the evidence held by the defendant company and shift the burden of proof, where appropriate.[287]

II. Types of remedies

The General Comment recommends that States parties should provide judicial and/or non-judicial remedies as part of meeting the *State obligation* to provide corporate human rights victims with access to effective remedies. Considering the centrality of judicial remedies, States parties should ensure that those violators are criminally accountable. The General Comment also recommends administrative sanctions such as denial of the awarding of contracts under public procurement regimes to those companies that

287 Ibid., paras. 39-48.

fail to provide information on the social and/or environmental impacts of their activities or those that have not ensured human rights due diligence to mitigate any negative impacts on the enjoyment of Covenant rights, as well as denying access to export credit and other forms of State support for companies that might have been engaged in conduct leading to a violation of Covenant rights.[288] Civil remedies also play an important role in ensuring access to justice for corporate human rights abuse victims.[289] As for Indigenous Peoples, it is important to ensure access to justice, through recognition of their customary laws, traditions and practices, in particular in relation to their customary ownership over their lands and natural resources in judicial proceedings.[290]

Non-judicial remedies also serve as a complimentary means to provide effective remedies to corporate human rights victims. These alternative non-judicial remedies should be adequately coordinated with available judicial remedies.[291] Stares parties thus have the discretion to utilize a wide range of administrative and quasi-judicial mechanisms with a view to regulating and adjudicating aspects of business activity, including labour inspectorates and tribunals, consumer and environmental protection agencies and financial supervision authorities. In this regard, the General Comment underlines the importance of extending the mandate of these bodies or creating new ones that address corporate human rights abuse complaints, including investigation of allegations of such corporate human rights abuses, imposing sanctions, as

---

288 Ibid., para. 50. See also International Centre for Settlement of Investment Disputes case No. ARB/07/26, *Urbaser S.A. and others v. Argentina* (award of 8 December 2016), paras. 1194 and 1195.

289 See supra note 271.

290 Supra note 236, CESCR-Committee General Comment No. 24 (2017) on State obligations under the International Covenant on Economic, Social and Cultural Rights in the context of business activities, UN Doc., E/C.12/GC/24, para. 52. See also UN Doc., A/68/279, para. 34 and Committee on the Elimination of Racial Discrimination, General Recommendation No. 31 (2005) on the prevention of racial discrimination in the administration and functioning of the criminal justice system, para. 5 (e).

291 Ibid., para. 53.

well as provision and enforcement of reparations for such corporate human rights abuse victims. National human rights institutions also play an important role in providing non-judicial remedies for corporate human rights abuse victims. Hence, they should be empowered to receive claims of corporate human rights abuses. [292]

Where State-based non-judicial mechanisms exist providing for alternative non-judicial remedies, such non-judicial mechanisms should: be credible and effectively contribute to the prevention of, and reparation for corporate human rights abuses; and be accessible to all and their decisions should be enforceable.[293] Non-judicial remedies/mechanisms for Indigenous victims of corporate human rights abuse should be developed with the participation of Indigenous Peoples concerned.[294] This is quite important, considering that only a very small number of States have ratified the ILO Indigenous and Tribal Peoples Convention (No. 169).[295]

Non-judicial mechanisms should be made available for victims located outside the States parties' territory through their access to the national human rights institutions or Ombudspersons. These corporate human rights abuse victims should also be able to have access to complaints mechanisms established under international organizations such as the National Contact Points under the OECD Guidelines for Multinational Enterprises.[296]

---

292 Ibid., para. 54.

293 Ibid., para. 55.

294 Ibid., para. 56.

295 There are currently only 24 States parties to the Convention. See the following ILO webpage: https://www.ilo.org/dyn/normlex/en/f?p=1000:11300:0::NO:11300:P11300_INSTRUMENT_ID:312314. (Accessed as of 7 September 2024).

296 Supra note 236, CESCR-Committee General Comment No. 24 (2017) on State obligations under the International Covenant on Economic, Social and Cultural Rights in the context of business activities, UN Doc., E/C.12/GC/24, para. 57.

C. Interim Conclusions

In the General Comment, the CESCR-Committee reaffirms that the States parties to the ICESCR have the *obligations/duties* to respect, protect and fulfil economic, social and cultural rights in the context of business activities.

The CESCR-Committee has used the duty to respect, protect and fulfil typology to clarify such *State obligations* to respect, protect and fulfil economic, social and cultural rights (Covenant rights) in relation to business activities. The *State obligation* to protect from corporate human rights abuse lies at the heart of these *State obligations*. The *State obligation* to protect refers to the duty of States parties to take all necessary measures aimed at ensuring that the human rights of the rights-holders under their territories and/or jurisdictions are protected from being violated by third parties, including business enterprises. Conceptually, this *State obligation* to protect from corporate human rights abuse has an indirect nature, in that corporate human rights abuses do not constitute human rights violations by States parties *per se*, unless they fail to take all necessary measures to protect people under their territories and jurisdictions from such corporate human rights abuses. In the case of States parties' failing to take such necessary protection measures, it may amount to a direct violation of the State obligation to protect.

In this General Comment, the CESCR-Committee reaffirms its well-established opinion that while States parties have the *State obligations* to respect, protect and fulfil human rights under the ICESCR/international human rights law, business enterprises have also the *Corporate responsibility* to respect human rights.

The CESCR-Committee also affirms the States parties' extraterritorial obligations under the ICESCR in relation to business activities. As such, States parties are required to exercise the extraterritorial obligations with a view to identifying, preventing, investigating, mitigating, and redressing corporate human rights harms as far as such exercise of extraterritorial obligations does not infringe on the sovereignty or diminish the capacity to uphold the international obligations of host States under the Covenant. In this regard, it is worth noting that the General Comment anchors the extraterritorial obligations in the framework of public international law. As such, the General Comment establishes that the duty of the Member States of the United Nations "*to take joint and separate action in cooperation with the Organization*" to achieve the purposes set forth in article 55 of the United Nations Charter, including "*universal respect for, and observance of, human rights and fundamental freedoms for all without distinction as to race, sex, language, or religion*" is expressed without any territorial limitation. Furthermore, the General Comment highlights the acknowledgment of the extraterritorial scope of core human rights treaties by the International Court of Justice, as well as the extended application of customary international law prohibiting a State from allowing its territory to be used to cause damage on the territory of another State under international environmental law to international human rights law.

In relation to the extraterritorial obligation to respect in the context of business activities, the CESCR-Committee establishes that international human rights obligations under the Covenant take precedence over the obligation stemming from trade or investment agreement. However, it can be critiqued that the CESCR-Committee has confused between what *must* be done (obligations) and what *should* be done (recommendations and/or suggestions for policy options) by States parties when it comes to the extraterritorial obligation of States parties to respect in the context of business activities. This is particularly true when the General Comment discusses the primacy of human rights obligations under the Covenant over the obligation following from trade or investment agreements in the context of the extraterritorial obligation to respect. It is submitted that considering the primacy of human rights obligations under the Covenant over the obligations flowing from trade or investment agreements, the State parties to the ICESCR are *obligated* not to conclude trade and/or investment agreements that could potentially conflict with Covenant provisions. When concluding such trade and/or investment agreements, States parties *should* consider taking measures such as undertaking human rights impact assessments, as well as explicitly referring to human rights obligations therein.

As part of the States parties' obligations to respect, protect and fulfil the economic, social and cultural rights recognized in the ICESCR in the context of business activities, the General Comment clarifies that the States parties to the ICESCR must take a range of measures, including a legislative measure mandating business enterprises to carry out human rights due diligence in their own operations and in their supply chains. The main components of the *State obligations* in this regard include: direct regulation and intervention, and regulation of privatization of public goods and services; direct provision of goods and services essential to the enjoyment of Covenant rights; as well as provision of effective remedies when corporate human rights abuses occur. This is an important interpretative guidance, as it provides States parties with the clarity on how to concretize the *State obligations* to respect, protect and fulfil Covenant rights in the context of business activities, as well as with the opportunity to codify the relevant international standards regarding the *Corporate responsibility* to respect human rights on the domestic law plane.

More specifically, the General Comment establishes that under *the State obligation* to protect, the States parties to the ICESCR have the duty to adopt a legal framework that obligates business enterprises to exercise human rights due diligence to identify, prevent and mitigate corporate abuse of Covenant rights and hold the perpetrators of such corporate human rights abuses to account for the human rights harms caused or contributed to by their own operations and by those entities under their control. It also recommends that the States parties to the ICESCR impose human rights due diligence requirements on business enterprises with a view to preventing abuses of Covenant rights in their supply chains. This interpretative guidance has been informed by the UN Guiding Principles on Business and Human

Rights (*Combination/zebra* standards), particularly regarding the white stripe of the *Combination/zebra* standards, *i.e.*, the *Corporate responsibility* to respect human rights, whose core element is for business enterprises to conduct human rights due diligence to identify, prevent, mitigate and account for how they address their adverse human rights impacts. However, it should be noted that the General Comment confuses the content of the UN Guiding Principles on Business and Human Rights: under the *State duty* to protect contained therein (*the black stripe*), States parties *must* adopt all necessary legislative, administrative, policy and judicial measures to ensure that corporate human rights abuses do not occur, as well as remedy corporate human rights harms if they occur. Under the *Corporate responsibility* to respect human rights (*the white stripe*) requires business enterprises to conduct human rights due diligence not only in their own operations but also in their supply chains. Instead, the General Comment interprets that the States parties to the ICESCR must adopt a specific legal framework mandating business enterprises to conduct human rights due diligence only in their own operations, and that States parties *should* impose human rights due diligence requirements for business enterprises to carry out in their supply chains. It is however submitted that the correct interpretative guidance on the *Corporate responsibility* to respect human rights contained in the UN Guiding Principles on Business and Human Rights must clearly indicate that while the States parties to the ICESCR *must* adopt legislative measures, including mandatory human rights due diligence law under the *State duty* to protect, the specific nature of such legislative measures should be left to the discretion of the States parties. Accordingly, the States parties to the ICESCR are recommended to adopt law mandating business enterprises to carry out human rights due diligence both in their own operations and in their supply chains.

When it comes to required protection measures against corporate human rights abuse, the General Comment provides a range of recommended policy choices/options for the States parties to the ICESCR, which can serve as standards/yardsticks to gauge as to whether the States parties make the full effort to meet the *State obligation* to protect from corporate abuses of Covenant rights. These recommendations and policy options can also serve other useful purposes such as providing the clarity on the contours of the *State duty* to protect from corporate human rights abuse and the *Corporate responsibility* to respect human rights, in particular regarding its core element, *i.e.,* for business enterprises to carry out human rights due diligence in their own operations and in the supply chain in order to identify, prevent, investigate, mitigate and redress the corporate human rights harms.

It is also worth noting that the international standards on the *Corporate responsibility* to respect human rights contained in the UN Guiding Principles on Business and Human Rights (Combination/zebra standards) have the functions of not only embracing very abstractly formulated norms, but also enabling more effectively for the interaction with other legally binding norms and standards.[297] The white stripe of these Combination/zebra standards contained in the UN Guiding Principles on Business and Human Rights, namely the *Corporate responsibility* to respect human rights provides an important normative substance for the States parties to the ICESCR, when it comes to concrete and specific legislative measures that the States parties should take in meeting the *State obligation* to protect from corporate human rights abuse.[298] This is particularly important considering the fact that the so-called hard norm part of the *State obligations* to respect, protect, and fulfil in the context of business activities under the current international human rights law regime do not cover the *Corporate responsibility* to respect human rights. Hence, the *Corporate responsibility* to respect human rights as an international standard serve to complement the existing norms, which can be distinguished from isolated standing-alone soft law notions, as well as from mere factual assessments. The international standards on the *Corporate responsibility* to respect human rights on the international law plane contained

297 Supra note 2, Eibe Riedel, 'Standards as Sources,' German Yearbook of International Law (GYIL) vol. 63 (220), 369-417 at 388-417.

298 Ibid., p. 406.

in the Combination/zebra standards on business and human rights (the UN Guiding Principles on Business and Human Rights) therefore represent "*normal typical, average social evaluations of practice reason*," when it comes to what is expected of business enterprises in society. This will further offer "*common sense solutions*" that can be easily accepted by many States, and prepare the ground for shaping future legal developments.[299]

With respect to the *State obligation* to provide effective remedies against corporate human rights abuses, the General Comment highlights the centrality of judicial mechanisms. Non-judicial mechanisms such as national human rights institutions, labour inspectorates and tribunals, consumer and environmental protection agencies and financial supervision authorities could play an important complementary role in providing effective remedies against corporate human rights abuses. It is crucial that both judicial and non-judicial mechanisms should be credible, independent, and effectively contribute to the prevention of, and reparation for such corporate human rights abuses.

Among the groups that are disproportionately affected by the adverse impacts of business activities, Indigenous Peoples enjoy special treatment in the General Comment. In recognition of the special relationship existing between Indigenous Peoples and their traditional territories, which form the basis of their distinct identities and cultures, the General Comment specifically refers to the *State duty* to obtain the free, prior, informed consent of Indigenous Peoples (the duty to consult) with regard to decisions affecting the enjoyment of Covenant rights by Indigenous Peoples, in particular those decisions affecting the right to traditional territories, lands and resources. However, it should be critiqued that the General Comment has confusingly mixed the *State obligation* and the *Corporate responsibility* to respect in this regard: there is the lack of clarity as to whether States parties *must* consult Indigenous Peoples and *must* obtain the free, prior, and informed consent

299 For the role of standards, see ibid., p. 416.

before it permits business enterprises to extract natural resources on the traditional lands and territories of Indigenous Peoples. The General Comment simply interprets that the States parties *should* ensure that, where appropriate, the impacts of business activities on Indigenous Peoples' rights, particularly those actual or potential adverse impacts on Indigenous Peoples' rights to land, resources, territories, cultural heritage, traditional knowledge and culture are incorporated into human rights impact assessments.

Part 3

Voluntary vs. Legally Binding Approach

Chapter 5: Existing International Voluntary Guidelines on Business and Human Rights

There are currently two prevailing approaches regarding how to address the negative impacts of business activities on the enjoyment of human rights. The first approach is to encourage business enterprises to respect human rights through voluntary efforts to identify, prevent, mitigate, and redress the human rights harms that they have caused and/or have contributed to, as well as those harms that are directly linked to their operations, products or services by their business relationships. This approach is a logical consequence of the interpretation that business enterprises currently do not bear the *obligation* to respect human rights, but merely have the *responsibility* to respect human rights on the international law plane, which is expected of them as social organs carrying out specialized functions in society.

To strengthen such *Corporate responsibility* to respect human rights, a number of voluntary initiatives[300] have been developed by business enterprises

300 For examples, see the Voluntary Principles on Security and Human Rights. It can be accessed

themselves in different business sectors and industries. International organizations have also adopted various guidelines/guiding principles aimed at encouraging business enterprises to respect human rights. The most prominent guidelines among these are: Guiding Principles on Business and Human Rights: Implementing the United Nations Protect, Respect and Remedy Framework (UN Guiding Principles on Business and Human Rights)[301]; OECD Guidelines for Multinational Enterprises on Responsible Business Conduct[302]; and ILO Tripartite Declaration of Principles Concerning Multinational Enterprises and Social Policy.[303] The United Nations Global Compact also serves as a source of guidance regarding the corporate respect of human rights.[304]

In contrast, the second approach seeks to impose direct legal obligations on business enterprises on the international law plane, in particular on transnational corporations/multinational enterprises. This approach is

---

at the following webpage: https://www.voluntaryprinciples.org/wp-content/uploads/2023/10/Voluntary-Principles_ENGLISH.pdf. (Accessed as of 8 September 2024); the Kimberley Process Certification Scheme. For the details of the Kimberly process, see its official website: https://www.kimberleyprocess.com/. (Accessed as of 8 September 2024); the Extractive Industries Transparency Initiative (EITI). The 2023 EITI Standard can be accessed at the following webpage: https://eiti.org/sites/default/files/2024-04/2023%20EITI%20Standard_Parts1-2-3.pdf. (Accessed as of 8 September 2024).

301 Supra note 4, Guiding Principles on Business and Human Rights: Implementing the United Nations Protect, Respect and Remedy Framework, Office of the United Nations High Commissioner for Human Rights, UN Publication, HR/PUB/11/04: it can be accessed at: https://www.ohchr.org/en/publications/reference-publications/guiding-principles-business-and-human-rights. (Accessed as of 8 September 2024).

302 OECD (2023), *OECD Guidelines for Multinational Enterprises on Responsible Business Conduct*, OECD Publishing, Paris, https://doi.org/10.1787/81f92357-en. (Accessed as of 8 September 2024).

303 ILO (2023), *ILO Tripartite Declaration of Principles concerning Multinational Enterprises and Social Policy*. It can be accessed at the following webpage: https://www.ilo.org/publications/tripartite-declaration-principles-concerning-multinational-enterprises-and-3. (Accessed as of 8 September 2024).

304 In addition to principles related to human rights, the UN Global Compact has also principles related to labour rights, environmental protection and anti-corruption. For details, consult the following webpage: https://unglobalcompact.org/what-is-gc/mission/principles. (Accessed as of 8 September 2024).

anchored in the belief that simply to rely on businesses' voluntary *bona fide* gestures to respect human rights without imposing direct obligations to respect human rights, particularly on transnational corporations that enjoy a huge level of influence and power over people's everyday lives have proven to be of limited effect in practice, when it comes to preventing and protecting from corporate human rights abuse.

The then UN Sub-Commission on the Promotion and Protection of Human Rights (hereinafter referred to as the then UN Sub-Commission) played a pioneering role in having identified internationally binding norms that could be imposed as direct legal obligations on business enterprises on the international law plane: Norms on the Responsibilities of Transnational Corporations and Other Business Enterprises with Regard to Human Rights (UN Norms on Business and Human Rights).[305] Although the UN Norms on Business and Human Rights were not eventually endorsed by the then United Nations Commission on Human Rights (hereinafter referred to as the then UN Commission on Human Rights), they represented an important attempt by the international community to identify relevant international norms and standards on business and human rights, which was premised on the theory that business enterprises also have the *obligation* to respect human rights on the international law plane, in addition to those international human rights *obligations* held by States.

Moreover, the United Nations Human Rights Council (hereinafter referred to as the UN Human Rights Council) has been elaborating an international treaty that seeks to regulate the activities of transnational corporations and other business enterprises with respect to human rights in

---

305 Supra note 39, 'Norms on Business and Human Rights, the then Sub-Commission on the Promotion and Protection of Human Rights,' UN Doc., E/CN.4/Sub.2/2003/12/Rev.2. It can be accessed at the following webpage: https://documents.un.org/doc/undoc/gen/g03/160/08/pdf/g0316008.pdf. (Accessed as of 12 September 2024); UN Doc., E/CN.4/Sub.2/RES/2003/16. It can be accessed at the following webpage: https://ap.ohchr.org/documents/dpage_e.aspx?si=E/CN.4/Sub.2/RES/2003/16. (Accessed as of 12 September 2024).

international human rights law, which led to the establishment of an open-ended intergovernmental working group on transnational corporations and other business enterprises with respect to human rights in 2014.[306] This working group meets annually in Geneva and has managed, with unprecedented speed, to produce the draft treaty texts.

The present chapter seeks to provide an overview of these existing international voluntary guidelines/guiding principles on business and human rights. The subsequent chapter (Chapter 6) aims to provide an overview of the main tenets of the other approach that seeks to impose direct legal obligations on business enterprises on the international law plane. It shall include explanations on the content of the UN Norms on Business and Human Rights. It shall also explore the main points of contention that have thus far emerged from the process of elaborating a future international treaty on business and human rights in the framework of the open-ended intergovernmental working group on transnational corporations and other business enterprises with respect to human rights.

A. OECD Guidelines for Multinational Enterprises

The Organization of Economic Cooperation and Development (OECD) adopted the "Guidelines for Multinational Enterprises on Responsible Business Conduct" (hereinafter referred to as OECD Guidelines for MNEs) in 1976, which was a part of the 1976 OECD Declaration on International Investment and Multinational Enterprises. The OECD Guidelines for MNEs are a set of recommendations on responsible business conduct, which aims at encouraging adhering Governments to address responsible business conduct to multinational enterprises (MNEs) operating

306 UN Doc., A/HRC/RES/26/9. It can be accessed at the following webpage: https://documents.un.org/doc/undoc/gen/g14/082/52/pdf/g1408252.pdf. (Accessed as of 8 September 2024).

in or from adhering States. As such, they clarify adhering Governments' expectations on responsible business conduct *vis-à-vis* multinational enterprises. They also have the objective of assisting MNEs in ensuring that their operations are aligned with government policies.[307]

The OECD Guidelines for MNEs have been updated six times since its adoption in 1976.[308] The most recent updates in 2011 and 2023 are of great significance when it comes to addressing the *Corporate responsibility* to respect human rights, which included a stand-alone chapter on human rights in alignment with the UN Guiding Principles on Business and Human Rights. The Chapter on Human Rights of the 2011 update was informed by the UN Guiding Principles on Business and Human Rights. As such, it

---

307 For detailed explanation on the OECD Guidelines for MNEs, see generally "OECD Guidelines for Multination Enterprises: Responsible Business Conduct Matters", at: http://mneguidelines.oecd.org/MNEguidelines_RBCmatters.pdf. (Accessed as of 8 September 2024). For a general exposition, see supra note 9, Andrew Clapham, Human Rights Obligations of Non-State Actors, Oxford University Press (2006), pp. 59-107; Jernej Letnar Cernic, 'Corporate Responsibility for Human Rights: A Critical Analysis of the OECD Guidelines for Multinational Enterprises,' Hanse Law Review, vol. 4, No. 1 (2008), pp71-102; Gefion Schuler, 'Effective Governance through Decentralized Soft Implementation: The OECD Guidelines for Multinational Enterprises,' German Law Journal, vol. 9, Issue 11: Special issue – The exercise of Public Authority by International Institutions (2008), pp.1753-1778; John Ruggie and Tamaryn Nelson, 'Human Rights and the OECD Guidelines for Multinational Enterprises – Normative Innovations and Implementation Challenges,' The Brown Journal of World Affairs, vol. XXII, Issue I, Fall/Winter 2015, pp. 99-128.

308 Of particular note, the 1st revision included recommendations in relation to employment and labour relations, mainly based on the ILO Tripartite Declaration of Principles concerning Multinational Enterprises and Social Policy. The 3rd revision in 1991 added a chapter on environmental protection. The 4th revision added chapters on combating bribery and the protection of consumer interests. The 5th revision most relevant to the present thesis included a stand-alone chapter on human rights in alignment with the UN Guiding Principles on Business and Human Rights. The 6th revision in 2023 provides updated recommendations on climate change, biodiversity, technology, business integrity and supply chain due diligence, as well as updated implementation procedures for the National Contact Points for Responsible Business Conduct. See supra note 312, OECD, *OECD Guidelines for Multinational Enterprises on Responsible Business Conduct*, OECD Publishing, Paris, https://doi.org/10.1787/81f92357-en. (Accessed as of 8 September 2024). See also OECD presentation on the 2023 edition of the OECD Guidelines for MNEs (Available at the following webpage: https://mneguidelines.oecd.org/mneguidelines/OECD-WEBINAR-070923-MNE-GUIDELINES.pdf – accessed as of 9 September 2024).

refers to explicit reference to the three pillars of the *State duty* to protect, the *Corporate responsibility* to respect human rights, and access to remedy. As such, it provides the *Corporate responsibility* to respect human rights as set out in the UN Guiding Principles on Business and Human Rights. In other words, business enterprises "*should avoid infringing on the human rights of others and should address adverse human rights impacts with which they are involved.*"[309] It further specifies the responsibility of business enterprises to identify, prevent, mitigate, and redress the adverse human rights impacts caused and/or contributed to by their own operations, as well as those that are directly linked to their operations, products or services by their business relationships. Towards this end, business enterprises should make publicly available the commitment to such *Corporate responsibility* to respect human rights and should conduct human rights due diligence "as appropriate to their size, the nature and context of operations and the severity of the risks of adverse human rights impacts."[310]

I. Main content

The OECD Guidelines for MNEs are unique in that they offer guidance on responsible business conduct on a comprehensive range of topics in alignment of relevant international agreements, including international human rights and environment agreements, as well as with the Convention

---

309 Ibid., Chapter IV: Human Rights.

310 Ibid. In addition to revising the OECD Guidelines for MNEs, the OECD has also updated the OECD Policy Framework for Investment in 2015 to include a strengthened chapter with recommendations on how Governments can enable responsible business conduct through regulation, facilitation, cooperation, promotion and leading by example. The Policy Framework for Investment and the OECD Guidelines for MNEs constitute an integral part of the OECD's approach to sustainable investment policy. There also exist a variety of sectoral guidance on due diligence, including OECD Due Diligence Guidance for Responsible Supply Chains from Conflict-Affected and High-Risk Areas (Minerals Guidance); Recommendation of the Council on the OECD-FAO Guidance for Responsible Agriculture Supply Chains; Recommendation of the Council on the Due Diligence Guidance for Meaningful Stakeholder Engagement in the Extractive Sector; and OECD Due Diligence Guidance for Responsible Supply Chains in the Garment and Footwear Sector.

on Combating Bribery of Foreign Public Officials in International Business Transactions and the G20/OECD Principles of Corporate Governance. The labour chapter has also been closely aligned to the ILO fundamental Conventions and the ILO Tripartite Declaration of Principles Concerning Multinational Enterprises and Social Policy of 1977. They are government-backed recommendations on responsible business conduct, which form an important part of voluntary guidance reflecting expectations of responsible business conduct on the part of multinational enterprises with in-built implementation mechanisms. They also adopt a comprehensive approach to due diligence and responsible supply chain management thus representing good practice for all business enterprises. As such, the OECD Guidelines for MNEs contain recommendations on responsible business conduct covering a broad range of topics such as information disclosure, human rights, employment and labour, environment, anti-corruption, consumer interests, science and technology, competition, and taxation.

As noted above, the OECD Guidelines for MNEs added a separate chapter on human rights consistent with the UN Guiding Principles on Business and Human Rights in 2011. Particularly relevant to the *Corporate responsibility* to respect human rights, additional provisions on internet freedom and stakeholder engagement were also added in the 2011 update. The OECD Guidelines for MNEs also contain recommendations on how to avoid causing or contributing to adverse human rights impacts through their own activities and how to address such impacts when they occur, including carrying out human rights due diligence in their own operations and in their supply chains. Moreover, the OECD Guidelines for MNEs recommend that enterprises should encourage, where practicable, business partners, including suppliers and sub-contractors, to apply principles of responsible business conduct covering the entire spectrum of impacts caused by, and contributed to by the enterprise, as well as those directly linked to enterprise operations, products, or services by a business relationship. The 2023 update has further strengthened Chapter IV: Human rights through, in its Commentary, paying special attention to the *Corporate responsibility* to respect human rights regarding issues related to at-risk individuals and groups, human rights defenders, Indigenous Peoples, and context of armed conflict.[311]

Accordingly, the OECD Guidelines for MNEs have become converged more closely with the UN Guiding Principles on Business and Human Rights, particularly when it comes to the *Corporate responsibility* to respect human rights, which continues to serve as the most authoritative and important international standard thereon.

II. Enforcement mechanisms

The OECD Guidelines for MNEs are the only *Corporate responsibility* instrument that has a built-in grievance mechanism called the National Contact Points (NCPs). The NCPs act as a forum for discussion for all matters relating to the OECD Guidelines for MNEs and contribute to the resolution of issues that arise relating to their implementation.

The 1984 revision saw inclusion, for the first time, of an obligation to set up a National Contact Point, which would undertake promotional activities, handle enquires, and contribute to resolving issues that arose relating to the implementation of the OECD Guidelines for MNEs in specific instances. The 2000 revision introduced a new "*specific instances*" mechanism, a detailed guidance on the role and functions of NCPs, which allowed the NCPs a stronger role to deal with all matters relating to the OECD Guidelines for MNEs, including resolving issues related to their non-observance by companies.[312]

---

311 Supra note 307, OECD, *OECD Guidelines for Multinational Enterprises on Responsible Business Conduct*, OECD Publishing, Paris, https://doi.org/10.1787/81f92357-en. (Accessed as of 8 September 2024). See II.A.10-15.

312 According to OECD, "*Since the introduction of the chapter on human rights to the Guidelines in 2011 specific instance proceedings have resulted in stronger human rights policies and due diligence processes in a number of companies. NCPs have handled specific instances dealing with a wide range of human rights issues such as the rights of indigenous peoples,*

Since the 2011 update, the role of NCPs in supporting the implementation of the OECD Guidelines for MNEs has been strengthened. In addition, OECD Ministers and G7 Leaders made calls in 2015 to strengthen the performance of NCPs, including through voluntary peer reviews and the exchange of best practices. This has resulted in an OECD Action Plan to strengthen NCPs, which focuses on peer reviews and capacity building, peer learning and the development of tools to support NCPs in delivering their mandate. The Action Plan was approved by the Investment Committee of OECD in 2016. The most recent 2023 update has further strengthened the NCP system by: adding new effectiveness criteria; providing for mandatory periodic peer reviews; and revising initial assessment criteria. Under this updated version, NCPs will always make a public statement. Recommendations and follow-up by the NCPs will be the norm. The principles of transparency and confidentiality have also been updated. [313]

The NCPs as a built-in grievance State-based non-judicial mechanism under the OECD Guidelines for MNEs provide an important avenue for corporate human rights abuse victims to have access to remedies at the national level. As such, the NCPs can handle corporate human rights abuse allegations in "specific instances" through provision of "good offices", which includes "*a range of approaches to support agreement between parties, ranging from informal dialogue to professional mediation*."[314] The "specific

---

lethal injections, and the right to privacy." 'Implementing OECD Guidelines for Multinational Enterprises: The National Contact Points from 2000 to 2015,' OECD (2016). It can be accessed at the following OECD webpage: http://mneguidelines.oecd.org/15-Years-of-the-National-Contact-Points-Highlights.pdf. (Accessed as of 9 September 2024).

313 OECD Presentation on the 2023 edition of the OECD Guidelines for MNEs (Available at the following webpage: https://mneguidelines.oecd.org/mneguidelines/OECD-WEBINAR-070923-MNE-GUIDELINES.pdf – accessed as of 9 September 2024).

314 In addition to facilitating the resolution of the issues raised in "specific instances" through "good offices", the NCPs can also make recommendations to the parties to the "specific instance" on ways to implement the recommendations of the OECD Guidelines for MNEs. See supra note 312, Executive Summary of OECD, 'National Contact Points for Responsible Business Conduct Providing access to remedy: 20 years and the road ahead.' It can be accessed at the following webpage: https://mneguidelines.oecd.org/NCPs-for-RBC-providing-access-to-

instances" process is set out in the 'Procedural Guidance' attached to the OECD Guidelines for MNEs, under which any individual, organization or community with an interest in the matter may report to the NCPs concerned issues related to the implementation of the OECD Guidelines for MNEs. When such a submission is made, the NCPs follow a three-step process; initial assessment, good offices, including provision of mediation and conciliation, and conclusion. They can pursue follow-up, if appropriate.[315]

It is worth noting that the OECD Guidelines for MNEs is currently the only international standards on the *Corporate responsibility* to respect human rights, which contains such a built-in grievance mechanism. As such, the NCPs play an increasingly important role in concretizing the *Corporate responsibility* to respect human rights particularly in terms of ensuring for access to remedy against corporate human rights abuse cases on the domestic law plane. The fact that in the past 20 years, the current existing 49 NCPs have collectively handled over 500 cases[316] attests to this increased role being played by the OECD Guidelines for MNEs, particularly in the context of the *Corporate responsibility* to respect human rights.

There are, however, still some remaining challenges in terms of the effectiveness of the NCPs' role in this regard, which include: lack of visibility and accessibility; and difficulties in handling and managing "specific instances" cases efficiently, which led to the delay in resolving many cases. Another important challenge is for the NCPs to ensure that parties can engage fairly and safely in the "specific instances" process without fear of intimidation and reprisals.[317]

---

remedy-20-years-and-the-road-ahead.pdf. (Accessed as of 9 September 2024).

315 Ibid., p. 15.

316 Supra note 312, Executive Summary of OECD, 'National Contact Points for Responsible Business Conduct Providing access to remedy: 20 years and the road ahead.'

317 Ibid., pp. 28-34. See also OECD, 'Annual Report on the OECD Guidelines for Multinational Enterprises 2018,' p. 8; supra note 9, Andrew Clapham, Human Rights Obligations of Non-State Actors, Oxford University Press (2006), pp. 207-209. Non-governmental Organization,

Moreover, as part of an ongoing effort to ensure more effective implementation of the OECD Guidelines for MNEs, work on due diligence for responsible global supply chains has been expanding since 2009, which began with the work on responsible mineral supply chains. The outcome of such work led to the development of the OECD Due Diligence Guidance for Responsible Supply Chains of Minerals from Conflict-Affected and High-Risk Areas in 2011. The OECD work to develop guidance to help enterprises to conduct due diligence for responsible business conduct and supply chains has expanded to cover the sectors of agriculture, garment and footwear, and finance.[318]

In parallel, OECD has developed in 2018 Due Diligence Guidance for Responsible Business Conduct in response to the G7 Leaders' Declaration adopted on 7-8 June 2015, which "*recognized the importance of establishing a common understanding on due diligence, in particular for small and medium-sized enterprises*".[319] The G7 Declaration also encouraged business enterprises doing active business and headquartered in their countries to carry out due diligence in their supply chains. G20 Leaders also triggered OECD to prepare the Guidance on due diligence in the supply chain by committing themselves to enhancing the implementation of labour, social and environmental standards and human rights in order to achieve sustainable inclusive supply chains. As such, they underlined the importance of the responsibility of business enterprises to conduct due diligence in the supply

---

OECD WATCH has been assessing the performances of the currently 51 NCPs against 38 key performance indicators on complaints handling procedures (specific instances cases), organisation and communication. For individual NCP evaluations, see the following OECD Watch webpage: https://www.oecdwatch.org/ncp/. (Accessed as of 9 September 2024).

318 See OECD-FAO Guidance for Responsible Agricultural Supply Chains: OECD Due Diligence Guidance for Responsible Supply Chains in the Garment and Footwear Sector. The OECD has also developed a draft paper on 'Due Diligence for Responsible Business Conduct in General Corporate Lending and Securities Underwriting,' OECD (2019), Annual Report on the OECD Guidelines for Multinational Enterprises 2018, p. 11.

319 See Foreword, OECD (2018), OECD Due Diligence Guidance for Responsible Business Conduct

chain.[320] The outcome of all these guidance has informed the 2023 update of the OECD Guidelines for MNEs, which specifies the responsibility of business enterprises to conduct human rights and environmental due diligence not only in their own operations but also in their supply chains.

It is submitted that the guidance on conducting human rights and environmental due diligence in their own operations and in their supply chains contained in the OECD Guidelines for MNEs can serve as an important international standard on the *Corporate responsibility* to respect human rights, which can inform the elaboration of mandatory human rights due diligence law on the domestic law plane. This may potentially serve as the basis for the *Corporate responsibility* to respect human rights on the international law plane to mature into the general principles of international law.

The important role being played by the OECD Guidelines for MNEs in remedying against corporate human rights abuses in the context of the "*specific instances*" process of the NCPs points to the importance of the argument for strengthening the national human rights protection ecosystem aimed at ensuring that business enterprises are obligated to respect human rights on the domestic law plane. This may also provide the strong argument for those who advocate the voluntary approach when it comes to addressing the negative impacts of business activities on the enjoyment of human rights on the international law plane, which can work as the counter-argument against codifying the *Corporate responsibility* to respect human rights as the direct legal obligation of business enterprises under the future treaty that is

---

320 Ibid. See also supra note 317, OECD, 'Annual Report on the OECD Guidelines for Multinational Enterprises 2018,' p. 9: According to OECD, the Guidance is "*the first governmental backed reference on due diligence which is relevant for all types of companies and helps companies respond to the expectations set out in the Guidelines [the OECD Guidelines for MNEs] that they carry out due diligence to identify, prevent and mitigate real and potential adverse impacts across their operations and business relationships and to account for how those impacts are addressed.*"

being elaborated under the auspices of the United Nations Human Rights Council.

B. ILO Tripartite Declaration of Principles Concerning Multinational Enterprises and Social Policy

The International Labour Organization (ILO) adopted the Tripartite Declaration of Principles concerning Multinational Enterprises and Social Policy[321] (hereinafter referred to as ILO Tripartite MNE Declaration) in 1977, which aimed at promoting labour standards and principles in the corporate world. The ILO Tripartite MNE Declaration addresses labour standards and principles in the following five principal areas: general policies; employment; training; conditions of work and life; and industrial relations. It was amended twice in 2000 and 2006, and was revised in 2017, the latter of which took into account the latest developments in labour standards since 2006. It also considered developments by other actors, including the UN Guiding Principles on Business and Human Rights endorsed by the United Nations Human Rights Council in 2011 and the 2030 Agenda for Sustainable Development. Its unique feature lies in the fact that it is the only global instrument that addresses corporate social responsibility and sustainable business practices, which was elaborated and adopted in a tripartite manner involving governments, employers, and workers. As such, it recognizes different roles and responsibilities of government, multinational and national enterprises, and other social actors for the purpose of achieving inclusive economic growth and decent work.[322] It is worth noting that unlike other UN specialized agencies that are inter-governmental, the ILO, as one of

321 International Labour Organization Tripartite Declaration of Principles concerning Multinational Enterprises and Social Policy. It can be accessed at the following ILO webpage: https://www.ilo.org/publications/tripartite-declaration-principles-concerning-multinational-enterprises-and-3. (Accessed as of 9 September 2024).

322 For further details, see, http://www.ilo.org/global/about-the-ilo/newsroom/news/WCMS_547615/lang--en/index.htm. (Accessed as of 9 September 2024).

the oldest international organizations in 105 years of its existence has the unique tripartite system where governments, trade unions and employer associations collectively develop international labour norms and standards. This tripartite system has enabled ILO to develop a vast number of treaties and recommendations.[323]

The 2017 revised ILO Tripartite MNE Declaration added principles designed to address specific decent work issues related to social security, forced labour, transition from the informal to formal economy, wages, access to remedy and compensation of victims. In line with the UN Guiding Principles on Business and Human Rights, it also sought to provide guidance on due diligence processes in achieving decent work, sustainable businesses, more inclusive growth and better sharing of the benefits of foreign direct investment.[324] The ILO tripartite MNE Declaration was further amended following ILO's inclusion of a safe and healthy working environment in the ILO's framework of fundamental principles and rights at work in 2022.[325]

As part of implementation measures, the ILO Governing Body has the overall role in overseeing the effective implementation of the ILO Tripartite MNE Declaration. In discharging that role, the ILO Governing Body has adopted a range of operational tools, including a regional follow-up mechanism, tripartite-appointed national focal points, company-union dialogue, and interpretation procedures of the principles of the ILO Tripartite MNE Declaration.[326]

---

323 For ILO standards as source of international law, see supra note 2, Eibe Riedel, 'Standards as Sources,' German Yearbook of International Law (GYIL) vol. 63 (220), 369-417 at 400-404.

324 Supra note 321.

325 Ibid.

326 For general, see the following ILO webpage: https://www.ilo.org/ilo-department-sustainable-enterprises-productivity-and-just-transition/areas-work/tripartite-declaration-principles-concerning-multinational-enterprises-and. (Accessed as of 9 September 2024).

I. Main content

At the outset, the ILO Tripartite MNE Declaration sets forth its aim and scope by contextualizing the reasons for the need for multinational enterprises, governments, workers' and employers' organizations to apply principles contained therein. It is based on the legal rules contained in ILO fundamental treaties, as well as the recommendations in the field of labour rights. Hence, it can be said that it is *Combination/zebra* standards related to what *must* be done and what *should* done in the area of labour rights, in particular in relation to business activities like the UN Guiding Principles on Business and Human Rights.

The ILO Tripartite MNE Declaration specifically refers to both the positive contributions and negative aspects of the activities of multinational enterprises, when it comes to multinational enterprises' playing a role in promoting decent work, inclusive economic growth and sustainable development. Accordingly, its main aim is to "*encourage the positive contribution which multinational enterprises can make to economic and social progress and the realization of decent work for all.*"[327] It also aims to minimize the negative impacts and the difficulties that can be caused by the way multinational enterprises operate and are organized. In this regard, the ILO Tripartite MNE Declaration emphasizes that such an aim can be furthered by the appropriate national legal framework in the area of labour law and administration, as well as by cooperation of all actors concerned, including governments, workers' organizations and employers' organizations.

In terms of its scope of application, the ILO Tripartite MNE Declaration implies that it should apply not only to multinational enterprises but also to national enterprises by clarifying that the principles contained

327 Supra note 321, ILO Tripartite Declaration of Principles concerning Multinational Enterprise and Social Policy, para. 2.

therein do not purport to introduce or maintain "*inequalities of treatment between multinational and national enterprises.*"[328] In this regard, it is interesting to note that the ILO Tripartite MNE Declaration only provides for a working definition of multinational enterprises for the purposes of facilitating its understanding:

> "*Multinational enterprises include enterprises-whether fully or partially state-owned or privately owned-which own or control production, distribution, services or other facilities outside the country in which they are based. They may be large or small; and can have their headquarters in any part of the world. The degree of autonomy of entities within multinational enterprises in relation to each other varies widely from one such enterprise to another, depending on the nature of the links between such entities and their fields of activity and having regard to the great diversity in the form of ownership, in the size, in the nature and location of the operation the enterprises concerned.*"[329]

Accordingly, the term, multinational enterprises, refers to the various entities in relation to distribution of responsibilities in the expectation that they will cooperate and assist one another. It can be argued that such recognition in the ILO Tripartite MNE Declaration of the fact that multinational enterprises operate through various relationships with other enterprises such as suppliers and contractors as part of their overall production process may have facilitated incorporating the core element of the *Corporate responsibility* to respect human rights, *i.e.*, conducting human rights due diligence in their own operations and in their supply chains, provided for in the UN Guiding Principles on Business and Human Rights.

The ILO Tripartite MNE Declaration sets out the frameworks as

---

328 Ibid., para. 5.
329 Ibid., para. 6.

"General Policies," in which multinational enterprises should apply the principles elaborated therein. All concerned to the ILO Tripartite MNE Declaration should respect the following overarching principles: respect of national sovereignty of States, particularly by complying with national laws and regulations. Due regard should also be had to local practices, as well as respect of relevant international standards, including the International Bill of Human Rights (the Universal Declaration of Human Rights and the International Covenants on Civil and Political Rights, and on Economic, Social and Cultural Rights), the ILO Constitution and its principles. The ILO Tripartite MNE Declaration emphasizes the need for all parties concerned to contribute to the realization of the ILO Declaration on Fundamental Principles and Rights at Work because though being a member of the ILO, States have the obligation to respect, promote and realize the fundamental principles and rights in the areas of freedom of association and the right to collective bargaining, the elimination of all forms of forced or compulsory labour, the abolition of child labour, and the elimination of discrimination in respect of employment and occupation.

The 2017 amended ILO Tripartite MNE Declaration incorporates fully the UN Guiding Principles on Business and Human Rights through incorporating the State obligations to respect, protect and fulfil human rights in relation to business activities, the *Corporate responsibility* to respect human rights, in particular through conducting human rights due diligence, highlighting the importance of carrying out human rights impact assessments in this regard, and the need to provide effective remedies against corporate human rights abuses.

The ILO Tripartite MNE Declaration emphasizes the importance of multinational enterprises' complying with national laws. In addition, in recognition of the extraterritorial nature of the activities of multinational enterprises, it recommends that Governments of both home and host States promote good social practice in accordance with the Declaration, as well as having regard to relevant international standards.[330]

The ILO Tripartite MNE Declaration addresses the following substantive areas: employment, training, conditions of work and life, and industrial relations. As regards employment, it highlights the contribution that can be made by multinational enterprises to employment promotion. It also addresses the Government obligations related to the right to social security and the multinational enterprises' complementary role in establishing public social security systems, the principles related to the elimination of forced or compulsory labour, the abolition of child labour, equality of opportunity and treatment, and security of employment. As such, the ILO Tripartite MNE Declaration specifies the responsibility for multinational enterprises in these areas. [331]

In relation to training, the ILO Tripartite MNE Declaration recommends that the Governments develop national policies for vocational training and guidance closely linked to employment, and that multinational enterprises provide training aimed at developing useful skills and promoting career opportunities and lifelong learning.[332]

Regarding the issue of conditions of work and life, the ILO Tripartite MNE Declaration addresses the issues related to wages, benefits and conditions of work, particularly emphasizing that no discrimination between workers in MNEs and workers employed by national enterprises in the host country. It specifies the *State obligation* and the responsibility of multinational enterprises to ensure the occupational safety and health.[333]

The ILO Tripartite MNE Declaration provides for the *State duties* and the *responsibilities* of multinational enterprises in relation to the right to freedom of association, the right to organize, collective bargaining,

---

330 Ibid., para. 12.
331 Ibid., paras. 13-36.
332 Ibid., paras. 37-40.
333 Ibid., paras. 41-46.

consultation, access to remedy and examination of grievances, as well as settlement of industrial disputes,[334] which represents the characteristics of the Declaration as "*Combination/zebra standards*".

II. Enforcement mechanisms[335]

The ILO Governing Body has the overall mandate to promote the ILO Tripartite MNE Declaration, mainly through regular reviews of the overall strategy and underlying activities aimed at promoting it.

The ILO Tripartite MNE Declaration has also envisaged promotional mechanisms, including regional follow-up mechanism, tripartite national focal points, and promotional actions by the ILO, including provision of technical assistance, information and guidance aimed at promoting it. The regional follow-up mechanism seeks to produce a regional report that is primarily based on inputs from governments, employers' organizations and workers' organizations in ILO member States. These inputs are provided based on a questionnaire and a special session is dedicated during ILO regional meetings, in which these inputs are discussed, through a tripartite dialogue forum identifying further promotional activities at the regional level. This regional follow-up reporting is conducted with a four-year cycle, which presents a report to the ILO Governing Body at the end of each cycle.

National constituents (Governments, employers' organizations and workers' organizations) are also encouraged to appoint national focal points on a tripartite basis to promote the ILO Tripartite MNE Declaration at the national level. Such national focal points could: raise awareness about the

---

334 Ibid., paras. 47-68.

335 For the details, supra note 321, see ANNEX II of International Labour Organization Tripartite Declaration of Principles concerning Multinational Enterprises and Social Policy. It can be accessed at the following ILO webpage: https://www.ilo.org/publications/tripartite-declaration-principles-concerning-multinational-enterprises-and-3. (Accessed as of 9 September 2024).

principles of the ILO Tripartite MNE Declaration among Government ministries and agencies, multinational enterprises and employers' and workers' organizations; organize capacity-building events; and develop online information and dialogue platforms in local languages. They are also recommended to organize tripartite-plus dialogue platforms to discuss opportunities and identify challenges presented by the activities of multinational enterprises in the national context. The actions of the national focal points should be conducted in a transparent, accessible and accountable manner. They should also communicate and collaborate with their counterparts in other countries in order to exchange ideas and raise awareness of the ILO Tripartite MNE Declaration globally. They are encouraged to inform the ILO of their activities on a regular basis and the ILO can provide support to Member States to establish national focal points and develop the promotional and dialogue facilitation activities of the national focal points.

The ILO also provides country-level technical assistance to Governments, employers' organizations and workers' organizations on the application of the principles contained in the ILO Tripartite MNE Declaration. Toward this end, the ILO Helpdesk for Business and International Labour Standards has been established.

The ILO Tripartite MNE Declaration also introduced in 2017 a mechanism called "Company-union dialogue", which aims to support dialogues involving multinational enterprises and the representatives of the workers affected, in particular trade unions, on the application of the principles of the ILO Tripartite MNE Declaration. With the voluntary agreement of company and union, the ILO will provide a neutral dialogue forum to discuss issues of mutual concern. The "Company-union dialogue" process is conducted in strict confidentiality and based on consensus of the parties, the content of which cannot be used for any binding procedure.

The ILO Tripartite MNE Declaration has another enforcement mechanism, called 'Interpretation Procedure', whose purpose is to interpret the provisions of the ILO Tripartite MNE Declaration to resolve a disagreement on their meaning arising from an actual situation. This procedure is limited to the interpretation of the ILO Tripartite MNE Declaration. It cannot therefore be invoked in respect of: national law and practice; international labour Conventions and Recommendations; and matters falling under the ILO freedom of association procedures. It is submitted that this "Interpretation Procedure" has the potential of providing interpretative guidance on the *Corporate responsibility* of business enterprises (multinational enterprises) to respect human rights contained in the ILO Tripartite MNE Declaration, which can serve as interpretation aides by the national court systems.

The added value of the ILO Tripartite MNE Declaration lies in the fact that it constitutes "*Combination/zebra* standards," which contains both the *State obligations to respect, protect and fulfil* labour rights, as well as international standards on the *Corporate responsibility* to respect labour rights. Accordingly, it can serve as interpretation guidance and aide, when it comes to clarifying the contours of the *Corporate responsibility* to respect labour rights impacted by the activities of business enterprises, particularly MNEs.[336]

C. The UN Guiding Principles on Business and Human Rights

The then Commission on Human Rights had addressed the issue of business and human rights since the late 1990s. First, the then United Nations Sub-Commission on the Promotion and Protection of Human Rights

336 C.f. A scholar has argued that the ILO MNE Declaration offers an evidence of human rights obligations of corporations on the international law plane. Jernej Letnar Černič, 'Corporate responsibility for human rights: Analyzing the ILO Tripartite Declaration of Principles Concerning Multinational Enterprises and Social Policy,' Miskolc Journal of International Law, Volume 6 (2009) No. 1., pp. 24-34 at p. 26.

(hereinafter referred to as the then Sub-Commission), a subsidiary expert body of the then Commission on Human Rights had begun examining the negative impacts of transnational corporations on the enjoyment of human rights in 1999 through its inter-sessional working group on the working methods and activities of transnational corporations. During its first session in 1999, the inter-sessional Working Group decided to develop '*a code of conduct for transnational corporations (TNCs) based on the human rights standards.*'[337]

After four years of deliberations on the draft code of conduct, initially prepared by Mr. Weissbrodt, a former member of the then Sub-Commission, the then Sub-Commission presented the "*Norms on the Responsibilities of Transnational Corporations and Other Business Enterprises with Regard to Human Rights*" in 2003, which were forwarded to the then Commission on Human Rights for endorsement.[338] The Norms essentially sought to "*impose on companies, directly under international law, the same range of human rights duties*"[339] that States have, which led to a deeply divisive debate evoking little support from Governments.[340] Consequently, the then Commission on Human Rights reacted coldly to the Norms emphasizing the fact that it did

---

337 UN Doc., E/CN.4/Sub.2/1999/9, para. 32. It can be accessed at the following webpage: https://digitallibrary.un.org/record/277965?ln=en&v=pdf. (Accessed as of 12 September 2024).

338 Supra note 39, 'Norms on Business and Human Rights, the then Sub-Commission on the Promotion and Protection of Human Rights,' UN Doc., E/CN.4/Sub.2/2003/12/Rev.2. It can be accessed at the following webpage: https://documents.un.org/doc/undoc/gen/g03/160/08/pdf/g0316008.pdf. (Accessed as of 12 September 2024. The draft Norms highlighted the State's obligation to protect human rights abuses by transnational corporations and other business enterprises. At the same time, the Norms enshrined the responsibility of transnational corporations and other business enterprises to respect and observe human rights within their respective sphere of influence. The Norms also provided for a complaint mechanism for cases of corporate violations. For detailed explanation on the development trajectory of the Norms. For further details, see infra Chapter 6. A.

339 'Report of the Special Representative of the Secretary-General on the issue of human rights and transnational corporations and other business enterprises, John Ruggie: Guiding Principles on Business and Human Rights: Implementing the United Nations "Protect, Respect and Remedy" Framework,' UN Doc., A/HRC/17/31, para. 2. It can be accessed at the following webpage: https://documents.un.org/doc/undoc/gen/g11/121/90/pdf/g1112190.pdf. (Accessed as of 12 September 2024).

340 Ibid., para. 3. See also infra Chapter 6. A.

not request the then Sub-Commission to prepare such Norms thus having no legal standing to do so. Instead, the then Commission on Human Rights requested the Office of the United Nations High Commissioner for Human Rights (OHCHR) to compile a further report on the subject matter, which was presented to it in 2005.[341]

In 2005, the then Commission on Human Rights passed a resolution entitled "*Human rights and transnational corporations and other business enterprises*" effectively ignoring the Norms of the then Sub-Commission and requesting instead the United Nations Secretary-General to appoint a special representative for human rights and transnational corporations and other business enterprises.[342]

Pursuant to the resolution, Mr. John Ruggie was appointed as the Special Representative of the Secretary-General for human rights and transnational corporations and other business enterprises. In 2008, he presented his interim report, *Protect, Respect and Remedy: A Framework for Business and Human Rights*, which consisted of three core principles: the *State duty* to protect human rights; the *Corporate responsibility* to respect human rights; and access to remedy. The United Nations Human Rights Council[343] (hereinafter referred to as the Human Rights Council) welcomed this

---

341 See 'Report of the United Nations High Commissioner on Human Rights on the responsibilities of transnational corporations and related business enterprises with regard to human rights,' UN Doc., E/CN.4/2005/91. It can be accessed at the following webpage: https://documents.un.org/doc/undoc/gen/g05/110/27/pdf/g0511027.pdf. (Accessed as of 12 September 2024).

342 UN Doc., E/CN.4/RES/2005/69. It can be accessed at the following webpage: https://ap.ohchr.org/documents/alldocs.aspx?doc_id=11160. (Accessed as of 12 September 2024).

343 In 2006, through UN reform, the then Commission on Human Rights have been transformed into the UN Human Rights Council. Previously the then Commission on Human Rights was one of the functional commissions under the UN Economic and Social Council. Initially, a proposal was made to elevate the Human Rights Council to the status equivalent to the UN Security Council considering that the respect of human rights is one of the main purposes of the United Nations Charter. However, this proposal did not see the light of day. Instead, Member States agreed to establish the Human Rights Council as a subsidiary body of the United Nations General Assembly. The notable difference of the Human Rights Council from

framework, which distinguished between *State obligation* to protect and *Corporate responsibility* to respect human rights.

In 2011, Mr. Ruggie presented the UN Guiding Principles on Business and Human Rights to the Human Rights Council, which contained the same three pillars of: the *State duty* to protect; the *Corporate responsibility* to respect human rights; and access to remedy. The Human Rights Council unanimously endorsed the UN Guiding Principles on Business and Human Rights.[344] This endorsement by the UN Human Rights Council not only "*effectively established the Guiding Principles as the authoritative global standard for preventing and addressing adverse impacts on human rights arising from business-related activity*"[345], but also it indicated a strong signal that to ensure the *Corporate responsibility* to respect human rights through voluntary guidelines could be a more appropriate approach to addressing the issue of business and human rights at the international level. Through the same resolution, the Human Rights Council also created a working group on the issue of human rights and transnational corporations and other business enterprises, which had the overall mandate of assisting States and the corporate sector in operationalizing and implementing the UN Guiding

---

the then Commission on Human Rights is the way, in which members of the Human Rights Council are selected. Previously under the then Commission on Human Rights, each regional group agreed on the countries from their respective region to fill in the vacancies of the 53 seats. Unlike the previous practice, to become a member of the 47-member Human Rights Council, States have to submit their candidacy to the General Assembly, which elects, based on the commitment and situation of human rights of the candidate countries. A new mechanism called universal periodic review, which reviews the human rights situation of all 193 UN Member States every four and a half years (initially every four years) was also established under the Human Rights Council as a new international human rights protection mechanism.

344 Supra note 339, 'Report of the Special Representative of the Secretary-General on the issue of human rights and transnational corporations and other business enterprises, John Ruggie: Guiding Principles on Business and Human Rights: Implementing the United Nations "Protect, Respect and Remedy" Framework,' UN Doc., A/HRC/17/31.

345 Para. 1, Report of the Working Group on the issue of human rights and transnational corporations and other business enterprises, UN Doc., A/HRC/20/29. It can be accessed at the following webpage: https://documents.un.org/doc/undoc/gen/g12/128/48/pdf/g1212848.pdf. (Accessed as of 12 September 2024).

Principles on Business and Human Rights.[346]

The defining characteristic of the UN Guiding Principles on Business and Human Rights lies in the fact that it clearly differentiates the *State duty* to protect from the *Corporate responsibility* to respect human rights that business enterprises have as social organs performing specialized functions in society. The UN Guiding Principles on Business and Human Rights also place a strong emphasis on the needs both for States and business enterprises to ensure that victims of corporate human rights abuses have effective remedies. Hence, it constitutes an emblematic "*Combination/zebra* standards" containing both the treaty norm on the *State duty* to protect (the black stripe) from corporate human rights abuse and an international standard on the *Corporate responsibility* to respect human rights (the white stripe).[347] The normative contribution of the UN Guiding Principles on Business and Human Rights "*lies not in the creation of new international law obligations but in elaborating the implications of existing standards and practices for States and businesses*."[348]

As such, the UN Guiding Principles on Business and Human Rights "*highlight what steps States need to take in order to ensure the respect of business for human rights; provide a blueprint for companies on how to know and show that they respect human rights, and reduce the risk of causing or contributing to human rights-related harm; indicate steps that States and business need to take to ensure effective remedy for those whose rights have been adversely affected; and comprise a set of benchmarks to enable stakeholders to assess and promote the respect of business, and its*

346 UN Doc., A/HRC/RES/17/4. It can be accessed at the following webpage: https://documents.un.org/doc/resolution/gen/g11/144/71/pdf/g1114471.pdf. (Accessed as of 12 September 2024). For information on the background and context of the mandate of the working group on the issue of human rights and transnational corporations and other business enterprises, see Ibid., Paras. 6-21.

347 See supra note 273.

348 Supra note 259, para. 14. See also infra note 369.

accountability, for human rights and engage with the issue."[349]

Benchmarks as well as indicators can serve as tools to monitor the implementation of not only the *State obligations* to respect, protect and fulfil human rights, but also the *Corporate responsibility* to respect human rights in relation to business activities. Establishing such benchmarks and indicators constitutes a core element of meeting the *State obligations*. As such, the CESCR-Committee, for instance, highlights that the core obligations of the right to health include the State obligation to adopt and implement a national public health strategy and plan of action that shall include, among others, rights to health indicators and benchmarks, by which progress can be monitored.[350] Accordingly, in order to meet the *State obligations* to respect, protect and fulfil human rights in relation to business activities, as well as the *Corporate responsibility* to respect human rights contained in the UN Guiding Principles on Business and Human Rights, relevant government authorities should identify appropriate benchmarks and indicators in national strategies and plans of action aimed at implementing such *State obligations* to respect, protect and fulfil human rights in the context of business activities and the *Corporate responsibility* to respect human rights.

The structure of the UN Guiding Principles on Business and Human Rights consists of General Principles; Foundational Principles; and Operational Principles under the three pillars, i.e., the *State duty* to protect human rights; the *Corporate responsibility* to respect human rights; and access to remedy. In total, there are 31 Principles; 2 Foundational Principles and 8 Operational Principles under the *State duty* to protect human rights pillar; 5 Foundational Principles and 9 Operational Principles under the

---

349 Report of the Working Group on the issue of human rights and transnational corporations and other business enterprises to the UN General Assembly (10 August 2012), UN Doc., A/67/285, para.6. It can be accessed at the following webpage: https://documents.un.org/doc/undoc/gen/n12/459/11/pdf/n1245911.pdf. (Accessed as of 12 September 2024).

350 CESCR-Committee General Comment No. 14 on the right to health, UN Doc., E/C.12/2000/4, paras. 43(f), 52, 53, 56-58, and 63.

Corporate responsibility to respect human rights pillar; and 1 Foundational Principle and 6 Operational Principles under the access to remedy pillar. The Special Representative of the Secretary-General, the author of the UN Guiding Principles on Business and Human Rights stated that they "*were intended to help generate a new regulatory dynamic, one in which public and private governance systems, corporate as well as civil, each come to add distinct value, compensate for one another's weaknesses, and play mutually reinforcing roles-out of which a more comprehensive and effective global regime might evolve.*"[351] For its effective implementation of the principles contained in the UN Guiding Principles on Business and Human Rights, the need for adopting "a smart mix of measures" is emphasized. The Special Representative underscored that a smart mix means "*a combination of voluntary and mandatory, as well as national and international measures.*"[352] This clearly indicates that the legal nature of the UN Guiding Principles on Business and Human Rights is the "*Combination/zebra* standards" that contain the international obligations of States in the context of business activities and the international standard of the *Corporate responsibility* to respect human rights on the international law plane.[353]

The UN Guiding Principles on Business and Human Rights apply to all States and all business enterprises, regardless of their size, sector, location, ownership and structure. They reaffirm the international obligations of States in relation to business activities and clarify the newly emerging international standard on the *Corporate responsibility* to respect human rights. As such, the Commentary to the UN Guiding Principles on Business and Human Rights explicitly states that nothing in the Guidelines should be read "*as creating new international law obligations or as limiting or undermining any legal*

---

351 John Ruggie, 'Keynote Address at the December 2019 Finnish EU Council Presidency Conference.' It can be accessed at the following webpage: https://shiftproject.org/resource/john-ruggie-keynote-finland2019/ . (Accessed as of 13 September 2024).

352 Ibid.

353 See supra note 273 and infra note 354.

obligations a State may have undertaken or be subject to under international law with regard to human rights".[354]

I. The State Duty to Protect

1. Foundational Principles

It is well established that States under international human rights law have the duty to protect the people under their territories and/or jurisdictions from violations of human rights by third parties, including business enterprises. When it comes to corporate human rights abuse, the UN Guiding Principles on Business and Human Rights reaffirms this *State duty* to protect. Principle 1 of the Guiding Principles on Business and Human Rights provides that: "*States must protect against human rights abuse within their territory and/or jurisdiction by third parties, including business enterprises. This requires taking appropriate steps to prevent, investigate, punish and redress such abuse through effective policies, legislation, regulations and adjudication.*"[355]

Under this *State duty* to protect, States must take a range of necessary legislative, administrative, policy, judicial and other measures aimed at preventing and redressing corporate human rights abuse. As such, this *State duty* to protect is "*a standard of conduct*," which means that "*States are not per se responsible for human rights abuse by private actors.*"[356] The failure of States to take necessary measures to prevent, investigate, punish and redress corporate human rights abuse can constitute a breach of this international

---

354 Guiding Principles on Business and Human Rights: Implementing the United Nations Protect, Respect and Remedy Framework, Office of the United Nations High Commissioner for Human Rights, UN Publication, HR/PUB/11/04, see General Principles, at p. 1. It can be accessed at the following webpage: https://www.ohchr.org/sites/default/files/Documents/Publications/GuidingPrinciplesBusinessHR_EN.pdf. (Accessed as of 13 September 2024).

355 Ibid., Principle 1.

356 Ibid., see the Commentary to Principle 1 at p. 3.

State obligation to protect. When it comes to deciding on the appropriateness of these measures, States enjoy a general level of discretion. However, States should take into account the full range of permissible preventative and remedial measures, including legislation, regulations, policies and adjudication, when meeting this *State duty* to protect.[357]

Under the *State duty* to protect, States should set out the clear expectation that business enterprises domiciled in their territory and/or jurisdiction respect human rights throughout their operations.[358] This principle touches upon the extraterritorial obligation of States to regulate the business activities outside the territory that may have caused or contributed to human rights harms. Under the international human rights law, States are required to exercise the extraterritorial obligations with a view to identifying, preventing, investigating, mitigating, and redressing corporate human rights harms as far as such exercise of extraterritorial obligations does not infringe on the sovereignty or diminish the capacity to uphold the international obligations of host States.[359] In this regard, States have adopted a variety of domestic measures that have extraterritorial implications, including requirements for 'parent' companies to report on the global operations, as well as direct extraterritorial legislation. The example of the latter is the US Alien Tort Claims Act that allows victims of corporate human rights abuse committed by companies domiciled in the US to sue those companies under a

---

357 Ibid. The Commentary highlights in this regard the related State duty to promote and protect the rule of law, including equality before the law and fairness in its application, which allows States to provide for accountability, legal certainty and procedural and legal transparency.

358 Supra note 354, Guiding Principles on Business and Human Rights: Implementing the United Nations Protect, Respect and Remedy Framework, Office of the United Nations High Commissioner for Human Rights, UN Publication, HR/PUB/11/04, Principle 2.

359 See supra Chapter 4.C: Interim Conclusions at p. 146. See also supra note 354, Guiding Principles on Business and Human Rights: Implementing the United Nations Protect, Respect and Remedy Framework, Office of the United Nations High Commissioner for Human Rights, UN Publication, HR/PUB/11/04, at pp. 3-4. The Commentary to Principle 2 states that States have the choice to regulate the extraterritorial activities of businesses domiciled in their territory and/or jurisdiction.

suit of civil tort action in the courts of the United States.[360]

2. Operational Principles

The Operational Principles provided for the *State duty* to protect pillar under the UN Guiding Principles on Business and Human Rights address the requirement of States to ensure that their general regulatory frameworks and policies are geared toward corporate respect of human rights. As such, States are required to: enforce laws designed for corporate respect of human rights through periodic assessment of their adequacy; and ensure that other laws and policies governing business enterprises do not constrain but enable corporate respect of human rights; provide guidance on corporate respect of human rights; and encourage, and require where appropriate, business enterprises to communicate how they address human rights impacts. The Operational Principles also address: the state-business nexus regarding the special duties of business enterprises owned or controlled by States, which requires States to take additional steps to protect from corporate human rights abuse by state-owned companies, including through, where appropriate, requiring human rights due diligence; the need for adequate oversight in the case of privatization of public services; the need to promote corporate respect of human rights when conducting commercial transactions with business enterprises; the heightened risks of gross human rights abuses in conflict-affected areas; and the need for States to ensure policy coherence.[361] States should also maintain adequate domestic policy space to meet their human rights obligations when concluding investment treaties or contacts with other States or business enterprises.[362] States should ensure that multilateral institutions, of which they are members do not constrain the ability of their

---

360 For the details on the US Alien Tort Claims Act, see infra Chapter 8.

361 Supra note 354, Guiding Principles on Business and Human Rights: Implementing the United Nations Protect, Respect and Remedy Framework, Office of the United Nations High Commissioner for Human Rights, UN Publication, HR/PUB/11/04, Principles 3-8.

362 Ibid., Principle 9.

member States to meet their *State duty* to protect or hinder corporate respect of human rights. States should also encourage those multilateral institutions to promote corporate respect of human rights within their respective mandates and capacities.[363]

II. The Corporate Responsibility to Respect

The UN Guiding Principles on Business and Human Rights envisage the three-part *Corporate responsibility* to respect human rights: a policy commitment to meet the responsibility to respect human rights; a human rights due diligence process to identify, prevent, mitigate and account for how a business enterprise addresses its adverse human rights impacts; and the remediation processes of adverse human rights impacts that it has caused or contributed to through their own activities, as well as those that are directly linked to their operations, products or services by their business relationships.[364] It should be emphasized, at the outset, that this *Corporate responsibility* to respect human rights, as a global standard of expected business conduct, exists independently of the *State duty* to protect from corporate human rights abuse. As such, it does not diminish the *State obligation* to protect. It is also over and above compliance with national laws and regulations of both home and host countries.[365] Business enterprises should therefore respect human rights in their own operations and in their supply chains in accordance with such an international human rights standard on the *Corporate responsibility* to respect human rights, in addition to complying with national laws and regulations. In case that the *Corporate responsibility* to respect human rights has been incorporated into national laws and regulations, it becomes the national-level legal obligation to respect human rights on the domestic law plane.[366]

---

363 Ibid., Principle 10.

364 Ibid., Principles 11-24, in particular Principle 15.

365 Ibid., See the Commentary to Principle 11.

366 For national examples of mandatory human rights due diligence law, see infra, Chapter 8.

1. Foundational Principles

The UN Guiding Principles on Business and Human Rights lay out five foundational principles, which clarifies the essential components of the *Corporate responsibility* to respect human rights: first and foremost, corporate respect of human rights means that business enterprises "*should avoid infringing on the human rights of others and address adverse human rights impacts with which they are involved.*"[367] In order to address adverse human rights impacts, they should have in place appropriate policies and processes depending on their size and circumstances with a view to identifying, preventing, mitigating, and remedying adverse human rights impacts caused by their own activities or contributed to, as well as those that are directly linked to their operations, products or services, even if they have not contributed to those impacts. In this regard, it is important to bear in mind that although business enterprises may undertake other commitments or activities to support and promote human rights, for instance, as part of effecting the corporate social responsibility policy, they cannot offset a failure to respect human rights throughout their operations. Business enterprises should not undermine States' abilities to meet their own human rights obligations, including weakening the integrity of judicial processes.[368]

The *Corporate responsibility* to respect human rights refers to internationally recognized human rights, those rights that found expressions in the International Bill of Human Rights and in the ILO Declaration on Fundamental Principles and Rights at Work.[369] The *Corporate responsibility* to respect human rights is distinct from issues of legal liability and enforcement. Business enterprises may also need to consider additional international human rights standards that address the rights of individuals belonging to specific groups or populations such as Indigenous Peoples,

---

367 Ibid., Principle 11.
368 Ibid., See the Commentary to Principle 11.
369 Ibid., Principle 12.

women, minorities, children, persons with disabilities and migrant workers. In situations of armed conflict, business enterprises should also respect international humanitarian law standards.[370]

The essence of the *Corporate responsibility* to respect human rights is that business enterprises should "*act with due diligence to avoid infringing on the rights of others and to address adverse impacts with which they are involved.*"[371]

This *Corporate responsibility* to respect human rights applies to all business enterprises "*regardless of their size, sector, operational context, ownership and structure.*" Business enterprises can adopt various means designed to meet the *Corporate responsibility* to respect human rights, the scale and complexity of which depends on these factors and the severity of the enterprise's adverse human rights impacts.[372] This explicit clarification on the scope of the application of the *Corporate responsibility* to respect human rights to all business enterprises can provide an inspiration for the elaboration of a future international treaty on business and human rights, which is currently being deliberated under the auspices of the Human Rights Council's open-ended intergovernmental working group on transnational corporations and other business enterprises with respect to human rights. The issue of the scope of application of the future treaty is indeed being debated in the deliberations on the draft text of such a future international treaty on business and human rights.[373] The severity of adverse human rights impacts should be judged "*by their scale, scope and irremediable character.*"[374]

---

370 Ibid., See the Commentary on Principle 12.

371 Supra note 339, 'Report of the Special Representative of the Secretary-General on the issue of human rights and transnational corporations and other business enterprises, John Ruggie: Guiding Principles on Business and Human Rights: Implementing the United Nations "Protect, Respect and Remedy" Framework,' UN Doc., A/HRC/17/31, para. 6.

372 Supra note 354, Principle 14.

373 For the details, see infra Chapter 7.

374 Supra note 354, See the Commentary to Principle 14.

As such, in order for business enterprises to meet the *Corporate responsibility* to respect human rights, they should put in place policies and processes appropriate to their size and circumstances, including a policy commitment to respect human rights, a human rights due diligence process designed to identify, prevent, mitigate and account for the ways in which their adverse human rights impacts are addressed, and remediation processes against such adverse human rights impacts. In other words, "*business enterprises need to know and show that they respect human rights.*"[375]

2. Operational Principles

The Operational Principles of the *Corporate responsibility* to respect human rights further specify the three-part *Corporate responsibility* to respect human rights: firstly, with respect to a policy commitment, business enterprises should prepare a policy commitment that serves as the basis for embedding the *Corporate responsibility* to respect human rights throughout their entire operations[376]; secondly, business enterprises should conduct human rights due diligence, which constitutes the most essential element of the *Corporate responsibility* to respect human rights pillar. As such, business enterprises should carry out human rights due diligence in order to identify, prevent, mitigate and account for how they address their adverse human rights impacts[377]; and thirdly, business enterprises should provide for or cooperate in remediation of the adverse impacts caused or contributed to, and those that are directly linked to their operations, products or services, even if they have not contributed to those impacts.[378]

---

375 Ibid. See the Commentary to Principle 15.

376 Ibid., see Principle 16.

377 Ibid., see Principles 17-21, which further specify that human rights due diligence processes should include: assessing actual and potential human rights impacts; integrating and acting upon the findings; tracking responses; and communicating how impacts are addressed. They should be ongoing in recognition that the human rights risks may change over time due to the evolution of the business enterprise's operations and operating context.

378 Ibid., Principle 23.

III. Access to Remedy

1. Foundational Principle

The *State duty* to protect from corporate human rights abuse will become meaningless unless States take appropriate steps to ensure, through judicial, administrative, legislative, or other appropriate means, that when corporate human rights abuses occur within their territory and/or jurisdiction, such corporate human rights abuse victims have access to effective remedy. Hence, it can be said that remediation is considered to matter the most for corporate human rights abuse victims.[379] Access to effective remedy has both procedural and substantive aspects: the aim of substantive forms of remedies is generally to counteract or make good human rights harms, and remedy may include "*apologies, restitution, rehabilitation, financial or non-financial compensation and punitive sanctions (whether criminal or administrative, such as fines), as well as the prevention of harm through, for example, injunctions or guarantees of non-repetition.*"[380] For those substantive forms of remedies to be considered effective, procedures for remedy provision should be "*impartial, protected from corruption and free from political or other attempts to influence the outcome.*"[381]

The UN Guiding Principles on Business and Human Rights envisage three main mechanisms that corporate human rights abuse victims can utilize in their pursuit of remediation of the corporate human rights harms suffered: state-based judicial mechanisms; state-based non-judicial grievance mechanisms; and non-state-based grievance mechanisms.[382]

---

379 Ibid., Principle 25.

380 Ibid. See the Commentary to Principle 25.

381 Ibid.

382 Ibid. The Commentary defines grievance as follows: "*For the purpose of these Guiding Principles, a grievance is understood to be a perceived injustice evoking an individual's or a group's sense of entitlement, which may be based on law, contract, explicit or implicit promises, customary practice, or general notions of fairness of aggrieved communities.*"

2. Operational Principles

The Operational Principles on the access to remedy pillar (Principles 26-31) of the UN Guiding Principles on Business and Human Rights further clarify the specific features of different kinds of mechanisms along with a detailed explanation on the effectiveness criteria for non-judicial grievance mechanisms in Principle 31.

a. State-based judicial mechanisms

Effective judicial mechanisms constitute a core element when it comes to ensuring access to remedy against corporate human rights harms. As such, States should ensure the effectiveness of judicial mechanisms, including considering means aimed at reducing legal practical and other barriers that could lead to a denial of access to remedy.[383] Such judicial mechanisms should be impartial and should function with integrity, and should have the ability to accord due process.

Legal barriers can arise in situations where legal responsibility is attributed among members of a corporate group that facilitates the avoidance of appropriate accountability; where there are no effective judicial recourse both in host and home States; and where certain groups such as Indigenous Peoples are discriminated against in terms of legal protection. Practical and procedural barriers on the other hand include: the extremely high costs of bringing claims; the lack of legal representation, owing to a lack of resources or lack of incentives for lawyers to advise claimants; the lack of adequate options for aggregating claims such as class actions; and lack of resources and expertise of prosecutors to investigate individual and business involvement in business-related human rights abuses (crimes).[384] To establish effectively

---

383 Ibid., Principle 26. See also the Commentary to Principle 26.

384 For more details, see ibid.

functioning judicial mechanisms, States should pay close attention to the additional cultural, social, physical and financial impediments to accessing such judicial mechanisms faced by individuals from groups at heightened risk of vulnerability or marginalization such as Indigenous Peoples.[385]

b. State-based non-judicial grievance mechanisms

State-based non-judicial grievance mechanisms can also play an essential complementary role in providing effective remedies against corporate human rights harms.[386] These mechanisms should take the forms of administrative, legislative and other non-judicial mechanisms, which can serve as important mechanisms to fill the gaps in the provision of remedy against business-related human rights abuses. To ensure their effectiveness, States should ensure that these mechanisms meet the effectiveness criteria set out in Principle 31 of the UN Guiding Principles on Business and Human Rights. Independent national human rights institutions fully compliant with the UN principles relating to the status of national human rights institutions (the Paris Principles) can play a particularly important role. Moreover, as with judicial mechanisms, States should reduce any barriers, including any imbalances between the parties to business-related human rights claims, and also address the additional needs for individuals from certain groups at a heightened risk of vulnerability or marginalization to have access to effective remedies. [387]

c. Non-State-based grievance mechanisms

States should facilitate access to effective non-State-based grievance mechanisms, including those administered by a business enterprise alone or with stakeholders, by an industry association or a multi-stakeholder, as well

385 Ibid.

386 Ibid., Principle 27.

387 Ibid. See the Commentary to Principle 27.

as regional and international human rights bodies.[388] The benefits of these non-State-based grievance mechanisms are: *"speed of access and remediation, reduced costs and/or transnational reach."*[389]

Operational-level grievance mechanisms play an important role when it comes to preventing grievances from escalating. As such, States are encouraged to ensure that business enterprises establish or participate in effective operational-level grievance mechanisms.[390] These mechanisms perform two key functions: firstly, to support the identification of adverse human rights impacts; and secondly, to prevent corporate human rights harms from compounding and grievances from escalating. They are usually administered by enterprises alone or in collaboration with relevant stakeholders, as well as through recourse to a mutually acceptable external expert or body, and they should be accessible. Their effectiveness should be ensured, which depends on *"the demands of scale, resource, sector, culture and other parameters."*[391] When serving as complements to wider stakeholder engagement and collective bargaining processes, operational-level grievance mechanisms should not be used to undermine the role of legitimate trade unions in addressing labour disputes, nor to preclude access to judicial and other non-judicial grievance mechanisms.[392]

d. Effectiveness criteria

With the aim of ensuring that non-judicial grievance mechanisms effectively function, the UN Guiding Principles on Business and Human

388 Ibid., Principle 28.

389 Ibid., see the Commentary to Principle 28.

390 Ibid., Principle 29.

391 Ibid., see the Commentary to Principle 29.

392 Ibid. The UN Guiding Principles on Business and Human Rights also highlights the importance of ensuring that industry, multi-stakeholder and other collaborative initiatives based on respect for human rights-related standards make available effective grievance mechanisms therein. (Principle 30).

Rights suggest the key 8 effectiveness criteria,[393] the first 7 of which apply to state-based judicial mechanisms, state-based non-judicial grievance mechanisms, and non-state-based grievance mechanisms, and the last criterion applies specifically to operational-level grievance mechanisms: firstly, non-judicial mechanisms should be legitimate, which means that they should enable trust from the stakeholders groups for whose use they are intended, and be accountable for the fair conduct of grievance processes; secondly, they should be accessible and provide adequate assistance for those who may face barriers to access. Barriers to access in this regard may include "*a lack of awareness of the mechanism, language, literacy, costs, physical location and fears of reprisal*"[394]; thirdly, they should be predictable. In other words, they should provide "*a clear and known procedure with an indicative time frame for each stage, and clarity on the types of process and outcome available and means of monitoring implementation*"[395]; fourthly, they should be equitable in terms of the parties' having equitable "*access to sources of information, advice and expertise to engage in a grievance process on fair, informed and respectful terms.*"[396] This is of particular importance because in grievances or disputes between business enterprises and affected stakeholders, usually the latter has much less access to information and expert resources, and often lacks the financial resources to pay for them[397]; fifthly, they should be transparent by "*keeping parties to a grievance informed about its progress*", and provide "*sufficient information about the mechanism's performance to build confidence in its effectiveness and meet any public interest at stake*"[398]; sixthly, they should be rights-compatible, which means that the outcomes of grievances resolution have human rights implications, and they should be fully in line with internationally recognized human rights norms and standards[399];

393 Ibid., Principle 31.
394 Ibid., see the Commentary to Principle 31.
395 Ibid., Principle 31(c).
396 Ibid., Principle 31(d).
397 Ibid., see the Commentary to Principle 31(d).
398 Ibid., Principle 31(e).
399 Ibid., see the Commentary to Principle 31(e).

seventhly, there should be regular analysis of the frequency, patterns and causes of grievances, which will enable the institution administering the mechanism to identify lessons for the purposes of not only improving the mechanism itself but also preventing future grievances and harms. In this way, they should serve as a source of continuous learning[400]; and lastly, operational-level grievance mechanisms should be based on engagement and dialogue with the affected stakeholder groups as a means to addressing and resolving grievances.[401]

D. Interim Conclusions

A host of international voluntary guidelines have been developed, which serves to provide guidance both for States and business enterprises on how to address the negative impacts of business activities on the enjoyment of human rights. These Guidance/Guidelines address both the *State obligation* to protect from corporate human rights abuse and *the Corporate responsibility* to respect human rights, which perfectly exemplifies the existing "*Combination/zebra* standards" on business and human rights such as the UN Guiding Principles on Business and Human Rights. Considering their voluntary nature, the implementation and operationalization of such guidance/guidelines, particularly on the *Corporate responsibility* to respect human rights on the ground depends a great deal on the willingness and commitment of States and business enterprises. Therefore, these guidelines can have a full meaning, only when the guidance provided for in these Guidelines is followed up and observed both by States as part of meeting their international human rights obligations in relation to business activities and by business enterprises in their efforts to respect human rights in their own activities and in their supply chains.

---

400 Ibid., Principle 31(f) and the Commentary thereto.
401 Ibid., Principle 31 (h) and the Commentary thereto.

Conducting human rights due diligence lies at the heart of such *Corporate responsibility* to respect human rights. Human rights due diligence can be understood, *de minimis*, as the process by which "*business enterprises can identify, prevent, mitigate and account for how they address their actual and potential adverse impacts as an integral part of business decision-making and risk management systems*."[402] Business enterprises can, as part of this human rights due diligence process, include actions such as conducting human rights impacts assessments, incorporation of the findings of such human right impact assessments into company operations, and communication both internally and externally on how they address actual and potential adverse human rights impacts. All these core elements of human rights due diligence are provided in the UN Guiding Principles on Business and Human Rights, the most recent and comprehensive international "*Combination/zebra* standards" on *the Corporate responsibility* to respect human rights.

With the adoption of the UN Guiding Principles on Business and Human Rights in 2011 by the UN Human Rights Council, there has been an increasing convergence of these voluntary guidelines/guidance on business and human rights, in particular in relation to the *Corporate responsibility* to respect human rights. For instance, the 2011 update of the OECD Guidelines for MNEs and the 2013 revised ILO MNE Declaration have incorporated the *Corporate responsibility* to respect human rights contained in the UN Guiding Principles on Business and Human Rights, which is currently the most authoritative and important international standard on the *Corporate* responsibility to respect human rights. Hence, it can be said that the *Combination/zebra* standards on business and human rights, in particular on the *Corporate responsibility* to respect human rights, are in the process of being concretized.

402 Supra note 307, OECD (2023), *OECD Guidelines for Multinational Enterprises on Responsible Business Conduct*, OECD Publishing, Paris, https://doi.org/10.1787/81f92357-en. (Accessed as of 8 September 2024), Commentary on General Principles, para. 15 at page 17.

The effectiveness of these Guidelines/Guidance depends largely on what kinds of built-in implementation/follow-up mechanisms are put in place. The OECD Guidelines for MNEs and the ILO MNE Declaration, for instance, have similar built-in implementation mechanisms such as National Contact Points (NCPs) under the former and National Focal Points (NFPs) under the latter. However, it is submitted that whether these NCPs or NFPs effectively function in a way that increases the level of implementation of those guidance is still being called into question when it comes to them serving as an adequate avenue of provision of remedy against corporate human rights abuse.[403]

It is also submitted that the OECD Guidelines for MNEs represent an important set of guidance for responsible business conduct to be observed on a voluntary basis. Various implementation mechanisms built in the OECD Guidelines for MNEs can serve as the useful tools to ensure that business enterprises meet their *Corporate responsibility* to respect human rights. In this regard, it is critically important to ensure for the transparent and participatory process involving Governments, business, trade unions and civil society in the actual operations of such implementation mechanisms, including National Contact Points, which is central to the evolution and the success of the OECD Guidelines for MNEs.

In terms of the nature of the ILO Tripartite MNE Declaration, an academic scholar argues that it provides the legal basis for the international obligations for companies to respect labour rights (human rights), making

---

403 Supra note 9, Andrew Clapham, Human Rights Obligations of Non-State Actors, Oxford University Press (2006), pp. 211-225. See also OECD Watch, 'State of Remedy 2023,' p.3. It notes some positive developments observed during 2023 regarding complaints handling by National Contact Points under the OECD Guidelines for MNEs but expressed concerns that NCPs' failure to meet the expectations in the Procedures for NCPs in the OECD Guidelines for MNEs (formerly the Procedural Guidance) risks undermining the effectiveness of the NCP compliant system. It can be accessed at the following webpage: https://www.oecdwatch.org/state-of-remedy-2023/. (Accessed as of 18 September 2024).

an assessment that it is "*an authoritative interpretation of some of the International Labour Conventions and customary international law relevant to labour rights.*"[404] He concludes that "*the Declaration provides material evidence that international labour law regime has come to include human rights obligations for national and multinational enterprises.*"[405] In this regard, it is submitted that even though the ILO Tripartite MNE Declaration contains international labour rights norms that are considered to be part of customary international law such as prohibition of uncompensated or abusive forced labour applicable in the context of both international and non-international armed conflicts,[406] the most part of the standards referred in the ILO Tripartite MNE Declaration still remains to be voluntary. In fact, it can be critiqued that the ILO Tripartite MNE Declaration has erroneously obfuscated the *State obligations* and the *Corporate responsibility* to respect human rights (labour rights). For instance, when the ILO Tripartite MNE Declaration has incorporated the UN Guiding Principles on Business and Human Rights through its latest amendment in 2017, it has included the *State duty* to provide access to remedy to victims of corporate human rights abuse as a recommendation, not as an obligation, which has been retained in the 2023 revised edition. As such, paragraph 64 of the ILO Tripartite MNE Declaration provides that "*As part of their duty to protect against business-related human rights abuses, Governments* ***should*** (emphasis added) *take appropriate steps to ensure, through judicial, administrative, legislative or other appropriate means, that when such abuses occur within their territory*

---

404 Supra note 9, Andrew Clapham, Human Rights Obligations of Non-State Actors, Oxford University Press (2006), pp. 211-225.

405 Ibid., pp. 211-225, in particular p. 215.

406 For the legal nature of the prohibition of uncompensated or abusive forced labour under international humanitarian law, see the following webpage: https://ihl-databases.icrc.org/en/customary-ihl/v1/rule95. (Accessed as of 18 September 2024). Labour rights contained in the ILO Conventions No. 87 concerning the Freedom of Association and Protection of the Right to Organize and No. 98 concerning the Application of the Principles of the Right to Organize and Bargain Collectively can be said that they constitute part of customary international law, which provides the basis for the *State obligations* and for the *Corporate responsibility* to respect human rights in the framework of the ILO Tripartite MNE Declaration.

and/or jurisdictions any affected worker or workers have access to effective remedy."[407] This runs the risk of diluting the existing *State obligation* to remedy against human rights harms caused by business activities under the current international human rights law regime.

With regard to enforcement mechanism, it is worth noting that the ILO Tripartite MNE Declaration is focusing mostly on promotional actions to be undertaken both by the National Focal Points and by the ILO itself. It is understandable that it focuses on such promotional activities, considering the voluntary nature of the ILO Tripartite MNE Declaration. However, this casts serious doubt as to whether the ILO Tripartite MNE Declaration can bring about real practical impact, when it comes to addressing the negative impacts of business activities on the enjoyment of human rights, in particular labour rights on the ground.

The UN Guiding Principles on Business and Human Rights is the most recent and comprehensive, perhaps the most authoritative voluntary guidance when it comes to the international human rights standards on business and human rights. The added value of the UN Guiding Principles on Business and Human Rights lies in the fact that they make a clear distinction between the *State obligation* to protect and the *Corporate responsibility* to respect human rights constituting as the "*Combination/zebra* standards" on business and human rights. As such, they clarify the distinct but yet complementary *State obligation* to protect from corporate human rights abuse and the *Corporate responsibility* to respect human rights under the existing international human rights law regime. They also address another crucial element of the requirement to provide effective remedies when corporate human rights abuses occur, as part of the *State obligation* to protect and the *Corporate responsibility* to respect human rights. It is submitted that it is

407 Supra note 321, ILO (2023), *ILO Tripartite Declaration of Principles concerning Multinational Enterprises and Social Policy*, para. 64.

critically important to operationalize the UN Guiding Principles on Business and Human Rights on the ground by clarifying what must be done and what should be done both by States and business enterprises.

When it comes to the *Corporate responsibility* to respect human rights, greater efforts should be made to clarify what are the minimum requirements for conducting human rights due diligence in different sectors and industries. Parallel efforts should also be made to clarify what States are obligated to do concretely to meet the *State duty* to protect from corporate human rights abuse. In this regard, UN treaty monitoring bodies[408] can play a critically important role as they can provide an authoritative interpretation of what is the content of the *State obligations* to respect, protect and fulfil human rights in relation to business activities under the respective treaties, whose implementation by States parties they are mandated to monitor and oversee. Regional and national-level practices such as the enactment of mandatory human rights due diligence law could also be of high relevance in terms of clarifying what measures must be taken by States as part of fulfilling their international obligations to respect, protect and fulfil human rights in relation to business activities. For instance, an increasing number of States have and/or are legislating mandatory human rights due diligence by business enterprises under this *State obligation* to protect from corporate human rights abuse. [409]

Ensuring the effectiveness of the UN Guiding Principles on Business and Human rights, particularly from the perspective of preventing and remedying human rights harms caused by business activities or contributed to, and those that are directly linked to their operations, products or services lies at the core of the spirit and letter of the guidance contained therein.

---

408 See supra Chapters. 3-4.
409 See infra Chapter 8. A.

The ultimate objective of both legally binding rules and voluntary Guidance/Guidelines on business and human rights is therefore to prevent, identify, investigate, mitigate and remedy the human rights harms caused by business activities. Bearing this in mind, it is submitted that a combination of these two sets of rules and voluntary Guidance/Guidelines on the international law plane as "*Combination/zebra standards*," which contains the *State duty* to protect (*the black stripe*), the *Corporate responsibility* to respect human rights (*the white stripe*), and access to remedy (both *the black stripe* referring to the *State obligation* to ensure that victims of corporate human rights abuse have access to remedy against it and *the white stripe* referring to the *responsibility* of business enterprises to remedy human rights harms caused or contributed to by their own business activities, and those that are directly linked to their operations, products or services by their business relationships[410] should be promoted. The most critical element in designing any internationally legally binding rules on business and human rights lies in the fact that such rules must ensure that business enterprises establish an effective and satisfactory remedy mechanism on the international law plane, whether it be judicial or quasi-judicial or non-judicial in nature, which will, in turn, enable corporate human rights abuse victims to have adequate and effective remedies against corporate human rights harms.

---

410 See supra note 354.

Chapter 6: Global Efforts to Impose Direct Obligation on Companies to Respect Human Rights

A. The Norms on Human Rights Responsibilities of Companies

The then United Nations Sub-Commission on the Promotion and Protection of Human Rights (hereinafter referred to as the then UN Sub-Commission) had addressed the issue of the impacts of business activities, in particular those of transnational corporations on the enjoyment of human rights through its inter-sessional working group established in 1998.

Prior to the establishment of an inter-sessional working group on the working methods and activities of transnational corporations in 1997, the then UN Sub-Commission had asked one of its members to present a working document[411] on the issue of human rights and transnational corporations to its 1998 session, which led to the establishment of an inter-sessional working group for a three-year period. The mandate of the inter-sessional working group was, *inter alia*, to identify issues and examine information regarding the effects of transnational corporations on human rights, and to assess the compatibility of investment agreements with human rights agreements. The mandate was also to make recommendations regarding the working methods and activities of transnational corporations with the aim of ensuring for human rights protection, taking into consideration the scope of the State obligation to regulate transnational corporations.[412] As such, the mandate of the inter-sessional working group narrowly focused on examining the working methods and activities of transnational corporations that might have

---

411 UN Doc., E/CN.4/Sub.2/1998/6. It can be accessed at the following webpage: https://documents.un.org/doc/undoc/gen/g98/128/35/pdf/g9812835.pdf. (Accessed as of 18 September 2024).

412 UN Doc., E/CN.4/Sub.2/RES/1998/8. It can be accessed at the following webpage: https://ap.ohchr.org/documents/alldocs.aspx?doc_id=8140. (Accessed as of 18 September 2024).

negative impacts on the enjoyment of human rights. This narrowly defined mandate focusing only on transnational corporations had triggered a great deal debate as to whether the Norms on the responsibilities of transnational corporations and other business enterprises with regard to human rights adopted in 2003 by the then UN Sub-commission should apply only to transnational corporations or to all other business enterprises.

The inter-sessional working group's mandate was extended for a further three-year period in 2001, because it had not completed its tasks. Its renewed mandate had not only clarified the mandate of the inter-sessional working group to draft relevant norms, but also added new activities, including: compiling a list of human rights instruments and norms in relation to transnational corporations; contributing to the drafting of norms relevant to transnational corporations and other economic units, whose activities had an impact on human rights; and analyzing and drafting norms aimed at establishing a monitoring mechanism that would apply sanctions to transnational corporations, when appropriate.[413]

Pursuant to the renewed mandate, the inter-sessional working group completed the Norms and Commentary (Human Rights Principles and Responsibilities for Transnational Corporations and Other Business Enterprises with Commentary on the Principles)[414] and submitted them to the then UN Sub-commission in 2002. The then UN Sub-commission, in turn, asked that the Norms and Commentary be disseminated as widely as possible so as to encourage Governments, inter-governmental organizations, non-governmental organizations (NGOs), transnational corporations and other business enterprises, unions and other interested parties to submit

---

413 UN Doc., E/CN.4/Sub.2/RES/2001/3. It can be accessed at the following webpage: https://ap.ohchr.org/documents/alldocs.aspx?doc_id=8220. (Accessed as of 18 September 2024).

414 UN Doc., E/CN.4/Sub.2/2002/WG.2/WP.1/Add.2. It can be accessed at the following webpage: http://hrlibrary.umn.edu/PrinciplesWithCommentary5final.html.

suggestions, observations and recommendations.[415]

In 2003, the then UN Sub-commission approved the Norms in its resolution, 2003/16,[416] through which it also submitted the Norms to the then United Nations Commission on Human Rights (hereinafter referred to as the then UN Commission on Human Rights) for eventual endorsement. In the same resolution, the then UN Sub-commission asked the then UN Commission on Human Rights to invite Governments, United Nations bodies, specialized agencies, NGOs and other interested parties to provide the latter with comments on the Norms for the March-April session of the then UN Commission on Human Rights in 2005.[417]

I. General and Specific Obligations

The Norms on the responsibilities of transnational corporations and other business enterprises with regard to human rights (hereinafter referred to as the Norms on Business and Human Rights) were premised on the notion that business enterprises have an international obligation to respect human rights. The legal basis was drawn from the Universal Declaration of Human Rights.[418] The Preamble of UDHR emphasizes that not only Governments

---

415 UN Doc., E/CN.4/Sub.2/RES/2002/8. It can be accessed at the following webpage: https://ap.ohchr.org/documents/alldocs.aspx?doc_id=8260. (Accessed as of 18 September 2024).

416 UN Doc., E/CN.4/Sub.2/RES/2003/16. It can be accessed at the following webpage : https://ap.ohchr.org/documents/dpage_e.aspx?si=E/CN.4/Sub.2/RES/2003/16. (Accessed as of 18 September 2024).

417 For a detailed exposition of the drafting history of the Norms, see supra note 9, David Weissbrodt and Muria Kruger, 'Norms on the Responsibilities of Transnational Corporations and Other Business Enterprises with Regard to Human Rights,' 97 Am. J. Int'l L. 901 (2003), available at: https://scholarship.law.umn.edu/cgi/viewcontent.cgi?article=1247&context=faculty_articles (Accessed as of 18 September 2024).

418 The then UN Sub-commission used the following part of the Preamble of the Universal Declaration of Human Rights as the basis for the international obligation for business enterprises to respect human rights: "a common standard of achievement for all peoples and all nations, to the end that Governments, *other organs of society and individuals* (emphasis added) shall strive, by teaching and education to promote respect for human rights and freedoms, and, by progressive measures, to secure universal and effective recognition and observance, including

but also other organs of society and individuals shall strive to promote respect of human rights. Based on this Preamble, the then UN Sub-commission took the view that business enterprises, as social organs having specialized functions in society, are also *obligated* to respect human rights on the international law plane. As such, the Norms on Business and Human Rights explicitly reaffirmed that "*transnational corporations and other business enterprises, their officers – including managers, members of corporate boards or directors and other executives – and persons working for them have, inter alia, human rights obligations and responsibilities.*"[419]

However, this view had been subjected to intense debate, as the majority of States[420] were of the opinion that business enterprises did not bear an international obligation to respect human rights on the international law plane, except for a few cases where international human rights norms such as customary international law, *ius cogens,* and certain international norms related to international crimes such as war crimes, genocide, and crimes

---

of equal rights of women and men and the promotion of social progress and better standards of life in larger freedom". As such, the Norms recognizes in its Preamble the following: "Even though States have the primary responsibility to promote, secure the fulfilment of, respect, ensure respect of and protect human rights, transnational corporations and other business enterprises, as organs of society, are also responsible for promoting and securing the human rights set forth in the Universal Declaration of Human Rights". See Preamble, 'Norms on the responsibilities of transnational corporations and other business enterprises with regard to human rights', UN Doc, E/CN.4/Sub.2/2003/12/Rev.2 of 26 August 2003. It can be accessed at the following webpage: https://documents.un.org/doc/undoc/gen/g03/160/08/pdf/g0316008.pdf. (Accessed as of 19 September 2024).

419 Ibid.

420 The then Commission on Human Rights, in its Decision 2004/115, rejected the Norms on Business and Human Rights using the terminology of "responsibility" to indicate that business enterprises do not have the obligation to respect human rights on the international law plane. This draft decision (E/CN.4/2004/L.73/Rev.1) was supported by the following States: Australia, Belgium, the Czech Republic, Ethiopia, Ghana, Hungary, Ireland, Japan, Mexico, Norway, South Africa, Sweden and the United Kingdom of Great Britain and Northern Ireland. Austria, Bangladesh, Croatia, Denmark, Equatorial Guinea, Finland, France, Germany, Guatemala, Iceland, Italy, Luxembourg, the Netherlands, Nigeria, Poland, Spain and Switzerland. UN Doc., E/CN.4/2004/127, pp. 332-333, 436, 563 and 590. It can be accessed at the following webpage: https://documents.un.org/doc/undoc/gen/g04/162/00/pdf/g0416200.pdf. (Accessed as of 19 September 2024).

against humanity could be directly applied.

As part of the general obligations, the Norms on Business and Human Rights highlight the primary duty of Governments to respect, protect and fulfil human rights. Therein, the Norms on Business and Human Rights place a particular emphasis on the *State duty* to protect from human rights abuses by third parties, including business enterprises (corporate human rights abuses). In addition to these State obligations, the Norms on Business and Human Rights explicitly provide that business enterprises also bear an international-level *obligation* to respect human rights by enunciating that "*within their respective spheres of activity and influence, transnational corporations and other business enterprises have the* ***obligation*** (emphasis added) *to promote, secure the fulfilment of, respect, ensure respect of and protect human rights recognized in international as well as national law.*"[421]

As such, the Norms on Business and Human Rights explicitly provide for the *obligation* of transnational corporations and other business enterprises to respect the whole gamut of human rights, covering the right to equal treatment and non-discrimination, workers' rights, including prohibition of forced and compulsory labour, protection from economic exploitation of children, provision of a healthy and safe working environment, just and favourable working conditions and protection of the rights to association and collective action such as collective bargaining and the right to strike, economic, social and cultural rights, as well as civil and political rights.

The Norms on Business and Human Rights also provide for the *obligation* of business enterprises in relation to consumer and environmental protection. Furthermore, the Norms on Business and Human Rights provide that transnational corporations and other business enterprises *shall* not engage or benefit from war crimes, crimes against humanity, genocide, torture,

---

421 Supra note 418., para. 1.

enforced disappearance, and international crimes. The Norms on Business and Human Rights further specifically provide that security arrangements for the operations of business enterprises must observe international human rights and international humanitarian law and standards.[422]

II. General Provisions of Implementation

The Norms on Business and Human Rights envisaged implementation measures, including requirements of business enterprises to adopt, disseminate and implement their internal rules of operation in compliance with the Norms on Business and Human Rights and to periodically report on and take other measures aimed at fully implementing the Norms on Business and Human Rights, and incorporate the Norms on Business and Human Rights in their contracts or other arrangements and dealings with contractors, sub-contractors, suppliers, licensees, distributors or natural or other legal persons.

The Norms on Business and Human Rights also envisaged periodic monitoring by existing United Nations and other international and national mechanisms, including any such future mechanisms, to be conducted in a transparent and independent manner, taking into account input from stakeholders.

In addition, the Norms on Business and Human Rights reiterated the *State duty* to protect from corporate human rights abuse through imposing the obligation on States to establish and reinforce the legal and administrative framework with a view to ensuring for the implementation of the Norms on Business and Human Rights at the national level.

The Norms on Business and Human Rights further provided for the

422 Ibid., paras. 3-4.

requirement that business enterprises shall provide prompt, effective and adequate reparation to those adversely affected by failures to comply with the Norms.

In sum, the Norms on Business and Human Rights represents the very first but failed attempt on the international law plane to explicitly impose the obligation on business enterprises to respect human rights, based on the abstractly worded Preamble of the Universal Declaration of Human Rights thus deviating from the traditional view that while States bear the *obligations* to respect, protect and fulfil human rights in relation to business activities, corporations have only the *responsibility* to respect human rights except that business enterprises are also subjected to customary international law and *ius cogens* on the international law plane. This has resulted in the refusal of the then Commission on Human Rights to endorse the Norms on Business and Human Rights.

B. The United Nations Human Rights Council Treaty-Making Process

I. The Evolutionary Trajectory

With increased power of the corporate sector, in particular that of transnational corporations, there have been growing demands to regulate the activities of transnational corporations and other business enterprises that have significant negative impacts on the enjoyment of human rights on the international law plane.

In response to such demands, business enterprises have taken the voluntary initiatives to respect human rights within their own spheres of influence. At the international level, a host of voluntary Guidelines/Guidance has been developed, which aims at providing for international standards/ guidance on the *Corporate* responsibility to respect human rights.[423] However, there exist the gaps in international human rights norms when it comes to ensuring corporate accountability for corporate human rights harms on the international law plane.

In recognition of the existing gap between the social and environmental commitments voluntarily made by business enterprises and the actual effects of their activities on the enjoyment of human rights, as well as on the environment,[424] some States and non-governmental organizations have increasingly been making calls to conclude an international instrument on business and human rights that applies directly to business enterprises on the international law plane. These calls are primarily based on the notion that such voluntary initiatives and commitments by businesses themselves, as well as other voluntary Guidelines/Guidance, including the UN Guiding Principles on Business and Human Rights, the OECD MNE Guidelines and the ILO Tripartite MNE Declaration have brought about only limited effect, when it comes to ensuring the *Corporate* responsibility to respect human rights.

Attempts have been made at the international level to examine the impacts of transnational corporations on various areas, including economic and social development, the environment and human rights, which traces back to 1972 when the United Nations formed a Group of Eminent Persons to "*study the impact of multinational corporations on economic development and international relations*."[425] The goal of this Group was to create a "*focal*

---

423 See supra Chapter 5.

424 Martens and Seitz, The Struggle for a UN Treaty: Towards global regulation on human rights and business, published by Global Policy Forum and Rosa Luxembourg Stiftung -New York Office, at p.7. It can be accessed at the following webpage: https://archive.globalpolicy.org/images/pdfs/UN_Treaty_online.pdf. (Accessed as of 12 September 2024). The paper notes that "*since the end of 2013, this demand has been supported by an alliance of several hundred civil society organizations. They represent a broad spectrum ranging from international human rights organizations to worker associations, environmental and developmental organizations, academics and human rights activists, and also include local groups that represent the victims of corporate human rights abuses*." (p. 8)

425 Sagafi-Nejad, The UN and Transnational Corporations: From Code of Conduct to Global Compact, (Indiana University Press, 2008), p. 52; Moran, The United Nations and Transnational Corporations: a review and a perspective, p. 2.

point" within the United Nations to develop the institutions needed for a new economic order. The report of the Group led to the establishment of the Commission on Transnational Corporations (TNCs) and the United Nations Centre on Transnational Corporations (UNCTC)[426] in New York in 1974.

The UNCTC made numerous controversial recommendations at the time, including urging TNCs to refuse to comply with apartheid in South Africa. However, the policy issue deemed the most significant and controversial at the UNCTC was its work on drafting a code of conduct for TNCs, which was demanded by the Group of 77 developing countries with the support from the socialist bloc. On the contrary, the countries of the market economy had favoured a voluntary code of conduct for TNCs over a binding instrument, which essentially was a reflection of the ideological rift between these two groups of States: while the former had believed in Government-directed development thus advocating for a binding instrument to regulate the activities of TNCs, the latter had preferred the primacy of the market mechanism as they had viewed that TNCs were yielding positive contributions to economic development in host countries. This ideological rift served as a harbinger that there would be a long-winding road ahead towards the adoption of a binding code of conduct for TNCs on the international law plane.

As predicted, the UNCTC had struggled for almost the subsequent two decades (1975-1992) regarding the issue of this binding code of conduct for TNCs when the UN Commission on TNCs was eventually dissolved in 1992 without having had been able to adopt such a code of conduct for TNCs.

While the work of the UN Commission on TNCs was carried out

---

426 According to Moran, the main mandate of the UNCTC "*included providing information, analysing policy, and offering advisory services, technical assistance and capacity-building.*" Ibid., p. 2.

in response to the need for a new international economic order[427] largely focusing on the role and implications of TNCs in economic development in host States, that focus had been shifted when the then Sub-Commission on Prevention of Discrimination and Protection of Minorities, a subsidiary body of the then UN Commission on Human Rights (predecessor to the UN Human Rights Council) requested the United Nations Secretary-General to prepare three reports on transnational corporations (TNCs) and human rights. These attempts to continue discussion on the subject matter in UN human rights fora had resulted in shifting the focus of the international community on the need to develop an international instrument to regulate the activities of TNCs that have negative impacts on the enjoyment of human rights.[428]

In 1999, the then Sub-Commission on the Promotion and Protection of Human Rights[429] established an inter-sessional working group on the activities of TNCs on the enjoyment of human rights, tasking it to explore the working methods and activities of transnational corporations. During its first session in 1999, the inter-sessional working group decided that it would develop "*a code of conduct for TNCs based on the human rights standards*".[430] The then UN Sub-commission forwarded the "*Norms on the Responsibilities of Transnational and Other Business Enterprises with Regard to Human Rights*" to the then UN Commission on Human Rights for endorsement.[431] The then Commission on Human Rights reacted rather

---

427 For a general exposition on the new international economic order, see Michael Hudson, Global Fracture: The New International Economic Order, Pluto Press (2005); Mohamed Bedjaoui, Towards a new international economic order, UNESCO (1979); P.N. Agarwala, The New International Economic Order: An overview, Pergamon (1983); Edwin P Reubens, The Challenge Of The New International Economic Order, (2021)(Routledge).

428 UN Docs., E/CN.4/Sub.2/1995/11, E/CN.4/Sub.2/1996/12, and E/CN.4/Sub.2/1998/6.

429 The then Sub-Commission on Prevention of Discrimination and Protection of Minorities renamed itself as the Sub-Commission on the Promotion and Protection of Human Rights in 1998.

430 Supra note 412.

431 UN Doc., E/CN.4/Sub.2/2003/12/Rev.2. The Norms highlighted the *State obligation* to protect from corporate human rights abuses committed by transnational corporations and other business enterprises. At the same time, the Norms enshrined the responsibility of transnational

coldly to the Norms emphasizing that it did not request the then UN Sub-commission to prepare the Norms thus having no legal standing. Instead, the then UN Commission on Human Rights requested the Office of the United Nations High Commissioner for Human Rights (OHCHR) to compile a further report on the subject matter, which was presented to the then UN Commission on Human Rights in 2005.

In addition, the then UN Commission on Human Rights passed a resolution[432] on "*Human rights and transnational corporations and other business enterprises*" ignoring the Norms, in which it requested the United Nations Secretary-General to appoint a special representative for human rights and transnational corporations and other business enterprises. Pursuant to the resolution, Mr. John Ruggie was appointed as the Special Representative of the Secretary-General for human rights and transnational corporations and other business enterprises. In 2008, he presented a report, entitled "*Protect, Respect and Remedy: a Framework for Business and Human Rights*",[433] which comprised three core pillars: the *State duty* to protect human rights; the *Corporate responsibility* to respect human rights; and access to remedy. The UN Human Rights Council welcomed this framework, which made a clear distinction between the *State duty* to protect and the *Corporate responsibility* to respect human rights.

In 2011, Mr. Ruggie presented *the UN Guiding Principles on Business and Human Rights* to the UN Human Rights Council, which contained the same three core pillars of the *State duty* to protect; the *Corporate*

---

corporations and other business enterprises to respect and observe human rights within their respective sphere of influence. The Norms also provided for a complaint mechanism for cases of corporate human rights violations.

432 See supra note 417.

433 John Ruggie, 'Protect, Respect and Remedy: a Framework for Business and Human Rights,' Report of the Special Representative of the Secretary-General on the issue of human rights and transnational corporations and other business enterprises, UN Doc., A/HRC/8/5, para. 25. It can be accessed at the following webpage: https://documents.un.org/doc/undoc/gen/g08/128/61/pdf/g0812861.pdf. (Accessed as of 12 September 2024).

responsibility to respect human rights; and access to remedy. The UN Human Rights Council endorsed unanimously the UN Guiding Principles on Business and Human Rights[434] and created a working group on the issue of human rights and transnational corporations and other business enterprises with the mandate of assisting States and the corporate sector in operationalizing and implementing them.[435] This endorsement by the UN Human Rights Council sent a strong signal that to ensure the *Corporate responsibility* to respect human rights through voluntary Guidance/ Guidelines was a more appropriate path to be pursued on the international law plane, at least for the time being.

However, as years have progressed, an increasing number of Governments and civil society actors have argued that voluntary Guidance/ Guidelines such as the UN Guiding Principles on Business and Human Rights have brought out only limited effect when it comes to addressing corporate human rights abuses, in particular those committed by transnational corporations. Along the lines of this view, Ecuador supported by 85 countries made a statement advocating for an internationally legally binding instrument on business and human rights during the September session of the UN Human Rights Council in 2013, in which it was emphasized that "*soft law instruments such as the Guiding Principles and the creation of the Working Group with limited powers to undertake monitoring of corporate compliance with the Principles are only a partial answer to the pressing issues relating to human rights abuses by transnational corporations. These principles and mechanisms fell short of addressing properly the problem of lack of accountability regarding transnational corporations worldwide and the*

434 'Report of the Special Representative of the Secretary-General on the issue of human rights and transnational corporations and other business enterprises, John Ruggie: Guiding Principles on Business and Human Rights: Implementing the United Nations "Protect, Respect and Remedy" Framework,' UN Doc., A/HRC/17/31.

435 UN Doc., A/HRC/RES/17/4. It can be accessed at the following webpage: https://documents.un.org/doc/resolution/gen/g11/144/71/pdf/g1114471.pdf. (Accessed as of 12 September 2024).

absence of adequate legal remedies for victims."[436]

As follow-up to the statement, Ecuador and South Africa proposed a resolution in 2014 to establish an open-ended inter-governmental working group on transnational corporations and other business enterprises with respect to human rights (hereinafter referred to as the OEIGWG), whose mandate is to elaborate an internationally legally binding instrument to regulate, in international human rights law, the activities of transnational corporations and other business enterprises. This resolution was adopted by the UN Human Rights Council on 26 June 2014.[437] According to some commentators, this resolution marked an historical milestone ushering in the beginning of the treaty process in the framework of the UN Human Rights Council on business and human rights.[438]

Divergent views have been expressed on the need for such an internationally treaty on business and human rights, among States, civil society, and business associations, during the period leading to the adoption of the above resolution, at the time of adoption of the resolution, as well as during the deliberations of the OEIGWG. Ongoing debates on the utility of concluding such an international treaty on business and human rights are continuing, even when a number of the draft texts[439] were proposed by the Chairperson of the OEIGWG.

---

436 It can be accessed at the following webpage: https://media.business-humanrights.org/media/documents/files/media/documents/statement-unhrc-legally-binding.pdf. (Accessed as of 12 September 2024).

437 UN Doc., A/HRC/RES/26/9.

438 Supra note 424, p. 7.

439 After the 4th session of the OEIGWG, it proposed two draft treaty texts, the first one in the main treaty and the second one in the form of an optional protocol. On 16 July 2019, the Chairperson of the OEIGWG has presented the revised draft. It can be accessed at the following webpage: https://www.ohchr.org/Documents/HRBodies/HRCouncil/WGTransCorp/OEIGWG_RevisedDraft_LBI.pdf. (Accessed as of 24 September 2024).

1. Business Enterprises as Subject of International Law

Traditionally, international law was understood to govern the international relations among States thus narrowly considering States as subject of international law. This definition of international law has been evolved and expanded to cover the international human rights law regime, under which individuals hold rights (rights-holders) while States bear duties to respect, protect and fulfil human rights (duty-bearers).

The issue of business enterprises as subject of international law should be examined from the perspective as to what legal capacities that business enterprises have as participants in the international norm development process such as the legal capacity to enter into international treaties/agreements. Therefore, from the outset, it is necessary to clarify whether companies have the legal capacity to become a party to an international agreement. Whether States only can ratify a future international treaty on business and human rights or whether companies can also ratify the future treaty is a critical factor when it comes to determining the added value of such a future treaty on business and human rights, in particular in connection with imposition of direct obligations for companies to respect human rights on the international law plane.

States, individuals, international organizations, transnational corporations, armed opposition groups, and non-governmental organizations are currently governed by or subjected to international law. As such, these actors are considered to have the legal personality under international law to hold rights and bear duties, as well as to exercise such rights and duties. This means that in practical terms, they can have various legal capacities: to bring claims before international and national courts to enforce their rights, for example, before the International Court of Justice; to enter into binding agreements under international law; and to enjoy immunity from the jurisdiction of foreign courts, for example, immunity for acts of State or diplomatic immunities and privileges. They can also be subjected to certain obligations under international law, for example, the *State obligations* to respect, protect and fulfil human rights under international human rights law. An international law scholar defined 'subject of the law' as "*an entity capable of possessing international rights and duties and having the capacity to maintain its rights by bringing international claims.*"[440] While noting that this definition is circular as the indicia referred to depends on the existence of a legal person, he further specified that "*An entity of a type recognized by customary law as capable of possessing rights and duties and of bringing international claims, and having these capacities conferred upon it is a legal person.*"[441]

The subject matter of "subjects of international law" has been examined from the perspective of the traditional understanding of international law as the rules governing the relations between States. Flowing from this conception of international law, States have been considered to be the primary subject of international law having all the legal capacities "*to make claims in respect of breaches of international law; to make treaties and agreements valid on the international law plane; and to enjoy privileges and immunities from national jurisdictions.*"[442]

The notion of "subjects of international law" has been extended to other categories such as individuals and non-governmental organizations as the conception of international law has evolved to encompass the relations, for example, between States and individuals under international human rights law and under international humanitarian law.[443]

---

440 Supra note 62, Ian Brownlie, Principles of Public International Law(4th Ed.), Oxford University Press (1990), p. 58.

441 Ibid.

442 Ibid.

443 Regarding this traditional approach, Prof. Eibe Riedel notes that "*the sovereignty dogma and its insistence on the domaine réservé, coupled with the notion of non-intrusion into the internal affairs for which the UN was not to have powers of intervention, except in exceptional circumstances laid down in article 2(7) [of the] UN Charter, still pervaded international law generally, and also shaped the UN Charter approach to human rights protection. Subsequent*

Another prominent international law scholar proposed an alternative approach to the issue of subjects of international law arguing that the traditional approach to linking the concept of subjects of international law to the legal personality had not necessarily served a useful purpose, rather it had obfuscated the discussion rendering the definition of subjects of international law circular and confusing. Accordingly, a distinction should be made between the concept of legal personality and the legal capacities attendant to it.[444]

States, individuals, armed opposition groups, or other legal entities such as corporations having different legal capacities on the international law plane can therefore be classed as subjects of international law without examining whether these entities have the legal personality under international law in a circular fashion. As such, the rights, powers and duties (legal capacities) of different subjects of international law vary according to their status and functions. For example, an individual has the right to freedom from torture under international law, while States have the duty under international human rights law not to torture individuals. This right to freedom from torture is a right protected both under customary international law and *ius cogens*,[445] as well as under treaty law, for instance, under the International Covenant on Civil and Political Rights and the Convention against Torture and Other Cruel, Inhuman or Degrading Treatment or Punishment (hereinafter referred to as the CAT). Individuals and business enterprises in addition to States have therefore a duty to respect the right to freedom from torture as they are

---

developments have, however, brought about a fundamental change of approach: the UDHR gradually became entrenched as binding customary international law in most of its provisions, with the exception perhaps of the right to property, which was not taken up in the two Covenants of 1966", Eibe Riedel, 'Rethinking Human Rights – Real Reforms in Procedure and Substance?', in J. Delbrück et al. (Eds.), Aus Kiel in die Welt. Kiel's contribution to international law, Essays in honour of the 100th Anniversary of the Walther-Schücking Institute of International Law, University of Kiel, Berlin 2014, at 423.

444 Supra note 9, Andrew Clapham, Human Rights Obligations of Non-State Actors, Oxford University Press (2006), pp. 59-83.

445 Supra note 2, Eibe Riedel, 'Standards as Sources,' German Yearbook of International Law (GYIL) vol. 63 (220), 369-417.

subjected to obligation under customary international law and *ius cogens*.

Traditionally under international human rights law, individuals hold rights (right-holders), and States bear duties (duty-bearers). However, increasingly non-state actors such as international organizations, transnational corporations and armed opposition groups are also subjected to obligations under international human rights law. Therefore, companies do have the legal obligation, for example, to respect the right to freedom from torture, and not to commit genocide and slavery.

In addition to being duty-bearers under international human rights law, a question can arise as to whether companies as subject of international law have the legal capacity to enter into an international agreement such as a future international treaty on business and human rights. While States have all the main legal capacities, other subjects of international law such as business enterprises have the legal capacity of a very restricted kind. Accordingly, companies do only have the limited legal capacity to hold rights and bear duties under certain situations, particularly under customary international law, but do not have the legal capacity in general to enter into agreements on the international law plane.

Corporations, whether private or public corporations, engage in economic activity in one or more States (host State) other than the State under the law which, they are incorporated (home State). The resources of these transnational corporations in certain cases far exceed those of smaller States. These transnational corporations also enjoy powerful diplomatic backing from Governments. Due to the fact that such corporations can make agreements, including concession agreements with the Governments of host states, it has been argued that the relations of host States and corporations should be treated on the international law plane. However, it has been argued that that business enterprises do not have the legal capacity to enter into agreements on the international law plane. [446]

This limited legal capacity or lack thereof becomes a critical issue when the added value of a future treaty on business and human rights, as one of the stated main purposes of the future treaty is to impose the direct obligation to respect human rights on business enterprises at the international level. In the absence of such a legal capacity for companies to enter into or ratify the future international treaty on business and human rights, the future treaty may not serve as a useful instrument to impose the direct obligation on companies to respect human rights on the international law plane.

It also signifies that the future treaty's added value lies only in the fact that it constitutes an important attempt to codify and clarify the content of the existing *State obligations* to respect, protect and fulfil human rights in relation to business activities. This will lend support to an important counterargument against such an international treaty on business and human rights. It will, instead, bolster the argument that there is no critical need to conclude such an international treaty on business and human rights, unless there is real added value such as imposing direct legal obligations on companies to respect human rights on the international law plane, against violations of which, there must effective remedies be provided. This line of argument emphasizes that it is more critical to strengthen domestic implementation measures as part of States' meeting their obligations to respect, protect and fulfil human rights in relation to business activities. In this vein, it can be argued that without the capacity for companies to ratify the future treaty, an international-level direct obligation to respect human rights can be simply imposed in the future treaty with strong built-in enforcement mechanisms. However, this may lead to a situation whereby the required number of ratifications that will trigger the treaty to come into force cannot be easily secured, as a result of which, the future treaty will become devoid of practical use for corporate human rights abuse victims.

---

446 Supra note 62, Ian Brownlie, Principles of Public International Law(4th Ed.), Oxford University Press (1990), p. 67.

On a related matter, it is equally important to make a clear distinction between the legal capacity for companies to make/ratify a future treaty on business and human rights as subject of international law and their right to sue States, based on provisions in bilateral investment agreements on investor-state dispute settlement (ISDS). It has been criticized that corporations have undue powers to sue States under ISDS, which could lead to transnational corporations' negatively impacting on a wide range of human rights. The then United Nations Independent Expert on the promotion of a democratic and equitable international order, Mr. *Alfred de Zayas* highlighted this issue as follows: "*the investor-state-dispute settlement mechanism (ISDS), the recently proposed Investment Court System (ICS), and the WTO dispute settlement mechanism suffer from systemic business-bias and often fail to consider the human rights impacts in their awards and decisions*."[447]

Accordingly, as much as an international treaty can create such a right for companies to sue States under ISDS, a future international treaty on business and human rights can also create the direct obligations for companies to respect human rights on the international law plane. However, this does not necessarily lead to the conclusion that companies have the legal capacity to make/ratify such a future treaty on business and human rights on the international law plane. This may serve as somewhat a strong argument for concluding the future treaty on business and human rights, when it comes to examining its added-value. However, on a closer examination, it becomes clear that this argument is weak at best and meaningless at worst from a practical perspective. Although States can create the direct international obligation for companies to respect human rights through such an international treaty on business and human rights, the effective enforcement of such a direct international obligation of companies to respect human

447 See "*Statement of the Independent Expert on the promotion of a democratic and equitable international order at the Human Rights Council 33rd session*." It can be accessed at the following webpage: https://www.ohchr.org/en/2016/09/statement-mr-alfred-maurice-de-zayas-independent-expert-promotion-democratic-and-equitable. (Accessed as of 24 September 2024).

rights will only have limited effect unless strong enforcement mechanisms are provided for in the treaty itself. Essentially, the enforcement of such a direct international obligation of companies to respect human rights will be more effectively achieved on the domestic law plane through adoption of legislative, administrative, policy and judicial measures necessary to ensure that companies respect human rights under the existing *State obligation* to protect from corporate human rights abuse.

Moreover, as argued above, if there will be no sufficient number of ratifications of the future treaty, it will take a very long time for the treaty to come into force, which will, in turn, significantly diminish the utility of such a future treaty. Viewed from the experience of the International Convention on the Rights of All Migrant Workers and Members of Their Families, there is a long road ahead to secure the necessary number of ratifications, which trigger the future treaty to come into force. Even if the treaty comes into force after the required number of ratifications, this will present a skewed situation whereby host States may ratify the future treaty on business and human rights, but very few, if not no, home States will ratify the future treaty. Considering strong resistance on the resolution to establish the OEIGWG from States where a large bulk of transnational corporations are registered, this situation is likely to occur.

II. The UN Human Rights Council Open-Ended Intergovernmental Working Group on Transnational Corporations and Other Business Enterprises with Respect to Human Rights

On 26 June 2014, the UN Human Rights Council passed a resolution,[448]

448 Supra note 316, UN Doc., A/HRC/RES/26/9. The resolution was passed by 20 in favour (Algeria, Benin, Burkina Faso, China, Cuba, Ethiopia, India, Indonesia, Côte d'Ivoire, Kazakhstan, Kenya, Morocco, Namibia, Pakistan, the Philippines, Republic of the Congo, Russian Federation, South Africa, Venezuela, and Viet Nam), 14 against (Australia, the Czech Republic, Estonia, France, Germany, the United Kingdom of Great Britain and Northern Ireland, Ireland, Italy, Japan, Montenegro, North Macedonia, Romania, the Republic of Korea and the United States of America), and 13 abstained

by which an open-ended inter-governmental working group on transnational corporations and other business enterprises with respect to human rights was established. The mandate of this working group is to elaborate on an internationally legally binding instrument to regulate, in international human rights law, the activities of transnational corporations and other business enterprises.

The resolution specifically requested that the first two sessions of the working group should be dedicated to conducting constructive deliberations on the content, scope, nature and form of the future instrument. The resolution further requested the Chairperson-Rapporteur of the working group to prepare elements for the legally binding instrument for substantive negotiations to start from the third session in 2017, taking into account the discussions held at the first two sessions.[449]

Some States, most prominently the United States of America (US) and the European Union (EU), opposed to such a resolution arguing that the process for concluding an internationally legally binding instrument on business and human rights will undermine the implementation process of the United Nations Guiding Principles on Business and Human Rights. This opposition subscribes to the notion that what was more critical at that stage was not to conclude an international treaty on business and human rights rather to strengthen the implementation of the UN Guiding Principles on Business and Human Rights that explicitly enshrined the *State obligation* to protect from corporate human rights abuse, the *Corporate responsibility* to respect human rights, as well as provision of remedy against such corporate human rights abuse.

(Argentina, Botswana, Brazil, Chile, Costa Rica, Gabon, Kuwait, the Maldives, Mexico, Peru, Saudi Arabia, Sierra Leone and the United Arab Emirates).

449 The Working Group held its first and second sessions respectively from 6-10 July 2015, and from 24-28 October 2016.

One day later on 27 June 2016, another resolution was passed in the field of business and human rights by the UN Human Rights Council, which opted for continuing the mandate of the UN Working Group on Business and Human Rights for another three years. This resolution further reaffirmed the content of the UN Guiding Principles on Business and Human Rights emphasizing the need for strengthening domestic implementation measures, including improved access to remedies for victims of business-related human rights abuses.[450]

In this regard, India advocated for a complementary approach emphasizing that the two resolutions were not mutually exclusive considering that there was a need for the international community to bridge the protection gaps at the international level, particularly when States were not adequately equipped to regulate gross corporate human rights abuses through enforcement of national laws.[451] This statement was premised on the fact that the primary responsibility to regulate the activities of transnational corporations and other business enterprises that had negative impacts on the enjoyment of human rights rested with States at the national level. It also implicitly advocated for the need to strengthen the national human rights protection framework to effectively implement the *State obligation* to protect from corporate human rights abuse under international human rights law. It further implied that as a complementary means to achieving this goal, the international community should consider the possibility of making an international treaty to regulate the activities of business enterprises with respect to human rights, in particular those of transnational corporations.

---

450 UN Doc., A/HRC/RES/26/22. This resolution represented the opposing school of thought to the one advocating for an international treaty on business and human rights that would provide for the Corporate obligation to respect human rights on the international law plane. It can be accessed at the following webpage: https://documents.un.org/doc/undoc/gen/g14/083/82/pdf/g1408382.pdf. (Accessed as of 24 September 2024).

451 Statement by the Permanent Mission of India to the United Nations Human Rights Council (2014).

The US vehemently opposed to the conclusion of such an international treaty on business and human rights by specifically arguing that the resolution constituted a threat to the UN Guiding Principles on Business and Human Rights. As a result, the US made it clear that it would not participate in an inter-governmental working group while calling upon other States also not to participate in the session.[452] Essentially, the US argument against an international treaty in this field was also premised on the theory that the primary responsibility to regulate the activities of business enterprises rested with the Governments at the national level. Hence, the US was of the view that a new international treaty on business and human rights would not have any added value, when it came to the intended primary objectives of the future treaty, namely, to prevent, protect from, and remedy against corporate human rights abuses.

The present thesis also subscribes to the argument that there would be little added value of concluding an international treaty on business and human rights at this stage as the existing international human rights law regime is adequate in terms of providing for the *State obligations* to respect, protect and fulfil human rights in the context of business activities. What is woefully lacking is the full implementation of such *State obligations* on the domestic law plane. It is therefore important to strengthen the national human rights protection system, through which international "*Combination/ zebra* standards" such as the UN Guiding Principles on Business and Human Rights that contain both treaty norms on *the State obligations* to respect, protect and fulfil human rights in relation to business activities, as well as soft law standards on the *Corporate responsibility* to respect human rights must and should be effectively implemented.

452 Statement by the Permanent Mission of the U.S. to the United Nations Human Rights Council (2014).

1. Scope of Application

a. Transnational Corporations vs. All Businesses

The three main areas of contention have featured prominently in the context of the first session of the working group to elaborate an international legally binding instrument on human rights and business: firstly, whether the future treaty should cover only transnational corporations or all other business enterprises; secondly, whether the future treaty shall provide for the extraterritorial obligation of States (home State); and thirdly, whether the future treaty should impose direct international legal obligations on companies to respect human rights.

The issue as to whether the application of the future treaty to be elaborated by the OEIGWG should be limited to transnational corporations or extended to all other business enterprises has quickly become a major point of contention from the very first session of the OEIGWG. The European Union strongly argued that the future treaty should not only cover transnational corporations but also all other business enterprises as many corporate human rights abuses were committed at the domestic level.[453] Non-governmental organizations also argued in favour of the future treaty that would regulate the activities of all business enterprises, including state-owned enterprises. State-owned enterprises (SOEs) of a transnational character or with transnational operations were deemed to be within the scope of the mandate of the OEIGWG.[454]

---

453 UN Doc., A/HRC/31/50, paras. 12-20. It can be accessed at the following webpage: https://documents.un.org/doc/undoc/gen/g16/018/22/pdf/g1601822.pdf. (Accessed as of 24 September 2024).

454 Submission by BIAC, ICC, IOE and WBCSD to the Open-ended Working Group on Business and Human Rights, "UN Treaty Process on Business and Human Rights, Further considerations by the international business community on a way forward" dated 29 September 2016,which noted that "*most of the world's economies with a high share of SOEs among their largest enterprises are important players in international trade in goods and services*."

Alternatively, a hybrid approach was suggested, i.e., the future treaty should cover all other business enterprises, but at the same time, provide for specific measures to address the particular challenges of transnational corporations having due regard to the large asymmetric power dynamics between States and transnational corporations, whose activities had important impacts on the enjoyment of human rights.[455]

Some businesses also advocated that the scope of the future treaty should cover not only transnational corporations but also all companies by arguing that a victim-centred approach required all actors to prevent, mitigate and remedy adverse human rights impacts. It did not matter from the perspective of corporate human rights abuse victims as to whether their suffering resulted from the action of a domestic company or a transnational one, a privately held entity or publicly traded one, whose shareholders included sovereigns or that which was financed by sovereign assets. The central issue for corporate human rights abuse victims was that the negative impact of the company's action must be mitigated and remedied.[456]

The revised draft legally binding instrument, in international human rights law, to regulate the activities of transnational corporations and other business enterprises settled this debate by providing that "*This (Legally Binding Instrument) shall apply, except as stated otherwise, to* ***all*** *(emphasis added) business activities, including particularly but not limited to those of a transnational character.*"[457] This is an important improvement from the 2018 zero draft legally binding instrument, viewed particularly from the perspective of the European Union that has been consistently arguing that the

455 Supra note 453, UN Doc., A/HRC/31/50, paras. 12-36.

456 Supra note 454.

457 Article 3 of the revised draft legally binding instrument to regulate, in international human rights law, the activities of transnational corporations and other business enterprises in July 2019. It can be accessed at the following OHCHR webpage: https://www.ohchr.org/Documents/HRBodies/HRCouncil/WGTransCorp/OEIGWG_RevisedDraft_LBI.pdf). (Accessed as of 24 September 2024).

future treaty shall apply to all business enterprises, not limited to transnational corporations, or to business activities of a transnational character.[458] However, the debates had continued during the fifth session of the OEIGWG that took place from 14 to 18 October 2019 with regard to the scope of the revised draft legally binding instrument. Some delegations have continued arguing that the extension of the scope of the draft treaty to include all business activities would exceed the parameters of resolution 26/9. Some other delegations highlighted the fact that a stronger focus needed being placed on business activities of a transnational character while they believed that the expanded scope of application was compatible with resolution 26/9. On the contrary, most delegations and organizations welcomed such an expansion of the scope of the future treaty to cover all business activities in the conviction that it would enhance the rights-holders' chance of having access to remedy against corporate human rights abuses.[459] At the same time, a proposal was made by one delegation that business activities to be covered by the future treaty should be expanded to "*economic or other activity*."[460] The latest third revised draft legally binding instrument introduced further clarity to the scope of the future treaty by explicitly providing that "*This (Legally Binding Instrument) shall apply to all business activities, including business activities*

---

458 The 2018 zero draft legally binding instrument, in international human rights law, to regulate the activities of transnational corporations and other business enterprises limited its scope of application to "*human rights violations in the context of any business activities of a transnational character*." Article 3 (1) of the zero draft legally binding instrument. It can be accessed at the following OHCHR webpage: https://www.ohchr.org/Documents/HRBodies/HRCouncil/WGTransCorp/Session3/DraftLBI.pdf). (Accessed as of 24 September 2024). In this regard, one academician viewed this expansion of scope of application as a welcome development as it would improve the treaty's chances of success. Nadia Bernaz, "*Clearer, Stronger, Better? – Unpacking the 2019 Draft Business and Human Rights Treaty.*" It can be accessed at the following webpage: http://rightsasusual.com/?p=1339.(Accessed as of 24 September 2024).

459 'Report on the fifth session of the open-ended intergovernmental working group on transnational corporations and other business enterprises with respect to human rights.' UN Doc., A/HRC/43/55, para. 16. It can be accessed at the following webpage: https://documents.un.org/doc/undoc/gen/g20/003/88/pdf/g2000388.pdf. (Accessed as of 26 September 2024).

460 Ibid., para. 36.

of [a] transnational character."[461] Despite such clarity in the draft texts of the future treaty, the continuing debate on the scope of the future treaty has served as one of the major hindering factors to the conclusion of the future treaty, which has been evidently manifested during the 9th session of the OEIGWG that took place from 23 to 27 October 2023.[462] This debate has continued during the most recent 10th session of the OEIGWG that took place from 16 to 20 December 2024.[463]

It is submitted that it is critically important that the future treaty on business and human rights should apply to transnational corporations and all other business enterprises, including state-owned enterprises (SOEs) and domestic business enterprises, whose activities can cause adverse human rights impacts.[464] To exclude such domestic business enterprises from the scope of application of the future treaty will render it ineffective, as it will fail to cover the vast majority of corporate human rights abuses.[465]

---

461 Article 3 of the 3rd revised draft legally binding instrument to regulate, in international human rights law, the activities of transnational corporations and other business enterprises dated 17 August 2021. It can be accessed at the following OHCHR webpage: https://www.ohchr.org/Documents/HRBodies/HRCouncil/WGTransCorp/Session6/LBI3rdDRAFT.pdf). (Accessed as of 26 September 2024).

462 'Report of the ninth session of the open-ended intergovernmental working group on transnational corporations and other business enterprises with respect to human rights,' UN Doc., A/HRC/55/59, paras. 12-27. It can be accessed at the following OHCHR webpage: https://documents.un.org/doc/undoc/gen/g23/264/16/pdf/g2326416.pdf. (Accessed as of 26 September 2024).

463 'Report of the tenth session of the open-ended intergovernmental working group on transnational corporations and other business enterprises with respect to human rights,' UN Doc., A/HRC/58/46, para. 20. It can be accessed at the following OHCHR webpage: https://docs.un.org/en/A/HRC/58/46. (Accessed as of 4 March 2025).

464 If these SOEs are under State's direct control or act as State agents although they are engaged in activities of a private character, their actions should be considered "State actions." Therefore, they are subjected to the obligation to respect human rights as they are mere State agents thus invoking the *State obligations* to respect, protect and fulfil human rights under international human rights law.

465 Margaret Jungk, a former member of the UN Working Group on Business and Human rights pointed out that "*the vast majority of economic activity is carried out by small-scale companies, ones you've never heard of, mostly in the informal sector. Their goods don't travel across borders, and when they exploit their workers or harm communities, you don't hear about it.*" "*Why do we know so little about corporate human rights abuses?*" available at: http://www.

b. Extraterritorial Obligation

Under international human rights law, States have the classic tripartite duty to respect, protect and fulfil human rights of the people under their territories and/or jurisdictions.[466] The duty to respect requires States to refrain from violating the rights of individuals. In other words, it is a negative duty not to infringe on the rights of individuals under their territories and/or jurisdictions. The duty to protect requires States to protect from human rights violations by third parties, including individuals and legal entities such as business enterprises. The *duty* to fulfil requires States to take necessary measures to facilitate and promote the enjoyment of rights, and in certain situations to directly provide goods and services essential to such enjoyment. The obligation to fulfil has three dimensions: the duty to facilitate, the duty to promote and the duty to provide.

The *State duty* to protect is of primary importance in the context of business activities. The UN Human Rights Committee, an expert body tasked with monitoring the implementation by the States parties to the International Covenant on Civil and Political Rights(ICCPR) of the rights provided for therein explains this *State duty* to protect as follows in its General Comment 31:

> *"The positive obligations on States Parties to ensure Covenant rights will only be fully discharged if individuals are protected by the State, not just against violations of Covenant rights by its agents, but also against acts committed by private persons or entities that would impair the enjoyment of Covenant rights in so far as they are amenable to application between private persons or entities. There may be circumstances in which a failure to ensure Covenant rights as required by article 2 would give rise to violations by States Parties of those rights as a result of States*

---

huffingtonpost.com/margaret-jungk/why-do-we-know-so-little-_b_8687196.html (Accessed as of 24 September 2024).

466 For details, see supra note 17.

> *Parties' permitting or failing to take appropriate measures or exercise due diligence to prevent, punish, investigate or redress the harm caused by such acts by private persons or entities.*"[467]

Essentially what this duty to protect requires States to do is for States to not only take appropriate measures or exercise due diligence to prevent, punish, investigate or redress the harm caused by acts by private persons or entities with a view to ensuring that those private persons or entities do not violate the human rights of other persons.

Similarly, the Committee on Economic Social and Cultural Rights specifies the *State duty* to protect in regard to corporations in General Comment on State obligations under the International Covenant on Economic, Social and Cultural Rights in the context of business activities as "*the obligation to adopt legislative, administrative, educational, as well as other appropriate measures to ensure effective protection against Covenant rights violations linked to business activities,*" as well as "*a positive duty to adopt a legal framework requiring business entities to exercise human rights due diligence in order to identify, prevent and mitigate the risks of violations of Covenant rights, to avoid such rights being abused, and to account for the negative impacts caused or contributed to by their decisions and operations and those of entities they control on the enjoyment of Covenant rights.*"[468] As such, the General Comment clarifies that this *State obligation* to protect not only applies domestically but also extends extraterritorially, to the extent

---

467 CCPR-Committee General Comment No. 31 on 'The Nature of the General Legal Obligation Imposed on States Parties to the Covenant,' UN Doc., CCPR/C/21/Rev.1/Add.13, para 8. It can be accessed at the following webpage: https://tbinternet.ohchr.org/_layouts/15/treatybodyexternal/Download.aspx?symbolno=CCPR%2FC%2F21%2FRev.1%2FAdd.13&Lang=en. (Accessed as of 26 September 2024).

468 The Committee on Economic, Social and Cultural Rights, General Comment No. 24 on 'State obligations under the International Covenant on Economic, Social and Cultural Rights in the context of business activities,' UN Doc., E/C.12/GC/24, paras. 14 and 16. It can be accessed at the following webpage: https://documents.un.org/doc/undoc/gen/g17/237/17/pdf/g1723717.pdf . (Accessed as of 26 September 2024). For further details, see supra Chapter 4.

compatible with international law.[469] The extraterritorial obligation was previously affirmed by the CESCR-Committee in its 2011 Statement, which emphasized that States were required to take necessary steps to prevent human rights violations abroad by corporations, over which they might exercise influence without infringing the sovereignty or diminishing the obligations of the host States under the ICESCR.[470]

It is worth noting that the General Comment emphasizes that as part of meeting the *State duty* to protect, States must adopt a legal framework requiring business enterprises to conduct human rights due diligence in their own activities and in the supply chain, which is a core element of the *Corporate responsibility* to respect human rights laid out as an international standard in the UN Guiding Principles on Business and Human Rights (Combination/zebra standards).

With respect to the extraterritorial obligation of States, the principle of respect of national sovereignty under international law was highlighted. During the first session of the OEIGWG, it was shown that Russia's position on the future treaty on business and human rights was noticeably less supportive of the treaty process,[471] as compared to the previous year when it

---

469 Ibid., paras. 25-37.

470 CESCR-Committee Statement No. 19, on the obligations of States Parties regarding the corporate sector and economic, social and cultural rights, UN Doc., E/C.12/2011/1, para. 5. It can be accessed at the following webpage: https://tbinternet.ohchr.org/_layouts/15/treatybodyexternal/Download.aspx?symbolno=E%2FC.12%2F2011%2F1&Lang=en. (Accessed as of 26 September 2024).

471 'Report on the first session of the open-ended intergovernmental working group on transnational corporations and other business enterprises with respect to human rights.' UN Doc., A/HRC/31/50, paras. 21-36 and 67-77. It can be accessed at the following webpage: https://documents.un.org/doc/undoc/gen/g16/018/22/pdf/g1601822.pdf. (Accessed as of 26 September 2024). The statements delivered by the Russian Federation during the session can be accessed at the following webpages: https://www.ohchr.org/sites/default/files/Documents/HRBodies/HRCouncil/WGTransCorp/Session1/GeneralComments/States/RussianFederation.pdf and https://www.ohchr.org/sites/default/files/Documents/HRBodies/HRCouncil/WGTransCorp/Session1/Panel4/States/RussianFederation.pdf. (Accessed as of 26 September 2024).

supported the adoption of resolution 26/9. As such, Russia argued that the debate on the possible content of such a future treaty on business and human rights was premature. Instead, the debate should focus on the feasibility of such a future treaty emphasizing that all efforts in this regard should be based on a gradual evolution of the UN Guiding Principles on Business and Human Rights.

Business representatives were also Sceptical about the inclusion of the extraterritorial obligation in the future treaty. They were concerned that it might lead to decreasing pressure on States to create a functioning national legal system. Furthermore, if the future treaty were to choose the path to limiting its application only to transnational corporations, it would result in completely exempting non-transnational corporations from the scope of application of the future treaty, arguing that creating the functioning national legal systems, not the introduction of the extraterritorial obligation, should be the focus of the future treaty.[472]

The discussions on the extraterritorial obligation of States to protect from corporate human rights abuse revolve around the *State duty* to provide effective remedies against corporate human rights abuses. As such, it has been strongly argued that the future treaty should elaborate on ways to increase pressure on States to improve their national human rights protection systems, including the judicial systems that would be enabled to provide effective remedies against corporate human rights abuses.[473]

---

472 See Letter by the Confederation of German Employers' Associations (BDA) to the state secretary of the Germany Foreign Office Stephan Steinlein dated 19 June 2014, re-quoted from footnote 10 of supra note 447, Martens and Seitz, Martens and Seitz, The Struggle for a UN Treaty: Towards global regulation on human rights and business, published by Global Policy Forum and Rosa Luxembourg Stiftung -New York Office, at p.7. It can be accessed at the following webpage: https://archive.globalpolicy.org/images/pdfs/UN_Treaty_online.pdf. (Accessed as of 26 September 2024).

473 Supra note 471, paras. 67-77.

In this regard, the revised draft legally binding instrument, in international human rights law, to regulate the activities of transnational corporations and other business enterprises has included strengthened provisions on the protection of human rights defenders, gender-sensitive support services, non-judicial grievance mechanisms and the reversal of the burden of proof.[474] Debates have been continuing regarding the details of Article 4 of the 3rd revised draft legally binding instrument. As such, whereas several NGOs strongly argue for including the reversal of burden of proof by making it obligatory, some State delegations and business organizations expressed concern that such a provision could possibly contravene the presumption of innocence principle depending on the situation, as well as the principle of due process protected both under domestic and international law.[475]

Two opposing views about the extraterritorial obligation have continued being expressed in the framework of the OEIGWG: one school of thought has argued for the inclusion of a specific provision/s on the extraterritorial obligation of States to protect while the other school of thought has opposed to including it in in the future treaty.[476] A question here arises as to whether there is added value of making a future treaty on business and human rights, in particular in relation to the discussion on the need to explicitly include the

---

474 Supra note 459, 'Report on the fifth session of the open-ended intergovernmental working group on transnational corporations and other business enterprises with respect to human rights,' UN Doc., A/HRC/43/55, para. 40. It can be accessed at: https://documents.un.org/doc/undoc/gen/g20/003/88/pdf/g2000388.pdf. See also supra note 488, Article 4 of the 3rd revised draft legally binding instrument to regulate, in international human rights law, the activities of transnational corporations and other business enterprises dated 17 August 2021. It can be accessed at the following OHCHR webpage: https://www.ohchr.org/Documents/HRBodies/HRCouncil/WGTransCorp/Session6/LBI3rdDRAFT.pdf). (Accessed as of 26 September 2024).

475 Ibid., paras. 44-58.

476 "Report of the third session of the open-ended intergovernmental working group on transnational corporations and other business enterprises with respect to human rights," UN Doc., A/HRC/37/67, para. 28. It can be accessed at the following webpage: https://documents.un.org/doc/undoc/gen/g18/017/50/pdf/g1801750.pdf. (Accessed as of 26 September 2024).

extraterritorial obligation therein. The extraterritorial obligation of States to protect from corporate human rights abuse already exists under international human rights law. It can arguably be said that the added value lies in the fact that the future treaty on business and human rights can explicitly codify the content of the *State obligation* to protect from corporate human rights abuse, including the extraterritorial obligation of States to protect from corporate human rights abuse, as treaty norms. Such a codification of the extraterritorial obligation of States to protect from corporate human rights abuse is important, considering that there exist a diversity of views as to whether the extraterritorial obligation constitutes an integral part of the *State duty* to protect from corporate human rights abuse on the international law plane.[477]

In this regard, it should be emphasized that, even in the case of codification of such extraterritorial obligations of States as a treaty norm in the future treaty, the specific content of the extraterritorial obligations of States applicable to business activities should be further clarified by the treaty monitoring bodies such as the Committee on Economic, Social and Cultural Rights. It should also be emphasized that the extraterritorial obligation of States to protect from corporate human rights abuses can be effectively realized only when States adopt the necessary legislative, administrative, policy, judicial and other measures on the domestic law plane.

c. Direct Obligation

States have the *duty/obligation* to protect from corporate human rights abuse under international human rights law, while companies have the *responsibility* to respect human rights. This means that business enterprises "*should avoid infringing on the human rights of others and should address adverse human rights impacts with which they are involved.*"[478]

---

477 See supra note 471.

478 Supra note 354, Principle 11.

Focused discussions have continued in the framework of the OEIGWG as to whether the direct obligation of companies to respect human rights should be included in the future treaty on business and human rights. The main argument in favour of including such direct international obligation of companies to respect human rights is premised on the view that to rely on the States' national systems to incorporate international human rights norms into the national law proves to have had limited effect in practice when it comes to preventing corporate human rights abuses. This is particularly evident where States have a weak or non-functioning governance system, including the unwilling judiciary, which is incapable of regulating the activities of business enterprises that have significant negative impacts on the enjoyment of human rights and holding them to account for their human rights abuses. The opponents of imposing such direct obligation (legal liability) on companies, in particular on TNCs have argued that even with the direct obligation of companies to respect human rights on the international law plane, States ultimately have to intervene in ensuring compliance with such direct international obligation, including through enforcement of judicial and non-judicial remedies on the domestic law plane. Along the same lines, the United States of America has expressed its opposition to imposing such direct international obligation on companies to respect human rights, noting that the obligation had to remain with Governments, and that a future treaty on business and human rights on the international law plane imposing the direct obligation on companies to respect human rights would not solve the basic problem that the success or failure of such a future treaty ultimately would depend on implementation of the future treaty at the domestic level.[479]

---

479 See Statements of US delegates during the 4th UN Forum on Business and Human Rights, Geneva (delivered during the session on: "The United Nations treaty process on business and human rights: business and other perspectives" and on side event "Connecting the Guiding Principles with the business and human rights treaty process", re-quoted from footnote 10 of supra note 447, Martens and Seitz, The Struggle for a UN Treaty: Towards global regulation on human rights and business, published by Global Policy Forum and Rosa Luxembourg Stiftung -New York Office, at p.7. It can be accessed at the following webpage: https://archive.globalpolicy.org/images/pdfs/UN_Treaty_online.pdf. (Accessed as of 12 September 2024).

For a different reason, a non-governmental organization warned against granting transnational corporations international legal status that would further strengthen their position. It was primarily concerned about the ongoing corporate capture of policy spaces both internationally and nationally, while noting that in some countries, transnational corporations have captured territories, and the administrative, legislative and adjudicatory systems. Hence, to give transnational corporations international legal status would further perpetuate such corporate capture of human rights.[480]

The revised draft legally binding instrument, in international human rights law, to regulate the activities of transnational corporations and other business enterprises has not contained a provision imposing such a direct international obligation on companies to respect human rights. The Preamble makes this explicit by underlining that "*all business enterprises, regardless of their size, sector, operational context, ownership and structure have the* ***responsibility*** (emphasis added) *to respect all human rights, including by avoiding causing or contributing to adverse human rights impacts through their own activities and addressing such impacts when they occur, as well as by preventing or mitigating adverse human rights impacts that are directly linked to their operations, products or services by their business relationships*".[481]

---

480 Supra note 471, 'Report of the first session of the open-ended intergovernmental working group on transnational corporations and other business enterprises with respect to human rights.' UN Doc., A/HRC/31/50, paras. 60-61. It can be accessed at the following webpage: https://documents.un.org/doc/undoc/gen/g16/018/22/pdf/g1601822.pdf. (Accessed as of 26 September 2024). See also The oral statement of FIAN delivered during Panel III discussion. It can be accessed at the following webpage: https://www.ohchr.org/sites/default/files/Documents/HRBodies/HRCouncil/WGTransCorp/Session3/OralInterventions/FIAN-SID-Subject3.Generalobligations.pdf. (Accessed as of 26 September 2024).

481 Preamble of the revised draft legally binding instrument to regulate, in international human rights law, the activities of transnational corporations and other business enterprises in July 2019. It can be accessed at the following OHCHR webpage: https://www.ohchr.org/Documents/HRBodies/HRCouncil/WGTransCorp/OEIGWG_RevisedDraft_LBI.pdf. (Accessed as of 26 September 2024. Cf. see PP.12 of the Preamble of the Updated draft legally binding instrument. It can be accessed at the following OHCHR webpage: https://www.ohchr.org/sites/default/files/documents/hrbodies/hrcouncil/igwg-transcorp/session9/igwg-9th-updated-draft-lbi-track-

From the perspective of those who have argued for imposing such direct obligations to respect human rights on business enterprises on the international law plane, this represents a setback from the zero draft legally binding instrument, which had indicated in the Preamble that business enterprises "*shall respect all human rights, including by avoiding causing or contributing to adverse human rights impacts through their own activities and addressing such impacts when they occur.*"[482] The third revised draft legally binding instrument, in international human rights law, to regulate the activities of transnational corporations and other business enterprises has made this issue become even more ambiguous. While the Preamble of the draft instrument implicitly mentions companies' direct obligations on the international law plane,[483] no such specific direct obligations of companies to respect human rights on the international law plane are however provided in the main body of the text. Instead, the revised draft legally binding instrument has an extensive provision on legal liability (Article 6), which requires the future States parties to the instrument to "*provide for a comprehensive and adequate system of legal liability for human rights violations or abuses in the context of business activities, including those of a transnational character*"

---

changes.pdf. (Accessed as of 26 September 2024).

482 Preamble of the 2018 zero draft legally binding instrument, in international human rights law, to regulate the activities of transnational corporations and other business enterprises. It can be accessed at the following OHCHR webpage: https://www.ohchr.org/Documents/HRBodies/HRCouncil/WGTransCorp/Session3/DraftLBI.pdf. (Accessed as of 26 September 2024). For a comparative analysis between the 2018 zero draft and the revised draft legally binding instrument, see generally supra note 485, Nadia Bernaz, 'Clearer, Stronger, Better? – Unpacking the 2019 Draft Business and Human Rights Treaty.' It can be accessed at the following webpage: http://rightsasusual.com/?p=1339. (Accessed as of 26 September 2024).

483 PP11 of Preamble of the 3rd revised draft legally binding instrument to regulate, in international human rights law, the activities of transnational corporations and other business enterprises dated 17 August 2021 provides that "*Underlining that business enterprises, regardless of their size, sector, location, operational context, ownership and structure have the obligation to respect internationally recognized human rights, including by avoiding causing or contributing to human rights abuses through their own activities and addressing such abuses when they occur, as well as by preventing or mitigating human rights abuses that are directly linked to their operations, products or services by their business relationships*". It can be accessed at the following OHCHR webpage: https://www.ohchr.org/Documents/HRBodies/HRCouncil/WGTransCorp/Session6/LBI3rdDRAFT.pdf. (Accessed as of 26 September 2024).

through domestic law.[484] This stance of the draft legally binding instrument has continued. Article 8 of the updated draft legally binding instrument hence contains detailed draft provisions on legal liability without mentioning about the direct international obligation of business enterprises to respect human rights on the international law plane.[485]

Hence, the revised draft legally binding instrument squarely focuses on the implementation of the *State obligations* to respect, protect and fulfil human rights in relation to business activities on the domestic law plane, in particular the *State duty* to protect from corporate human rights abuse, rather than on imposing the direct legal obligation on business enterprises to respect human rights on the international law plane.[486] The fact that the future treaty will fall short of imposing the direct international legal obligations on business enterprises to respect human rights will lend important support to the argument that the future treaty does have no real added-value because it simply codifies the existing *State obligations* to respect, protect and fulfil human rights in relation to business activities.

---

484 Article 6 of the Revised draft legally binding instrument to regulate, in international human rights law, the activities of transnational corporations and other business enterprises in July 2019. It can be accessed at the following OHCHR webpage: https://www.ohchr.org/Documents/HRBodies/HRCouncil/WGTransCorp/OEIGWG_RevisedDraft_LBI.pdf). (Accessed as of 26 September 2024).

485 The Updated draft legally binding instrument to regulate, in international human rights law, the activities of transnational corporations and other business enterprises. It can be accessed at the following OHCHR webpage: https://www.ohchr.org/sites/default/files/documents/hrbodies/hrcouncil/igwg-transcorp/session9/igwg-9th-updated-draft-lbi-track-changes.pdf (Accessed as of 26 September 2024).

486 For the details on the deliberations on Article 6 of the Revised draft legally binding instrument, see supra note 471, 'Report on the first session of the open-ended intergovernmental working group on transnational corporations and other business enterprises with respect to human rights.' UN Doc., A/HRC/31/50, paras. 69-77. It can be accessed at the following webpage: https://documents.un.org/doc/undoc/gen/g16/018/22/pdf/g1601822.pdf. (Accessed as of 26 September 2024).

2. Form and Content

During the discussions of the OEIGWG, various views have been expressed on the possible elements of the future treaty. However, there have been little discussion, if no discussion at all, held on the form of such a future treaty on business and human rights. During its second session, a mention was made to the potential forms of the future treaty: "a detailed treaty setting out both substantive and procedural matters; a framework treaty setting out key principles and approaches; a core treaty with a series of annexes dealing with supervisory mechanisms and further developments in international law; or an optional protocol to existing human rights treaties."[487]

a. An Overarching General Framework Convention

Some proposals to adopt a general framework convention on business and human rights had been made. For instance, the International Commission of Jurists advocated for a general declaration or framework convention that should focus on defining the standards, or those that had insufficiently been considered by the UN Guiding Principles on Business and Human Rights. These would include: a clear definition of corporate human rights abuses; standards for human rights due diligence; remedies for victims; and international cooperation in establishing accountability for corporate human rights abuses.[488] It is believed that the advantage of such a general framework convention lies in the fact that it will be easier to achieve political consensus over general principles, and that detailed legal obligations can be further

487 Report on the second session of the Open-ended intergovernmental working group on transnational corporations and other business enterprises with respect to human rights, para. 98. It can be accessed at the following webpage: https://documents.un.org/doc/undoc/gen/g17/000/94/pdf/g1700094.pdf (Accessed as of 19 October 2024).

488 International Commission of Jurists (ICJ), 'Needs and Options for a New International Instrument in the Field of Business and Human Rights,' pp. 37-43. It can be accessed at the following webpage: https://www.icj.org/wp-content/uploads/2014/06/NeedsandOptionsinternationalinst_ICJReportFinalelecvers.compressed.pdf (Accessed as of 19 October 2024).

elaborated at a later stage in the form of optional protocols.

Similarly, a non-governmental organization proposed "a living treaty" consisting of basic standards and principles, as well as process-oriented elements, which would enable the flexible growth of binding standards (rules). A human rights academic proposed, in this regard, mechanisms for norm development and decision-making in the case of disputes.[489]

Per contra, some legal experts were Sceptical about this path to adopting a general framework convention. Most notably, the late Mr. John Ruggie, who was the author of the UN Guiding Principles on Business and Human Rights had argued that an overarching general framework convention on business and human rights would not be an appropriate form of a treaty, considering the complexity of the issues. He further emphasized that such an overarching general framework convention was politically non-negotiable and the eventual implementation of such a treaty would fail at the domestic level. He further highlighted that the core challenge was that "*business and human rights is not so discrete an issue-area as to lend itself to a single set of detailed treaty obligations*." He cautioned against the danger that an overarching general framework convention would be so highly abstract that "*it would be devoid of substance, of little practical use to real people in real places, and with high potential for generating serious backlash against any form of further international legalization in this domain*."[490]

---

489 Supra note 424, Martens and Seitz, The Struggle for a UN Treaty: Towards global regulation on human rights and business, published by Global Policy Forum and Rosa Luxembourg Stiftung -New York Office, at p.7. It can be accessed at the following webpage: https://archive.globalpolicy.org/images/pdfs/UN_Treaty_online.pdf. (Accessed as of 26 September 2024).

490 John Ruggie, 'The Past as Prologue? A Moment of Truth for UN Business and Human Rights Treaty, Institute for Human Rights and Business.' It can be accessed at the following webpage: https://www.hks.harvard.edu/sites/default/files/centers/mrcbg/programs/cri/files/Treaty_Final.pdf. (Accessed as of 19 October 2024).

b. Thematically focused Individual Conventions or an Optional Protocol to an Existing Human Rights Agreement

An alternative form for the future treaty as compared to having a general framework convention is to have a set of shorter instruments that have specific content or to conclude a future treaty in the form of an optional protocol to the existing human rights instruments such as the International Covenant on Economic, Social and Cultural Rights and/or the International Covenant on Civil and Political Rights. A non-governmental organization suggested that such a protocol should require States to adopt national legislation that provides for measures to prevent and to ensure liability for corporate human rights abuse.[491]

Eventually, the OEIGWG has considered an approach to concluding a treaty that has both substantive and procedural matters along with an option protocol that is similar to the Optional Protocol to the Convention against Torture (OP-CAT), whereby the ratification of an optional protocol will obligate States Parties to establish a national implementation mechanism at the domestic level.[492]

---

491 Supra note 488, International Commission of Jurists, 'Needs and Options for a New International Instrument in the Field of Business and Human Rights,' p. 43.

492 The Chairperson-rapporteur of the OEIGWG has proposed the elements of the future treaty in anticipation of the third. It can be accessed at the following OHCHR webpage: https://www.ohchr.org/sites/default/files/Documents/HRBodies/HRCouncil/WGTransCorp/Session3/LegallyBindingInstrumentTNCs_OBEs.pdf. In advance of the fourth session of the OEIGWG, the Chairperson-rapporteur also proposed the zero draft legally binding instrument to regulate, in international human rights law, the activities of transnational corporations and other business enterprises. (It can be accessed at the following OHCHR webpage: https://www.ohchr.org/sites/default/files/Documents/HRBodies/HRCouncil/WGTransCorp/Session3/DraftLBI.pdf. (Accessed as of 19 October 2024). The draft optional protocol to the treaty was proposed. It can be accessed at the following OHCHR webpage: https://www.ohchr.org/sites/default/files/Documents/HRBodies/HRCouncil/WGTransCorp/Session4/ZeroDraftOPLegally.pdf. (Accessed as of 19 October 2024). In advance of the 5th session of the OEIGWG, the Chairperson-rapporteur also proposed the revised draft legally binding instrument to regulate, in international human rights law, the activities of transnational corporations and other business enterprises in July 2019. It can be accessed at the following OHCHR webpage: https://www.ohchr.org/sites/default/files/Documents/HRBodies/HRCouncil/WGTransCorp/

3. Possible Elements

Olivier de Schutter, the former Special Rapporteur on the right to food and the current Special Rapporteur on extreme poverty and a former expert member of the Committee on Economic, Social and Cultural Rights identified four possible options for a future treaty: firstly, to clarify and strengthen the *State obligation* to protect from human rights abuses, including extraterritoriality; secondly, to oblige States, through a framework convention, to report on the adoption and implementation of national action plans on business and human rights; thirdly, to impose direct obligation on transnational corporations (TNCs) and establish a new mechanism to monitor compliance with such direct obligation; and fourthly, to impose the duty of mutual legal assistance on States to ensure effective remedies for corporate human rights abuse victims. He proposed, as a preferred option, a combined instrument that renewed the *State obligation* to protect, including extraterritoriality, as well as to impose the *State duty* of mutual judicial assistance aimed at ensuring effective remedies for corporate human rights abuse victims. He argued that this combined instrument would represent an improvement for corporate human rights abuse victims, and that it would be considered politically more feasible as such a treaty would not be fundamentally new, and it would build on the existing *State duty* to protect under international human rights law.[493]

In addition to the suggested extraterritorial obligation of States to be included in the future treaty, the discussions of the OEIGWG have indicated that the following elements should be included as the basic elements for the future treaty: firstly, direct obligation at the international level to comply not

---

OEIGWG_RevisedDraft_LBI.pdf (Accessed as of 19 October 2024). However, eventually, the update revised legally binding instrument did not contain any optional protocol to the main treaty.

493 de Schutter, 'Toward a New Treaty on Business and Human Rights,' Business and Human Rights Journal, Vol. 1 (1), pp. 41-67.

only with human rights standards, but also with environmental, health and labour standards, as well as international humanitarian law; and secondly, rights of individuals and affected communities by corporate human rights abuses such as provision of remedies to the harms caused by corporate human rights abuses, including prevention, detection, investigation, punishment and redress, which will help establish accountability for corporate human rights abuses, including that for parent companies of transnational corporations in home States through piercing the corporate veil. The importance of judicial cooperation between States in this regard was also highlighted as an important element to be included in the future treaty. Furthermore, civil society organizations strongly advocated for the inclusion of international implementation mechanisms, including the possible creation of an international tribunal to adjudicate corporate human rights abuse cases.[494]

During the discussions of the OEIGWG, a vast number of statements have focused on the possible elements of a future treaty on business and human rights. In relation to the issue as to which corporate human rights abuse should be addressed by a future treaty, differing views were expressed. Several participants argued for the inclusion of all corporate human rights abuses because to limit the scope of the future treaty to gross human rights violations would send the wrong message that other violations would be tolerated. Similarly, some States and experts emphasized that human rights were universal, indivisible, and interdependent, as recognized in the Vienna Declaration and Programme of Action (VDPA) thus pointing to the need to include all corporate human rights abuses. It was also proposed that the future treaty should develop an adequate methodology to identify corporate accountability, and place an emphasis on victim's rights in order to ensure that corporate human rights victims have access to effective remedies against

---

494 See generally, supra note 487, Report on the second session of the Open-ended intergovernmental working group on transnational corporations and other business enterprises with respect to human rights, para. 98. It can be accessed at the following webpage: https://documents.un.org/doc/undoc/gen/g17/000/94/pdf/g1700094.pdf (Accessed as of 19 October 2024).

corporate human rights abuses.[495] A range of concrete suggestions have also been made and reflected in the updated draft legally binding instrument to regulate, in international human rights law, the activities of transnational corporations and other business enterprises, including mutual legal assistance and international cooperation.[496]

The third session of the OEIGWG has had the draft elements of the future treaty for deliberations, during which extensive discussions on all elements have been discussed. Still diverse and oftentimes opposing views on what should be included in the future treaty were expressed during this session, including on the general framework and scope of application, as well as substantive elements encompassing general obligations, preventive measures, legal liability, access to justice, effective remedy and guarantees of non-repetition, jurisdiction, international cooperation, mechanisms for promotion, implementation and monitoring, and general provisions.[497]

The most recent updated draft legally binding instrument contained the following substantive areas: rights of victims, including protection of victims. Under this rubric, victims shall enjoy the human rights and fundamental freedoms. More specifically, the draft legally binding instrument contained provisions on a range of victims' rights, including the right to be treated humanely and with respect and in dignity, the rights to life, personal integrity, freedom of expression and opinion, peaceful assembly and association, and freedom of movement, the right to access to effective remedies such as restitution, compensation, rehabilitation, reparation, satisfaction, guarantees

---

495 For further details on the discussion, see UN Doc. A/HRC/31/50.

496 Supra note 485: https://www.ohchr.org/sites/default/files/Documents/HRBodies/HRCouncil/WGTransCorp/OEIGWG_RevisedDraft_LBI.pdf (Accessed as of 19 October 2023). See Articles 12-13.

497 'Report of the third session of the open-ended inter-governmental working group on transnational corporations and other business enterprises with respect to human rights,' UN Doc., A/HRC/37/67, paras. 37-126. It can be accessed at the following webpage: https://documents.un.org/doc/undoc/gen/g18/017/50/pdf/g1801750.pdf. (Accessed as of 19 October 2024).

of non-repetition, injunction, environmental remediation, and ecological restoration, the right to submit claims, the right to be protected from unlawful interference against their privacy, and from intimidations and reprisals, the right to access information, as well as the right to participation, transparency and independence in reparation processes.

Similarly, it provided for the obligation of States to adopt adequate and effective measures aimed at guaranteeing a safe and enabling environment for persons, groups and organizations to promote and defend human rights and the environment, and to be able to exercise their human rights free from any threat, intimidation, violence, insecurity, harassment, or reprisals. For the purposes of preventing corporate human rights abuses from occurring, the updated draft legally binding instrument also explicitly provides for the obligation of States parties to adopt appropriate legislative, regulatory, and other measures, including legislating mandatory human rights due diligence by business enterprises in their own operations and in the supply chain. With respect to access to remedy, an emphasis has also been laid on the need to reduce barriers faced by corporate human rights abuse victims in accessing effective remedies. It further obligates States parties to establish legal liability for corporate human rights abuses in the forms of criminal, civil or administrative liability as appropriate. Regarding jurisdiction, the updated draft legally-binding instrument clearly establishes the extraterritorial obligation of States parties to regulate the activities occurring in other States (host States) of business enterprises registered in their own jurisdictions (home States). No statute of limitations shall apply to the commencement of legal proceedings in relation to human rights abuses which constitute the most serious crimes of concern to the international community as a whole, including war crimes, crimes against humanity or crimes of genocide. It also clarifies that in the absence of specific procedural rules regarding claims before the competent national court by the future treaty (applicable law), the law of that competent court seized on the matter shall apply. On mutual legal assistance, it also provides for the obligation of States to render mutual assistance in criminal, civil or administrative proceedings. It also provides for the obligation to cooperate in good faith to enable the obligations contained in the treaty (international cooperation). It further specifically provides that States parties carry out the obligations under the treaty in a manner consistent with fully respecting the principle of sovereign equality and territorial integrity of States. It also contains provisions relating to implementation, and institutional arrangements, including establishment of a committee of experts (a treaty monitoring body) to oversee the implementation of the provisions of the future treaty by its States parties and the International Fund for Victims.[498]

a. Definition of Legal Responsibilities

During the discussions of the OEIGWG, it became clear that there was a clear need to clarify the legal responsibilities for transnational corporations and other business enterprises in the future treaty. It is therefore vital to establish standards of legal liability, including: a focus on victims; a differentiation between various types of responsibilities, including criminal, civil or administrative; and the flexibility for States to apply standards in national systems. It was also suggested in that regard that the future treaty should incorporate the obligations of States in order to clearly define and incorporate in national criminal law all forms of harmful corporate conduct, and that it should include sanctions for corporate human rights abuses that were not defined as criminal acts, as well as standards of complicity or conspiracy and the explicit recognition of the legal responsibility of a company as a legal person, not excluding the individual legal responsibility of directors and managers.[499]

---

498 See the following webpage: https://www.ohchr.org/sites/default/files/documents/hrbodies/hrcouncil/igwg-transcorp/session9/igwg-9th-updated-draft-lbi-track-changes.pdf (Accessed as of 19 October 2024). Cf. The revised draft legally binding instrument to regulate, in international human rights law, the activities of transnational corporations and other business enterprises in July 2019. It can be accessed at the following OHCHR webpage: https://www.ohchr.org/Documents/HRBodies/HRCouncil/WGTransCorp/OEIGWG_RevisedDraft_LBI.pdf. (Accessed as of 19 October 2024). This revised draft legally binding instrument seemed to have adopted the similar approach proposed by de Schutter when it came to the form of the treaty.

499 'Report of the first session of the open-ended inter-governmental working group on

b. Human Rights Due Diligence

It is essential that the future treaty should include not only the *State obligation* to protect from corporate human rights abuse, but also the *Corporate responsibility* to respect human rights, in particular the responsibility for companies to exercise human rights due diligence in their own operations and in their supply chains, as an integral component of such *Corporate responsibility* to respect human rights. Companies tend to exercise human rights due diligence when it becomes a legally binding obligation, *de minimis*, on the domestic law plane, if not on the international law plane. Such national-level obligation to conduct human rights due diligence requires business enterprises to assess human rights impacts of their activities on the enjoyment of human rights (human rights impacts assessments), which will help companies to identify and prevent adverse human rights impacts.[500]

In this regard, it is worth noting that even though the requirement of human rights due diligence were to be explicitly included in the future treaty, that international obligation still lies with the States as part of the *State obligation* to protect from corporate human rights abuse whereas business enterprises only hold the *Corporate responsibility* to respect human rights on the international law plane. As such, the updated draft legally binding instrument has included an extensive provision requiring States parties to ensure that companies conduct mandatory human rights due diligence. States parties shall therefore "*ensure that their domestic legislation requires all persons conducting business activities, including those of a transnational*

---

transnational corporations and other business enterprises with respect to human rights,' UN Doc., A/HRC/31/50, paras. 88-90. It can be accessed at the following webpage: https://documents.un.org/doc/undoc/gen/g16/018/22/pdf/g1601822.pdf. (Accessed as of 20 October 2024).

500 During the first session of the OEIGWG, the importance of the due diligence approach was highlighted as follows: "*The due diligence approach was essential as it went far beyond national or international liability and dealt with the expectations of society, which have more serious economic impacts than a long legal process*." Ibid., para. 89.

character, in their territory or jurisdiction, to respect human rights and prevent human rights violations or abuses."[501]

Human rights due diligence comprises the following elements: identification and assessment of real and potential human rights harms to be caused and contributed to by business activities; taking appropriate actions with the aim of preventing such adverse human rights impacts; monitoring the human rights impacts of business activities, including those under contractual relationships; and communication of those measures adopted to prevent and address such adverse human rights impacts to external stakeholders.[502]

Together with provision on legal liability, provisions on human rights due diligence forms the essential elements of the future treaty. It is worth noting that the updated draft legally binding instrument has been more closely aligned with the UN Guiding Principles on Business and Human Rights,[503] when it comes to the requirement on human rights due diligence. It is also worth noting that if adopted, the future treaty will have led to a transformation of an international human rights law standard on the *Corporate responsibility* to respect human rights into a treaty norm

---

501 Article 5(1), of the revised draft legally binding instrument to regulate, in international human rights law, the activities of transnational corporations and other business enterprises in July 2019. It can be accessed at the following OHCHR webpage: https://www.ohchr.org/Documents/HRBodies/HRCouncil/WGTransCorp/OEIGWG_RevisedDraft_LBI.pdf (Accessed as of 20 October 2024).

502 Ibid. Article 5(2). See also Article 5(3), which further provides for possible measures to be taken in connection with human rights due diligence. These measures include: conducting human rights and environmental impact assessments; public and periodic report on financial and non-financial matters; integration of human rights due diligence requirements in contractual relationships; and adoption and implementation of enhanced human rights due diligence measures to prevent human rights abuses in occupied or conflict-affected areas. Cf. supra note 485, Article 6.4 on mandatory human rights due diligence requirement for companies of the Updated draft legally binding instrument: https://www.ohchr.org/sites/default/files/documents/hrbodies/hrcouncil/igwg-transcorp/session9/igwg-9th-updated-draft-lbi-track-changes.pdf (Accessed as of 20 October 2024).

503 See supra note 395.

concretizing what is required on the domestic law plane on the part of States parties to meet the *State obligation* to protect from corporate human rights abuse. However, the 5th session of the OEIGWG has shown that there is still a great deal divergence to be converged on the provisions on human rights due diligence, including debates on the need to link legal liability on prevention (human rights due diligence), the too broad and prescriptive language that may restrict States' flexibility regarding the means available to them to implement those obligations on the domestic law plane, the need to use accepted language found under other international instruments such as the ILO Indigenous and Tribal Peoples Convention (ILO Convention No. 169), as well as the need to expand the scope of protection and the list of protected groups.[504] The updated draft legally binding instrument compiled by the Chairperson of the OEIGWG after the conclusion of its 9th session in 2023 is still subject to ongoing debates.[505]

c. Monitoring and Implementation Mechanisms

The discussions of the OEIGWG have been placing a greater emphasis on the need to provide effective judicial and non-judicial remedies for victims of business-related human rights abuses. It has therefore been strongly argued that a future treaty on business and human rights should complement existing national, regional and international efforts, as well as ensure the full scope of remedies with clear mechanisms for redress. It has also been emphasized that the future treaty should call for collaboration, capacity-building and mutual assistance on due diligence investigations, administration of justice and

---

504 For detailed deliberations on Article 5, see 'Report on the fifth session of the open-ended intergovernmental working group on transnational corporations and other business enterprises with respect to human rights,' UN Doc., A/HRC/43/55, paras. 59-68. It can be accessed at the following OHCHR webpage: https://documents.un.org/doc/undoc/gen/g20/003/88/pdf/g2000388.pdf (Accessed as of 20 October 2024).

505 Supra note 485, Article 6.4 on mandatory human rights due diligence requirement for companies of the Updated draft legally binding instrument: https://www.ohchr.org/sites/default/files/documents/hrbodies/hrcouncil/igwg-transcorp/session9/igwg-9th-updated-draft-lbi-track-changes.pdf (Accessed as of 20 October 2024).

enforcement of judgments.[506] NGOs also strongly advocated for a treaty that would provide access to justice and effective remedy mechanisms, including administrative, non-judicial and judicial remedies. They further emphasized that the lack of remedy mechanisms in the home State of the corporation was recognized as a barrier to access to justice. Hence, the principle of complementarity between the home and the host State jurisdiction should be included in the future treaty. Others called for effective enforcement bodies such as a committee for compliance oversight or a public centre for control of transnational corporations. Some NGOs went so far as to call for a world court or tribunal that could receive claims, adjudicate and enforce judgments, and operate in complementarity with national and regional instruments.[507]

The revised draft legally binding instrument contained provisions on institutional arrangements: the future treaty shall establish a committee (treaty monitoring body) to oversee compliance with the treaty by States parties. The draft optional protocol also envisaged the obligation of the States parties to establish national implementation mechanism to ensure the effective implementation of the provisions and compliance of the future treaty.[508] As seen above, the most recent updated draft legally binding instrument has dropped the idea of an optional protocol. Instead, it contains a provision to establish an International Fund for Victims.[509]

---

506 Supra note 499, 'Report of the first session of the open-ended inter-governmental working group on transnational corporations and other business enterprises with respect to human rights,' UN Doc., A/HRC/31/50, paras. 98-105. It can be accessed at the following webpage: https://documents.un.org/doc/undoc/gen/g16/018/22/pdf/g1601822.pdf. (Accessed as of 20 October 2024).

507 Ibid., para. 105.

508 Supra note 501, Article 13 of the revised draft legally binding instrument to regulate, in international human rights law, the activities of transnational corporations and other business enterprises in July 2019. It can be accessed at the following OHCHR webpage: https://www.ohchr.org/Documents/HRBodies/HRCouncil/WGTransCorp/OEIGWG_RevisedDraft_LBI.pdf (Accessed as of 20 October 2024). The draft optional protocol to the treaty can be accessed at the following OHCHR webpage: https://www.ohchr.org/Documents/HRBodies/HRCouncil/WGTransCorp/Session4/ZeroDraftOPLegally.pdf (Accessed as of 20 October 2024).

509 Supra note 485, Article 6.4 on mandatory human rights due diligence requirement for

d. Extraterritorial Obligation

The *State obligation* to protect from corporate human rights abuse through adoption of legislative, administrative, judicial, and educational/ promotional measures, as well as other appropriate measures under international human rights law is well established. The discussions of the OEIGWG have been focusing on the issue of the extraterritorial obligation of States (home States) to regulate corporate human rights abuses that occur in the host states. It has been highlighted that the gaps existed concerning the extraterritorial obligation of States to respect, protect and fulfil human rights obligations in relation to business activities, in particular on jurisdiction. In this regard, it has been recommended that the principle of *forum non conveniens* should be abolished with a view to ensuring accountability for such corporate human rights abuses when applying the extraterritorial obligation of home States.

In an effort to operationalize such extraterritorial obligation of home States, the following elements were suggested to be included in the future treaty: creation of prevention, disclosure and reporting requirements; removing obstacles to the exercise of jurisdiction such as *forum non conveniens*; and facilitating cross-border cooperation in investigation and mutually recognizing national judgments.[510] The draft legally binding instrument provides that States parties are obligated to provide jurisdiction to the courts of the State where: a) corporate human rights abuses occurred; or b) the victims of such corporate human rights abuses are domiciled; or c) the

---

companies of the updated draft legally binding instrument: https://www.ohchr.org/sites/default/files/documents/hrbodies/hrcouncil/igwg-transcorp/session9/igwg-9th-updated-draft-lbi-track-changes.pdf (Accessed as of 20 October 2024).

510 Supra note 499, 'Report of the first session of the open-ended inter-governmental working group on transnational corporations and other business enterprises with respect to human rights,' UN Doc., A/HRC/31/50, para. 71. It can be accessed at the following webpage: https://documents.un.org/doc/undoc/gen/g16/018/22/pdf/g1601822.pdf. (Accessed as of 20 October 2024).

business enterprises alleged to have committed such corporate human rights abuses are domiciled. As such, the future treaty contains the extraterritorial obligation of home States to regulate the activities of business enterprises that occur in another States if those business enterprises are under the jurisdiction of the home States.[511]

As it is vital to strengthen the national legislative and judicial system to meet the *State obligation* to protect from corporate human rights abuse, including extraterritorial obligation, the thesis highlights the need to establish a stable and predictable legal framework backed up by well-defined laws to promote the enjoyment of human rights, including awareness-raising and dissemination in the corporate world. As such, it emphasizes that barriers to access to justice such as the principle of *forum non conveniens* should be eliminated in order to ensure that corporate human rights abuse victims are able to bring cases in the home States of transnational corporations.

e. Relationship Between the Future Treaty and Trade and Investment Agreements

The issue of possible conflict between the future treaty and trade and investment agreements has been addressed during the deliberations of the OEIGWG. In this regard, it has been suggested that a future treaty could declare, in its Preamble, that human rights enjoy normative supremacy and that such an instrument could include a section requiring States to include human rights labour and environmental standards in bilateral investment

---

511 Supra note 501, Article 7 of the revised draft legally binding instrument to regulate, in international human rights law, the activities of transnational corporations and other business enterprises in July 2019. It can be accessed at the following OHCHR webpage: https://www.ohchr.org/Documents/HRBodies/HRCouncil/WGTransCorp/OEIGWG_RevisedDraft_LBI.pdf (Accessed as of 20 October 2024). C.f., Supra note 485, Article 6.4 on mandatory human rights due diligence requirement for companies of the Updated draft legally binding instrument: https://www.ohchr.org/sites/default/files/documents/hrbodies/hrcouncil/igwg-transcorp/session9/igwg-9th-updated-draft-lbi-track-changes.pdf (Accessed as of 20 October 2024).

agreements.[512] More specifically, noting that there existed an imbalance between the right of transnational corporations provided for in investor-state dispute mechanisms of investment agreements and the responsibility of such TNCs to respect human rights, it has been suggested that the future treaty should allow victims access to courts in the home States of the investors and/or that it should establish an international mechanism to consider business-related human rights abuses. The future treaty should also provide guidance regarding the development of trade and investment instruments, including stipulating the requirement of *ex ante* and *ex post facto* human rights impact assessments and setting out investor obligations.[513]

The revised draft legally binding instrument has, however, not included specific provisions on the relationship between the future treaty and trade

---

512 Supra note 499, 'Report of the first session of the open-ended inter-governmental working group on transnational corporations and other business enterprises with respect to human rights,' UN Doc., A/HRC/31/50, paras. 93 and 97. It can be accessed at the following webpage: https://documents.un.org/doc/undoc/gen/g16/018/22/pdf/g1601822.pdf. (Accessed as of 24 October 2024).

513 Supra note 487, Report on the second session of the Open-ended intergovernmental working group on transnational corporations and other business enterprises with respect to human rights, para. 26. It can be accessed at the following webpage: https://documents.un.org/doc/undoc/gen/g17/000/94/pdf/g1700094.pdf (Accessed as of 24 October 2024). When resolving the conflict between provisions of bilateral investment treaty and provisions of international human rights treaty, the following potential interpretative approaches could be applied by the International Centre for Settlement of Investor Disputes (ICSID): evasion; harmonious interpretation; and prioritization. Dispute settlement decisions issued by the ICSID in the framework of State-Investor disputes indicate that the ICSID ignored or failed to assess the argument by the States that they had taken measures disputed by investors as part of their human rights obligations under international human rights treaties or under the national legal framework (evasion). It is currently not clear as to whether human rights norms should prevail over provisions of bilateral investment treaties, even if the ICSID were to apply the prioritization interpretative approach. Therefore, the argument that the primacy of human rights norms over provisions of bilateral investment treaties must be explicitly provided for in the future treaty on business and human rights can lend clarity and guidance as to how the ICSID should apply the prioritization interpretative approach to the cases at hand. For a detailed analysis, see Johannes Hendrik Fahner and Matthew Happold, 'The Human Rights Defence In International Investment Arbitration: Exploring The Limits of Systemic Integration,' International and Comparative Law Quarterly (ICLQ) vol. 68, July 2019 pp. 741-759.

and investment agreements. Instead, it has opted for the provision in general terms that any bilateral and multilateral agreements shall be compatible and interpreted in accordance with the obligations under the future treaty.[514] The 2023 updated draft legally binding instrument has maintained the same approach to including a provision requiring that trade and investment agreements be interpreted and implemented in a manner that would not undermine or restrict the capacity of States parties to fulfil their obligations under the treaty.[515] This may be viewed as a setback by those proponents who had been advocating that the future treaty provisions should prevail over trade and investment agreements. In fact, the 2018 zero draft had proposed a stronger language in that regard as follows "*States Parties agree that any future trade and investment agreements they negotiate, whether amongst themselves or with third parties, shall not contain any provisions that conflict with the implementation of this Convention and shall ensure upholding human rights in the context of business activities by parties benefiting from such agreements.*"[516]

---

514 Supra note 501, Article 12 of the revised draft legally binding instrument to regulate, in international human rights law, the activities of transnational corporations and other business enterprises in July 2019. It can be accessed at the following OHCHR webpage: https://www.ohchr.org/Documents/HRBodies/HRCouncil/WGTransCorp/OEIGWG_RevisedDraft_LBI.pdf (Accessed as of 20 October 2024).

515 Supra note 485, Article 14.5 of the updated draft legally binding instrument: https://www.ohchr.org/sites/default/files/documents/hrbodies/hrcouncil/igwg-transcorp/session9/igwg-9th-updated-draft-lbi-track-changes.pdf (Accessed as of 20 October 2024).
Supra note 526, Article 13.6 of the zero draft legally binding instrument to regulate, in international human rights law, the activities of transnational corporations and other business enterprises. It can be accessed at the following OHCHR webpage: https://www.ohchr.org/sites/default/files/Documents/HRBodies/HRCouncil/WGTransCorp/Session3/DraftLBI.pdf. (Accessed as of 24 October 2024).

516 Supra note 492, Article 13.6 of the zero draft legally binding instrument to regulate, in international human rights law, the activities of transnational corporations and other business enterprises. It can be accessed at the following OHCHR webpage: https://www.ohchr.org/sites/default/files/Documents/HRBodies/HRCouncil/WGTransCorp/Session3/DraftLBI.pdf. (Accessed as of 24 October 2024). For an argument for a human rights primacy clause to be included in the future treaty, see '*Briefing Paper on the Zero Draft: Unpacking Arguments Against A Treaty*', Treaty Alliance Germany, at the following: https://www.business-humanrights.org/sites/default/files/documents/TreatyAllianceGermany_CounterArguments_Briefing_2-2019_en.pdf. (Accessed as of 24 October 2024).

4. The Added-Value

a. Codification and Clarification

The proponents of the future treaty have argued that the future treaty could serve as a complementary means to enhancing the corporate respect of human rights. It has been argued that while the UN Guiding Principles on Business and Human Rights has included the *State duty* to protect from corporate human rights abuse and the *Corporate responsibility* to respect human rights, there is still a need to codify the *State obligations* to respect, protect and fulfil human rights in relation to business activities in an international treaty. Such an international treaty could also clarify the content of the existing *State obligation* to protect from corporate human rights abuse, including clarifying the extraterritorial obligation of States. On the contrary, some Governments and business associations are of the opinion that in order to increase the corporate respect of human rights, further efforts should first be devoted to the full implementation of the UN Guiding Principles on Business and Human Rights at the national level.[517]

Parallel and complimentary efforts could also be made at the international level to conclude a future treaty on business and human rights, provided that there is added value in concluding such a treaty. The main added value of such a future treaty would be that the imposition of the direct international obligations on business enterprises to respect human rights on the international law plane coupled with strong built-in enforcement mechanisms of such obligations, including setting up a tribunal where corporate human rights abuse victims can bring their claims would eventually increase the level of protection against corporate human rights harm in complementarity with the protections provided against such corporate human rights harm on the domestic law plane. However, as has repeatedly been

517 Supra notes 436-439.

noted in this thesis, under the existing international human rights law regime, States have already the *obligations* to respect, protect and fulfil human rights in relation to business activities.

b. Establishment of International-level Enforcement Mechanisms

As noted above, the updated draft legally binding instrument envisages the establishment of a monitoring body of the future treaty (treaty body) designed to monitor the level of implementation of the treaty obligations by future States parties to the future treaty along with the establishment of the International Fund for corporate human rights victims. This will provide a certain form of legally non-binding international-level redress against corporate human rights abuses.[518] However, without the strong enforcement/implementation mechanisms and processes to address corporate human rights abuses such as an international dispute settlement tribunal that can adjudicate corporate human rights violation cases and enforce appropriate remedies on the international law plane, the future treaty will have very limited effect when it comes to protecting corporate human rights abuse victims. It is therefore critical that the future treaty provide for strong enforcement mechanisms aimed at remedying such human rights violations at the international level, including compensation, restitution, rehabilitation and guarantee of Non-recurrence. It should also be emphasized that even with such strong treaty-level enforcement mechanisms, the national-level enforcement is key to fully respecting the right of corporate human rights abuse victims to have access to effective remedies. Considering that in the absence of the direct obligations of business enterprises to respect human rights on the international law plane under the updated draft legally binding instrument, in international human rights law, to regulate the activities of transnational corporations and other business activities, the present thesis therefore argues that there will be very

---

518 Supra note 485, Article 15 of the updated draft legally binding instrument: https://www.ohchr.org/sites/default/files/documents/hrbodies/hrcouncil/igwg-transcorp/session9/igwg-9th-updated-draft-lbi-track-changes.pdf (Accessed as of 20 October 2024).

little added value in concluding such a future treaty on business and human rights.

C. Interim Conclusions

The then UN Sub-commission had played a pioneering role in clarifying the human rights norms that were relevant to addressing the negative impacts of business activities on the enjoyment of human rights. The adoption of the Norms on the responsibilities of transnational corporations and other business enterprises with regard to human rights marked a milestone in the process of clarifying the content of the *State obligations* to respect, protect and fulfil human rights in relation to business activities. However, the then UN Sub-commission had adopted too broad an interpretative approach to claiming that business enterprises had also the *obligation* to respect human rights under international human rights law, which led to a regrettable situation where its own parent body, the then UN Commission on Human Rights had not endorsed the Norms, despite the fact that the Norms themselves constituted a very important body of international human rights norms and standards on business and human rights.

It is submitted that the inter-sessional working group of the then UN Sub-commission fell short of clearly specifying the legal basis, based on which the direct legal obligations can be imposed on business enterprises under international human rights law. It is true that certain norms identified in the Norms can be directly applied to business enterprises, including those norms relevant to international crimes, customary international law, and peremptory norms (*ius cogens*). However, the mere existence of such norms that can be directly applied to non-state actors such as business enterprises cannot automatically lead to the conclusion that the direct international-level legal obligations can be imposed on business enterprises. Currently under international human rights law, States have the *obligations* to respect, protect and fulfil human rights in the context of business activities, whilst business enterprises have only the *responsibility* to respect human rights.

Despite unsuccessful attempts to craft the framework of international human rights norms that can be directly imposed on business enterprises, the momentum to create an international human rights instrument that would impose the direct legal obligations on business enterprises on the international law plane had persisted. This is somewhat surprising, when seen from the perspective that the pre-dominant mood of the international community had been that a more effective way to address the negative impacts of business activities on the enjoyment of human rights was through strengthening the existing *State duty* to protect from corporate human rights abuse on the domestic law plane and through voluntary observance of international standards on the *Corporate responsibility* to respect human rights by business enterprises themselves. However, the persisting arguments from some States and civil society organizations that there was still a real need to create an international human rights treaty to address corporate human rights abuses led to the establishment of the open-ended inter-governmental Working Group to elaborate, in international law a legally binding instrument to regulate the activities of transnational corporations and other business enterprises (OEIGWG) under the auspices of the UN Human Rights Council.

A closer examination of the current updated draft legally binding instrument on business and human rights shows that it is not designed to impose the direct legal obligations on business enterprises to respect human rights on the international law plane. The draft instrument rather focuses on what must and should be done in order to meet the *State obligations* to respect, protect and fulfil human rights in relation to business activities, under which the *Corporate responsibility* to respect human rights is addressed as part of the *State duty* to protect from corporate human rights abuse. It is submitted that there is little added-value of concluding an international treaty on business and human rights at this stage as the existing international human rights law regime is adequate in terms of providing for the *State obligations* to respect, protect and fulfil human rights in relation to business activities. What is lacking is the full implementation of such *State obligations* on the domestic law plane. Unless the future treaty on business and human rights imposes the direct international obligations on business enterprises to respect human rights and creates an international mechanism such as an international-level dispute settlement body/tribunal that can review and adjudicate allegations of corporate human rights abuses and provide enforceable remedies against corporate human rights violations, it would end up in concluding an international instrument with little practical added-value for corporate human rights abuse victims. Consequently, it is most likely that States would not ratify it. In this regard, it is worth noting that the attitude towards the future treaty may likely change at least at the European Union (EU) level as the EU now enacted the Corporate Sustainability Due Diligence Directive on 25 July 2024.[519] Some European States such as France and Germany also enacted the mandatory human rights due diligence laws.[520]

With respect to the scope of the application of a future treaty, it is submitted that the future treaty should not only apply to transnational corporations but also to all business enterprises. At the same time, the particular challenges caused by the activities of transnational corporations on the enjoyment of human rights should explicitly be acknowledged. However, considering that there exist the vast number of non-transnational

---

519 DIRECTIVE (EU) 2024/1760 OF THE EUROPEAN PARLIAMENT AND OF THE COUNCIL of 13 June 2024 on corporate sustainability due diligence and amending Directive (EU) 2019/1937 and Regulation (EU) 2023/2859. Official Journal of the European Union. It can be accessed at the following webpage: https://eur-lex.europa.eu/legal-content/EN/TXT/HTML/?uri=OJ:L_202401760. (Accessed as of 31 October 2024). The European Union during the 10th session of the OEIGWG explicitly stated that it would support the adoption of the binding international treaty on business and human rights. See the oral statement of the European Union made during the 10th session of the OEIGWG, which can be accessed at the following webpage: https://www.ohchr.org/sites/default/files/documents/hrbodies/hrcouncil/igwg-transcorp/session10/1-general-statements/igos/igwg-10th-general-statement-eu.pdf. Refer also to the following webpage of Business and Human Rights Resource Centre: https://www.business-humanrights.org/en/latest-news/day-1-monday-16-december/. (Accessed as of 4 March 2025.

520 For the details of such laws, see infra Chapter 8.

corporations, including state-owned enterprises, whose activities could cause significant negative impacts on the enjoyment of human rights, the future treaty should cover all business enterprises. Furthermore, the need to cover all business enterprises becomes even more acute, when seen from the perspective of protection of corporate human rights abuse victims. The central issue for corporate human rights abuse victims is that corporate human rights abuses must be investigated, mitigated, and remedied. Accordingly, it is vital that all business enterprises should be required to: avoid causing or contributing to adverse human rights impacts through their own activities, and address such impacts when they occur; and seek to prevent or mitigate adverse human rights impacts that are directly linked to their operations, products or services by their business relationships, even if they have not contributed to those impacts. The fact that the current updated draft legally binding instrument of OEIGWG has expanded its scope of application to the activities of all business enterprises is a welcome development from the zero draft legally binding instrument that has narrowly limited such scope of application to the business activities of a transnational character.

The extraterritorial obligation of States (home States) is an essential component of the *State duty* to protect from corporate human rights abuse. This extraterritorial obligation already exists as an integral part of the general *State obligations* to respect, protect and fulfil human rights on the international human rights law plane, which leads to the conclusion that there is no real need to make an additional international treaty to simply reaffirm such *State obligations* to respect, protect and fulfil human rights in the context of business activities, including the extraterritorial obligations of States. Potentially, one can find value in codifying and clarifying the content of such *State duty* to protect from corporate human rights abuse, including through the codification of the extraterritorial obligation to protect from corporate human rights abuse into the future treaty. However, it is submitted that the current international human rights law regime provides the clear legal basis for such extraterritorial obligation to regulate the activities of business enterprises overseas as part of the *State duty* to protect from corporate human rights abuse. In addition, the clarification of the specific content of the State obligations to respect, protect and fulfil human rights in the context of business activities could be provided by the existing treaty monitoring bodies under international human rights treaties such as the Committee on Economic, Social and Cultural Rights. It is equally important to acknowledge in this regard that the implementation of such extraterritorial obligation of States to protect from corporate human rights abuse ultimately rests with States themselves on the domestic law plane. Furthermore, considering that a large number of States parties to the existing human rights treaties lack capacity and resources to meet the reporting obligations to concerned treaty bodies, the additional reporting obligation to be created on the States parties to the future treaty on business and human rights may divert the resources of States parties from those required to provide national-level needed protection for corporate human rights abuse victims.[521]

In relation to the direct legal obligations for companies to respect human rights on the international law plane, it is concluded that although companies do not have the direct obligation to respect human rights under the current international human rights law regime, they are subjected to the direct obligation to respect human rights under customary international law such as freedom from torture, slavery, genocide and crimes against humanity. Some human rights scholars and experts argue that most human rights provided under the Universal Declaration of Human Rights, if not all, are considered to have reached the status of customary international law. It is, therefore, submitted that instead of overly focusing on creating the direct obligation for companies to respect human rights on the international law plane through a treaty-making process, it is more critically important to strengthen the capacities of States to regulate the activities of companies on the domestic law plane through appropriate policy, legislative, administrative, judicial,

521 Supra note 2, Eibe Riedel, 'Standards as Sources,' German Yearbook of International Law (GYIL) vol. 63 (220), 369-417, at 378-379.

promotional and educational measures. The current updated draft legally binding instrument of OEIGWG clearly points to the need to strengthen the national human rights framework because the provisions contained in the draft instrument are exclusively focused on the *State obligations* to respect, protect and fulfil human rights in relation to business activities, including provision of effective remedies against corporate human rights abuse.

It is also submitted that it is premature to strive to conclude an international treaty on business and human rights without clearly articulating the added-value. It is hence concluded that there is a critical need to strengthen the national human rights protection system, in particular strengthening legislative and judicial measures, with a view to ensuring that the *State duty* to protect from corporate human rights abuse, including measures to fully realize the *extraterritorial obligation* of States, is effectively fulfilled. Accordingly, in the absence of such clear added-value, States must take effective national measures to identify, prevent, mitigate and redress against the corporate human rights harms, both domestically and extraterritorially, to the extent consistent with international law. Toward this end, States must adopt legislative, administrative, policy, judicial, promotional, and educational and other measures necessary to ensure effective protection against corporate human rights abuse. As part of meeting the *State duty* to protect from corporate human rights abuse, States must ensure that business enterprises conduct human rights due diligence in their own operations and the supply chain to avoid causing adverse human rights impacts. States must also ensure that corporate human rights abuse victims have remedy against such business-related human rights harms.[522]

522 Supra note 232, CESCR-Committee General Comment No. 24 (2017) on State obligations under the International Covenant on Economic, Social and Cultural Rights in the context of business activities, UN Doc., E/C.12/GC/24, paras. 17-18.

Part 4

Human Rights Council Mechanisms
Relevant to Business and Human Rights

Chapter 7: Human Rights Council Mechanisms

With the unanimous endorsement by the Human Rights Council in 2011 of the UN Guiding Principles on Business and Human Rights, increasing attention has been paid to the issue of business and human rights by international human rights mechanisms. The Human Rights Council has specifically established the Working Group on the issue of human rights and transnational corporations and other business enterprises (the Working Group on Business and Human Rights), which has the principal objective of implementing the UN Guiding Principles on Business and Human Rights. The Working Group on Business and Human Rights is part of the special procedures of the Human Rights Council. Other special procedure mandate holders have also increasingly been addressing the relevant human rights implications that business activities may have on the rights that fall within their respective mandates.

The universal periodic review of the Human Rights Council (hereinafter referred to as the UPR), an inter-governmental peer review process that reviews the human rights situations of all 193 UN Member States every four and a half years, has also been addressing business and human rights-related issues.

An increasing number of UPR recommendations related to the issue of business and human rights have thus been made to the States under review, particularly since its second cycle reviews.

The present chapter seeks to analyze the works of these Human Rights Council mechanisms such as special procedures and the universal periodic review on the human rights impacts of business activities with a focus on the work of the Working Group on Business and Human Rights and the Annual Forum on Business and Human Rights, which is held annually under the guidance of the Working Group on Business and Human Rights.[523]

A. The Working Group on the Issue of Human Rights and Transnational Corporations and Other Business Enterprises

I. The Mandate and Working Methods

In its resolution 17/4 of 2011, the Human Rights Council established the Working Group on the issue of human rights and transnational corporations and other business enterprises, whose mandate has been renewed in 2014, 2017 and 2020 respectively through resolutions 26/22, 35/7 and 44/15.

The main mandate of the Working Group on Business and Human Rights, as set out in resolution in 17/4, is to promote the effective dissemination and implementation of the Guiding Principles on Business and Human Rights: Implementing the United Nations "Protect, Respect and Remedy" Framework. The Human Rights Council also requested the Working Group on Business and Human Rights to identify and promote good practices and

---

523 Treaty bodies' works on the issue of business and human rights are analyzed separately in Chapters 3 and 4.

lessons learned on the implementation of the UN Guiding Principles on Business and Human Rights. In addition, the Working Group on Business and Human Rights was called upon to provide support for efforts to promote capacity-building, in particular through provision of advice and recommendations related to the development of national law and policies on business and human rights.

Furthermore, the Working Group on Business and Human Rights was asked to explore options and recommendations aimed at enhancing access to effective remedies for those, whose human rights are affected by corporate activities, including those in conflict areas, at the national, regional and international levels. The Human Rights Council further authorized the Working Group on Business and Human Rights to conduct country visits asking the latter to respond promptly to invitations from States for such visits. As an essential component of the working methods of the Working Group on Business and Human Rights, the Human Rights Council emphasized the importance of integrating a gender perspective throughout its work. The Human Rights Council also emphasized the importance of working in close cooperation and coordination with other relevant special procedures of the Human Rights Council, treaty bodies, as well as with relevant international bodies and regional human rights organizations.

The development of a regular dialogue and identification of possible areas of cooperation with Governments also constitutes a crucial component of the mandate of the Working Group on Business and Human Rights. The Working Group on Business and Human Rights was further given the mandate to guide the work of the Forum on Business and Human Rights, created under the auspices of the Human Rights Council, as well as to report to the Human Rights Council and the General Assembly on an annual basis.[524]

---

524 For further details, see UN Doc., A/HRC/RES/17/4. It can be accessed at the following

The Human Rights Council extended the mandate of the Working Group on Business and Human Rights in 2014 for a period of three years through resolution 26/22. One notable addition to the mandate in this extension was to explicitly provide the Working Group on Business and Human Rights with the mandate to process individual communications on business-related human rights violations and abuses. Paragraph 12 of resolution 26/22 encourages "*all States, relevant United Nations agencies, funds and programmes, treaty bodies and civil society actors, including non-governmental organizations, as well as public and private businesses to cooperate fully with the Working Group in the fulfilment of its mandate by, inter alia, responding to communications transmitted, and for States to reply favourably to requests for visits by the Working Group.*"[525] The Working Group on Business and Human Rights as part of the United Nations special procedures was not initially given an explicit mandate to process individual communications as one of its working methods in its founding resolution 17/4, unlike other special procedures mandate holders. This explicit mandate to process individual communications is therefore considered to be significant in that it has allowed the Working Group on Business and Human Rights to monitor not only States' fulfilment of their international obligations in relation to business activities but also business enterprises' meeting their *Corporate responsibility* to respect human rights by directly fielding queries and clarifications to them.

The Human Rights Council extended the mandate of the Working Group on Business and Human Rights for a second time in 2017 for a period of three years through resolution 35/7. Of note is that the Working Group on Business and Human Rights was requested "*to give due consideration*

---

webpage: https://documents.un.org/doc/resolution/gen/g11/144/71/pdf/g1114471.pdf. (Accessed as of 19 January 2025).

525 UN Doc., A/HRC/RES/26/22. It can be accessed at the following webpage: https://documents.un.org/doc/undoc/gen/g14/083/82/pdf/g1408382.pdf. (Accessed as of 19 January 2025).

to the implementation of the Guiding Principles in the context of the 2030 Agenda for Sustainable Development."[526] The 2030 Agenda for Sustainable Development, adopted unanimously in 2015 by all UN Member States, with its 17 Goals (Sustainable Development Goals – SDGs), 169 targets and 231 indicators provide international guidance and direction for global and national development policies. They also offer renewed opportunities to bridge the divide between human rights and development. As such, it is notable that the 2030 Agenda is explicitly anchored in human rights and grounded in the Universal Declaration of Human Rights, international human rights treaties, as well as other relevant international human rights standards such as the Declaration on the Right to Development.[527] As such, through this renewed mandate, the Working Group on Business and Human Rights has been enabled to explore the linkages between the implementation of the Guiding Principles on Business and Human Rights and achievements of Sustainable Development Goals (SDGs).

In the meantime, before a further extension for three years in 2020 through resolution 44/15,[528] which has now become a routine exercise, the Human Rights Council passed resolutions[529] aimed at improving access to effective remedies against corporate human rights abuses in recognition of the critical importance of providing effective remedies for corporate human rights

---

526 UN Doc., A/HRC/RES/35/7. It can be accessed at the following webpage: https://documents.un.org/doc/undoc/gen/g17/191/47/pdf/g1719147.pdf. (Accessed as of 19 January 2025).

527 'Transforming our world: the 2030 Agenda for Sustainable Development,' UN Doc., A/RES/70/1. It can be accessed at the following webpage: https://www.un.org/en/development/desa/population/migration/generalassembly/docs/globalcompact/A_RES_70_1_E.pdf (Accessed as of 11 November 2024).

528 UN Doc., A/HRC/RES/44/15. It can be accessed at the following webpage: https://documents.un.org/doc/undoc/gen/g20/189/66/pdf/g2018966.pdf. (Accessed as of 19 January 2025).

529 UN Doc., A/HRC/RES/32/10. It can be accessed at the following webpage: https://documents.un.org/doc/undoc/gen/g16/155/72/pdf/g1615572.pdf. (Accessed as of 19 January 2025). UN Doc., A/HRC/RES/38/13. It can be accessed at the following webpage: https://documents.un.org/doc/undoc/gen/g18/221/90/pdf/g1822190.pdf. (Accessed as of 19 January 2025).

abuse victims who have been faced with an array of practical obstacles and barriers, when it comes to accessing such effective remedies against corporate human rights abuses. Since then, the need for enhanced accountability and improved accessibility to effective remedies against corporate human rights abuses has become an integral part of the resolution extending the mandate of the Working Group on Business and Human Rights.

The 2020 extension of the mandate of the Working Group on Business and Human Rights contained the following notable elements: firstly, the resolution (44/15) recognizes the relevance of the UN Guiding Principles on Business and Human Rights to global crises such as the COVID-19 pandemic emphasizing the need for States to ensure responsible business conduct during the COVID-19 pandemic crisis and a recovery; secondly, the resolution encouraged business enterprises to conduct human rights due diligence, in particular with regard to the recently recognized human right by the Human Rights Council to the enjoyment of a safe, clean, healthy and sustainable environment, as well as to hold meaningful and inclusive consultations with groups to be potentially affected by business activities and other relevant stakeholders. This is an important acknowledgment of the recognition of the importance of mandating human rights due diligence as part of the *Corporate responsibility* to respect human rights, as well as to meet the *State obligation* to protect from corporate human rights abuse on the international law plane, which may eventually lead to the development of customary international law on the *Corporate responsibility* to respect human rights; thirdly, the resolution emphasizes the importance of ensuring gender equality, in particular with regard to multiple forms of discrimination and barriers in seeking access to effective remedies against corporate human rights abuses; fourthly, it highlights the valuable role to be played by civil society, including non-governmental organizations, and national human rights institutions in implementing the UN Guiding Principles on Business and Human Rights at the country level, while expressing concern about reports of intimidation against corporate human rights abuse victims, witnesses and their legal representatives; and fifthly, it mandated a holding of a panel discussion in

2021 during the 47th session of the Human Rights Council to take stock of progress made over the past 10 years, as well as to discuss possible future steps aimed at improving future implementation on the occasion of the 10th anniversary of the UN Guiding Principles on Business and Human Rights.[530]

It is the following components of the Working Group on Business and Human Rights' broad mandate to operationalize the UN Guiding Principles on Business and Human Rights that have featured most prominently: provision of capacity-building; provision of advice and recommendations, in particular regarding the development of domestic legislation and policies on business and human rights; exploration of options and recommendations aimed at enhancing effective access to remedies against corporate human rights abuse; and integration of a gender perspective throughout its work with special attention being paid to persons living in vulnerable situations.[531] It is worth noting that the Human Rights Council has adopted an eclectic and gradual approach by setting the priorities for the work of the Working Group on Business and Human Rights in an indirect manner through routinely (every three years) extending its mandate, at each extension of which the Human Rights Council has encouraged the Working Group on Business and Human Rights to thematically focus on certain elements of the *State duty* to protect pillar, the *Corporate responsibility* to respect human rights pillar and the access to remedy pillar contained in the UN Guiding Principles on Business and Human Rights.

Based on the above eclectic and gradual approach promoted by the Human Rights Council to operationalizing the UN Guiding Principles on Business and Human Rights, the Working Group on Business and

530 For further details, see UN Doc., A/HRC/RES/44/15. It can be accessed at the following webpage: https://documents.un.org/doc/undoc/gen/g20/189/66/pdf/g2018966.pdf. (Accessed as of 19 January 2025).

531 UN Doc., A/HRC/RES/17/4. It can be accessed at the following webpage: https://documents.un.org/doc/resolution/gen/g11/144/71/pdf/g1114471.pdf. (Accessed as of 19 January 2025).

Human Rights has initially been focusing its work on "*global dissemination, promoting implementation, and embedding in global governance frameworks*,"[532] along with addressing thematic issues with the aim of assisting both States and business enterprises in implementing the UN Guiding Principles on Business and Human Rights. Anchored in the mandate of the Working Group on Business and Human Rights given by relevant HRC resolutions.

The Working Group on Business and Human Rights has further identified challenges related to effective implementation of the UN Guiding Principles on Business and Human Rights. Such challenges for business enterprises include the incorporation of human rights into risk management and due diligence processes, supply chains and grievance mechanisms when meeting the *Corporate responsibility* to respect human rights. In the case of States, it has been identified that "*advancing policy coherence, identifying roles for national and subnational public agencies, and building capacity of public accountability bodies and judicial and non-judicial mechanisms*"[533] will constitute the main challenges. These identified challenges have served as indicators of what the Working Group on Business and Human Rights should focus its work on fulfilling its mandate in the coming years through adopting an eclectic and gradual approach to the operationalization of the UN Guiding Principles on Business and Human Rights.

II. Operationalization of the UN Guiding Principles on Business and Human Rights

Based on the broad mandate given by the Human Rights Council,

---

532 'Report of the Working Group on the issue of human rights and transnational corporations and other business enterprises' to the UN Human Rights Council, UN Doc., A/HRC/20/29, paras. 36 and 71. It can be accessed at the following webpage: https://documents.un.org/doc/undoc/gen/g12/128/48/pdf/g1212848.pdf (Accessed as of 11 November 2024).

533 Ibid., para. 71.

the Working Group on Business and Human Rights has focused on a wide range of key topics aimed at operationalizing the UN Guiding Principles on Business and Human Rights. Initially the Working Group on Human Rights has focused its attention on the dissemination and integration of the UN Guiding Principles on Business and Human Rights into global governance mechanisms and several business-led voluntary initiatives. It took a gradual approach to clarifying what those principles contained in the UN Guiding Principles on Business and Human Rights specifically mean, when it comes to the *State obligations* in relation to business activities and the *Corporate responsibility* to respect human rights.

Accordingly, the Working Group on Business and Human Rights prepared the strategy designed to effectively disseminate and implement the UN Guiding Principles on Business and Human Rights as its core mandate, which has been based on the three overarching principles: 1) to use the UN Guiding Principles on Business and Human Rights as a common reference point in the field of business and human rights; 2) to use the UN Guiding Principles on Business and Human Rights with a view to securing enhanced accountability for human rights harms/abuses caused by business enterprises; and 3) to build an environment conducive/receptive to the effective implementation of the UN Guiding Principles on Business and Human Rights. In addition, it presented its preliminary thoughts and ideas on future work streams and focus criteria, in which the three main work streams have been identified: global dissemination, promoting implementation, and integration (embedding) of the UN Guiding Principles on Business and Human Rights in global governance frameworks. It also articulated the inclusive and consultative approach as its principal approach when it comes to its engagement with stakeholders.[534]

In terms of the working methods, it is worth noting that considering

---

534 Ibid., paras. 63-83.

the initial lack of the explicit mandate to process individual communications, the Working Group on Business and Human Rights clarified that it would not address alleged individual cases of corporate human rights abuses, although it would take into account such cases in order to inform recommendations to States, business and other actors on the implementation of the UN Guiding Principles on Business and Human Rights.[535] As part of its guiding role in the preparation of the Annual Forum on Business and Human Rights mandated by resolution 17/4, the Working Group on Business and Human Rights has decided to hold the very first annual forum from 4 to 5 December 2012.[536] The Forum on Business and Human Rights has since been providing a largest global public forum to discuss a whole range of issues related to the *State duty* to protect, the *Corporate responsibility* to respect human rights and access to remedy of the UN Guiding Principles on Business and Human Rights having had discussions with different thematic focus at each session.

In relation to the embedding of the UN Guiding Principles on Business and Human Rights in global governance frameworks, the Working Group on Business and Human Rights noted the following initiatives: the UNCTAD Investment Policy Framework for Sustainable Development; the Voluntary Guidelines on the Responsible Governance of Tenure of Land, Fisheries and Forests endorsed by the UN Committee on World Food Security; the revised Sustainability Framework of the International Finance Corporation, all of which have referenced the UN Guiding Principles on Business and Human Rights.[537] As such, an increasing number of global

---

535 Pursuant to HRC resolution 26/22 of 2014, the Working Group on Business and Human Rights was given the mandate to process individual communications like other special procedures of the Human Rights Council. UN Doc., A/HRC/RES/26/22, para. 11. It can be accessed at the following webpage: https://documents.un.org/doc/undoc/gen/g14/083/82/pdf/g1408382.pdf (Accessed as of 11 November 2024).

536 Supra note 532, UN Doc., A/HRC/20/29, para. 90.

537 'Report of the Working Group on the issue of human rights and transnational corporations and other business enterprises,' UN Doc., A/67/285, paras. 15-27. It can be accessed at the following webpage: https://documents.un.org/doc/undoc/gen/n12/459/11/pdf/n1245911.pdf (Accessed as of 11 November 2024).

governance frameworks on business and human rights have converged with the UN Guiding Principles on Business and Human rights incorporating notably the international standard on the *Corporate responsibility* to respect human rights contained in the UN Guiding Principles on Business and Human Rights since. This is an indication that the UN Guiding Principles on Business and Human Rights constitute the most authoritative international *Combination/zebra* standards on business and human rights.

Efforts by treaty bodies such as the CESCR's statement on the obligations of States parties to the Covenant regarding the corporate sector and economic, social and cultural rights and the General Comment 24 on State obligations under the International Covenant on Economic, Social and Cultural Rights in the context of business activities, as well as the General Comment of the CRC-Committee on child rights and the business sector have informed the work of the Working Group on Business and Human Rights, in particular when it comes to clarifying the due diligence dimensions of the *Corporate responsibility* to respect human rights contained in the UN Guiding Principles on Business and Human Rights In addition, continued efforts by special procedures of the Human Rights Council to address the human rights-related impacts of business activities have informed the work of the Working Group on Business and Human Rights as the former has been clarifying the impacts of business activities on the enjoyment of the rights that fall under their respective mandate, and have been making specific references to the UN Guiding Principles on Business and Human Rights, in doing so. It can be said that the Working Group on Business and Human Rights has prioritized its work on encouraging the international human rights ecosystem, including UN entities to embed the UN Guiding Principles on Business and Human Rights in UN policies, programmes and activities.

As such, the Working Group on Business and Human Rights took note of other inter-governmental initiatives that sought to align them with the UN Guiding Principles on Business and Human Rights, including: the revised Guidelines for Multinational Enterprises of the Organization for

Economic Cooperation and Development (OECD); the OECD Council recommendation on common approaches for officially supported export credits and environmental and social due diligence; the efforts of the OECD network of National Contact Points to implement the OECD Guidelines for Multinational Enterprises; a Global Forum on Responsible Business Conduct, scheduled to be launched by the OECD Investment Committee in 2013; and the OECD Due Diligence Guidance for Responsible Supply Chains of Minerals from Conflict-affected and High-risk Areas.

The Working Group on Business and Human Rights also noted sector or industry-specific guidance tools, including: the European Commission's project to develop guidance based on the Guiding Principles on Business and Human Rights for the oil and gas, information and communications strategy, and employment and recruitment sectors, as well as for small and medium-sized enterprises; that the OECD Investment Committee was developing guidance for enterprises relating to the financial, extractive, information and communications technology, and agriculture sectors; the UNICEF pilot workbook designed to provide guidance to companies on how to meet their *Corporate responsibility* to respect the human rights of children in the workplace, marketplace and community in line with the United Nations Guiding Principles on Business and Human Rights and the Children's Rights and Business Principles; the International Council on Mining and Metals on how human rights due diligence can be integrated into corporate risk management processes within the mining and metals industry; the oil and gas industry launched projects to produce guidance on human rights impact assessments and due diligence processes; the International Trade Union Federation's guidance for trade unionists on the United Nations Guiding Principles on Business and Human Rights and how they can be used for dialogue and engagement with Government and business; the International Federation of Human Rights (FIDH) updated guide for NGOs and victims on recourse mechanisms for human rights abuses. In an effort to increase convergence, avoid duplication, and maintain the integrity of the United Nations Guiding Principles on Business and Human Rights, the

Working Group on Business and Human Rights sought to provide guidance on interpretation and feedback on specific tools through clarification on interpretation of the United Nations Guiding Principles on Business and Human Rights and establishing a set of simple criteria aimed at ensuring that guidance tools are aligned with them.[538]

The Working Group on Business and Human Rights further noted that the European Union (EU) had aligned the EU definition of corporate social responsibility with the UN Guiding Principles on Business and Human Rights. The European Commission strategy for the implementation of the UN Guiding Principles on Business and Human Rights by EU Member States and enterprises had embedded key concepts of the UN Guiding Principles on Business and Human Rights. The Steering Committee for Human Rights of the Council of Europe (CoE) also stressed the central place of the UN Guiding Principles on Business and Human Rights as an authoritative reference point for its work on corporate social responsibility in the field of human rights.[539] As shall be seen in the subsequent chapter, efforts of the European Union to align its own guidance on business and human rights have borne some fruits as it managed to enact regional mandatory human rights due diligence law, i.e., the EU Corporate Sustainability Due Diligence Directive in April 2024, which are largely aligned with the UN Guiding Principles on Business and Human Rights. Other regional human rights bodies such as ASEAN Intergovernmental Commission on Human Rights and the General Assembly of the Organization of American States have also made some efforts to embed the UN Guiding Principles on Business and Human Rights in their work.[540]

Furthermore, private and multi-stakeholder initiatives, including the Fair Labor Association, the Global Network Initiative and the Voluntary

---

538 Ibid., para. 22.
539 Ibid., paras. 23-24.
540 Ibid., paras. 25-26.

Principles on Security and Human Rights, the Thun Group of banks and the International Council on Mining and Metals have made references to the UN Guiding Principles on Business and Human Rights in order to align their guidance tools with the UN Guiding Principles on Business and Human Rights.[541]

In the area of reporting and disclosure, existing reporting initiatives, including the Global Reporting Initiative, the World Bank Environmental and Social Safeguard Policy, the Equator Principles Association of the credit risk management framework and the Committee on World Food Security of the principles on responsible agricultural investment have aligned their respective guidelines for reporting and disclosure with the UN Guiding Principles on Business and Human Rights, particularly regarding company disclosure on the management approach to human rights, supply chain disclosure, including with reference to human rights performance of suppliers and other business partners and grievance mechanisms.[542]

As for dissemination of the UN Guiding Principles on Business and Human Rights, there is a need for ongoing efforts to disseminate as the Working Group on Business and Human Rights highlighted that there had been insufficient efforts to disseminate it across all regions and all stakeholder groups.[543]

As for implementation efforts, while highlighting that the ultimate and overarching objective of the strategy of the Working Group on Business and Human Rights was effective implementation of the UN Guiding Principles on Business and Human Rights, it had embarked on two specific projects that focused on supporting Governments in the elaboration of national plans of action to implement the UN Guiding Principles on Business and Human

---

541 Ibid., para. 28.
542 Ibid., paras. 29-30.
543 Ibid., paras. 32-38.

Rights, as well as supporting peer discussion and learning among States and business enterprises on implementation efforts. In this regard, it noted that the large number of Governments had failed to take initial steps towards implementation of the UN Guiding Principles on Business and Human Rights. Further in recognition of the importance of effective remedies as an essential element to implementation of the UN Guiding Principles on Business and Human Rights, it emphasized that both States and business enterprises should make more efforts.[544] Towards this end, the UN Working Group on Business and Human Rights developed guidance on how to devise the national action plan on business and human rights.[545]

The following categories of allegations of human rights violations linked to business activities attracted the attention of the Working Group on Business and Human Rights. These corporate human rights abuses were related to the rights to life, self-determination, and liberty and security, the rights not to be subjected to slavery or forced labour, freedom of association, assembly and expression, protection for the child, non-discrimination, health, food, adequate housing, education and just conditions of work and the right to join trade unions, as well as rights associated International Labour Organization core conventions and the rights of minorities.[546] This clearly indicates that the full range of human rights, including both civil and political rights and economic, social and cultural rights can be impacted by business activities.

In ongoing efforts to clarify how the *Combination/zebra* standards contained in the UN Guiding Principles on Business and Human Rights could be applied and related to in a variety of diverse thematic issues

---

544 Ibid., paras. 39-48.

545 It can be accessed at the following OHCHR webpage: https://www.ohchr.org/sites/default/files/Documents/Issues/Business/UNWG__NAPGuidance.pdf. (Accessed as of 25 November 2024).

546 Supra note 532, paras. 50 and 65.

and contexts, the Working Group on Business and Human Rights has subsequently addressed key business and human rights-related thematic issues ranging from anti-corruption,[547] conflict,[548] corporate human rights due diligence,[549] integration of a gender perspective,[550] the need to ensure policy coherence,[551] the relationship to trade and investment support to business enterprises,[552] the role of the state as an economic actor,[553] human rights defenders and civic space[554] to sustainable development.[555]

More specifically, the Working Group on Business and Human Rights

---

547 'Report of the Working Group on transnational corporations and other business enterprises: Connecting the business and human rights and other anti-corruption agendas,' UN Doc., A/HRC/44/43. It can be accessed at the following webpage: https://documents.un.org/doc/undoc/gen/g20/150/03/pdf/g2015003.pdf. (Accessed as of 28 November 2024).

548 'Report of the Working Group on transnational corporations and other business enterprises: Business, human rights and conflict-affected regions – towards tightened action,' UN Doc., A/75/212. It can be accessed at the following webpage: https://documents.un.org/doc/undoc/gen/n20/190/21/pdf/n2019021.pdf . (Accessed as of 28 November 2024).

549 'Report of the Working Group on transnational corporations and other business enterprises,' UN Doc., A/73/163. It can be accessed at the following webpage: https://documents.un.org/doc/undoc/gen/n18/224/87/pdf/n1822487.pdf. (Accessed as of 28 November 2024).

550 'Report of the Working Group on transnational corporations and other business enterprises: Gender dimensions of the Guiding Principles on Business and Human Rights,' UN Doc., A/HRC/41/43. It can be accessed at the following webpage: https://documents.un.org/doc/undoc/gen/g19/146/08/pdf/g1914608.pdf. (Accessed as of 28 November 2024).

551 'Report of the Working Group on transnational corporations and other business enterprises,' UN Doc., A/74/198. It can be accessed at the following webpage: https://documents.un.org/doc/undoc/gen/n19/224/00/pdf/n1922400.pdf. (Accessed as of 28 November 2024).

552 'Report of the Working Group on transnational corporations and other business enterprises,' UN Doc., A/HRC/38/48. It can be accessed at the following webpage: https://documents.un.org/doc/undoc/gen/g18/123/33/pdf/g1812333.pdf. (Accessed as of 28 November 2024).

553 Ibid.

554 'Report of the Working Group on transnational corporations and other business enterprises: The Guiding Principles on Business and Human Rights – guidance on ensuring respect for human rights defenders,' UN Doc., A/HRC/47/39/Add.2. It can be accessed at the following webpage: https://documents.un.org/doc/undoc/gen/g21/161/49/pdf/g2116149.pdf. (Accessed as of 28 November 2024).

555 For a stock-taking of the 10th anniversary of the UN Guiding Principles on Business and Human Rights, see 'Report of the Working Group on transnational corporations and other business enterprises: Guiding Principles on Business and Human Rights at 10 – taking stock of the first decade,' UN Doc., A/HRC/47/39. It can be accessed at the following webpage: https://documents.un.org/doc/undoc/gen/g21/093/82/pdf/g2109382.pdf. (Accessed as of 28 November 2024).

has opined that ensuring policy coherence is relevant to all three Pillars of the UN Guiding Principles on Business and Human Rights. Towards this end, the Working Group on Business and Human Rights recommended that States should build operational capacity and ensure accountability across all relevant government entities when fulfilling *the State duty* to protect from corporate human rights abuse, as well as that States establish consistent and clear guidelines and methodologies, which should be used, enforced, and monitored.

The Working Group on Business and Human Rights explicitly noted that despite significant adverse human rights impacts caused by trade, the imports and exports of goods in the global supply chain, very little had been done by States' fulfilling their obligations under Principle 4 of the UN Guiding Principles on Business and Human Rights. As such, it was recommended that States should do more to align trade promotion with the UN Guiding Principles on Business and Human Rights. The Working Group on Business and Human Rights also noted that States had done more in conditioning trade support to business commitments not to engage in bribery and to act with integrity, which must be expanded to cover commitments from business to respect human rights. In the area of export credits, there had been some progress in the framework of the 2016 updated OECD recommendations on common approaches to export credit, which included a requirement for export credit agencies to require applicants to conduct human rights due diligence, in particular regarding projects that posed severe human rights risks. However, there was still room for reform of these OECD Common Approaches to align closer to the UN Guiding Principles on Business and Human Rights. In this regard, it is worth noting that export and import controls and restrictions had proven to be a promising path to fulfilling the *State duty* to protect from corporate human rights abuses.

Such controls and restrictions could trigger business enterprises to engage in stronger human rights due diligence as States could restrict the export and import of goods that were produced by violating human rights such as forced labour.[556]

For the specific purposes of integrating a gender perspective, the Working Group on Business and Human Rights developed the gender framework and the gender guidance for the UN Guiding Principles on Business and Human Rights. The gender framework has three-step cycle: gender-responsive assessment, gender-transformative measures and gender transformative remedies, which is grounded in the notion that firstly, a gender-responsive assessment of laws, policies, norms, and standards must be first done to identify whether they are directly or indirectly discriminatory towards women. In adopting this gender-responsive assessment, both States and businesses should take into account the differentiated, inter-sectional and disproportionate adverse impacts on women's rights, as well as existing discriminatory norms and patriarchal power structures; secondly, States and businesses must take transformative measures that should bring about change to existing patriarchal norms and unequal power structures; and thirdly, States and businesses must provide remedies that could change discriminatory power structures and reduce gender inequality.[557] Conducting a gender-responsive assessment consists of the following elements: "*review whether laws, policies, norms, standards and practices are directly or indirectly discriminatory towards women; assess how the State or business enterprise's current and future actions or omissions might adversely affect women; collect sex-disaggregated data; consider intersectionality [of discrimination against women]; ensure the meaningful participation of women and women's*

556 For further details, see 'Report of the Working Group on transnational corporations and other business enterprises: Human rights-compatinble international investment agreements,' UN Doc., A/76/238. It can be accessed at the following webpage: https://documents.un.org/doc/undoc/gen/n21/208/09/pdf/n2120809.pdf. (Accessed as of 28 November 2024).

557 For detailed explanation on the gender framework and the gender guidance, including context, their objectives, methodology, their scope and limitation, and challenges, see supra note 586, 'Report of the Working Group on transnational corporations and other business enterprises: Gender dimensions of the Guiding Principles on Business and Human Rights,' UN Doc., A/HRC/41/43. It can be accessed at the following webpage: https://documents.un.org/doc/undoc/gen/g19/146/08/pdf/g1914608.pdf. (Accessed as of 28 November 2024).

organizations in the assessment process; engage gender-sensitive experts to conduct impact assessment; and evaluate the effectiveness of gender-transformative measures and remedies."[558]

The Gender Framework for the UN Guiding Principles on Business and Human Rights suggests the following actions as part of gender-transformative remedies: "*Offer a range of preventive, redressive and deterrent remedies; engage women's organizations and gender-sensitive experts to identify appropriate remedies; address both specific and systematic abuses affecting women; propose remedies that could change discriminatory power structures and reduce violence against women; and engage with Governments and other stakeholders to reform discriminatory laws.*"[559] It has also issued "Gender Guidance for the UN Guiding Principles on Business and Human Rights," which has been annexed to the above Gender Framework.[560]

With respect to state support for trade, export and investment promotion, the Working Group on Business and Human Rights has made a host of recommendations primarily to States in order to bring closer alignment of state practices into the UN Guiding Principles on Business and Human Rights: *firstly*, States should require business enterprises to demonstrate an awareness of and commitment to the UN Guiding Principles on Business and Human Rights as a pre-requisite for receiving state support and benefits relating to trade and export promotion. Participation in trade missions, eligibility for trade advocacy and generalized export assistance should be used as tools to raise awareness of business-related human rights risks in the relevant contexts with a particular focus on the risks faced by vulnerable groups and individuals. In this regard, the situation of human

---

558 Ibid., p. 11, 'Gender framework for the Guiding Principles on Business and Human Rights'

559 Ibid.

560 Ibid., Annex 'Gender guidance for the Guiding Principles on Business and Human Rights'. Under each Guiding Principle, a range of illustrative actions have been suggested.

rights defenders and trade unions can serve as a concrete benchmark; *secondly*, States should expand the requirement for businesses to make integrity and anti-corruption pledges to include a commitment to respect human rights and an alignment of business activities with the UN Guiding Principles on Business and Human Rights; *thirdly*, States should consider a withdrawal of state support from companies in the event that they have been found to have caused or contributed to or been directly linked to adverse human rights impacts; *fourthly*, States should more actively consider using withdrawal of trade support in order to create incentives for companies to respect human rights and engage in human rights due diligence and legitimate remediation processes; *fifthly*, with respect to export credit, States and their export credit agencies should ensure that their practices are aligned with the UN Guiding Principles on Business and Human Rights. For participants in the OECD Export Credit Group, those States are encouraged to look beyond the OECD Common Approaches with a view to aligning export credit activity with the UN Guiding Principles on Business and Human Rights. Export credit agencies should also develop useful models of human rights screening and due diligence; *sixthly*, export credit agencies should focus on the issue of enabling access to remedy. They should also evaluate, support and incentivize the quality of the grievance mechanisms of their clients/ applicants at the operational level. Export credit agencies should also establish effective complaints mechanisms that are readily available by affected parties, rights-holders and communities; *seventhly*, export credit agencies should conduct review of their current transparency and disclosure policies, and revise them to make more information public; *eighthly*, States should identify more innovative measures to prevent trade in goods that are connected to serious human rights risks in global supply chains; and *ninthly*, States should use various multinational fora that exist for export credit agencies to engage in developing good practices and further commitments relating to the UN Guiding Principles on Business and Human Rights such as the Berne Union, the international Working Group on Export Credits, the European Union and the BRICS Export Credit Forum.[561]

It is concluded that the Working Group on Business and Human Rights has rightly focused its work on the operationalization of the UN Guiding Principles on Business and Human Rights, the most authoritative international *Combination/zebra* standards on business and human rights, through offering a range of suggestions for the integration of such international standards into global governance mechanisms and several business-led voluntary initiatives. As such, it is worth noting that the Working Group on Business and Human Rights has provided guidance on a range of thematic issues, including how to incorporate a gender perspective, how to ensure inter-governmental policy coherence in meeting the *State duty* to protect from corporate human rights abuse, the nexus between support for trade and export and human rights obligations to respect, protect and fulfil human rights in relation to business activities, as well as guidance on how to develop national policy framework on business and human rights such as development of national action plan on business and human rights. The Working Group on Business and Human Rights has significantly contributed to clarifying what it entails under the *State duty* to protect pillar of the UN Guiding Principles on Business and Human Rights by providing an array of guidance aimed at helping States operationalize the *State duty* to protect pillar at the national level. However, it can be said that the Working Group on Business and Human rights has yet to provide further clarity and adequate guidance on how to operationalize the *Corporate responsibility* to respect Pillar and the access to remedy Pillar of the UN Guiding Principles on Business and Human Rights.

---

561 For details on recommendations, see supra note 552, 'Report of the Working Group on transnational corporations and other business enterprises,' UN Doc., A/HRC/38/48. It can be accessed at the following webpage: https://documents.un.org/doc/undoc/gen/g18/123/33/pdf/g1812333.pdf. (Accessed as of 28 November 2024). The Working Group on Business and Human Rights recommended to civil society actors that they should seek greater alignment of State policies and regulations with the UN Guiding Principles on Business and Human Rights in relation to issues of human rights, export credits and trade promotion. They should also carry out continuing advocacy on these issues. The Working Group on Business and Human Rights also encouraged businesses to work in partnership with trade promotion entities to develop and disseminate effective guidance on how business respect for human rights can be demonstrated in cross-border trade.

B. The Annual Forum on Business and Human Rights

The UN Annual Forum on Business and Human Rights (the UN Annual Forum on BHR) established by the Human Rights Council in 2011 has become the world's largest global gathering on business and human rights. The three-day conference is held annually in Geneva, normally in November. As specified in HRC resolution 17/4, the UN Annual Forum on BHR serves as a key global platform for stakeholders to "*discuss trends and challenges in the implementation of the [UN] Guiding Principles and promote dialogue and cooperation on issues linked to business and human rights*."[562] It is open to States, business enterprises and associations, civil society organizations, trade unions, victims, academics, students, the media and any other relevant stakeholder. It is guided by the Working Group on Business and Human Rights. Moreover, as of 2017 (resolution 35/7), the Working Group on Business and Human Rights also has a mandate "*to chair the Forum and submit a report on the proceedings and thematic recommendations of the Forum for consideration by the Human Rights Council*."[563]

I. Main Activities and Outcomes

The UN Forum on Business and Human Rights have addressed a whole array of business and human rights-related issues with the central aim of assisting States in operationalizing the UN Guiding Principles on Business and Human Rights at the national level. It has addressed issues ranging from trends and challenges in implementing the UN Guiding Principles on Business and Human Rights,[564] enhancing the dissemination

---

562 UN Doc., A/HRC/RES/17/4. It can be accessed at the following webpage: https://documents.un.org/doc/resolution/gen/g11/144/71/pdf/g1114471.pdf. (Accessed as of 29 November 2024).

563 UN Doc., A/HRC/RES/35/7. It can be accessed at the following webpage: https://documents.un.org/doc/undoc/gen/g17/191/47/pdf/g1719147.pdf. (Accessed as of 29 November 2024).

564 For further details, see UN Doc., A/HRC/FBHR/2012/4. It can be accessed at the following webpage: https://documents.un.org/doc/undoc/gen/g13/102/88/pdf/g1310288.pdf. (Accessed as of 29 November 2024).

and implementation of the UN Guiding Principles on Business and Human Rights and promoting multi-stakeholder dialogue and cooperation on business and human rights,[565] advancing business and human rights globally,[566] tracking progress and ensuring coherence in the implementation of the UN Guiding Principles on Business and Human Rights,[567] the role of leadership and leverage in embedding human rights in the rules and relationships that drive the global economy,[568] realizing access to effective remedy,[569] the need for companies to exercise human rights due diligence to prevent adverse impacts on people,[570] meeting the *State duty* to protect from corporate human rights abuse with a focus on strengthening accountability,[571] prevention of business-related human rights abuse as the key to a sustainable future for people and planet,[572] taking stock of the decade and envisioning the next decade with a view to increasing the implementation of the UN Guiding Principles on Business and Human Rights,[573] strengthening accountability to

---

565 For further details, see UN Doc., A/HRC/FBHR/2013/4. It can be accessed at the following webpage: https://www.ohchr.org/sites/default/files/Documents/Issues/Business/ForumSession2/A-HRC-FBHR-2013-4_en.pdf. (Accessed as of 29 November 2024).

566 For further details, see UN Doc., A/HRC/FBHR/2014/3. It can be accessed at the following webpage: https://documents.un.org/doc/undoc/gen/g15/019/83/pdf/g1501983.pdf. (Accessed as of 29 November 2024).

567 For further details, see UN Doc., A/HRC/FBHR/2015/2. It can be accessed at the following webpage: https://documents.un.org/doc/undoc/gen/g16/021/77/pdf/g1602177.pdf. (Accessed as of 29 November 2024).

568 For further details, see UN Doc., A/HRC/FBHR/2016/2. It can be accessed at the following webpage: https://documents.un.org/doc/undoc/gen/g17/097/76/pdf/g1709776.pdf. (Accessed as of 29 November 2024).

569 For further details, see UN Doc., A/HRC/38/49. It can be accessed at the following webpage: https://documents.un.org/doc/undoc/gen/g18/116/09/pdf/g1811609.pdf. (Accessed as of 29 November 2024).

570 For further details, see UN Doc., A/HRC/41/49. It can be accessed at the following webpage: https://documents.un.org/doc/undoc/gen/g19/120/49/pdf/g1912049.pdf. (Accessed as of 29 November 2024).

571 For further details, see UN Doc., A/HRC/44/56. It can be accessed at the following webpage: https://documents.un.org/doc/undoc/gen/g20/154/85/pdf/g2015485.pdf. (Accessed as of 29 November 2024).

572 For further details, see UN Doc., A/HRC/47/50. It can be accessed at the following webpage: https://documents.un.org/doc/undoc/gen/g21/095/76/pdf/g2109576.pdf. (Accessed as of 29 November 2024).

573 For further details, refer to the following OHCHR webpage: https://www.ohchr.org/en/

advance business respect for people and the planet in the next decade,[574] to effective change in implementing obligations, responsibilities and remedies.[575] The latest Annual Forum was held in November, 2024 with the theme focusing on "a smart mix of measures" aimed at protecting human rights in the context of business activities.[576]

C. The Special Procedures

With the adoption of the UN Guiding Principles on Business and Human Rights, a number of Human Rights Council special procedures mandate holders, in particular thematic mandate holders have been attempting to address the interlinkages between their respective thematic mandates and business and human rights-related issues. For example, the Special Rapporteur on the issue of human rights obligations relating to the enjoyment of a safe, clean, healthy and sustainable environment has addressed the responsibility of business in relation to the right to a healthy environment by highlighting the importance of undertaking human rights due diligence with a good set of safeguards for the protection of human rights and the environment.[577] The Special Rapporteur on the right to privacy has also addressed security and surveillance, health data and the use of personal data by business enterprises,

---

events/forums/2021/10th-un-forum-business-and-human-rights. (Accessed as of 29 November 2024).

574 For further details, refer to the following OHCHR webpage: https://www.ohchr.org/en/events/forums/2022/11th-un-forum-business-and-human-rights. (Accessed as of 29 November 2024).

575 For further details, refer to the following OHCHR webpage: https://www.ohchr.org/en/events/sessions/2023/12th-united-nations-forum-business-and-human-rights. (Accessed as of 29 November 2024).

576 For further details, refer to the following OHCHR webpage: https://www.ohchr.org/en/events/sessions/2024/13th-united-nations-forum-business-and-human-rights. (Accessed as of 29 November 2024).

577 For further details, see UN Doc., A/HRC/43/54. It can be accessed at the following webpage: https://documents.un.org/doc/undoc/gen/g20/018/23/pdf/g2001823.pdf. (Accessed as of 29 November 2024).

which has had impacts on the protection of the right to privacy.[578] The Special Rapporteur on toxics and human rights has examined hundreds of cases of alleged human rights abuses by businesses and the extraterritorial obligations of States and responsibilities of transnational corporations in relation to adverse effects suffered from exposure to hazardous substances because of business activities.[579] The Special Rapporteur on the rights of Indigenous Peoples has addressed the drastic increase in attacks and acts of violence against, criminalization of and threats targeted at Indigenous Peoples, in particular those arising in the context of large-scale projects involving extractive industries, agribusiness, infrastructure, hydroelectric dams and logging.[580]

In spite of the above efforts by special procedures to clarify what should be done to meet the *State obligations* to respect, protect and fulfil human rights in relation to business activities, as well as the *Corporate responsibility* to respect human rights, there is a further need to incorporate and implement such *State obligations* and the *Corporate responsibility* to respect human rights at the national level.

It is also submitted that the works of special procedures mandate holders have contributed to providing a further clarification and understanding of how business activities can impact on the whole spectrum of human rights, which will, in turn, assist States in operationalizing the UN Guiding Principles on Business and Human Rights at the national level. However, there is a still need for special procedures mandate holders

---

578 For further details, see UN Doc., A/HRC/43/52. It can be accessed at the following webpage: https://documents.un.org/doc/undoc/gen/g20/071/66/pdf/g2007166.pdf. (Accessed as of 29 November 2024).

579 For further details, see UN Doc., A/75/290. It can be accessed at the following webpage: https://documents.un.org/doc/undoc/gen/n20/205/17/pdf/n2020517.pdf. (Accessed as of 29 November 2024).

580 For further details, see UN Doc., A/HRC/39/17. It can be accessed at the following webpage: https://documents.un.org/doc/undoc/gen/g18/246/34/pdf/g1824634.pdf. (Accessed as of 29 November 2024).

to provide further clear guidance on what '*must*' and '*should*' be done as part of meeting the *State obligations* to respect, protect and fulfil human rights in relation to business activities, as well as on what should be done by business enterprises' meeting the *Corporate responsibility* to respect human rights, in particular clarifying the essential steps to be taken for the purpose of conducting human rights due diligence in their own operations and in the supply chain, which constitutes the core element of the *Corporate responsibility* to respect human rights.

D. The Universal Periodic Review

The Universal Periodic Review (hereinafter referred to as the UPR) forms a part of international human rights protection mechanisms, which conducts peer reviews of the human rights situations of all 193 UN Member States every four and a half years in the framework of the UN Human Rights Council. The UPR was established as a novel mechanism, when the then UN Commission on Human Rights was transformed into the UN Human Rights Council in 2006 through General Assembly resolution.[581]

The bases of the UPR comprise three documents. Firstly, the State that will go through the review (State under review) will submit the national report, in which the State under review articulates its national human rights protection and promotion frameworks, as well as any achievements and challenges faced regarding human rights protection and promotion in the country. Secondly, the Office of the United Nations High Commissioner for Human Rights (OHCHR) is tasked to prepare a compilation report based on Concluding Observations and recommendations of UN Treaty Bodies, special procedures, and public official information of UN entities, relevant

581 UN Doc., A/RES/60/251. It can be accessed at the following webpage: https://documents.un.org/doc/undoc/gen/n05/502/66/pdf/n0550266.pdf. (Accessed as of 29 November 2024).

to the human rights situation of the State under review. Thirdly, OHCHR prepares a summary of inputs from stakeholders submitted for the specific UPR of the State under review. The UPR has thus far completed the three cycles of reviews of all UN Member States with a 100 per cent participation rate and the 4th cycle review started in November 2022 has just passed its half-way point.

The issue of business and human rights *per se* has not been focused in the first cycle UPR review. However, along with the endorsement of the UN Guiding Principles on Business and Human Rights in 2011, the issue of business and human rights has been increasingly addressed in the framework of the UPR, in particular starting from the second cycle review. As such, the issues related to business and human rights have been reflected in all three UPR documents and the number of recommendations related to business and human rights has noticeably increased since the third cycle review.[582]

The recommendations related to business and human rights of the second cycle UPR are mostly of a general nature recommending the States under review to adopt national action plan on business and human rights. The third cycle UPR witnessed that the recommendations related to business and human rights had increasingly become more specific and complex in substance, for instance, by recommending that the concerned State under review address business and human rights-related issues coupled with the issue of climate change and human rights and/or the issue of human rights and the environment. Furthermore, these recommendations tend to go beyond the adoption of a national action plan on business and human rights making substantively specific recommendations, for instance, recommending

582 For instance, during the course of the 3rd cycle reviews, a total of 39,217 UPR recommendations were made, 251 – as compared to 25 during the 1st cycle and 77 during the 2nd cycle – out of which were related to business and human rights, including those making references to the UN Guiding Principles on Business and Human Rights. Detailed information can be accessed at the following webpage: https://uhri.ohchr.org/en/search-human-rights-recommendations. (Accessed as of 29 November 2024).

enacting mandatory human rights due diligence law and regulating the activities of business activities extraterritorially as part of exercising their *State obligations* to protect from corporate human rights abuse.[583]

E. Interim Conclusions

The Working Group on Business and Human Rights was established with the principal aim of assisting States in operationalizing at the country level the UN Guiding Principles on Business and Human Rights. As such, the Human Rights Council has given concrete mandates to the Working Group on Business and Human Rights, first and foremost to: disseminate and raise the awareness of the UN Guiding Principles on Business and Human Rights, as well as to clarify and provide further guidance on the content of the UN Guiding Principles on Business and Human Rights.

The Working Group on Business and Human Rights has made a considerably high-level of progress in fulfilling the mandates given to it by the UN Human Rights Council. Of the most notable are: 1) the publication of the Guidance on how to prepare the National Action Plan on Business and Human Rights; 2) the clarification of what it means by corporate human rights due diligence; 3) the further clarification of the *State duty* to protect from corporate human rights abuse; 4) the ongoing provision of further guidance on access to remedy against corporate human rights abuse; and the development of further guidance on how to incorporate a gender perspective in relation to business and human rights issues. As such, the Working Group on Business and Human Rights has focused on providing guidance aimed at mostly helping States operationalize the *State duty* to protect pillar contained

583 As a prominent example, please refer to the recommendations given to China during its 3rd cycle UPR (Recommendations Nos. 28.130-28.133). It can be accessed at the following webpage: https://documents.un.org/doc/undoc/gen/g18/446/59/pdf/g1844659.pdf. (Accessed as of 29 November 2024).

in the UN Guiding Principles on Business and Human Rights. However, the Working Group on Business and Human rights needs to provide further clarity and guidance on how to operationalize the *Corporate responsibility* to respect and access to remedy Pillars of the UN Guiding Principles on Business and Human Rights, in particular clearly identifying what should be done by business enterprises when it comes to conducting human rights due diligence in their own operations and in their supply chains.

The Working Group on Business and Human Rights did not have the initial mandate of processing individual communications on corporate human rights abuses, despite the fact that it was part of the UN special procedures when first established in 2011. In 2015, when the mandate of the Working Group on Business and Human Rights was renewed, the Working Group on Business and Human Rights was given the mandate to address individual cases of business-related human rights abuses. This component of the mandate of the Working Group on Business and Human Rights is significant in the sense that it not only promotes the dissemination and operationalization of the UN Guiding Principles on Business and Human Rights, but also monitors corporate human rights abuses, which can contribute to facilitating provision of remedy for corporate human rights abuse victims. It is, however, submitted that the initial omission of such a mandate to process individual corporate human rights abuse cases has led the Working Group on Business and Human Rights to focusing more on the promotional aspect of its mandate. It should be noted, in this regard, that another important monitoring tool that the Working Group on Business and Human Rights can use, i.e., public condemnation on violations of human rights obligations by States in relation to business activities and corporate human rights abuses has been relatively under-utilized, as compared to other special procedures mandate holders, despite the recent increase of use of such public statements. It is therefore submitted that in order to more effectively fulfil its mandate, the Working Group on Business and Human Rights should strike a balance between its promotional and monitoring work.

The UN Annual Forum on Business and Human Rights guided by the Working Group on Business and Human Rights has also achieved an impressive level of visibility in the corporate sector, which must be acknowledged as one of the most significant contributions made thus far. As such, the Annual Forum on Business and Human Rights has successfully been serving as an important multi-stakeholder forum on business and human rights, whose main aim is to better operationalize the UN Guiding Principles on Business and Human Rights and share emerging promising practices on its implementation at the national and regional levels.

In this regard, it is submitted that resources should be strengthened within OHCHR, which will, in turn, allow the Working Group on Business and Human Rights to provide adequate guidance and advice on specific areas of critical importance, including individualized and tailored advice on such issues as corporate human rights due diligence, including how to effectively conduct human rights impact assessments, integrate findings of such human rights impact assessments into business operations, as well as report externally on company actions thereon.

United Nations special procedures mandate holders have been addressing the interlinkages between their respective thematic mandates and business and human rights-related issues, in particular since the endorsement of the UN Guiding Principles on Business and Human Rights by the Human Rights Council in 2011. It is submitted that this important body of work by special procedures mandate holders has provided a further clarification and understanding of how business activities can impact on the whole spectrum of human rights. As such, it will further assist States in meeting the *State obligations* to respect, protect and fulfil human rights in relation to business activities, as well as in operationalizing the UN Guiding Principles on Business and Human Rights at the national and regional levels. However, there is a still strong need for special procedures mandate holders to provide clear guidance on what *'must'* and *'should'* be done as part of meeting the *State obligations* to respect, protect and fulfil human rights in relation to business activities, as well as on what '*should*' be done by business enterprises to meet the *Corporate responsibility* to respect human rights, in particular clarifying the essential steps to be taken for the purpose of conducting human rights due diligence in their own operations and in the supply chain, which constitutes the core element of the *Corporate responsibility* to respect human rights. In this connection, it is critically important for special procedures mandate holders not to confuse measures to be taken and policy options/recommendations that can be taken by States as part of meeting the *State obligations* to respect, protect and fulfil human rights as well as of business enterprises' meeting the *Corporate responsibility* to respect human rights.

The universal periodic review of the Human Rights Council has also increasingly been addressing issues related to business and human rights. An increase in the number and substantive depth of business and human rights-related UPR recommendations, in particular since the third cycle review, is a welcome development. It is critically important that States implement these business and human rights-related UPR recommendations at the country level in full alignment of the UN Guiding Principles on Business and Human Rights.

Part 5

Strengthening National Human Rights Protection Mechanisms

Chapter 8: Strengthening the State Obligation to Protect from Corporate Human Rights Abuse and the Corporate Responsibility to Respect Human Rights

To prevent, identify, and redress corporate human rights abuse lies at the heart of the *State obligation* to protect from corporate human rights abuse. Towards this end, it is essential that States strengthen relevant national human rights protection frameworks aimed at addressing the negative impacts of business activities on the enjoyment of the whole spectrum of human rights.

The *State duty* to protect from corporate human rights abuse requires that States must take an array of legislative, administrative, policy, judicial and other measures necessary to ensure that third parties, including business enterprises under their territories and/or under their effective jurisdictions, do not violate human rights of others.

The *Corporate responsibility* to respect human rights is premised on the fact that as an organ of society that performs specialized functions should respect human rights that can be impacted by business activities. The core of the *Corporate responsibility* to respect human rights is for business enterprises to conduct human rights due diligence in their own operations and in the supply chain to avoid causing or contributing to adverse human rights impacts through their own activities and address such impacts when they occur, as well as to seek to prevent or mitigate adverse human rights impacts directly linked to their operations, products or services by their business relationships, even if they have not contributed to those impacts.[584]

This chapter seeks to explore various measures that States, as the primary duty-bearers, must take for the purposes of preventing, identifying and remedying corporate human rights harms. It focuses on emerging State practices in terms of legislative action designed to incorporate the UN Guiding Principles on Business and Human Rights in the domestic legal framework, in particular through the enactment of a law that mandates business enterprises to conduct human rights due diligence in their own operations and in the supply chain (mandatory human rights due diligence law). An examination of mandatory human rights due diligence law is inextricably linked to the *Corporate responsibility* to respect human rights, which enables such *Corporate responsibility* to respect human rights as an obligation to respect human rights on the domestic law plane. It also seeks to examine policy and judicial measures that States must and/or should take with a view to protecting rights-holders from corporate human rights abuse. It also highlights the importance of business enterprises' having in place company internal mechanisms that will facilitate corporate human rights abuse victims' being remedied against corporate human rights abuses.

584 See supra note 354, Principle 13.

A. Legislative Measures

I. Human Rights Due Diligence Law

States have put in place numerous legal frameworks aimed at preventing, identifying, mitigating and redressing against corporate human rights abuse. These legal frameworks have traditionally been framed not necessarily as human rights protection legal frameworks but rather as sectoral laws and regulations that have the specific aim of regulating certain categories of business activity that could bring about the negative impacts on the safety and well-being of individuals and/or on society, including the potential adverse impacts on the environment. The most fundamental legal framework at the domestic level is corporate law, through which the activities of commercial legal entities are regulated. There also exist a range of specific laws and regulations that address the actual and potential negative impacts of business activities on the enjoyment of human rights, including environmental protection law, data-protection law, anti-corruption law, anti-bribery law, consumer protection law, etc. Such laws and regulations are crucial to addressing the actual and potential negative impacts, which affect the whole spectrum of human rights, including civil, cultural, economic, political and social rights, as well as the right to enjoy a safe, clean, healthy and sustainable environment.[585]

With the unanimous endorsement of the UN Guiding Principles on Business and Human Rights by the UN Human Rights Council in 2011, States have embarked on efforts to integrate the UN Guiding Principles on Business and Human Rights into their own domestic legal and policy

585 During its 48th session, the United Nations Human Rights Council has adopted an historic resolution that explicitly recognizes the human right to a clean, healthy and sustainable environment. '*Resolution adopted by the Human Rights Council on 8 October 2021 (48/13): The human right to a clean, healthy and sustainable environment.*' UN Doc, A/HRC/RES/48/13. It can be accessed at the following webpage: https://documents.un.org/doc/undoc/gen/g21/289/50/pdf/g2128950.pdf. (Accessed as of 4 December 2024).

frameworks. To fulfil the *State duty* to protect from corporate human rights abuse, which constitutes a core pillar of the UN Guiding Principles on Business and Human Rights, an increasing number of States have adopted law that incorporates the responsibility of business enterprises to respect human rights as a legal obligation at least on the domestic law plane.

The core elements of the *Corporate responsibility* to respect human rights under the UN Guiding Principles on Business and Human Rights encompass the responsibilities of business enterprises to: set clearly a commitment at the highest level of management to respecting human rights; carry out human rights due diligence that includes conducting human rights impact assessments, incorporating results of such human rights impact assessments in operations, and tracking its implementation; as well as communicating the actions taken aimed at increasing the corporate respect of human rights both internally and externally; and remedying corporate human rights harms.[586]

Based on the standards set out in the UN Guiding Principles on Business and Human Rights (the *State duty* to protect from corporate human rights abuse; the *Corporate responsibility* to respect human rights; and provision of effective remedies against corporate human rights abuse), States have been focusing their efforts on enacting law that requires business enterprises to conduct mandatory human rights (and/or environmental) due diligence where there exist significant risks that business activities can cause adverse human rights impacts. This increasing importance of conducting human rights due diligence has been highlighted by the former UN Special Representative of the Secretary-General on the issue of business and human rights, the very author of the UN Guiding Principles on Business and Human Rights, who described the emerging practice of companies' conducting human rights due diligence in the supply chain as "*the new normal of human rights due*

586 Refer to supra Chapter 5. C.

diligence."[587] Increasing momentum has thus gathered to press Governments to adopt laws that require companies to conduct mandatory human rights due diligence.[588]

Human rights due diligence is defined as "*the process through which enterprises can identify, prevent, mitigate and account for how they address their actual and potential adverse impacts.*"[589] Although environmental due diligence has not been explicitly referenced in the UN Guiding Principles on Business and Human Rights, human rights due diligence is interpreted to encompass environmental aspects of companies' actual and potential adverse impacts on the entire spectrum of internationally recognized human rights, including the rights to health, water, food, as well as the rights of Indigenous Peoples.[590]

---

587 John Ruggie, 'The New Normal of Human Rights Due Diligence,' Op-Ed in Swiss Newspaper *HANDELSZEITUNG* of 22 March 2018. The English translation of the op-ed can be accessed at the following website: https://shiftproject.org/john-ruggie-weighs-in-on-swiss-debate-on-mandatory-human-rights-due-diligence/ (Accessed as of 4 December 2024).

588 One of the recent campaigns for legislating such mandatory human rights due diligence has come from 110 Catholic Bishops who have called for the legislation that should "*introduce mandatory environmental and human rights due diligence, that is, to identify, assess, stop, prevent and mitigate the risks and violations to the environment and all human rights throughout the supply chains of businesses and to substantially improve the possibilities of affected people to claim for compensation in national civil courts". 'Now more than ever, we need mandatory supply chain due diligence: to stop corporate abuse and guarantee global solidarity*' (06 July 2020), CIDSE. In the context of the COVID-19 pandemic crisis, the statement by the participating 110 Catholic Bishops emphasized the urgency of introducing such mandatory human rights due diligence, in particular in the supply chains of multinational corporations through legislative act. See the statement at the following website: https://www.cidse.org/wp-content/uploads/2020/07/EN-Bishop-Statement-HRDD-6-July-2020-1.pdf (Accessed as at 4 December 2024).

589 Supra note 354, Principle 17. See also Nicolas Bueno, '*The Swiss Popular Initiative on Responsible Business: From Responsibility to Liability*', which can be accessed as at the following webpage: https://papers.ssrn.com/sol3/papers.cfm?abstract_id=3125672. (Accessed as of 4 December 2024).

590 Nicolas Bueno, 'The Swiss Popular Initiative on Responsible Business: From Responsibility to Liability', which can be accessed at the following webpage: https://papers.ssrn.com/sol3/papers.cfm?abstract_id=3125672. (Accessed as of 4 December 2024). For further comments, See also Mirina Grosz, 'Menschenrechte als Vehikel für ökologische Unternehmensverantwortung' [2017] Pratique Juridique Actuelle 982. On the other hand, Chapter VII of the OECD Guidelines for Multinational Enterprises defines the conduct that multinational enterprises

II. Mandatory Human Rights Due Diligence Law: Emerging Examples

France adopted the *Duty of Vigilance* Law[591] in 2017, which has been incorporated by way of amending the existing Commercial Code (*code de commerce*). This law obligates certain business enterprises to be vigilant (a duty of vigilance) in order to prevent human rights and environmental harm to be caused by their subsidiaries and through their business relationships.[592] Specifically, the law requires those applicable companies "*to develop and implement a vigilance plan and account for how they identify, prevent and address human rights impacts in their global operations*."[593]

When it comes to the drawing-up of the required vigilance plan, the law provides for the five elements that need to be included therein: 1) a risks-mapping aimed at identifying, analyzing and prioritizing those risks; 2) regular evaluation procedures regarding the situation of subsidiaries, sub-contractors and suppliers; 3) actions needed to mitigate risks and to prevent serious harms; 4) an alert and complaint mechanism to be drawn up through a multi-stakeholders process; and 5) a monitoring scheme for implementation and evaluation of their effectiveness. The law specifies that this is not the

---

should adopt to take due account of the need to protect the environment.

591 LOI n° 2017-399 du 27 mars 2017 relative au devoir de vigilance des sociétés mères et des entreprises donneuses d'ordre (Law No. 2017-399 of 27 March 2017). It can be accessed at the following French official bulletin webpage: https://www.legifrance.gouv.fr/jorf/id/JORFTEXT000034290626/. (Accessed as of 4 December 2024). The unofficial English translated text of the law can be found on the following webpage: https://www.business-humanrights.org/en/latest-news/french-duty-of-vigilance-law-english-translation/. (Accessed as of 4 December 2024).

592 The law applies only to companies, including in their subsidiaries that have 5,000 employees in France or 10,000 employees overseas. See: https://vigilance-plan.org/mcdonalds-france-yves-rocher-nestle-france-france-televisions-primark-france-27-of-companies-would-have-failed-to-comply-with-the-french-law-on-the-duty-of-vigilance/ (Accessed as of 4 December 2024).

593 'Report of the Working Group on the issue of human rights and transnational corporations and other business enterprises to the United Nations General Assembly,' UN Doc., A/73/163, para. 67. It can be accessed at the following webpage: https://documents.un.org/doc/undoc/gen/n18/224/87/pdf/n1822487.pdf. (Accessed as of 4 December 2024). Article 1 of the French Duty of Vigilance Law.

exhaustive list of the elements that must be included as it provides that through a decree, the *State Council* may expand the above vigilance measures. The *State Council* may also further elaborate upon the methods for drawing up and implementing the vigilance plan, "*where appropriate in the context of multi-stakeholder initiatives within sectors or at territorial level*."[594]

The law further provides that the *State Council* issues a formal notice to the companies to prepare the required vigilance plans in accordance with the law. In the case of the failures by the companies to comply within three months from the issuance of the formal notice, the competent court may order the companies, including under a periodic penalty system, to comply with the requirements of drawing up the vigilance plans in accordance with the above required elements, provided that there is a request by any person with standing.[595]

Moreover, the law establishes the liability of the offender requiring it to compensate any damage that would have been prevented, if the offender had performed the duties required under the law. A torts claim can be brought before the competent court by any person with standing. The law further provides for the possibility of the court to order the publication, dissemination or display of its decision or an extract thereof, according to the court's specified terms. The court may further order the execution of its decision under a periodic penalty payment.[596]

The French Duty of Vigilance Law assumes a pioneering position in that it is the first comprehensive national law that specifically mandates companies to conduct human rights due diligence to prevent, identify and address human rights risks. It is worth noting that the law mandates companies to prepare the vigilance plan. The drafter of the law seems to

---

594 Supra note 591, Article 1 (I) of the French Duty of Vigilance Law.

595 Ibid., Article 1 (II) of the French Duty of Vigilance Law.

596 Ibid., Article 2 of the French Duty of Vigilance Law.

have paid close attention to the importance of effective enforcement of the law as a periodic penalty system has been embedded in the law both as a means to compel the companies to comply with the requirements of drawing up the vigilance plan,[597] as well as to ensure that corporate human rights abuse victims have access to remedies through them having the possibility of pursuing civil liability of companies that have violated the duty of vigilance thereby causing corporate human rights harms.[598]

Despite its pioneering position, the implementation of the law has been called into question. For instance, an official list of companies that would come under the purview of the law has yet to be published by the French Government.[599] In the absence of such an official list, French civil society organizations have prepared their own list of the companies that would be subject to the law with a view to monitoring their observance of the law. These civil society organizations have monitored 265 companies that would fall under the purview of the law. Recently, they have examined whether these companies have prepared the vigilance plan in compliance with the law. It was found that 72 companies out of their own listed 265 companies (around 27 per cent) were without a plan of vigilance.[600]

At the same time, an official working in the French Ministry for Europe and Foreign Affairs has drawn a lesson with regard to the enactment and implementation of the Duty of Vigilance Law, in which it was highlighted that "*An obligation can be more effective than incentives or voluntary measures, particularly with regard to companies that have not integrated*

---

597 Ibid., Article 1 (II) of the French Duty of Vigilance Law.

598 Ibid., Article 2 of the French Duty of Vigilance Law.

599 See: https://vigilance-plan.org/mcdonalds-france-yves-rocher-nestle-france-france-televisions-primark-france-27-of-companies-would-have-failed-to-comply-with-the-french-law-on-the-duty-of-vigilance/. (Accessed as of 4 December 2024).

600 '*Le radar du devoir de vigilance: Identifier les entreprises submises à la loi, 2020 edition*', Terre-Solidaire and Sherpa. It can be accessed at: https://plan-vigilance.org/wp-content/uploads/2020/06/2020-06-25-Radar-DDV-Edition-2020.pdf. (Accessed as of 4 December 2020).

responsible business conduct into the heart of their strategy as there is greater reputational and legal risk, even though the threat of a legal sanction remains potential. Such an obligation also reinforces companies already engaged in a business and human rights approach and leads them to promote and strengthen their business and human rights strategy. It also encourages them to participate in collective initiatives".[601]

The Netherlands has taken a slightly different approach as compared to France.[602] Instead of adopting general human rights due diligence legislation that would apply to companies in general as far as they do meet the threshold of application, it passed the law that required conducting human rights due diligence tailored to protect the rights of children. As such, the Dutch Parliament passed the Dutch Child Labour Duty of Care Act into law on 14 May 2019.[603] It is worth noting that as part of fulfilling an obligation to conduct mandatory human rights due diligence, companies based in the Netherlands should act in accordance with the ILO Guidance Tool for Business.[604] The law also provides for administrative and criminal fines for those companies that do not submit a declaration that they have conducted human rights due diligence, or that they fail to conduct human rights due

601 Odile Roussel, 'Paving the Way: The Pioneering role of the French Duty of Vigilance Law and the Relevance for EU-Level Mandatory Due Diligence'. It can be accessed at the following webpage: https://www.business-humanrights.org/en/blog/paving-the-way-the-pioneering-role-of-the-french-duty-of-vigilance-law-and-its-relevance-for-eu-level-mandatory-due-diligence/. (Accessed at 4 December 2024).

602 For a comparative analysis of the French and Dutch Laws, see the following article, 'Call for EU Human Rights Due Diligence Legislation: What Can Be Learnt from France and the Netherlands?', Blog of Dr. Ekaterina Aristova, https://www.business-humanrights.org/en/call-for-eu-human-rights-due-diligence-legislation-what-can-be-learnt-from-france-and-the-netherlands (Accessed as at 4 December 2024).

603 The original Dutch text of the law can be accessed at the following webpage: https://www.eerstekamer.nl/behandeling/20170207/gewijzigd_voorstel_van_wet/document3/f=/vkbkk8pud2zt.pdf . (Accessed as of 4 December 2024). The unofficial English translated text of the law can be found at the following webpage: https://www.ropesgray.com/-/media/files/alerts/2019/06/20190605_csr_alert_appendix/20190605_csr_alert_appendix.pdf?rev=c5d7ad3e13a741ab855eb30bc40e998b&hash=3A7ED519E9820C5B7E7617D8F16905CD. (Accessed as of 4 December 2024).

604 Ibid., Article 5(3) of the Dutch Child Labour Duty of Care Act.

diligence when required.[605]

Increasing momentum for establishing a general mandatory human rights due diligence legislative framework has been built up in the Netherlands. The Netherlands business community, business associations and political parties have openly requested the Dutch Government to come up with such a general mandatory human rights due diligence law in order to put an end to corporate human rights abuse and environmental harm.[606] In this regard, it should be noted that in compliance with the obligation of national transposition of the European Union Corporate Sustainability Due Diligence Directive (CSDDD),[607] which came into effect on 25 July 2024 within 2 years (namely by 26 July 2026), the Netherlands must establish a national legislative framework to obligate companies to conduct mandatory human rights due diligence in their operations and in their supply chains.

Switzerland has also attempted to elaborate on a legislative proposal on mandatory human rights due diligence and reform corporate liability. Swiss civil society organizations had launched "*the Responsible Business Initiative*"[608] with the stated aim of imposing legal obligations to incorporate respect for human rights and the environment on Swiss multi-national companies. The *Responsible Business Initiative* aimed to impose mandatory human rights due diligence on Swiss-based companies' activities abroad with civil liability for human rights violations. The Swiss Parliament made

---

605 Ibid., Articles 4 and 7 of the Dutch Child Labour Duty of Care Act.

606 See https://www.business-humanrights.org/en/netherlands-momentum-builds-towards-mandatory-due-diligence-regulation#c211314 (Accessed as of 4 December 2024).

607 'Directive (EU) 2024/1760 of the European Parliament and of the Council of 13 June 2024 on corporate sustainability due diligence and amending Directive (EU) 2019/1937 and Regulation (EU) 2023/2859 (Text with EEA relevance).' It can be accessed at the following EU's Official Journal webpage: https://eur-lex.europa.eu/eli/dir/2024/1760/oj. (Accessed as of 4 December 2024).

608 For the details on the "the Responsible Business Initiative," see the following webpage: https://konzernverantwortung.ch/wp-content/uploads/2022/02/kvi_factsheet_initiativtext_fr.pdf (Accessed as of 20 December 2024).

a counterproposal in 2018 to this civil society *Initiative*, which did not envisage due diligence except for child labour cases and trading of conflict minerals. Instead, the counter-proposal envisaged merely a public non-financial reporting.[609] The Swiss Federal Council had scheduled a popular vote on *the Responsible Business Initiative*, which was held on 29 November 2020.[610] The *Responsible Business Initiative* was rejected because it failed to achieve the majority vote of Swiss Cantons even though it managed to gain the majority of popular vote. Accordingly, the counter-proposal by the Swiss Parliament came into effect on 1 January 2022.[611] Civil society has continued with its campaign for legislating a mandatory human rights due diligence law, highlighting the fact that Switzerland will remain the only country with no mandatory human rights due diligence law with the adoption by the European Union in July 2024 of the Corporate Sustainability Due Diligence Directive (CSDDD).[612]

The proposal aimed at amending the Swiss Constitution (which would have been introduced as Article 101a of the Constitution, if successful) set out the general obligation of the Government to "*strengthen respect for human rights and the environment through business*." The proposal contained further two important substantive elements, when it came to mandatory human rights due diligence. The first element was to require Switzerland-based companies to

609 For a comparison between the Responsible Business Initiative and the counter-proposal by the Swiss Parliament, see the following webpage: https://www.pwc.ch/en/insights/sustainability/responsible-business-initiative-vs-counterproposal.html. (Accessed as of 20 December 2024).

610 The vote did not pass as it had reached the only majority of votes not the majority of cantons. For the details on the vote results, see the following webpage: https://www.bk.admin.ch/ch/d/pore/va/20201129/can636.html. (Accessed as of 20 December 2024).

611 The counter-proposal has been incorporated into Article 964, in particular 964(a) and 964(j)-(k) of the Swiss Code of Obligations. It can be accessed at the following webpage: https://www.fedlex.admin.ch/eli/cc/27/317_321_377/en#part_4/tit_32/chap_8/lvl_C. For a brief explanation on the counter-proposal, see the following webpage: https://www.bdo.ch/en-gb/insights/indirect-counter-proposal-to-the-responsible-business-initiative. (Accessed as of 20 December 2024).

612 For the continuing campaign, see the following webpage: https://responsabilite-multinationales.ch/notre-objectif/. (Accessed as of 20 December 2024).

conduct human rights and environmental due diligence both in Switzerland and abroad. The second element was to provide for the liability of the harm caused by companies under their control unless they could prove that they had taken due care to avoid such harm.[613] Moreover, the novel feature of this proposal was to contain an explicit provision in relation to the applicable laws. It provided that "*the provisions based on the principles of paragraphs a-c apply irrespective of the law applicable under private international law*".[614] According to a legal scholar, "*the introduction of a mandatory due diligence provision objectifies the expected conduct that Switzerland-based companies must apply with a view to preventing adverse human rights and environmental impacts in Switzerland and abroad.*"[615]

The German trajectory of developing a mandatory human rights due diligence law has been unique in the sense that a political party (the Green Party) has kick-started it. Civil society, including scholars and NGOs, has added further pressure to the German Government to enact a mandatory human rights due diligence law, which culminated in a campaign by a coalition of 64 civil society organizations calling for a supply chain law.[616]

On the part of the German Government, it responded to such calls for a mandatory human rights due diligence law, first by explicitly stating that

---

613 For a detailed scholarly explanation on the Initiative, See supra note 268, Nicolas Bueno, '*The Swiss Popular Initiative on Responsible Business: From Responsibility to Liability*', which can be accessed as at the following webpage: https://papers.ssrn.com/sol3/papers.cfm?abstract_id=3125672. (Accessed as of 20 December 2024). It has a comparative examination between other national laws, in particular the French Duty of Vigilance Law and the Swiss Responsible Business Initiative by showing the differences and similarities between the two legal texts. See, Chapter IV (C).

614 For the actual text of the proposal and its explanation, see 'The Initiative Text with Explanations' at the following webpage: https://konzernverantwortung.ch/wp-content/uploads/2022/02/kvi_factsheet_initiativtext_fr.pdf. (Accessed as of 20 December 2024).

615 Supra note 590, Nicolas Bueno, '*The Swiss Popular Initiative on Responsible Business: From Responsibility to Liability*,' pp. 13-14. It can be accessed as at the following webpage: https://papers.ssrn.com/sol3/papers.cfm?abstract_id=3125672. (Accessed as of 20 December 2024).

616 For the details, see https://www.business-humanrights.org/en/latest-news/german-due-diligence-law/. (Accessed as of 21 December 2024).

it would consider introducing such a human rights due diligence legislation if by 2020 less than 50 per cent of German companies with over 500 employees have human rights due diligence processes in place when it adopted the National Action Plan on Business and Human Rights. In February 2019, the German Federal Ministry for Economic Cooperation and Development (BMZ) prepared a draft legal proposal, which included an element on human rights due diligence for German companies. The Development Ministry's proposal contained a number of strong elements and had a comprehensive approach to the human rights responsibilities of German companies' foreign subsidiaries and contractors, including the scope of application (companies with more than 250 employees and 40 million Euros in annual turnover).

German civil society organizations, including *Germanwatch, Südwind, CorA and Venro* welcomed the proposed draft law and expressed their support for it, while cautioning against focusing such a law on labour rights abuses alone. They also questioned the draft law, in particular in connection with the issue as to whether and how foreign workers would get better access to justice in German courts. At the same time, they strongly emphasized the importance of not losing the opportunity to back the initiative, due to opposition from other ministries.[617]

Various German companies were supportive of such a law. Experiencing a textile disaster in Pakistan, KiK Suppliers, for example, was among those who had previously spoken out in favour of obligating mandatory human rights due diligence in the supply chain. According to Kik

617 For the details, see https://www.business-humanrights.org/en/will-germany-become-a-leader-in-the-drive-for-corporate-due-diligence-on-human-rights?utm_source=Business+%26+Human+Rights+Resource+Centre+Updates&utm_campaign=199fcfe071-EMAIL_CAMPAIGN_2019_02_18_06_20&utm_medium=email&utm_term=0_c0049647eb-199fcfe071-182077453&mc_cid=199fcfe071&mc_eid=1de65b4c6f. (Accessed as of 21 December 2024). See also https://www.business-humanrights.org/en/german-development-ministry-drafts-law-on-mandatory-human-rights-due-diligence-for-german-companies (Accessed as of 21 December 2024).

Suppliers, regulation would provide legal certainty and level the playing field from a business perspective. It, hence, encouraged all responsible companies to welcome such an approach in principle.

The Development Ministry's proposal should be seen in a broader context, in which several initiatives were calling for regulatory shifts towards mandatory corporate human rights due diligence in Europe. Subsequently in December 2019, the Minister of BMZ and the Federal Minister for Labour and Social Affairs (BMAS) announced that they would draft a human rights due diligence law.[618]

On 10 March 2020, the German Ministries of BMZ and BMAS published the key points of the draft law, entitled "*A Federal Law on Strengthening Corporate Due Diligence To Prevent Human Rights Violations In Global Value Chains (Due Diligence Act)*". The law was intended to obligate companies based in Germany with more than 500 employees to meet their responsibilities in the value chain, which explicitly pointed out that the corporate due diligence obligations in the draft law would be based on the requirements of the UN Guiding Principles on Business and Human Rights and the OECD Guidelines for MNEs. In this regard, it should be noted that the scope of application of the eventually adopted Act on Corporate Due Diligence in Supply Chains (*Lieferkettensorgfaltspflichtengesetz*)[619] has slightly been changed from the draft law.[620] As of 01 January 2023, the law has been applied to companies that have central administration, headquarters and

---

618 Ibid.

619 The law can be found at the following webpage of *Bundesgesetzblatt*: https://www.bgbl.de/xaver/bgbl/start.xav?startbk=Bundesanzeiger_BGBl&jumpTo=bgbl121s2959.pdf#__bgbl__%2F%2F*%5B%40attr_id%3D%27bgbl121s2959.pdf%27%5D__1734783832310. For more details of *Lieferkettensorgfaltspflichtengesetz*, see also the following webpage: https://www.bmas.de/DE/Service/Gesetze-und-Gesetzesvorhaben/Gesetz-Unternehmerische-Sorgfaltspflichten-Lieferketten/gesetz-unternehmerische-sorgfaltspflichten-lieferketten.html. (Accessed as of 21 December 2024).

620 For the initial Government draft law, see the following webpage: https://dserver.bundestag.de/btd/19/286/1928649.pdf. (Accessed as of 21 December 2024).

registered office and more than 3,000 employees, including those seconded to a foreign country in Germany. It also applies to foreign companies that have a branch office and more than 3,000 employees in Germany. As of 01 January 2024, the law will apply to companies that have more than 1,000 employees in Germany. [621]

As enforcement measures, the draft law had initially included a civil liability provision: a company would be liable for damages that were foreseeable and avoidable when meeting the due diligence obligation. In principle, the burden of proof lied with the plaintiff. Hence, a company would not be liable if its action would be deemed appropriate within the parameters of factual and legal responsibilities (obligation of effort). On the other hand, the adopted law of 11 June 2021 contained an explicit proviso that a violation of obligations arising under the Act shall not give rise to additional civil liability.[622] It can be critiqued that the law did not fully comply with the UN Guiding Principles on Business and Human Rights as the exclusion of such a civil liability provision would hamper the realization of the right of corporate human rights abuse victims to have access to remedies. In this regard, it is worth noting that with the adoption of the EU CSDDD, which contained a civil liability provision therein, Germany is required to transpose the EU CSDDD into its national legislative framework. Accordingly, Germany may have the option of amending the existing *Lieferkettensorgfaltspflichtengesetz* or adopting a new law in full compliance with the EU CSDDD, including providing for civil liability for breaches of human rights due diligence requirement. This will eventually lead to the enhanced level of protection of the right of corporate human rights abuse victims to have access to remedies against corporate human rights abuses.

---

621 For a brief summary of *Lieferkettensorgfaltspflichtengesetz*, see 'The German Parliament passed the "Act on Corporate Due Diligence in Supply Chains" on 11 June 2021,' at the following White & Case webpage: https://www.whitecase.com/publications/alert/german-parliament-passed-act-corporate-due-diligence-supply-chains-11-june-2021. (Accessed as of 21 December 2024).

622 Ibid.

The draft law also contained administrative enforcement measures, including electronic reporting procedures and enquiry procedures on a case-by-case basis of suspected serious infringements, which might result in an appropriate fine. In addition, the draft law provided for in-house enforcement measures, according to which, the management shall be responsible for the operational implementation of the due diligence obligations through company internal regulations, including adopting measures such as the appointment of a human rights officer within the company.

Uniquely, the German draft law contained a safe harbour provision, which encouraged companies to join and implement an officially recognized industry standard. If companies followed these officially recognized industry standards, their civil liabilities would be limited to intentional non-compliance of the law and gross negligence. The company's compliance with the relevant industry standard must be externally audited. The adopted law of 11 June 2021 however did not maintain those explicit safe harbour provisions contained in the draft law. [623]

The draft law further contained a provision that companies issued a certain level of fine due to the violation of due diligence obligation must be excluded from public procurement processes. Towards this end, the competent authority would maintain a register for those companies that had been fined. Procuring government entities must access this register above a certain volume of contracts. The competent authority must also provide information to the procuring authorities.[624]

On 12 February 2021, the Government approved a legislative proposal.

---

623 Ibid.

624 For details, see https://www.rph1.rw.fau.de/files/2020/06/key-points-german-due-diligence-law.pdf. (Accessed as of 24 August 2020). For the summary of timelines for the development of the German human rights due diligence law, see https://www.business-humanrights.org/en/latest-news/germany-draft-key-points-of-a-mandatory-human-rights-due-diligence-law/ (Accessed as at 24 August 2020).

Consequently, on 03 March 2021, the Parliament's lower house (*Bundestag*) debated the final text and referred it to the Bundestag's Labour and Social Affairs Committee on 22 April 2021. The Parliament's upper house (*Bundesrat*) discussed the matter on 07 May 2021 and agreed not to raise any objections to the Government draft. The law was adopted with 412 votes in favour, 159 against, and 59 abstentions on 11 June 2021.[625]

It is worth noting that some commentators have argued that the adopted law on mandatory human rights due diligence in the supply chains fell short of the standards contained in the UN Guiding Principles on Business and Human Rights, as far as the due diligence obligations with respect to the business activities of indirect suppliers are concerned.[626] As noted above, the fact that there is no possibility of civil liability for a violation of the obligations arising under the law could be considered a weak point when it comes to ensuring access to remedy for corporate human rights abuse victims. Civil society organizations have also argued that the future German Government should improve the law to bring it in alignment of the UN Guiding Principles on Business and Human Rights. The weaknesses of the

---

625 For a comparative analysis of mandatory human right due diligence law, see the following website: National & regional movements for mandatory human rights & environmental due diligence in Europe – Business & Human Rights Resource Centre (business-humanrights.org). (Accessed as of 21 December 2024).

626 See: https://www.business-humanrights.org/en/will-germany-become-a-leader-in-the-drive-for-corporate-due-diligence-on-human-rights?utm_source=Business+%26+Human+Rights+Resource+Centre+Updates&utm_campaign=199fcfe071-EMAIL_CAMPAIGN_2019_02_18_06_20&utm_medium=email&utm_term=0_c0049647eb-199fcfe071-182077453&mc_cid=199fcfe071&mc_eid=1de65b4c6f (Accessed as at 21 December 2024). See also https://www.business-humanrights.org/en/german-development-ministry-drafts-law-on-mandatory-human-rights-due-diligence-for-german-companies (Accessed as of 21 December 2024). It was clarified that "*Although the supply chain generally encompasses all of a company's indirect suppliers, principal due diligence obligations, such as conducting risk analysis and implementing further risk management including preventive and remedial measures as well as public reporting, per se, apply only in relation to the company's own business and its direct suppliers. Only where the company has substantiated knowledge of a possible infringement of a protected legal position by, or in the business context of, any of its indirect suppliers, do the aforementioned due diligence obligations also apply towards indirect suppliers' business.*"

adopted law identified by civil society groups include: that the law falls short of the requirements of the UN Guiding Principles on Business and Human Rights, in particular in terms of the scope of due diligence obligation, and the participation of affected stakeholders in the due diligence process and remediation; the lack of civil liability clause in the adopted law that would hinder corporate human rights abuse victims to access remedy against corporate human rights harms; that there exist major gaps in the definition of the protected human rights under the adopted law, in particular those relating to protection of gender equality and Indigenous Peoples' rights; and the lack of general environmental due diligence obligation that takes into account biodiversity and climate change, among others.[627]

At the regional level, there has been significant progress when it comes to legislating mandatory human rights due diligence obligation for business enterprises, particularly at the European Union (hereinafter referred to as the EU). The history of such efforts to legislate human rights due diligence obligation within the EU traces back to 2016 when members of eight national parliaments expressed support for EU legislation imposing on companies the duty to respect human rights in their global operations.[628]

Calls for such EU-level legislation on mandatory human rights due diligence has intensified in 2019 when a coalition of 107 non-governmental and civil society organizations called for a EU mandatory human rights and environmental due diligence legislation, which should aim to "*establish a corporate duty to respect human rights and the environment and require companies and financial institutions to identify, prevent, mitigate and account*

---

627 Initiative Lieferkettengesetz.de, 'Not there yet, but finally at the start: What the new Supply Chain Act delivers – and what it doesn't': https://lieferkettengesetz.de/wp-content/uploads/2021/06/Initiative-Lieferkettengesetz_Analysis_What-the-new-supply-chain-act-delivers.pdf. (Accessed as of 21 December 2024).

628 See the following webpage: https://corporatejustice.org/news/members-of-8-european-parliaments-support-duty-of-care-legislation-for-eu-corporations/. (Accessed as of 21 December 2024).

for abuses and harm in their domestic and global operations, activities, products, services, supply chains and exports."[629]

In response to such increasing calls for legislating a mandatory human rights and environmental due diligence directive at the EU level, the EU Commissioner for Justice announced, on 29 April 2020, that the European Commission was committed to introducing a new mandatory human rights and environmental due diligence legislation in 2021. Civil society swiftly welcomed the announcement encouraging the Commissioner for Justice to follow through his pledge with a robust legislation. A non-governmental organization that had been actively participating in the campaign for establishing a mandatory human rights due diligence legislation at the EU level remarked that "*such legislation would help to ensure robust and sustainable supply chains and help companies address their environmental, social and governance issues related to the Covid-19 crisis.*"[630]

Members of the European Parliament (MEPs) have started working on a European Parliament's position on the shape of the proposed human rights due diligence law. On 23 February 2022, the European Commission published EU legislative proposal for a Corporate Sustainability Due Diligence draft directive. On 1 December 2022, the EU Council adopted its general position, following which more than 20 leading business and networks urged Members of the European Parliament to adopt a text that was closely aligned with the UN Guiding Principles on Business and Human Rights and

---

629 'A Call for EU human rights environmental due diligence legislation', 02 December 2019, the full text of which can be accessible at the following webpage: https://corporatejustice.org/wp-content/uploads/2021/04/final_cso_eu_due_diligence_statement_2.12.19.pdf. (Accessed as of 21 December 2024).

630 'Important step towards greater corporate accountability as European Commission commits to new EU rules to regulate supply chains', Global Witness' press release dated 29 April 2020. It can be accessed at the following webpage: https://www.globalwitness.org/en/press-releases/important-step-towards-greater-corporate-accountability-european-commission-commits-new-eu-rules-regulate-supply-chains/?utm_source=hootsuite&utm_medium=twitter_ (Accessed as of 21 December 2024).

the OECD Guidelines for MNEs in April 2023. The European Parliament Legal Committee adopted its position on the European Union Corporate Sustainability Due Diligence Directive (CSDDD), which was adopted by the Plenary in June 2023. Trilogue discussions on a final law within the three EU institutions ensued.[631] With a considerable number of twists and turns, EU Member States finally confirmed the CSDDD on 24 May 2024. The CSDDD was published in the EU's Official Journal[632] on 5 July 2024 and came into effect on 25 July 2024.[633]

In terms of the scope of the proposed EU law on mandatory human rights due diligence, commentators drew their attention to the issue of board oversight. They argued for making board oversight an explicit requirement in the proposed law on mandatory human rights due diligence, which would allow the courts to interpret as to whether board directors had fulfilled their fiduciary duty in relation to human rights due diligence. The former Special Representative of the Secretary General on Business and Human Rights also took a somewhat expansive interpretative approach to this issue by arguing that if mandatory human rights due diligence legislation was detailed in incorporating the elements set out in the UN Guiding Principles on Business and Human Rights, in particular regarding stakeholder engagement and communication, it could be interpreted that "*a board would be failing in its own fiduciary responsibility if it did not exercise sufficient oversight, as is true for any other legal obligation of the company.*"[634] It would constitute an ideal

---

631 For detailed timelines of the EU legislative proposal, see https://www.business-humanrights.org/en/latest-news/eu-commissioner-for-justice-commits-to-legislation-on-mandatory-due-diligence-for-companies/ (Accessed as of 21 December 2024).

632 https://eur-lex.europa.eu/eli/dir/2024/1760/oj. (Accessed as of 21 December 2024).

633 For further details, see the following webpage: https://www.business-humanrights.org/en/latest-news/eu-csddd-political-agreement/. (Accessed as of 21 December 2024).

634 John Ruggie, 'European Commission Initiative on Mandatory Human Rights Due Diligence and Directors' Duties.' It can be accessed at the following webpage: https://media.business-humanrights.org/media/documents/EU_mHRDD_paper_John_Ruggie.pdf. See also Business and Human Rights Resources Centre, 'Responsibility from the top down: Why human rights due diligence must be a mandated concern of corporate boards.' It can be accessed at the following webpage: https://www.business-humanrights.org/en/latest-news/john-ruggie-

situation if explicit board oversight were to be required in the EU proposed law on mandatory human rights due diligence, through which a more effective enforcement of human rights due diligence requirement could be ensured. In the absence of such an explicit requirement of board oversight in relation to mandatory human rights due diligence, an expansive interpretative method should be employed whereby the existing board directors' fiduciary duty under the corporate law can be interpreted to encompass board oversight in relation to conducting human rights due diligence in their own company operations, as well as within the supply chain.

In addition to the above concerns of the draft EU mandatory human rights due diligence law, the finally adopted EU CSDDD has some gaps when measured against the international *Combination/zebra* standards of the UN Guiding Principles on Business and Human Rights, which included the reduced scope of companies covered, and the limited recognition of a company's downstream business partners' impacts and impacts caused by financial activities. Despite these gaps, the EU CSDDD is considered to be the international due diligence law most closely aligned with the UN Guiding Principles on Business and Human Rights. The most important features of the CSDDD are also: the explicit recognition of civil liability for breaches of due diligence duty, which gives more weight to the right of corporate human rights abuse victims to access remedies; provision of mandatory multi-stakeholder engagement; a broader array of measures, including support to small and medium enterprises (SMEs) and adjustments to a company's own harmful purchasing practices; and the obligation of companies, including those in finance industry to develop and implement transition plans for climate change mitigation.[635]

---

raises-concerns-about-adding-company-directors-duties-in-eu-mandatory-human-rights-due-diligence-legislation/. (Accessed as of 21 December 2024).

635 For further details, see the following webpage: https://www.business-humanrights.org/en/latest-news/bhrrc-comments-on-final-csddd-adoption/. (Accessed as of 21 December 2024).

With the adoption of the EU CSDDD, EU Member States must transpose it into its own national legislative frameworks within 2 years from 25 July 2024 when it came into force. The national transposition process will present the opportunity for EU Member States to bridge the gaps of the EU CSDDD thus bringing their own mandatory human rights due diligence legislative framework even closer to the international *Combination/zebra* standards on business and human rights (the UN Guiding Principles on Business and Human Rights) than the EU CSDDD. At the same time, there is still a grave risk that some States within the EU lobbied by the business community may attempt to derail or undermine the application of the EU CSDDD as demonstrated by the recent French Government's push for the indefinite postponement of the CSDDD and weakening of key provisions.[636] In fact, these efforts to weaken the application of the EU CSDDD have indeed materialized: on 26 February 2025, the European Commission published the so-called "*Omnibus simplification package*" aimed at amending the EU CSDDD and the Corporate Sustainability Reporting Directive (CSRD).[637] Specifically, the new proposal postpones the transposition deadline and the application of the EU CSDDD by 1 year for the group of companies falling under the scope of Articles 2(1)(a)-(b) and 2(2)(a)-(b) of the EU CSDDD.[638]

---

636 For details, see the following webpage of a French NGO, Sherpa: Corporate Sustainability Due Diligence Directive : France advocates for indefinite postponement, to the detriment of social and environemental justice – Sherpa. (Accessed as of 10 February 2025).

637 The European Commission, '*Proposal for a Directive of the European Parliament and of the Council amending Directives (EU)2022/2464 and (EU) 2024/1760 as regards the dates from which Member States are to apply certain corporate sustainability reporting and due diligence requirements.*' It can be accessed at the following webpage: https://commission.europa.eu/document/download/0affa9a8-2ac5-46a9-98f8-19205bf61eb5_en?filename=COM_2025_80_EN.pdf. (Accessed as of 4 March 2025).

638 According to Article 37 of the EU CSDDD, "Member States shall adopt and publish, by 26 July 2026, the laws, regulations and administrative provisions necessary to comply with this Directive." Further, Article 37(a) provides that "*from 26 July 2027 as regards companies referred to in Article 2(1), points (a) and (b), which are formed in accordance with the legislation of the Member State and that had more than 5 000 employees on average and generated a net worldwide turnover of more than EUR 1 500 000 000 in the last financial year preceding 26 July 2027 for which annual financial statements have been or should have been adopted, with the exception of the measures necessary to comply with Article 16, which Member States shall apply to those companies for financial years starting on or after 1 January 2028*" and Article

III. Extraterritorial Jurisdiction

The general international law principles governing extraterritorial jurisdiction by States have yet to be clearly defined. Currently, only the principle of non-intervention in internal affairs serves as an impediment to the exercise of extraterritorial jurisdiction by States over the activities of transnational corporations abroad. Hence, the question as to whether home States (where transnational corporations are headquartered) are required to exercise extraterritorial jurisdiction under international human rights law remains an open question. In this regard, it has been clarified that "*Under international law, direct assertions of jurisdiction over foreign companies and business activities must be justified according to one or more internationally recognized bases of jurisdiction: territoriality, nationality, the protective principle, passive personality and universality.*"[639] In addition, assertions of extraterritorial jurisdiction are generally subject to the requirement of 'reasonableness' in the way it is exercised. It can be said that in situations involving serious international crimes subject to universal jurisdiction, there arises an obligation on the part of companies. Moreover, in many cases, it is still not clear whether this obligation can be attached to juridical persons such as business enterprises or only to natural persons (individuals). It is also unclear as to what particular form such regulation can take, i.e., whether it should be

---

37(c) provides that "*from 26 July 2027 as regards companies referred to in Article 2(2), points (a) and (b), which are formed in accordance with the legislation of a third country and that generated a net turnover of more than EUR 1 500 000 000 in the Union, in the financial year preceding the last financial year preceding 26 July 2027, with the exception of the measures necessary to comply with Article 16, which Member States shall apply to those companies for financial years starting on or after 1 January 2028.*" According to the new proposal, Articles 37(a) and (c) will be removed and Articles 37(e) will be amended to postpone the transposition deadline by one year. Ibid., Article 2, and see Article 37 of the EU CSDDD. It can be accessed at the following webpage: https://eur-lex.europa.eu/eli/dir/2024/1760/oj/eng. (Accessed as of 4 March 2025).

639 Report of the United Nations High Commissioner for Human Rights to the United Nations Human Rights Council, 'Improving accountability and access to remedy for victims of business-related human rights abuse: explanatory notes for guidance,' UN Doc., A/HRC/19/Add.1, para. 32. It can be accessed at the following webpage: https://documents.un.org/doc/undoc/gen/g16/095/88/pdf/g1609588.pdf . (Accessed as of 10 January 2025).

criminal, civil or administrative regulation.[640]

A host of specific questions can be raised on how to regulate the extraterritorial activities of transnational corporations. For instance, there is the need to determine corporation nationality in order to establish which State has jurisdiction. There exists also the need to look beyond the formal separation of legal entities in a corporate group to be able to attribute liability (the question of piercing the corporate veil). Other key factor to exercise extraterritorial jurisdiction is as to whether there is real interest in home States requiring increased human rights reporting and impact assessments thus making it their domestic obligation for transnational corporations to respect human rights abroad.

Exercising extraterritorial jurisdiction to regulate the activities of transnational corporations can strengthen the States' obligation to provide effective remedies against corporate human rights abuses that occurred in other States (host States). It is therefore critically important that practical measures be adopted to strengthen victims' access to remedies in home States, including improving victims' access to law-making institutions.

The extraterritorial obligation of companies to respect human rights, in particular in the supply chain has increasingly been made an integral part of the newly emerging mandatory human rights due diligence law, which

---

640 Report of the Special Representative of the Secretary-General on the issue of human rights and transnational corporations and other business enterprises, 'Corporate responsibility under international law and issues in extraterritorial regulation: summary of legal workshops,', UN Doc., A/HRC/4/35/Add.2, paras. 39-52. It can be accessed at the following webpage : https://documents.un.org/doc/undoc/gen/g07/108/45/pdf/g0710845.pdf. (Accessed as of 10 January 2025). For a further detailed explication regarding extraterritorial obligation in relation to economic, social and cultural rights, see Elif Askin, 'Economic and Social Rights, Extraterritorial Application', Max Planck Encyclopedia of Public International Law, Oxford Public International Law (http://opil.ouplaw.com), Oxford University Press (2022): https://opil.ouplaw.com/view/10.1093/law-epil/9780199231690/law-9780199231690-e2213?print=pdf (Accessed as of 10 January 2025).

codifies the international law-level *Corporate responsibility* to respect human rights as a legal obligation to respect human rights on the domestic law plane.

Most of the existing mandatory human rights due diligence laws are based on the notion that home States can exercise extraterritorial jurisdiction obligating companies to respect human rights not only in their own operations but also in the supply chain.

B. Policy Measures

States should take an array of policy measures necessary to meet their obligations to protect people in their territories and/or under jurisdictions from corporate human rights abuse. With the adoption of the UN Guiding Principles on Business and Human Rights, States are increasingly articulating such business and human rights-related policy measures, in particular through adopting national action plans on business and human rights. National action plans on business and human rights are considered by many States to serve as a key instrument to operationalizing the UN Guiding Principles on Business and Human Rights. Such national action plans on business and human rights essentially have the function of mapping out a whole range of legislative, policy and regulatory options and priorities that would take their own national contexts and situations into consideration, while bearing in mind the importance of their related international obligations. Accordingly, this section focuses on the development of the national action plan on business and human rights, which aims to map out a whole range of legislative, policy, administrative, judicial and other measures relevant to business and human rights in a single consolidated document based on the international *Combination/zebra* standards contained in the UN Guiding Principles on Business and Human Rights.

I. Action Plan on Business and Human Rights

Action plans on business and human rights serve as important policy strategies for meeting States' international obligations to protect from corporate human rights abuse and ensure that business enterprises respect human rights under their territories and/or jurisdictions.

Such national action plans on business and human rights can make a qualitative contribution to the effective implementation of the UN Guiding Principles on Business and Human Rights at the national level. As such, they serve as a crucial tool for coordinated, coherent and organic implementation of the UN Guiding Principles on Business and Human Rights, *inter alia*, through a comprehensive assessment of needs and gaps for increased public accountability, as well as mobilization of resources aimed at improving national policy, legal and regulatory frameworks to prevent and protect against corporate human rights abuses.[641]

In recognition of the important role that such national action plans on business and human rights can play in operationalizing the UN Guiding Principles on Business and Human Rights at the national level, the UN Working Group on Business and Human Rights has issued guidance for States on how to develop national action plans on business and human rights. The guidance has highlighted the four essential elements indispensable for such national action plans to be effective: firstly, national action plans need to be based on the UN Guiding Principles on Business and Human Rights, in which the *State duty* to protect from corporate human rights abuse, the *Corporate responsibility* to respect human rights, and the access to remedy

641 'Report of the of the Working Group on the issue of human rights and transnational corporations and other business enterprises, submitted pursuant to Human Rights Council resolutions 17/4 and 26/22', UN Doc., A/69/263, para. 7. It can be accessed at the following webpage: https://documents.un.org/doc/undoc/gen/n14/495/68/pdf/n1449568.pdf. (Accessed as of 10 January 2025).

against corporate human rights abuse have been reflected. National action plans on business and human rights should also be underpinned by the core human rights principles of non-discrimination and equality; secondly, context-specific national action plans are needed where the actual and potential human rights abuses should be addressed, including adverse impacts of business activities occurring both within the territory and/or jurisdiction and outside the State's jurisdiction by defining realistic, deliverable measures aimed at preventing, identifying and remedying corporate human rights harms; thirdly, they should be developed in full inclusiveness and transparency through ensuring for the participation of relevant stakeholders in the process; and fourthly, national action plan development processes require regular review and update to ensure that they can adequately respond to changing contexts.[642]

A sizable number of States have already developed national action plans on business and human rights and a large number of States are also in the process of developing such national action plans on business and human rights.[643] A desk review of those plans has revealed the following elements: firstly, those national action plans on business and human rights have been adopted with the explicitly stated aim of operationalizing the UN Guiding Principles on Business and Human Rights in their respective countries. For instance, the UK national action plan on business and human rights initially adopted in 2013 and revised in 2016 has structured the action plan around the three pillars of the UN Guiding Principles on Business and Human Rights, namely the *State duty* to protect from corporate human rights abuse; the

642 For the details, see 'Guidance on National Action Plans on Business and Human Rights', UN Working Group on Business and Human Rights. It can be accessed at the following website: https://www.ohchr.org/Documents/Issues/Business/UNWG_NAPGuidance.pdf . (Accessed as of 10 January 2025).

643 The United Nations Working Group on Business and Human Rights has uploaded the available national action plans on business and human rights on the following webpage: https://www.ohchr.org/EN/Issues/Business/Pages/nationalactionplans.aspx. (Accessed as of 10 January 2025).

Corporate responsibility to respect human rights; and access to remedy.[644] Secondly, national action plans on business and human rights serve as a key bridge to leading to concrete legislative action in relation to the business and human rights agenda, in particular adoption of mandatory human rights due diligence law. For instance, Germany has used the effective implementation of its 2016 national action plan on business and human rights in the area of human rights due diligence as an indicator for the need to adopt a mandatory human rights due diligence legislation. As such, Germany adopted such a mandatory human rights due diligence law in 2019. The German National Action Plan on Business and Human Rights specifically stated in this regard as follows: "*The Federal Government expects all enterprises to introduce the processes described above in a manner commensurate with their size, the sector in which they operate and their position in supply and value chains. Their compliance will be reviewed annually from 2018. In the absence of adequate compliance, the Federal Government will consider further action, which may culminate in legislative measures and in a widening of the circle of enterprises to be reviewed.*"[645]

It can be assessed that through developing national action plans on business and human rights which articulates a whole range of legislative, administrative, policy, judicial and other necessary measures aimed at regulating business activities that might have the negative impact on the enjoyment of human rights, States have increasingly been taking concrete actions to operationalize and implement the international *Combination/ zebra* standards on business and human rights of the UN Guiding Principles on Business and Human Rights. This further indicates that the *State duty*

---

644 Ibid. See the following webpage: https://assets.publishing.service.gov.uk/government/uploads/system/uploads/attachment_data/file/522805/Good_Business_Implementing_the_UN_Guiding_Principles_on_Business_and_Human_Rights_updated_May_2016.pdf . (Accessed as of 10 January 2025).

645 For the National Action Plan on Business and Human Rights of Germany, see the following webpage: https://www.ohchr.org/Documents/Issues/Business/NationalPlans/NAP_Germany.pdf. (Accessed as of 10 January 2025).

to protect, the *Corporate responsibility* to respect human rights, as well as provision of access to remedy against corporate human rights abuse constitute not only the contemporary most authoritative international human rights standards, but also they have become the increasingly important national rules and guidance when it comes to regulating corporate human rights abuses on the domestic law plane.

C. Judicial Measures

I. Judicial Remedies Against Corporate Human Rights Abuse

When corporate human rights abuses occur, to have access to an effective remedy[646] matters the most for corporate human rights abuse victims. States must therefore establish administrative, civil and criminal liability for corporate human rights abuses. Without effective remedy[647]

646 Different terminologies such as the right to an effective remedy, access to effective remedies, access to justice, and corporate accountability are being interchangeably used, despite the fact that there exists a strong need for conceptual clarification of these terminologies. For further details, see 'Report of the Working Group on the issue of human rights and transnational corporations and other business enterprises,' UN Doc., A/72/162, paras. 13-17. It can be accessed at the following webpage: https://documents.un.org/doc/undoc/gen/n17/218/65/pdf/n1721865.pdf. (Accessed as of 10 January 2025).

647 As to the effectiveness of remedies, the UN Guiding Principles on Business and Human Rights sets out effectiveness criteria when it comes to non-judicial grievance mechanisms in its Principle 31. On the other hand, the UN Guiding Principles on Business and Human Rights do not explicitly set out effectiveness criteria for judicial mechanisms. Instead, Principle 26 of the Guiding Principles provides that "States should take appropriate steps to ensure the effectiveness of domestic judicial mechanisms (emphasis added) when addressing business-related human rights abuses, including considering ways to reduce legal, practical and other relevant barriers that could lead to a denial of access to remedy." The current international standards regarding access to remedy are that States should provide for "adequate, effective prompt reparation for harm suffered." See the Basic Principles and Guidelines on the Right to a Remedy and Reparation for Victims of Gross Violations of International Human Rights Law and Serious Violations of International Humanitarian Law (General Assembly resolution 60/147, annex), article I.2 (b) and VII, UN Doc., A/RES/60/147. It can be accessed at the following webpage: https://www.ohchr.org/sites/default/files/2021-08/N0549642.pdf . (Accessed as of 19 January 2025).

against corporate human rights abuse, other legislative, policy and administrative measures adopted with the aim of enhancing the *Corporate responsibility* to respect human rights could become hollow or meaningless. Accordingly, to ensure remediation against corporate human rights abuses lies at the heart of States' efforts to fulfil their international obligations to protect people in their territories and/or their jurisdictions from business-related human rights harms.[648]

On the international law plane, there currently exist no adjudicative mechanisms that allow victims of corporate human rights abuses judicial remedies. However, the non-existence of such international adjudicative mechanisms for corporate human rights abuse does not necessarily mean that business enterprises can escape from liability entirely. Whereas on the domestic law plane, a range of avenues are available to seek remedies against corporate human rights harms. These include state-based judicial mechanisms, state-based non-judicial mechanisms, non-state-based grievance mechanisms such as operational level grievance mechanisms aimed at ensuring legal accountability and remedies against business-related human rights harms. Among these, state-based judicial mechanisms are "at the core of ensuring access to remedy."[649]

---

648 For a detailed explanation on the importance of provision of effective remedy against business-related human rights harms under the UN Guiding Principles, see, paras. 32-51 of the annual report of the Working Group on the issue of human rights and transnational corporations and other business enterprises to the 26th session of the UN Human Rights Council, UN Doc., A/HRC/26/25. It can be accessed at the following webpage: https://documents.un.org/doc/undoc/gen/g14/141/00/pdf/g1414100.pdf. (Accessed as of 19 January 2025).

649 'Improving accountability and access to remedy for victims of business-related human rights abuse: Report of the United Nations High Commissioner for Human Rights,' UN Doc, A/HRC/32/19, para. 3. It can be accessed at the following webpage: https://documents.un.org/doc/undoc/gen/g16/093/78/pdf/g1609378.pdf. (Accessed as of 19 January 2025). The UN Working Group on Business and Human Rights promotes an overarching idea that rights-holders should be central to the entire remediation process, including to the question of effectiveness of remedies. See Ibid., paras. 18-25, 'Report of the Working Group on the issue of human rights and transnational corporations and other business enterprises,' UN Doc., A/72/162. It can be accessed at the following webpage: https://documents.un.org/doc/undoc/gen/n17/218/65/pdf/n1721865.pdf. (Accessed as of 19 January 2025). While judicial mechanisms

Most States with the strong and independent judiciary have put in place mechanisms, through which corporate human rights abuse victims can seek remedy either in a criminal or civil lawsuit. Despite the theoretical existence of such avenues, judicial measures to ensure effective remedy against corporate human rights abuses, however, appear to be having limited effect in practice.

Against this backdrop, the UN Guiding Principles on Business and Human Rights underscores the importance of providing effective remedies as an integral part of the *State duty* to protect from corporate human rights abuse. As such, Principle 25 of the Guiding Principles on Business and Human Rights explicitly states that "*States must take appropriate steps to ensure, through judicial, administrative, legislative or other appropriate means, that when such [corporate human rights] abuses occur within their territory and/or jurisdiction, those affected have access to effective remedy.*"[650]

In recognition of the fact that "*effective judicial mechanisms are at the core of ensuring access to remedy,*"[651] the UN Guiding Principles on Business and Human Rights further encourages States "*to take appropriate steps to ensure the effectiveness of domestic judicial mechanisms when addressing business-related human rights abuses, including considering ways to reduce legal, practical and other relevant barriers that could lead to a denial of access to remedy.*"[652] It has been argued that there are a number of challenges when

---

play a likely most important role in ensuring access to effective remedy against human rights abuses, one should not lose sight of the importance of having in place legislative and administrative reparations mechanisms and programmes. Criminal and civil judicial procedures may seek to apportion responsibility for material and moral harm and grant reparations to corporate human rights abuse victims, "they do not provide the proper framework for reparations and guarantees of non-repetition which may have the greatest transformative potential." For detailed explanations on advantage of reparations programmes crafted through legislative or administrative schemes, see Ibid., paras. 34-40, 84 of the 'Report of the Special Rapporteur on violence against women, its causes and consequences, Rashida Manjoo,' UN Doc., A/HRC/14/22.

650 Supra note 354, Principle 25.

651 Ibid., Principle 26 and its Commentary at page 28.

652 Ibid.

it comes to obtaining remedy through state-based judicial mechanisms. These challenges vary from jurisdiction to jurisdiction, but the following problems have been identified as persistent ones common to many jurisdictions, including: "*fragmented, poorly designed or incomplete legal regimes; lack of legal development; lack of awareness of the scope and operation of regimes; structural complexities within business enterprises; problems in gaining access to sufficient funding for private law claims; and a lack of enforcement*."[653]

It is therefore essential that the judiciary be independent and impartial, which will, in turn, enable the courts system to provide effective remedies against corporate human rights abuses with integrity, as well as in accordance with due process. The UN Guiding Principles on Business and Human Rights also emphasizes that courts must be "*independent of economic or political pressures from other State agents and from business actors*,"[654] highlighting the importance of States' ensuring that the provision of justice is rendered without the corruption of the judicial process.

In addition, States should ensure that they do not erect barriers for legitimate cases to be brought before the courts seeking remedies against corporate human rights abuses. The UN Guiding Principles on Business and Human Rights exemplifies those legal barriers, which include, *inter alia*: firstly, that corporate legal responsibility is attributed among members of a corporate group in a way that facilitates the avoidance of appropriate accountability; secondly, cases where claimants face a denial of justice in a host State and cannot access home State courts regardless of the merits of the claim; and thirdly, cases where certain groups such as Indigenous Peoples and migrants do not enjoy the same level of legal protection of their human rights

---

653 Supra note 649, 'Improving accountability and access to remedy for victims of business-related human rights abuse: Report of the United Nations High Commissioner for Human Rights,' para. 4, UN Doc, A/HRC/32/19. (Accessed as of 10 February 2025).

654 Supra note 354, Principle 26 and its Commentary at page 29.

as compared to the wider population.[655]

When it comes to practical and procedural barriers, the UN Guiding Principles on Business and Human Rights cites the following examples: the high costs of bringing claims coupled with lack of Government support; the difficulty in securing legal representatives, due to a lack of resources or of other incentives for lawyers; inadequate options for aggregating claims or enabling representative proceedings such as class actions and other collective action procedures; and lack of adequate resources, expertise and support on the part of State prosecutors to investigate individual and business involvement in human rights-related crimes.[656]

Moreover, imbalances among the parties to the claim in financial resources, access to information and expertise can lead to individuals from groups or populations' being at a heightened risk of vulnerability or marginalization, as well as them experiencing active discrimination or unintended discrimination. There is therefore a need to pay particular attention to the rights and specific needs of these groups or populations at each stage of the remedial process.[657]

Increasingly, cases alleging human rights violations in countries (host States) other than those countries where companies are registered as headquarters (home States) are being adjudicated in the courts of home States. These cases which are mostly civil torts cases based on the domestic legislation have been brought before the courts. A new phenomenon is that corporate human rights abuse victims are seeking remedies in the courts of home States on the grounds that those companies have infringed on the human rights of those corporate human rights abuse victims in violation of customary international law requesting home States courts to hear the cases

655 Ibid.

656 Ibid.

657 Ibid. Principles 26 and its Commentary at pp. 29-30.

because the courts have the extraterritorial jurisdiction. These avenues of judicial redress against corporate human rights abuses in home States offer an important, realistic option for corporate human rights abuse victims as in many instances, those corporate human rights abuse victims lack access to effective judicial remedies in host States, owing to the lack of a political will and insufficient legal capacity of local authorities.[658]

Of the most prominent example is the US Alien Tort Statute (ATS) of 1789 also known as the Alien Tort Claims Act (ATCA),[659] which provides the most singularly important legal basis for foreigners to sue multinational companies for a tort before US courts for human rights violations committed abroad. Under this Statute, US federal courts may hear civil cases lodged by a non-US citizen based on the claim that she or he is a victim of serious violation of "*the law of nations*" or "*a treaty of the United States*."[660] The use of this Statute was revived in 1980 for human rights cases after a long period of dormancy in the landmark case of *Filártiga v. Peña-Irala*,[661] where the

---

658 'Supra note 649, Corporate Accountability for Human Rights Abuses: A Guide for Victims and NGOs on Recourse Mechanisms', International Federation of Human Rights (FIDH). It can be accessed at the following webpage: https://www.fidh.org/IMG/pdf/corporate_accountability_guide_version_web.pdf. (Accessed as of 21 January 2025).

659 First Judiciary Act 1789 (ch. 20, §9(b)), as codified in 28 USC. § 1350. It provides that "The district courts shall have original jurisdiction of any civil action by an alien for a tort only, committed in violation of the law of nations or a treaty of the United States." Another US federal statutes that can be used by foreign nationals and or US nationals to bring the allegations of serious human rights violations committed by US-headquartered transnational corporations before the US courts exist, which includes the Torture Victim Protection Act, the Trafficking Victims Reauthorization Act. Further, corporate human rights abuse victims of foreign nationals can also bring state tort law claims against corporations for such torts as assault and battery, sexual assault, intentional infliction of emotional distress and wrongful death. For more details, see supra note 694, 'Corporate Accountability for Human Rights Abuses: A Guide for Victims and NGOs on Recourse Mechanisms', International Federation of Human Rights (FIDH). It can be accessed at the following webpage: https://www.fidh.org/IMG/pdf/corporate_accountability_guide_version_web.pdf. (Accessed as of 21 January 2025).

660 28 U.S.C. §1350, It provides that "*The district courts shall have original jurisdiction of any civil action by an alien for a tort only, committed in violation of the law of nations or a treaty of the United States*." It can be accessed at the following webpage: https://www.govinfo.gov/content/pkg/USCODE-2011-title28/pdf/USCODE-2011-title28.pdf. (Accessed as of 31 January 2025).

661 Filártiga v. Peña-Irala, 630 F.2d 876 (2d Cir. 1980). It can be accessed at the following webpage:

plaintiff (*Filártiga*) sued the defendant (*Peña-Irala*) under the ATCA alleging that the defendant who was Inspector-General of Police during the regime of Paraguayan President Alfredo Stroessner tortured the brother of the plaintiff. The suit was dismissed by the Eastern District Court of New York on the grounds that the court had no jurisdiction over the defendant. However, the US Federal Court of Appeals for the Second Circuit reversed the decision of the Eastern District Court of New York on the grounds that torture was a violation of the law of nations under the ATCA, which granted the US Federal Court of Appeals for the Second Circuit jurisdiction to hear the case. As a consequence, the US Federal Court of Appeals for the Second Circuit exercized personal jurisdiction over the defendant for torture committed in a foreign country.[662] It is worth noting that the ATCA in the case of *Filártiga v. Peña-Irala* had been used to litigate human rights violations committed by persons who were acting under colour of law as public officials. The scope of the ATCA then had been extended to cover human rights violations committed by persons acting outside any official capacity.[663] As such, the mid-1990s saw the application of the ATCA extended to cases of human rights violations committed abroad by US transnational corporations.[664] In 2004, in the case of Sosa v. Alvarez-Machain,[665] the U.S. Supreme Court heard an ATCA case, which was a transnational human rights case. In it, the Supreme

---

https://hrp.law.harvard.edu/wp-content/uploads/2011/04/filartiga-v-pena-irala.pdf. (Accessed as of 31 January 2025).

662 Ibid. See also Paula Alexander Becker, 'The Alien Tort Statute of 1789 and International Human Rights Violations: Kiobel v. Royal Dutch Petroleum Co.,' New England Journal of Entrepreneurship: Vol.17: No. 1, Article 6, p. 29. It can be accessed at the following webpage: https://www.academia.edu/72112666/The_Alien_Tort_Statute_of_1789_and_International_Human_Rights_Violations_Kiobel_v_Royal_Dutch_Petroleum_Co. (Accessed as of 31 January 2025).

663 *Kadić v. Karadžić*, 70 F.3d 232 (2d Cir. 1995). It can be accessed at the following webpage: https://casetext.com/case/kadic-v-karadzic-2. (Accessed as of 31 January 2025).

664 For further details, see supra note 658, 'Corporate Accountability for Human Rights Abuses: A Guide for Victims and NGOs on Recourse Mechanisms', International Federation of Human Rights (FIDH). It can be accessed at the following webpage: https://www.fidh.org/IMG/pdf/corporate_accountability_guide_version_web.pdf. (Accessed as of 31 January 2025).

665 Sosa v. Alvarez-Machain, 542 U.S. 692, 725 (2004). It can be accessed at the following webpage: https://supreme.justia.com/cases/federal/us/542/692/. (Accessed as of 08 February 2025).

Court clarified that all actions based upon "*a norm of international character accepted by the civilized world and defined with a specificity comparable to the features of 18th century paradigms*"[666] may be brought. As such, individuals may bring human rights cases under the ATCA for violation of universal, obligatory, specific and definable international norm such as the prohibitions of torture and genocide. However, the Supreme Court held that arbitrary detention as pled in the case of Sosa v. Alvarez-Machain did not constitute a violation of well-established customary international law thus dismissing the action.[667] Another important rule pronounced by the U.S. Supreme Court was concerned with the need to displace the presumption against extraterritoriality if the claims under the ATCA were to be successful. In the case of Kiobel v. Royal Dutch Petroleum of 2013, the Supreme Court held that "*even where the claims touch and concern the territory of the United States, they must do so with sufficient force to displace the presumption against extraterritorial application.*"[668]

In 2018, the US Supreme Court excluded foreign corporations from the reach of jurisdiction of the ATCA.[669] With regard to the question as to whether US corporations can be sued under the ATCA in the case of Nestle USA, Inc. v. Doe et al, No. 19-416, 593 U.S.- (2021) (Nestle), the US Supreme Court confirmed that the ATCA could not be applied extraterritorially to US corporations.[670]

---

666 Ibid., Part IV.

667 Ibid., Part IV. C.

668 Kiobel v. Royal Dutch Petroleum Co., 569 US 108 (2013) at p.125. It can be accessed at the following webpage: https://supreme.justia.com/cases/federal/us/569/108/. (Accessed as of 08 February 2025).

669 Jesner v. Arab Bank PLC., 584 U.S. (2018). It can be accessed at the following webpage: https://supreme.justia.com/cases/federal/us/584/16-499/. (Accessed as of 08 February 2025).

670 Nestle USA, Inc. v Doe et al, No. 19-416, 593 U.S. (2021). It can be accessed at the following webpage: https://www.supremecourt.gov/opinions/20pdf/19-416_i4dj.pdf. (Accessed as of 08 February 2025). For an analysis of the case, refer also to the following webpage: https://www.justsecurity.org/77012/the-surprisingly-broad-implications-of-nestle-usa-inc-v-doe-for-human-rights-litigation-and-extraterritoriality/. (Accessed as of 08 February 2025). For a general explanation on the ATCA and other US laws, see Beth Stephens et al, *International Human*

There also exist a host of obstacles to US courts recognizing such extraterritorial jurisdiction: under the *forum non conveniens* doctrine that cases should be heard in the most appropriate forum, which is generally the jurisdiction where human rights violations in case have occurred. This doctrine can serve as a significant barrier for corporate human rights abuse victims, because the court systems in host countries where the torts occurred in many cases are not equipped to provide effective remedy against such corporate human rights abuses. Hence, transnational corporate defendants invoke this doctrine not infrequently. In order for the court to apply the *forum non conveniens* doctrine, it must be convinced that another court exists where the plaintiff can seek remedy against the harm suffered and that an assessment of all the interests involved, including the public interest, leads to the conclusion that the alternative forum is most appropriate. The court also takes interests of the parties' to the suit and the jurisdiction, including: the accessibility of evidence, witness availability and other elements that would render a trial easy, rapid and less costly. Public interests of the jurisdiction include: the court's caseload, the interests of the forum in trying the case and the judge's familiarity with the applicable law. The burden of proof for these two elements of the *forum non conveniens* doctrine lie with the defendant.[671]

Rights Litigation in U.S. Courts (2nd ed.), Martinus Nijhoff Publishers, 2008). See also supra note 658, 'Corporate Accountability for Human Rights Abuses: A Guide for Victims and NGOs on Recourse Mechanisms', International Federation of Human Rights (FIDH), Chapter II (Judicial Mechanisms), Part I (Extraterritorial Civil Liability of Multinational Corporations for Human Rights Violations). It can be accessed at the following webpage: https://www.fidh.org/IMG/pdf/corporate_accountability_guide_version_web.pdf. ; Ralph G. Steinhardt, Special Edition Response, 'Losing the "Right" Way Preserves the Narrow Scope of the Alien Tort Statute: NESTLE USA, INC., v. John DOE,' Geo. Wash. L. Rev. (2021). It can be accessed at the following webpage: https://www.gwlr.org/losing-the-right-way-preserves-the-narrow-scope-of-the-ats/. (Accessed as of 08 February 2025).

671 Supra note 658, 'Corporate Accountability for Human Rights Abuses: A Guide for Victims and NGOs on Recourse Mechanisms', International Federation of Human Rights (FIDH), Chapter II (Judicial Mechanisms), Part I (Extraterritorial Civil Liability of Multinational Corporations for Human Rights Violations). It can be accessed at the following webpage: https://www.fidh.org/IMG/pdf/corporate_accountability_guide_version_web.pdf. (Accessed as of 08 February 2025). See also the following Corporate Accountability webpage: https://corporateaccountability.fidh.org/the-guide/judicial-mechanisms/extraterritorial-civil-liability-of-multinational-corporations-for-human-rights-violations/establishing-the-jurisdiction-of-a-us-court-and-

It is submitted that the ATCA and other US laws currently serve as the most practical and central extraterritorial legal basis for human rights abuse victims abroad to seek remedies against human rights harms caused by translational corporations headquartered in the United States of America. This is in spite of the fact that there is some uncertainty and recalcitrant decisions to limit the application of the ATCA to corporate human rights abuses that have occurred in foreign countries by the U.S. Courts.

II. Inter-State Judicial Cooperation

Inter-state judicial cooperation plays an important role in ensuring effective remedy against business-related human rights abuses. In cross-border human rights cases,[672] inter-state judicial cooperation can become a particularly important factor when it comes to corporate human rights abuse victims' seeking remedies. For instance, for those home States recognizing the extraterritorial jurisdiction aimed at regulating the activities of transnational corporations in other States (host States) thus providing some concrete avenues of remedies against corporate human rights harms before their national courts, it is critically important for corporate human rights abuse victims to be able to utilize arrangements that would facilitate inter-state judicial cooperation, including joint investigations, protection of witnesses and sensitive information and cross-border consultation and coordination. There seemingly exist a host of practical challenges that would undermine effective inter-state judicial cooperation, including: "*a lack of information about how to make a request to agencies in other States, a lack of opportunities*

---

determining-the-law-applicable-to-the-case/under-what-conditions-will-a-us-court-recognize-jurisdiction/applying-the-ats-to-private-individuals-and-multinational-corporations/. (Accessed as of 08 February 2025).

672 A "cross-border" case can be defined as "*one where the relevant facts have taken place in, the relevant actors are located in or the evidence needed to prove a case is located in more than one State*." See Box3: Key Concepts 3 on page 10 of UN Doc., A/HRC/32/19/Add.1. It can be accessed at the following webpage: https://documents.un.org/doc/undoc/gen/g16/095/88/pdf/g1609588.pdf. (Accessed as of 10 February 2025).

for cross-border consultation and coordination, differences of approach regarding issues of privacy and the protection of sensitive information, a lack of resources needed to process requests in a timely manner and a lack of awareness of investigative standards in other States."[673]

In recognition of the importance of inter-state judicial cooperation, the updated draft legally binding instrument to regulate, in international human rights law, the activities of transnational corporations and other business enterprises contains a comprehensive draft article that touches upon specific requirements regarding mutual legal assistance and international judicial cooperation.[674] The draft instrument essentially obligates the States Parties to the future treaty to render mutual legal assistance and international judicial cooperation under existing bilateral and international agreements on mutual legal assistance and international judicial cooperation, including the conclusion of agreements and treaties in the absence of such agreements. If concluded, these provisions on inter-state judicial cooperation can have the function of clarifying what the State obligation to protect from corporate human rights abuse, in particular in terms of adoption of necessary judicial measures entails as a treaty norm.

According to the updated draft legally binding instrument to regulate, in international human rights law, the activities of transnational corporations and other business enterprises, mutual legal assistance may include: "*taking evidence or statements from persons; executing searches and seizures;*

---

673 Supra note 639, 'Improving accountability and access to remedy for victims of business-related human rights abuse: Report of the United Nations High Commissioner for Human Rights,' para. 4, UN Doc, A/HRC/32/19. (Accessed as of 10 February 2025).

674 See: https://www.ohchr.org/sites/default/files/documents/hrbodies/hrcouncil/igwg-transcorp/session9/igwg-9th-updated-draft-lbi-track-changes.pdf (Accessed as of 10 February 2025). C.f., Article 12 of the 3rd Revised draft legally binding instrument to regulate, in international human rights law, the activities of transnational corporations and other business enterprises, which can be accessed at the following OHCHR webpage: https://www.ohchr.org/Documents/HRBodies/HRCouncil/WGTransCorp/Session6/LBI3rdDRAFT.pdf (Accessed on 10 February 2025).

examining objects and sites; providing information, evidentiary items and expert evaluations; providing originals or certified copies of relevant documents and records, including government, bank, financial, corporate or business records; identifying or tracing proceeds of crime, property, instrumentalities or other things for evidentiary purposes; facilitating the voluntary appearance of persons in the requesting State Party; facilitating the freezing and recovery of assets; assisting and protecting victims, their families, representatives and witnesses, consistent with international human rights legal standards and subject to international legal requirements, including those relating to the prohibition of torture and other forms of cruel, inhuman or degrading treatment or punishment; assisting in regard to the application of domestic law; and any other type of assistance that is not contrary to the domestic law of the requested State Party". International judicial cooperation is understood to include "*effective service of judicial documents; and provision of judicial comity consistent with domestic law.*"[675]

Moreover, the draft treaty requires the States Parties, to the fullest extent possible, to provide mutual legal assistance for criminal offences covered under the draft instrument and encourages the States Parties to proactively transmit and exchange information on those criminal offences among the States Parties without a prior request from another States Party. The draft treaty further encourages the States Parties to establish joint investigation bodies in relation to matters that are subject of investigations, prosecutions or judicial proceedings through bilateral or multilateral arrangements and/or agreements. The draft treaty also obligates the States Parties to the future treaty to designate a central authority that shall have the responsibility and power to receive requests for mutual legal assistance and either execute or transmit such requests to the competent authorities for execution in accordance with their domestic laws.[676]

---

675 Ibid., Article 12(5).
676 Ibid., Article 12(7)-(9).

The States Parties to the future treaty must recognize and enforce judgments of another State Party unless the defendant furnishes proof that he/she was not given reasonable notice and a fair opportunity to present his or her case; recognition and enforcement of foreign court's judgment is irreconcilable with an early judgment of the concerned State Party; and the foreign court's judgement is manifestly contrary to the *ordre pubic* of the State Party where its recognition and enforcement is sought.[677]

D. Interim Conclusions

Since the adoption of the UN Guiding Principles on Business and Human Rights in 2011, an increasing number of States have made and been making efforts to strengthen the *State duty* to protect from corporate human rights abuse. Among these efforts, legislating mandatory human rights due diligence at the national level as an essential component of the *Corporate responsibility* to respect human rights lies at the heart of such efforts. Such mandatory human rights due diligence law will bolster the arguments for making the *Corporate responsibility* to respect human rights a legal obligation on the international law plane. One of the most prominent examples is the Duty of Vigilance Law of France, which requires applicable companies under the scope of the Law to fulfil "the vigilance obligations", including the establishment of a vigilance plan, the effective implementation of such a vigilance plan and its publication, as well as mandatory reporting on its implementation. A host of other European States are following suit by having adopted such a mandatory human rights due diligence law or by contemplating to adopt one. At the regional level, the European Union has also taken the lead by adopting such mandatory human rights and environmental due diligence law in 2024, titled "Corporate Sustainability Due Diligence Directive (CSDDD). It can be critiqued that the EU CSDDD

677 Ibid., Article 12(10)-(11).

has some gaps when measured against the international *Combination/zebra* standards on business and human rights of the UN Guiding Principles on Business and Human Rights, as the former included the reduced scope of companies covered, and the limited recognition of a company's downstream business partners' impacts and impacts caused by financial activities. Despite these gaps, it can also be said that the EU CSDDD is considered to be the international (regional) due diligence law most closely aligned with the UN Guiding Principles on Business and Human Rights.

It is worth noting in this regard that the ongoing national transposition process (within 2 years from the adoption of the CSDDD on 25 July 2024) will further present the opportunity for EU Member States to bridging the gaps of the CSDDD thus bringing their own mandatory human rights due diligence legislative frameworks even closer to the international *Combination/zebra* standards on business and human rights (the UN Guiding Principles on Business and Human Rights) than the CSDDD itself. At the same time, there is still a grave risk that some EU Member States lobbied by the business community to derail or undermine the application of the CSDDD as recently demonstrated by the recent French Government's advocating for the indefinite postponement of the CSDDD, and for weakening its key provisions.[678]

It is submitted that taking such legislative measures must be an integral part of the fulfilment of the *State duty* to protect from corporate human rights abuse. Under the current international human rights law regime, a clear distinction exists between the *State duty* to protect from corporate human rights abuse and the *Corporate responsibility* to respect human rights. In the absence of the direct legal obligation for business enterprises to respect human rights on the international law plane, the most effective and practical way to ensure business respect of human rights is through the strengthening

---

678 For details, see the following webpage of a French NGO, Sherpa: Corporate Sustainability Due Diligence Directive : France advocates for indefinite postponement, to the detriment of social and environemental justice – Sherpa. (Accessed as of 10 February 2025).

of the *State duty* to protect from corporate human rights abuse on the domestic law plane. The adoption of laws in countries that mandate/obligate business enterprises to conduct human rights due diligence (mandatory human rights due diligence) in their own operations and in the supply chain is therefore a most welcome development as it will pave the way for the most effective operationalization and implementation of the UN Guiding Principles on Business and Human Rights (*Combination/zebra* standards) at the country level, whose three core pillars are: the *State duty* to protect, the *Corporate responsibility* to respect human rights, and access to remedy against corporate human rights abuses. It is critically important that such mandatory human rights due diligence law be developed in full alignment with the relevant international human rights norms and standards, in particular including the UN Guiding Principles on Business and Human Rights. Of equal importance is that such laws should be effectively enforced against those business enterprises that fail to comply with the requirement of conducting mandatory human rights due diligence in their own operations and in the supply chain. It is further expected that a proliferation of such national and regional laws of mandatory human rights due diligence would undoubtedly lend support to an early conclusion of a legally binding international treaty on business and human rights that is currently being deliberated under the auspices of the UN Human Rights Council.

When it comes to the extraterritoriality of such national human rights due diligence law, it is critical to ensure that the law allows corporate human rights abuse victims to have access to remedies against corporate human rights abuses. In this regard, it is important that a consistency in the law in different countries be achieved. In addition, the exercise of extraterritorial jurisdiction by home States and/or the possibility for corporate human rights abuse victims to seek remedies using home States' legal frameworks can serve a critically important function when it comes to fulfilling both States' duty to protect from corporate human rights abuse and the legal obligation of business enterprises to respect human rights, at a minimum, on the domestic law plane.

National action plans on business and human rights can serve as a roadmap for an array of legislative, policy, judicial measures that States must and should adopt as part of meeting their international obligations to respect, protect and fulfil human rights in relation to business activities under their territories and/or jurisdictions. A host of merits exist in developing such national human rights action plans on business and human rights. For instance, consultations with key stakeholders at the national level for the development of a national action plan on business and human rights can contribute significantly to raise the awareness of the importance of the *Corporate responsibility* to respect human rights coupled with the Government's international obligations to respect, protect and fulfil human rights in relation to business activities both within its territory and/or jurisdiction. This will further build the momentum for the development of legislative (such as enactment of a mandatory human rights and environmental due diligence law), administrative, policy and judicial measures aimed at enhancing the *Corporate responsibility* to respect human rights. However, it is important that States should ensure effective implementation of such national action plans on business and human rights, which should be developed based on the relevant international *Combination/zebra* standards on business and human rights contained in the UN Guiding Principles on Business and Human Rights with the aim of enhancing the *State duty* to protect from corporate human rights abuse and strengthening the *Corporate responsibility* to respect human rights on the ground. Towards this end, States may explore the possibility of seeking technical assistance from the Office of the United Nations High Commissioner for Human Rights (OHCHR) with a view to improving the national capacities to meet the international obligations to respect, protect and fulfil human rights in relation to business activities.

It is submitted that through developing national action plans on business and human rights which articulate a whole range of legislative, administrative, policy, judicial and other necessary measures aimed at regulating business activities that might have the negative impact on the enjoyment of human rights, States have increasingly been taking concrete actions to operationalize and implement the international *Combination/ zebra* standards on business and human rights of the UN Guiding Principles on Business and Human Rights. This indicates that the *State duty* to protect, the *Corporate responsibility* to respect human rights, as well as provision of access to remedy against corporate human rights abuse contained in the UN Guiding Principles on Business and Human Rights constitute not only the contemporary most authoritative international human rights standards, but also they have increasingly become important national rules and guidance, when it comes to regulating corporate human rights abuses on the domestic law plane.

It is submitted that effective access to remedies against corporate human rights abuse, including monetary compensation, restitution, public apologies, and promises of a non-repetition matters the most for corporate human rights abuse victims. Judicial remedies lie at the heart of remedies, which could be sought by such corporate human rights abuse victims using the national human rights protection frameworks that permit extraterritorial jurisdiction of the courts of home States. Such national legal frameworks such as the US Alien Torts Claims Act can serve as an important avenue of ensuring corporate accountability for and access to remedy against business-related human rights harms. It is also submitted that various policy and judicial measures, in particular state-based judicial mechanisms aimed at providing access to remedies for corporate human rights abuse victims need to be further strengthened at the national level.

In addition, inter-state judicial cooperation, including mutual legal assistance plays an important role in ensuring effective access to remedies against corporate human rights abuses. Considering that there exist a range of practical challenges that would hinder effective inter-state judicial cooperation, States must take a range of practical steps intended to enhance the ability of relevant State agencies to seek and obtain cooperation and assistance from their counterparts in other jurisdictions, including putting in place bilateral and multilateral arrangements for such inter-state judicial cooperation, enabling joint investigations through the establishment of joint investigation teams, ensuring access to information and training, development of centralized information repositories, and promoting awareness and facilitating networking between law enforcement practitioners amongst States, and recognition and enforcement of judgments among others.

Part 6

Conclusion

Chapter 9: Combination/zebra Standards on Business and Human Rights

The international community has been holding discussions on how to address the impacts of business activities on social development, the environment and human rights from the 1970s when the United Nations established the Commission on Transnational Corporations and the United Nations Centre on Transnational Corporations in 1974. Throughout its existence, the Commission on Transnational Corporations had attempted to establish a controversial 'code of conduct for transnational corporations' without success until 1992 when it was formally dissolved.

Since its dissolution, the focus of the debate/discussion has shifted to the one that has been focusing on how to address the impacts of the activities of transnational corporations on the enjoyment of human rights within the United Nations human rights fora. The accelerating process of globalization of the 1990s has further intensified the discussions/debates on the need to address the impacts of the activities of transnational corporations on the enjoyment of human rights through ensuring adequate regulation of their activities at the international level.

How the international community should approach to this issue has diverged when it comes to addressing such negative impacts of business activities on the enjoyment of human rights. On the one hand, a voluntary approach has been preferred, which is essentially based on the premise that it is more effective to prevent the negative human rights impacts of their activities from occurring, if business enterprises themselves take voluntary action aimed at respecting human rights. This approach has been strongly advocated for mostly by developed States, from where the vast majority of transnational corporations have originated, as well as by the corporate sector. On the other hand, some developing States along with non-governmental human rights organizations, workers' organizations, and Indigenous Peoples' organizations have been arguing for the establishment of corporate accountability on the international law plane for corporate human rights abuse.

The United Nations Human Rights Council's (the successor to the then UN Commission on Human Rights) initial response to such demands for internatinal-level regulation of the impacts of business activities seemed to lend more weight to the so-called voluntary approach. On the contrary, the then United Nations Sub-Commission on the Promotion and Protection of Human Rights of the then United Nations Commission on Human Rights had started looking into the impacts of the activities of transnational corporations and other business enterprises on the enjoyment of human rights from 1999, which led to the drafting of the UN Norms on Business and Human Rights in 2004. However, the then UN Commission on Human Rights, the parent body, did not endorse the then Sub-commission's Norms on the grounds that the former did not request the latter to draft such Norms on business and human rights. The then UN Commission on Human Rights requested the Office of the United Nations High Commissioner for Human Rights (OHCHR) to compile a report on the issue of business and human rights, which was presented to the then Commission on Human Rights in 2005. In 2006, the then UN Commission on Human Rights passed a resolution on "*Human rights and transnational corporations and other business enterprises*" ignoring the Norms of the then Sub-commission, in which it, instead, requested the Secretary-General of the United Nations to appoint a special representative for human rights and transnational corporations and other business enterprises.

The Secretary-General appointed late Mr. John Ruggie as his special representative for human rights and transnational corporations and other business enterprises, who, in 2008, presented "*Protect, Respect and Remedy: A Framework for Business and Human Rights*," composed of the three core pillars: the *State duty* to protect human rights; the *Corporate responsibility* to respect human rights; and access to remedy. The United Nations Human Rights Council welcomed this framework, which clearly distinguished between the *State duty* to protect human rights and the *Corporate responsibility* to respect human rights. In 2011, Mr. Ruggie presented the UN Guiding Principles on Business and Human Rights to the Human Rights Council, which contained the same three core pillars of the *State duty* to protect, the *Corporate responsibility* to respect human rights; and access to remedy. The Human Rights Council endorsed the UN Guiding Principles on Business and Human Rights as the authoritative international standards on business and human rights, while creating an expert working group on the issue of human rights and transnational corporations and other business enterprises, whose main mandate was to assist States and the corporate sector in operationalizing and implementing them at the national level. The unanimous endorsement of the UN Guiding Principles on Business and Human Rights by the Human Rights Council has sent a strong signal in that the international community considers that to ensure the *Corporate responsibility* to respect human rights through a voluntary approach is a more appropriate path to be pursued, at least, on the international law plane, as opposed to the so-called legal accountability approach attempted by the then UN Sub-Commission on the Promotion and Protection of Human rights through the identification of existing international human rights norms that could be directly applicable to business enterprises, in particular transnational corporations, on the international human rights law plane.

With the above historical evolutionary trajectory in mind, this final chapter, which serves as the conclusions of the thesis, seeks to identify not only existing relevant international standards (*Combination/zebra* standards)[679] on business and human rights but also international efforts to codify such international norms and standards on business and human rights into an international treaty on business and human rights.

The *State duty* to protect from corporate human rights abuse is explicitly provided for under international human rights law (treaties, customary international law and the general principles of international law and standards).[680] The most prominent is the Bill of International Human Rights made up of the Universal Declaration of Human Rights, the International Covenant on Economic, Social and Cultural Rights and the International Covenant on Civil and Political Rights. There are additional 7 other core international human rights treaties, which can serve as the important legal bases for the *State duty* to protect from corporate human rights abuse. A wide range of customary international law norms, the general principles of international law, and other relevant standards (*Combination/zebra* standards) such as the UN Guiding Principles on Business and Human Rights also provide for the *State duty* to protect from corporate human rights abuse.

When it comes to the *Corporate responsibility* to respect human rights, there currently exists no firm legal basis to impose direct obligation on business enterprises to respect human rights (corporate accountability). The exception to this is *ius cogens* as part of general principles of international

---

679 For detailed expositions on the main features and functions of the so-called combination standards (zebra standards) as sources, see supra note 2, Riedel, 'Standards as Sources,' at 396-417.

680 Ibid. Professor Riedel cogently proffered the theory that 'standards' should also be considered as sources along with the traditional 'hard law' sources triad, namely treaties, customary international law, and general principles of international law, contained in Article 38(1) of the Statute of the International Court of Justice.

law, in particular public interest norms[681] such as prohibition of piracy, slavery and genocide, which applies not only to States but to juridical persons such as business enterprises. In this regard, some commentators and scholars have argued that corporations/companies are increasingly being recognized as 'participants' on the international law plane with the capacity to bear some rights and duties. For instance, they have certain rights under bilateral investment treaties. They are also subject to duties under several civil liability conventions dealing with environmental pollution. Some efforts have also been made to impose direct legal obligation on business enterprises on the international law plane, including the Norms on Business and Human Rights of the then UN Sub-Commission on the Promotion and Protection of Human Rights. The United Nations Human Rights Council is also currently in the process of elaborating on a legally binding treaty to regulate, in international law, the activities of transnational corporations and other business enterprises.

Moreover, there exist a large number of the so-called 'soft law' standards (Combination/zebra standards) on the *Corporate responsibility* to respect human rights, which sets out the clear expectation that business enterprises as a social organ carrying out specialized functions in society should respect human rights throughout their entire operations and in the supply chain. The most recent and authoritative of which is the UN Guiding Principles on Business and Human Rights. The UN Guiding Principles on Business and Human Rights is unique in that it constitutes *Combination/zebra* standards whereby both the treaty norms on the *State duty/obligation* to protect from corporate human rights abuse and the international standards on the *Corporate responsibility* to respect human rights are included. In this regard, it is worth noting that through long-years of state practice to ensure for the *Corporate responsibility* to respect human rights via various

681 Supra note 2, Eibe Riedel, 'Standards as Sources,' German Yearbook of International Law (GYIL) vol. 63 (220), at 385-386.

means, including through adoption of resolutions and declarations within UN human rights fora such as the UN Human Rights Council and the UN General Assembly, such standards regarding the *Corporate responsibility* to respect human rights can be ripened into customary international law or be translated into a treaty norm. This will, in turn, provide a solid legal basis for the direct legal obligation for business enterprises to respect human rights on the international law plane. However, considering the emerging international standards as part of the international *Combination/zebra* standards on the *Corporate responsibility* to respect human rights, whose main component is to require business enterprises to conduct human rights due diligence in their own operations and in the supply chain, are being further made concrete through national-level legislative action, such *Combination/zebra* standards on business and human rights, in particular the *Corporate responsibility* to respect human rights could be used as important "yardsticks or signposts of legal development"[682] on the international law plane.

As such, a clear distinction should be made under the current international human rights law regime between the *State duty/obligation* to protect from corporate human rights abuse and the *Corporate responsibility* to respect human rights. The former is a well-established legal obligation as part of the *State duty* to respect, protect and fulfil (promote and provide) human rights under international human rights law. When it comes to the *State duty/obligation* to protect from corporate human rights abuse, international human rights treaties impose such an obligation on States parties in a myriad of ways: firstly, generalized obligations are imposed on States parties to take all necessary measures to protect from human rights abuse by third parties, including business enterprises. The *State duty/obligation* to protect from corporate human rights abuse can therefore be implied from these generalized obligations when they have voluntarily agreed to become a

---

682 Supra note 2, Eibe Riedel, 'Standards as Sources,' German Yearbook of International Law (GYIL) vol. 63 (220), at 388.

party to international human rights treaties; and secondly, some international human rights treaties make specific references to the obligation of States parties in relation to business enterprises and/or specific industries or sectors such as banking and finance, agricultural or media sectors.

By contrast, the *Corporate responsibility* to respect human rights is not a legal obligation *per se*. The *Corporate responsibility* to respect human rights is societal expectations placed on business enterprises to respect human rights in relation to their business operations that could impact on the enjoyment of the rights of the people. The concept of 'sphere of influence'[683] could serve a useful purpose in determining the degree and extent of such impacts on the enjoyment of the human rights of the people affected by business operations. This will further help identify corresponding responsibilities of companies to individual situations. The more proximate the sphere of influence of a company's operations is to the human rights impacts caused by company's operations, the more direct responsibility the company should bear. However, when it comes to protecting the rights of its suppliers or the rights of wider consumers, the *Corporate responsibility* to respect human rights becomes less strong, even though this does not necessarily mean that the *Corporate responsibility* to respect human rights ceases to exist in these cases. There is an alternative approach to using the concept of 'complicity' when it comes to identifying the *Corporate responsibility* to respect human rights, in particular the scope of "due diligence." This approach requires that companies should avoid complicity in human rights violations, for which they should act with "due diligence" to avoid knowingly contributing to human rights violations/abuses, regardless of a potential risk of legal liability. As such, "due diligence" will help companies to identify and act upon risks in a way that companies can

683 Supra note 158, John Ruggie, 'Report of the Special Representative of the Secretary-General on the Issue of Human Rights and Transnational Corporations and other Business Enterprises: Clarifying the Concepts of "Sphere of influence" and "Complicity",' UN Doc., A/HRC/8/16, para. 71. It can be accessed at the following webpage: https://documents.un.org/doc/undoc/gen/g08/134/78/pdf/g0813478.pdf. (Accessed as of 10 February 2025).

ensure that they do not knowingly contribute to such human rights violations/abuses or knowingly benefit from them.[684]

The core elements of the *Corporate responsibility* to respect human rights are comprehensively spelled out in the most prominent international '*Combination/zebra*' standards on business and human rights, namely the UN Guiding Principles on Business and Human Rights, which has the three principal components: a policy commitment to meet the responsibility to respect human rights; a human rights due diligence process to identify, prevent, mitigate and account for how a business enterprise addresses its adverse human rights impacts; and the remediation processes of adverse human rights impacts that it has caused or contributed to.

Human rights due diligence is considered to be a core element of the *Corporate responsibility* to respect human rights. Conducting human rights due diligence under the *Corporate responsibility* to respect human rights requires business enterprises to: carry out human rights impact assessments before initiating any business activity; adopting human rights policies whereby business enterprises commit themselves to the imperative of respecting human rights throughout their entire operations and beyond; and tracking human rights performance in order to not only adjust human rights policies to the changing business contexts but also to ensure for mechanisms that allow corporate human rights abuse victims to have access to remedies. Such human rights due diligence should not only be conducted in the context of companies' own operations, but also in the framework of the relationships associated with such company operations with a view to ensuring that companies are not complicit or implicated in human rights harms caused by third parties such as in the supply chain.[685] In this connection, it is also important to make a clear distinction that business enterprises hold the

684 Ibid.
685 Ibid., para. 72.

responsibility for their own adverse human rights impacts (human rights harms caused by their own operations) regardless of whether they have taken reasonable steps to prevent and mitigate such adverse human rights impacts while they hold the responsibility and its correlative responsibility to provide a remedy to the adverse human rights impacts (human rights harms) of third parties that resulted from their failure to act with reasonable due diligence, with which they have business relationships.[686]

The interpretative guidance of various treaty bodies also makes it clear that States have the primary obligations to respect, protect and fulfil human rights in relation to the activities of business enterprises, while acknowledging that the *Corporate responsibility* to respect human rights is not explicitly established in treaties. Nevertheless, through the interpretation of the *State obligation* to protect from corporate human rights abuse, treaty bodies have established the important principle of conducting due diligence on the part of States parties in order to prevent, punish, investigate or redress the human rights harms caused by acts of private persons or entities. This *State obligation* to exercise due diligence as part of the *State duty* to protect from corporate human rights abuse can serve as an inspiration for clarifying what can constitute core elements of human rights due diligence to be conducted by business enterprises as part of the *Corporate responsibility* to respect human rights, which is a legal obligation, at least, within the national legislative framework, if exists such mandatory human rights due diligence law in a given State party. As such, to take legislative measures such as enacting mandatory human rights due diligence law is considered to be an essential action that States parties must take, as part of meeting their international obligations to respect, protect and fulfil the human rights in relation to business activities under the international human rights treaties.

---

686 Supra note 354, Guiding Principles on Business and Human Rights: Implementing the United Nations Protect, Respect and Remedy Framework, Office of the United Nations High Commissioner for Human Rights, UN Publication, HR/PUB/11/04, Principles 17-21.

The interpretative guidance of treaty bodies also commonly emphasizes the importance of Stares parties' exercizing their extraterritorial obligations, as well as providing remedies against corporate human rights abuses through establishing various state-based judicial and non-judicial mechanisms, and non-state-based mechanisms, when it comes to ensuring that the *State duty/obligation* to protect from corporate human rights abuse is fully met.

Through issuing Concluding Observations, treaty bodies have also identified the *State obligations* to respect, protect and fulfil human rights in relation to business activities. It is worth noting that the recommendations given through these Concluding Observations have increasingly become more specific since the endorsement of the UN Guiding Principles on Business and Human Rights by the United Nations Human Rights Council in 2011. Along the lines of the interpretative guidance regarding States parties' obligations to respect, protect and fulfil human rights in relation to business activities, these Concluding Observations have also recommended that States parties must establish effective legislative frameworks that legally obligate business enterprises to conduct human rights due diligence in order to prevent, identify, mitigate and redress the adverse impacts of the activities of business enterprises on the enjoyment of human rights, as well as to prevent abuses of such rights in the supply chain. Similar to the interpretative guidance provided in General Comments, these Concluding Observations have also emphasized the importance of providing remedies against corporate human rights abuses, as well as that of States parties' exercising the extraterritorial obligation in order to regulate the activities of corporations abroad.

Treaty Bodies have also dealt with the *State obligations* to respect, protect and fulfil human rights in relation to business activities and the *Corporate responsibility* to respect human rights by issuing a host of General Comments. The States parties' legal obligations in relation to business activities flow mainly from *the State duty/obligation* to protect from corporate human rights abuse, which is of primordial importance when it comes to considering their obligations in relation to business activities under international human rights law. The *State duty/obligation* to protect refers to the obligation of States parties to take all necessary measures aimed at ensuring that the human rights of the rights-holders under their territories and/or jurisdictions are protected from being violated by third parties, including business enterprises. Conceptually, this *State duty/obligation* to protect from corporate human rights abuse has an indirect nature, in that corporate human rights abuses do not constitute human rights violations by States parties *per se*, unless they fail to take all necessary measures to protect people under their territories and/or jurisdictions from such corporate human rights abuses. In the case of States parties' failing to take such necessary protection measures, it may amount to a direct violation of their *State duty/obligation* to protect from corporate human rights abuse.

With respect to the direct legal obligation of business enterprises under the International Covenant on Economic, Social and Cultural Rights (ICESCR) (or under international human rights law), the CESCR-Committee affirmed the traditionally-held view that while States had the primary *obligations* to respect, protect and fulfil human rights under the ICESCR/international human rights law, business enterprises have also the *Corporate responsibility* to respect human rights independently of those State obligations. Currently under international human rights law, business enterprises do not have the direct legal obligation to respect human rights, except that they could be held legally liable under customary international law.

The CESCR-Committee affirmed the States parties' extraterritorial obligations under the ICESCR in relation to business activities. The CESCR-Committee made it explicit that States parties were required to exercise the extraterritorial obligations with a view to preventing, identifying, investigating and redressing corporate human rights abuses as far as such exercise of extraterritorial obligations did not infringe on the sovereignty or diminished the obligations of the host States under the International Covenant on Economic, Social and Cultural Rights. The CESCR-Committee has also clearly established that international human rights obligations under the ICESCR would take precedence over the obligation stemming from trade and investment treaties. However, it can be critiqued that the CESCR-Committee has confused between what '*must*' be done (obligations) and what '*should*' be done (recommendations and/or suggestions for policy options) by States parties when it came to the extraterritorial obligation of States parties to respect in relation to business activities. In particular, when the CESCR-Committee discussed the extraterritorial obligation to respect in relation to conclusion and negotiation of trade investment agreements or financial and tax treaties, it did not specify what was required under the obligation to respect in relation to business activities, but instead it simply suggested certain actions, for instance, identification of any potential conflict between their human rights obligations under the ICESCR and under trade or investment treaties, and conducting human rights impact assessments prior to concluding such trade and investment treaties.

As part of the States parties' obligations to respect, protect and fulfil the economic, social and cultural rights recognized in the ICESCR in relation to business activities, the General Comment provided a range of measures that need to be taken by the States parties, including taking legislative measure mandating business enterprises to conduct human rights due diligence in their own operations and in the supply chain. The main components of the State obligations in this regard included: direct regulation and intervention, and regulation of privatization of public good and services in line with the States parties' obligations under the Covenant; direct provision of goods and services essential to the enjoyment of Covenant rights; and provision of effective remedies when corporate human rights abuses occurred. Such an interpretative guidance will provide States parties with an opportunity to codify the relevant international standards on the *Corporate responsibility* to respect human rights at the national level. These standards on the *Corporate responsibility* to respect human rights have the functions of not only embracing very abstractly formulated norms, but also enabling more effectively for the interaction with other legally binding norms and standards.[687]

The *Combination/zebra* standards contained in the UN Guiding Principles on Business and Human Rights contains the component of the *Corporate responsibility* to respect human rights as an international standard, clarity of which can be provided by the CESCR-Committee through a General Comment as an interpretative aide for the States parties when it comes to what concrete legislative, administrative, policy and judicial measures must or should be taken by them in meeting their international obligations to respect, protect and fulfil human rights in relation to business activities.[688] This is particularly important considering the fact that the so-called hard norm part of the *State obligations* to respect, protect, and fulfil in relation to business activities under the current international human rights law regime do not precisely cover the *Corporate responsibility* to respect human rights. Hence, the *Corporate responsibility* to respect human rights as an international standard serves to complement the existing norms and principles, which can be distinguished from isolated standing-alone soft law notions, as well as from mere factual assessments. It is therefore be submitted that the international standard on the *Corporate responsibility* to respect human rights contained in the *Combination/zebra* standards on business and human rights (The UN Guiding Principles on Business and Human Rights) "*profess normal typical, average social evaluations of practice reason*" when it comes to what is expected of business enterprises in society, which can, in turn, offer "*common sense solutions*" that can be easily accepted by many States and prepare the ground for shaping future legal developments.[689]

With respect to provision of remedies against corporate human rights abuse, the General Comment also highlights the central role to be

687 Supra note 2, Eibe Riedel, 'Standards as Sources,' German Yearbook of International Law (GYIL) vol. 63 (220), 369-417 at 388-417.

688 Ibid., p. 406.

689 For the role of standards, see Ibid., at p. 416.

played by judicial mechanisms. Non-judicial mechanisms such as national human rights institutions, labour inspectorates and tribunals, consumer and environmental protection agencies and financial supervision authorities could play an important complementary role in providing remedies against corporate human rights abuses. It is crucial that both judicial and non-judicial mechanisms should be credible, independent and effectively contribute to the prevention of, and reparation for such corporate human rights abuses.

When it comes to required protection measures against corporate human rights abuse, the General Comment also suggests a whole range of policy choices/options for the States parties to the ICESCR. It is worth noting that the General Comment implicitly acknowledges the utility of *Combination/zebra* standards on business and human rights in this regard. These so-called *Combination/zebra* standards can serve as yardsticks for specific conduct patterns, which can be termed as 'standards of conduct.' These standards usually relate to technical rules and generally supplement binding principles and rules contained in treaties, customary international law and/or the general principles of international law. They are applied on a voluntary basis and States have the choice of applying these technical standards without going through the lengthy sometimes complex ratification process. These standards have also the advantage of being capable of adaptation to the changing circumstances.[690] Professor Riedel has also highlighted in this regard that "*these standards can either deal with issues not covered by binding treaty norms, or they can serve to supplement existing treaty law, facilitating its implementation.*"[691] These standards are, in practice,

---

690 For detailed expositions on the main features and functions of the so-called combination standards (zebra standards) as sources, see supra note 2, Riedel, 'Standards as Sources,' at 396-417.

691 Ibid., Eibe Riedel, 'Standards as Sources,' German Yearbook of International Law (GYIL) vol. 63 (220), 369-417 at 398. With respect to the unique features or utility of the so-called combination standards developed in the context of the International Labour Organization (ILO), Professor Riedel succinctly concluded that "*the ILO standards produced in the form of conventions, recommendations, declarations, resolutions, and statements to a large part remain below the level of binding law, but present very effective and ready-made programmatic,*

elaborated by expert bodies such as the CESCR-Committee set up by an international treaty. The General Comment No. 26 of the CESCR-Committee is a prime example of such an elaboration of standards, in particular those related to the *Corporate responsibility* to respect human rights. However, it is worth mentioning that an oversized focus laid in the General Comment on recommended policy choices/options may run the risk of blurring the lines between what constitutes measures that '*must*' be taken to meet the States parties' *obligations*, and that '*should*' be taken as recommended policy choices/options available for the States parties under the ICESCR.

Among the groups that are disproportionately affected by the adverse impacts of business activities, Indigenous Peoples have enjoyed special treatment in the General Comment. The General Comment emphasized the importance of respecting the principle of free, prior and informed consent of Indigenous Peoples in relation to matters affecting their rights, including their rights to lands, territories and resources. States parties should therefore ensure that business enterprises conduct good faith (*bona fide*) consultations with Indigenous Peoples as an essential part of conducting human rights impact assessments, which in turn constitutes a central component of human rights due diligence.

A host of international voluntary guidelines have been developed, which serves to provide guidance both for States and business enterprises on how to address the negative impacts of business activities on the enjoyment of human rights. These Guidance/Guidelines both address the *State duty* to protect from corporate human rights abuse and the *Corporate responsibility* to respect human rights (*Combination/zebra standards*). Considering their voluntary nature, the implementation and operationalization of such Guidance/Guidelines on the ground depends a great deal on the willingness

---

appellative or harmonising yardsticks, which provide rich incentive to shape regulation in national law by serving as signposts or model laws, or interpretation aids when it comes to interpreting open principles and rules," ibid., at 404.

and commitment of both States and business enterprises. Therefore, these Guidance/Guidelines will have a full meaning and effect only when the guidance provided for in those Guidelines is fully followed up and observed in practice.

The effectiveness of these Guidance/Guidelines also depends in large part on what kinds of in-built implementation/follow-up mechanisms there are. The OECD Guidelines for MNEs and the ILO MNE Declaration, for instance, have similar built-in implementation mechanisms such as National Contact Points (NCPs) under the OECD Guidelines for MNEs and National Focal Points (NFPs) under the ILO MNE Declaration. However, it should be noted that whether these NCPs or NFPs effectively function in a way that increases the level of implementation of these Guidance/Guidelines is still called into question, when it comes to them serving as an adequate avenue of provision of remedy against corporate human rights abuse.

The UN Guiding Principles on Business and Human Rights is the most recent and comprehensive, perhaps the most authoritative guidance when it comes to the international human rights standards on business and human rights. The added value of the UN Guiding Principles on Business and Human Rights lies in the fact that they make a clear distinction between the *State duty/obligation* to protect and the *Corporate responsibility* to respect human rights constituting as "*Combination/zebra standards*" on business and human rights. They clarify the distinct but yet complementary *State duty/obligation* to protect from corporate human rights abuse and the *Corporate responsibility* to respect human rights under the existing international human rights law regime. They also address another crucial element of the requirement to provide remedies against corporate human rights abuses as part of their respective *State duty/obligation* to protect and *Corporate responsibility* to respect human rights. It is submitted that the UN Guiding Principles on Business and Human Rights provide a broad framework for the *State duty/obligation* to protect from corporate human rights abuse and the *Corporate responsibility* to respect human rights under international human rights law. It is therefore critically important to operationalize this broad framework on the ground by clarifying what is required to implement those Guiding Principles related to business and human rights.

When it comes to the *Corporate responsibility* to respect human rights, greater efforts should be made to clarify what are the minimum requirements for conducting human rights due diligence in different sectors and industries of the UN Guiding Principles on Business and Human Rights. Parallel efforts should also be made to clarify what States are obligated to do concretely in order to meet their international obligations regarding their *State duty/obligation* to protect from corporate human rights abuse. In this regard, UN treaty monitoring bodies can play a critically important role as they can provide an authoritative interpretation of what is the content of the *State obligations* to respect, protect and fulfil human rights in relation to business activities under the respective treaties, whose implementation by States parties they are mandated to monitor and oversee. Regional and national-level practices could also be of high relevance in terms of clarifying what measures '*must*' be taken by States as part of fulfilling their international obligations to respect, protect and fulfil human rights in relation to business activities.

Preventing and remedying human rights harms caused by business activities are at the core of the spirit and letter of the UN Guiding Principles on Business and Human Rights. In this regard, an argument has been put forward that the voluntary Guidelines/Guidance have proven to be of limited effect, when it comes to redressing corporate human rights abuses. Conversely, another school of thought, particularly the one supported by the business community has argued that more time is needed to give full effect to the UN Guiding Principles on Business and Human Rights, because the negative impacts of business activities on the enjoyment of human rights will be better addressed once these Guiding Principles on Business and Human Rights are more widely accepted and operationalized by business enterprises themselves.

Bearing in mind the ultimate objective of both legally binding rules and voluntary guidelines on business and human rights, i.e., to prevent, identify, investigate, mitigate and remedy the human rights harms caused by business activities, a combination of these two sets of rules and guidelines both on the international and domestic law planes should be employed and promoted. Therefore, the most critical element to be considered in designing the international legally binding treaty on business and human rights should be to ensure that these international norms and standards establish an effective and satisfactory remedy mechanism on the international law plane, whether it be judicial or quasi-judicial or non-judicial in nature, which will, in turn, enable corporate human rights abuse victims to have access to remedies against corporate human rights abuses.

The then UN Sub-Commission had played a pioneering role in clarifying the international human rights norms[692] that are relevant to addressing the negative impacts of business activities on the enjoyment of human rights. The adoption of the Norms on the responsibilities of transnational corporations and other business enterprises with regard to human rights marked a milestone in the process of clarifying the content of the *State obligations* to respect, protect and fulfil human rights in relation to business activities. However, the then UN Sub-commission had adopted too broad an interpretative approach to claiming that business enterprises currently have the *obligation* to respect human rights on the international law plane. This had resulted in a regrettable situation where its own parent body, the then UN Commission on Human Rights had not endorsed the Norms, despite the fact that the Norms themselves constituted a very important body of international human rights norms and standards on business and human rights.

---

692 Supra note 418, 'Norms on the responsibilities of transnational corporations and other business enterprises with regard to human rights', UN Doc, E/CN.4/Sub.2/2003/12/Rev.2 of 26 August 2003. It can be accessed at the following webpage: https://documents.un.org/doc/undoc/gen/g03/160/08/pdf/g0316008.pdf. (Accessed as of 17 February 2025).

It is submitted that the inter-sessional working group of the then UN Sub-commission fell short of clearly specifying the legal basis, based on which the direct legal obligations can be imposed on business enterprises under international human rights law. Certain norms identified in the Norms can be directly applied to business enterprises, including those norms relevant to international crimes, customary international law, and peremptory norms (*ius cogens*). However, the mere existence of such norms that can be directly applied to non-state actors such as business enterprises cannot automatically lead to the conclusion that the direct legal obligations can be imposed on business enterprises on the international law plane.

Despite unsuccessful attempts to craft the framework of international human rights norms that can be directly imposed on business enterprises, the momentum to create an international human rights instrument that would impose the direct legal obligations on business enterprises on the international law plane had persisted, which led to the establishment of the open-ended inter-governmental working group (OEIGWG) to elaborate on a legally binding instrument to regulate, in international law, the activities of transnational corporations and other business enterprises in the framework of the UN Human Rights Council.

A closer examination of the current updated draft legally binding instrument on business and human rights points to the fact that it is not designed to impose the direct legal obligations on business enterprises to respect human rights on the international law plane. The draft instrument rather focuses on what '*must*' and '*should*' be done in order to meet the *State obligations* to respect, protect and fulfil human rights in relation to business activities. It is therefore submitted that there is little added value of concluding an international treaty on business and human rights at this stage as the existing international human rights law regime is adequate in terms of providing for *the State obligations* to respect, protect and fulfil human rights in relation to business activities. What is woefully lacking is the full implementation of such *State obligations* at the national level. Unless the future treaty on business and human rights creates an international mechanism such as an international-level dispute settlement body/tribunal that can review and adjudicate allegations of corporate human rights abuses and provide enforceable remedies against them, it would result in an international instrument with little practical added-value. Consequently, it is most likely that States would not ratify it. The attitude towards this future treaty may likely change at least at the European Union (EU) level as an increasing number of EU policy makers and legislators (Members of the European Parliament – MEPs) has been pushing the European Commission to formally engage in negotiating in the drafting of the future treaty on business and human rights at the UN level.[693] It is also worth noting that many European States such as France and Germany have also enacted the mandatory human rights due diligence laws.[694] Moreover, the EU also adopted the CSDDD in 2024 mandating applicable business enterprises to conduct human rights/ environmental due diligence in their own operations and in the supply chain in closer alignment with the UN Guiding Principles on Business and Human Rights. These regional and national-level development of mandatory human rights due diligence law may provide further impetus for concluding the future treaty on business and human rights.

With respect to the scope of the application of a future treaty, it is submitted that the future treaty should not only apply to transnational corporations but also to all business enterprises. In this regard, the particular

---

693 On 16 July 2020, 75 MEPs urged the European Union to "adopt a negotiation mandate to participate in the UN negotiations for a binding treaty on business and human rights". This call for the EU's participation in the negotiation of the binding treaty at the UN level may reflect the EU's confidence as the global leader on national legislation on human rights and environmental due diligence to be conducted by business enterprises. Hence, it may be logical for the EU to engage in the future binding treaty on business and human rights whose core content is to codify the State obligation to protect from corporate human rights abuse at the national level. See https://www.business-humanrights.org/sites/default/files/documents/2020-07-20%20-%20EU%20Parliament%20-%20Letter%20requesting%20a%20negociation%20mandate.pdf. (Accessed as of 17 February 2025).

694 See supra Chapter 8.

challenges caused by the activities of transnational corporations on the enjoyment of human rights should explicitly be acknowledged. However, considering that there exist the vast number of non-transnational corporations that can cause significant negative impacts on the enjoyment of human rights, the future treaty should cover all business enterprises. Furthermore, the need to cover all business enterprises becomes even more acute, when seen from the perspective of protection of corporate human rights abuse victims. The central issue for corporate human rights abuse victims is that corporate human rights abuses must be investigated, mitigated, and remedied. Accordingly, it is vital that all business enterprises should be required to identify, prevent, mitigate and remedy the human rights harms caused and contributed to by their business activities. The fact that the current updated draft legally binding instrument of the OEIGWG has expanded its scope of application to the activities of all business enterprises is a welcome development from the zero draft legally binding instrument that narrowly limited the scope of application of the future treaty to business activities of a transnational character.

The extraterritorial obligation of States (home States) is an essential component of the State obligation to protect from corporate human rights abuse. The extraterritorial obligation already exists as an integral part of the general obligations of States under international human rights law, which leads to the conclusion that there is no real need to make an additional international legally binding treaty to simply reaffirm such *State duty/obligation* to protect from corporate human rights abuse, including the extraterritorial obligation of States. Potentially, one can find value in codifying and clarifying the content of such *State duty/obligation* to protect from corporate human rights abuse, including through the codification of the extraterritorial obligation to protect from corporate human rights abuse in the future treaty. However, it is worth noting that such an articulation and elaboration of the content of the *State duty/obligation* to protect from corporate human rights abuse can easily be achieved by the existing treaty monitoring bodies under international human rights treaties such as the Committee on Economic, Social and Cultural Rights. It is equally important to acknowledge, in this regard, that the implementation of such extra obligation of States parties to protect from corporate human rights abuse ultimately rests with States themselves at the national level.

Furthermore, considering that a large number of States parties to the existing human rights treaties lack capacity and resources to meet the reporting obligations to concerned treaty bodies, the additional reporting obligation to be created on the States parties to the future treaty on business and human rights may serve as an obstacle to effective implementation of the future treaty norms, when it comes to actual protection from corporate human rights abuse.

It is therefore submitted that it is premature to strive to conclude an international legally binding treaty on human rights and business without clearly articulating the added value of such an international treaty. It is therefore concluded that there is a critical need to strengthen the national human rights protection system, in particular strengthening legislative and judicial measures, to ensure that the *State duty/obligation* to protect from corporate human rights abuse, including measures to fully realize the extraterritorial obligation of States, is effectively fulfilled. In the absence of such clear added value, efforts should be made that would focus on strengthening measures aimed at ensuring that States fulfil their obligation to protect from corporate human rights abuse at the national level. Towards this end, States must adopt legislative, administrative, policy, judicial, promotional and educational, and other measures necessary to ensure effective protection against corporate human rights abuse. States must not only exercise due diligence themselves in meeting this obligation to protect from corporate human rights abuse, but also, they must ensure that business enterprises conduct human rights due diligence in order not to impede the enjoyment of human rights of those who depend on their business activities or who may be negatively affected by them. States must also provide victims of such business-related human rights abuses with remedies when such victims suffer from human rights harms caused by business activities. The special procedures and the universal periodic review (UPR) of the Human Rights Council has been addressing business and human rights-related issues notably since the adoption of the UN Guiding Principles on Business and Human Rights. Of particular note is the establishment of the United Nations Working Group on Business and Human Rights, which has the principal aim of assisting States in operationalizing at the country level the UN Guiding Principles on Business and Human Rights.

It is submitted that the Working Group on Business and Human Rights has made a considerably high-level of progress in fulfilling the mandates given to it by the UN Human Rights Council. Of the most notable are: 1) the publication of the Guidance on how to prepare the National Action Plan on Business and Human Rights; 2) the clarification of what is meant by corporate human rights due diligence; 3) the further clarification of the *State duty* to protect from corporate human rights abuses; 4) the ongoing provision of further guidance on access to remedy against corporate human rights abuses; and the development of further guidance on how to incorporate a gender perspective in relation to business and human rights issues. The Working Group on Business and Human Rights has thus been focusing on providing guidance aimed at mostly helping States operationalize the *State duty* to protect pillar contained in the UN Guiding Principles on Business and Human Rights. However, there is a strong need for the Working Group on Business and Human rights to provide further clarity and guidance on how to operationalize the *Corporate responsibility* to respect and Access to remedy Pillars of the UN Guiding Principles on Business and Human Rights, in particular through clearly identifying what '*should*' be done by business enterprises, when it comes to conducting human rights due diligence in their own operations and in the supply chain.

It is worth noting that the Working Group on Business and Human Rights did not have the initial mandate of processing individual communications on corporate human rights abuses, despite the fact that it was part of the UN special procedures when first established in 2011. In 2015, when the mandate of the Working Group on Business and Human Rights was renewed, the Working Group on Business and Human Rights was given the mandate to address individual cases of business-related human rights abuses. This component of the mandate of the Working Group on Business and Human Rights is significant in the sense that it not only promotes the dissemination and operationalization of the UN Guiding Principles on Business and Human Rights, but also monitors corporate human rights abuses worldwide. It is therefore submitted that in order to more effectively fulfil its mandate, the Working Group on Business and Human Rights should strike a balance between its promotional and monitoring work.

The UN Annual Forum on Business and Human Rights guided by the Working Group on Business and Human Rights has also achieved an impressive level of visibility in the business community. In this regard, it is submitted that resources should be strengthened within OHCHR, which will, in turn, allow the Working Group on Business and Human Rights to provide adequate guidance and advice on specific areas of critical importance, including individualized and tailored advice on such issues as corporate human rights due diligence, including how to effectively conduct human rights impact assessments, integrate findings of such human rights impact assessments into business operations, as well as track and report both internally and externally on company actions thereon.

United Nations special procedures mandate holders have also been addressing the interlinkages between their respective thematic mandates and business and human rights-related issues. It is submitted that this important body of work by special procedures mandate holders will provide a further clarification and understanding of how business activities can impact on the whole spectrum of human rights. It will further assist States in meeting its international obligations to respect, protect and fulfil human rights in relation to business activities, as well as in operationalizing the UN Guiding Principles on Business and Human Rights at the country level. However, there is still a strong need for special procedures mandate holders to provide clear guidance on what '*must*' and '*should*' be done as part of meeting the *State obligations* to respect, protect and fulfil human rights in relation to business activities, as well as on what '*should*' be done by business enterprises' meeting the *Corporate responsibility* to respect human rights under the current international human rights law regime, in particular clarifying the essential steps that need to be taken for the purpose of conducting human rights due diligence in their own operations and in the supply chain. In this connection, it is critically important for special procedures mandate holders not to confuse measures that must be taken with policy options/recommendations that can be taken by States as part of meeting the *State obligations* to respect, protect and fulfil human rights, as well as of business enterprises' meeting the *Corporate responsibility* to respect human rights.

The universal periodic review has also increasingly been addressing issues related to business and human rights. An increase in the number and substantive depth of business and human rights-related UPR recommendations, in particular since the third cycle review is a welcome development. It is critically important that States implement these business and human rights-related UPR recommendations at the country level in full alignment of the UN Guiding Principles on Business and Human Rights.

Since the adoption of the UN Guiding Principles on Business and Human Rights in 2011, an increasing number of States have made and been making efforts to strengthen the *State duty* to protect from corporate human rights abuse. Legislating mandatory human rights due diligence at the national level as an essential component of the *Corporate responsibility* to respect human rights lies at the heart of such efforts. Such mandatory human rights due diligence law will bolster the arguments for making the *Corporate responsibility* to respect human rights a legal obligation on the international law plane. A host of European States[695] have adopted such a mandatory human rights due diligence law or been contemplating to adopt one. At the regional level, the European Union has also taken the lead by committing itself to developing such mandatory human rights and environmental due diligence law in 2021 that will be binding on all EU Member States. As such, the European Union adopted the Corporate Sustainability Due Diligence Directive in 2024.[696]

It is submitted that taking such legislative measures must be an integral part of the fulfilment of the *State duty* to protect from corporate human rights abuse. Under the current international human rights law regime, a clear distinction exists between the *State duty* to protect from corporate human rights abuse and the *Corporate responsibility* to respect human rights. In the absence of the direct legal obligation for business enterprises to respect human rights on the international law plane, the most effective and practical way to ensure business respect of human rights is through the strengthening of the *State duty* to protect from corporate human rights abuse on the domestic law plane. The adoption of laws in countries that mandate business enterprises to conduct human rights due diligence (mandatory human rights due diligence) in their own operations and in the supply chain is therefore a most welcome development as it will pave the way for the most effective operationalization and implementation of the UN Guiding Principles on Business and Human Rights at the country level. It is of central importance that such mandatory human rights due diligence law should be developed in full alignment with the relevant international human rights norms and standards, in particular including the UN Guiding Principles on Business and Human Rights (*Combination/zebra* standards). Of equal importance is that such laws should be effectively enforced against those business enterprises that fail to comply with the requirement of conducting mandatory human rights due diligence in their own operations and in the supply chain. It is further expected that a proliferation of such national and regional laws of mandatory human rights due diligence would lend support to an early conclusion of a legally binding international treaty on business and human rights that is currently being

695 See supra Chapter 8.
696 Supra note 607.

deliberated under the auspices of the UN Human Rights Council.

When it comes to the extraterritoriality of such national human rights due diligence law, it is critical to ensure that the law allows corporate human rights abuse victims to have access to remedies against corporate human rights abuses in home States. It is equally important that a consistency in the law in different countries be achieved when it comes to the possibility of corporate abuse victims' getting such remedies against corporate human rights abuses. The exercise of extraterritorial jurisdiction by home States and/or the possibility for corporate human rights abuse victims to seek remedies using home States' national legal frameworks can serve a critically important function when it comes to fulfilling both the *State duty/obligation* to protect from corporate human rights abuse on the international law plane and the legal obligation of business enterprises to respect human rights on the domestic law plane.

National action plans on business and human rights can serve as a roadmap for an array of legislative, policy, judicial measures that States must and should adopt as part of meeting their international obligations to respect, protect and fulfil human rights in relation to business activities under their territories and/or jurisdictions. A host of merits exist in developing such national human rights action plans on business and human rights. For instance, consultations with key stakeholders at the national level for the development of a national action plan on business and human rights can contribute significantly to raise the awareness of the importance of the *Corporate responsibility* to respect human rights coupled with the State's international obligations to respect, protect and fulfil human rights in relation to business activities both within its territory and/or jurisdiction. This will further build a momentum for the development of legislative (such as enactment of a mandatory human rights and environmental due diligence law), administrative, policy and judicial measures aimed at enhancing the *Corporate responsibility* to respect human rights. However, it is crucially important that States should ensure effective implementation of such national action plans on business and human rights, which should be developed based on the relevant international "*Combination/zebra* standards" on business and human rights contained in the UN Guiding Principles on Business and Human Rights with the aim of enhancing the *State duty* to protect from corporate human rights abuse and strengthening the *Corporate responsibility* to respect human rights on the ground.

It is submitted that effective access to remedies against corporate human rights abuse, including monetary compensation, restitution, public apologies, and promises of a non-repetition matters the most for corporate human rights abuse victims. Judicial remedies lie at the heart of such remedies, which could be sought by corporate human rights abuse victims using the national human rights protection frameworks that permit extraterritorial jurisdiction of the courts of home States. Such national legal frameworks can serve as an important avenue of ensuring corporate accountability for business-related human rights harms. Various policy and judicial measures, in particular state-based judicial mechanisms aimed at providing access to effective remedies for corporate human rights abuse victims need to be further strengthened at the national level.

Inter-state judicial cooperation, including mutual legal assistance, plays an important role in ensuring for remedies against corporate human rights abuses. Considering that there exist a range of practical challenges that would hinder effective inter-state judicial cooperation, States should take a range of practical steps intended to enhance the ability of relevant State agencies to seek and obtain cooperation and assistance from their counterparts in other jurisdictions, including putting in place bilateral and multilateral arrangements for such inter-state judicial cooperation, enabling joint investigations through the establishment of joint investigation teams, ensuring access to information and training, development of centralized information repositories, and promoting awareness and facilitating networking between law enforcement practitioners amongst States, and recognition and enforcement of judgments, among others.

This study has reaffirmed that there is a clear distinction between the *State duty* to protect from corporate human rights abuse (*obligation*) and the *Corporate responsibility* to respect human rights (*responsibility*) under the current international human rights law regime. These distinct but complementary norms and standards on business and human rights (*Combination/zebra* standards) serve as important legal bases for identifying what '*must*' and '*should*' be done on the part of States in order to fulfil their international obligations to respect, protect and fulfil human rights in relation to business activities, as well as what '*should*' be done on the part of business enterprises to effectively meet their responsibility to respect human rights.

The study also concludes that despite the fact that there currently exist a host of international voluntary Guidance/Guidelines related to business and human rights, as well as voluntary initiatives by business enterprises themselves aimed at increasing the level of corporate respect of human rights, there has been limited effect when it comes to remedying the corporate human rights harms suffered by corporate human rights abuse victims. It therefore suggests that the most practical and effective way to ensure corporate accountability for human rights abuse is to strengthen the national human rights protection system, which facilitates States' meeting the *State duty* to protect from corporate human rights abuse at the national level. Towards this end, States have taken a range of legislative, policy and judicial measures. Some efforts at the international and regional levels have also been made with the aim of increasing the level of corporate accountability for corporate human rights abuses. This study has shown that legislative measures both at the national and regional levels, in particular the enactment of mandatory human rights due diligence law, can constitute the critically most important element, when it comes to fulfilling the *State duty* to protect from corporate human rights abuse thus ensuring for corporate respect for human rights.

The study further concludes that a proliferation of mandatory human rights due diligence law will lend support to an early conclusion of a binding international human rights treaty on business and human rights that is currently being deliberated under the auspices of the UN Human Rights Council. Such an international treaty could potentially contribute to the effective enforcement of "*Combination/zebra* standards" on business and human rights both at the international and national levels, in particular through codifying the *Corporate responsibility* to respect human rights as a treaty norm on the international law plane. At the same time, the study concludes that there is little added value of concluding an international treaty on business and human rights at this stage as the existing international human rights law regime is adequate in terms of providing for *the State obligations* to respect, protect and fulfil human rights in relation to business activities. Unless such a future treaty on business and human rights creates an international mechanism such as an international-level dispute settlement body/tribunal that can review and adjudicate allegations of corporate human rights abuses and provide enforceable remedies against them, it would result in an international instrument with little practical added-value, which most likely lead to the situation where States would not ratify it.

The study has also explored the important role that international human rights mechanisms, including treaty bodies, special procedures and the UPR can play in ensuring corporate accountability for corporate human rights abuses both at the international and national levels. In this connection, the study concludes that it is critically important for these international human rights mechanisms to take care not to confuse measures that '*must*' be taken (obligations) and policy options/recommendations that '*should*' be taken by States as part of meeting the *State obligations* to respect, protect and fulfil human rights, as well as that of business enterprises' meeting the *Corporate responsibility* to respect human rights.

Bibliography

I. MONOGRAPHS

A Zerk, *Multinationals and Corporate Social Responsibility* (Cambridge University Press, 2006)

Andreas von Arnauld, *Völkerrecht* (C.F. Müller, 2019)

Andrew Clapham, *Human Rights Obligations of Non-State Actors* (Oxford University Press, 2006)

Bertrand Ramcharan, *The United Nations High Commissioner for Human Rights: The Challenges of International Protection* (Cambridge University Press, 2002)

Beth Stephens et al, *International Human Rights Litigation in U.S. Courts* (2nd ed.), Martinus Nijhoff Publishers, 2008)

Christian Tomuschat, *Human Rights Between Idealism and Realism* (Oxford University Press, 2008)

Christof Heyens/Frans Viljoen, *The Impact of the United Nations Human Rights Treaties on the Domestic Level* (The Hague, 2002)

Edwin P Reubens, *The Challenge Of The New International Economic Order*, (Routledge, 2021)

Eibe Riedel, *The Universality of Human Rights* (original title: *Die Universalität der Menschenrechte)*, Christian Koenig/Ralph Alexander Lorz (Eds.), Veröffentlichungen des Walther-Schücking-Institututs für Internationales Recht an der Universität Kiel, Bd. 143, (Duncker & Humboldt, Berlin, 2003)

Eibe Riedel, *Constitutionalism – Old Concepts, New Worlds, German Contributions to the VI.th World Congress of the International Association of Constitutional Law (IACL)*, (Berliner Wissenschaftsverlag, Berlin, 2005)

Eibe Riedel, *The Human Right to Water*, in Veröffentlichungen des Walther-Schücking-Instituts für Internationales Recht an der Universität Kiel, Festschrift Delbrück, Bd. 155, (Duncker & Humblot, Berlin, 2006)

Gudmundur Alfredsson/Asbjørn Eide (Eds.), *The Universal Declaration of Human Rights – A Common Standard of Achievement* (The Hague, 1999)

Henry Shue, *Basic Rights: Subsistence, Affluence and U.S. Foreign Policy*, (Princeton University

Press, 1996)

Henry J. Steiner/Philip Alston (Eds.), *International Human Rights in Context: Law, Politics, Morals* (Oxford University Press, 1996)

Henry J. Steiner, Philip Alston, and Ryan Goodman, *International Human Rights in Context* (Oxford University Press, 2008)

Ian Brownlie, *Principles of Public International Law* (Clarendon Press, 1990)

Justinian, *The Digest of Roman Law: Theft, Rapine, Damage and Insult*, translated by Colin Kolbert (Penguin Classics, 1979)

L. Hannikainen, *Peremptory Norms (Jus Cogens) in International Law* (Finnish Lawyers' Publishing Company, 1988)

Manfred Nowak, *Introduction to the International Human Rights Regime* (Martinus Nijhoff Publishers, 2003)

Manfred Nowak, *UN Covenant on Civil and Political Rights: CCPR Commentary* (N.P. Engel Verlag. 2005)

Mark W. Janis, *An Introduction to International Law*, (Little, Brown and Company, 1993)

Mary Ann Glendon, *A World Made New: Eleanor Roosevelt and The Universal Declaration of Human Rights* (Random House, 2001)

Matthew Craven, *The International Covenant on Economic, Social and Cultural Rights* (Turku/Abo, 1999)

Matthew Craven, *The International Covenant on Economic, Social and Cultural Rights – A Perspective on its Development* (Oxford University Press, 1995)

Michael Hudson, *Global Fracture: The New International Economic Order*, (Pluto Press, 2005)

Mohamed Bedjaoui, *Towards a new international economic order*, (UNESCO, 1979)

Philip Alston (Ed.), *The United Nations and Human Rights: A Critical Appraisal* (Oxford University Press, 1992)

Philip Alston/James Crawford (Eds.), *The Future of UN Human Rights Treaty Monitoring* (Cambridge University Press, 2000)

P.N. Agarwala, *The New International Economic Order: An overview*, (Pergamon, 1983)

R Higgins, *Problems and Process: International Law and How We Use It*, (Clarendon Oxford, 1994)

R Portmann, *Legal Personality in international Law* (CUP Cambridge, 2010)

Reinhard Zimmerman, *The Law of Obligations: Roman Foundations of the Civilian Tradition* (Clarendon Press, 1996)

Sagafi-Nejad, *The UN and Transnational Corporations: From Code of Conduct to Global Compact* (Indiana University Press, 2008)

Sarah Joseph/Jenny Schultz/Melissa Castan (Eds.), *The International Covenant on Civil and Political Rights – Cases, Materials, and Commentary* (Oxford University Press, 2000)

Stéphanie Bijlmakers, *Corporate Social Responsibility, Human Rights, and the Law* (Routledge, 2009)

Susan Marks and Andrew Clapham, *International Human Rights Lexicon* (Oxford University Press, 2005)

Walter Kälin/ Jörg Künzli, *The Legal Nature of Human Rights Obligations* (Oxford University Press, 2009)

II. ARTICLES

A. Nussberger, "Evaluating the ILO's Approach to Standard-Setting and Monitoring in the Field of Social Security", in E. Riedel (ed.), *Social Security as a Human Right*, (Berlin/ Heidelberg, 2007), pp. 103-116.

B. Simma, 'The Examination of State Reports' in E. Klein (ed.), *The Monitoring System of Human Rights Treaty Obligations*, Berlin, 1998, pp. 31-48

C. Scott, 'Multinational Enterprises and Emergent Jurisprudence on Violations of Economic, Social and Cultural Rights,' in Eide, Krause, Rosas (eds.), *Economic, Social and Cultural Rights – A Textbook*, (Dordrecht, 2001), pp. 563-595

Daniel Warmer, 'Can Multinational Corporations Be Responsible?' (12 November 2020) available at: https://www.swissinfo.ch/eng/can-multinational-corporations-be-responsible-/46152654

David Weissbrodt and Muria Kruger, 'Norms on the Responsibilities of Transnational Corporations and Other Business Enterprises with Regard to Human Rights,' 97 Am. J. Int'l L. 901 (2003), available at: https://scholarship.law.umn.edu/cgi/viewcontent.cgi?article=1247&context=faculty_articles

E. Renaud, "The Right to Social Security – Current Challenges in International Perspective", in E. Riedel (ed.), *Social Security as a Human Right*, (Berlin/Heidelberg, 2007), pp. 1-16

Ed Bates, 'History in International Human Rights Law' (Daniel Moeckli et al eds) (Oxford University Press, 2010)

Eibe Riedel, 'The Examination of State Reports,' in E. Klein (ed.), *The Monitoring System of Human Rights Treaty Obligations*, Berlin, 1998, pp. 31-48

Eibe Riedel, 'Commentary to Art.55(c) UN-Charter, in Simma (ed.): The Charter of the United Nations – A Commentary,' (Oxford University Press, 2002)

Eibe Riedel, 'Commentary to Art.68, UN-Charter, in Simma (ed.): The Charter of the United

Nations, A Commentary,' (Oxford University Press, 2002)

Eibe Riedel, 'International Law Shaping Constitutional Law – Realization of Economic, Social and Cultural Rights – Constitutionalism – Old Concepts, New Worlds, German Contributions to the VI.th World Congress of the International Association of Constitutional Law (IACL),' Eibe Riedel (ed.), (Berliner Wissenschaftsverlag Berlin, 2005)

Eibe Riedel, 'The Development of International Law: Alternatives to Treaty-Making? International Organizations and Non-State-Actors, Developments of International Law in Treaty Making, Rüdiger Wolfrum/Volker Röben (Eds.), Heidelberg (2005), pp. 301-318

Eibe Riedel, 'Monitoring the International Covenant on Economic, Social and Cultural Rights (1966),' in Politakis, George P. (ed.): *Protecting Labour Rights as Human Rights: Present and Future of International Supervision, International Colloquium on the 80th anniversary of the ILO Committee of Experts*, Geneva, pp. 24-25 November 2006, ILO Geneva 2007

Eibe Riedel, 'The Human Right to Social Security: Some Challenges,' in E. Riedel (ed.), *Social Security as a Human Right*, (Berlin/Heidelberg, 2007), pp.17-28

Eibe Riedel, 'The Human Rights to Health, Conceptual Foundations,' in Andrew Clapham/ Mary Robinson, et al. (eds.): *Realizing the Right to Health*, (Rüffer & Rub. Zürich, 2009), pp. 23-41

Eibe Riedel, 'The Committee on Economic, Social and Cultural Rights,' Max Planck Encyclopedia of Public International Law (MPEPIL), No. 765, (Oxford University Press, 2010)

Eibe Riedel, 'International Covenant on Economic, Social and Cultural Rights (1966),' in R. Wolfrum (ed.), Max Planck Encyclopedia of Public International Law (MPEPIL), (Oxford University Press, 2010), no. 836.

Eibe Riedel, 'Rethinking Human Rights – Real Reforms in Procedure and Substance?' in J. Delbrück et al. (eds.), Aus Kiel in die Welt. Kiel's contribution to international law, Essays in honour of the 100th Anniversary of the Walther-Schücking Institute of International Law, (University of Kiel, Berlin 2014), 423

Eibe Riedel, 'Core Obligations in Social Rights and Human Dignity,' pp. 79-91 in 'Von der Kultur der Verfassung' (Max-Emanuel Geis, Markus Winkler, Christian Bickenbach eds), Festschrift Für Friedhelm Hufen Zum 70. Geburtstag, C.H.Beck (2015, special print)

Eibe Riedel, 'Reflections on the UN Human Rights Covenants at Fifty' Archiv des Völkerrechts (AVR) (2016)

Eibe Riedel, 'Standards as Sources,' German Yearbook of International Law (GYIL) vol. 63

(220)

Eide Asbjørn, 'Realization of Social and Economic Rights and the Minimum Threshold Approach,' Human Rights Law Journal, 1989 Vol. 10, No. 1–2

Eide Asbjørn, 'Economic and Social Rights,' in J. Symonides (ed.), *Human Rights. Concept and Standards*, (Aldershot, 2000, reprinted 2005), pp.109-174

Elif Askin, 'Economic and Social Rights, Extraterritorial Application,' Max Planck Encyclopedia of Public International Law, Oxford Public International Law (http://opil.ouplaw.com), (Oxford University Press, 2022) available at: https://opil.ouplaw.com/view/10.1093/law-epil/9780199231690/law-9780199231690-e2213?print=pdf

Hurst Hannum, 'The Status of the Universal Declaration of Human Rights in National and International Law,' 25 Georgia Journal of International and Comparative Law (1995/1996) 287

J Alvarez, 'Are Corporations "Subjects" of International Law?' (2011) 9 Santa Clara Journal of International Law 1-35

Jernej Letnar Cernic, 'Corporate Responsibility for Human Rights: A Critical Analysis of the OECD Guidelines for Multinational Enteprises,' Hanse Law Review, vol. 4, No. 1 (2008), pp 71-102;

Johannes Hendrik Fahner and Matthew Happold, 'The Human Rights Defence In International Investment Arbitration: Exploring The Limits of Systemic Integration,' International and Comparative Law Quarterly (ICLQ) vol. 68, (July 2019)

John P. Humphrey, 'The Universal Declaration of Human Rights: its History, Impact and Judicial Character,' in Bertrand G. Ramcharan (ed.), *Human Rights, Thirty Years after the Universal Declaration* (Martinus Nijhoff, 1979)

John Ruggie, 'The New Normal of Human Rights Due Diligence,' Op-Ed in Swiss Newspaper *HANDELSZEITUNG* of 22 March 2018. The English translation of the op-ed can be accessed at the following website: https://shiftproject.org/john-ruggie-weighs-in-on-swiss-debate-on-mandatory-human-rights-due-diligence/

John Ruggie, 'Keynote Address at the December 2019 Finnish EU Council Presidency Conference,' available at: https://shiftproject.org/resource/john-ruggie-keynote-finland2019/

John Ruggie, 'The Past as Prologue? A Moment of Truth for UN Business and Human Rights Treaty, Institute for Human Rights and Business', available at: https://www.hks.harvard.edu/m-rcbg/CSRI/Treaty_Final.pdf

John Ruggie and Tamaryn Nelson, 'Human Rights and the OECD Guidelines for Multinational Enterprises – Normative Innovations and Implementation Challenges,' The Brown Journal of World Affairs, vol. XXII, Issue I, Fall/Winter 2015, pp. 99-

128.

Jonathan Bonnitcha and Robert McCorquodale, 'The Concept of 'Due Diligence' in the UN Guiding Principles on Business and Human Rights,' European Journal of International Law (EJIL) (2017) Vol. 28 No. 3, 899-919

L. Lamarche, 'The Right to Social Security in the International Covenant on Economic, Social and Cultural Rights,' in A. Chapman and S. Russell (eds.), *Core Obligations: Building a Framework for Economic, Social and Cultural Rights*, (Antwerp, 2002), pp. 87-114

M. Langford, "The Right to Social Security and Implications for Law, Policy and Practice", in E. Riedel (ed.), *Social Security as a Human Right*, (Berlin/Heidelberg, 2007), pp. 29-53

M. Scheinin, 'The Right to Social Security,' in A. Eide, C. Krause, A. Rosas (eds.), *Economic, Social and Cultural Rights – A Textbook*, (Dordrecht, 2001), pp. 211-222

Margaret Jungk,'Why do we know so little about corporate human rights abuses?' available at: http://www.huffingtonpost.com/margaret-jungk/why-do-we-know-so-little-_b_8687196.html

Martens and Seitz, 'The Struggle for a UN Treaty: Towards global regulation on human rights and business,' Global Policy Forum and Rosa Luxembourg Stiftung – New York Office (https://www.globalpolicy.org/home/270-general/52867-new-publication-the-struggle-for-a-un-treaty.html

Mirina Grosz, 'Menschenrechte als Vehikel für ökologische Unternehmensverantwortung' [2017] Pratique Juridique Actuelle 982

Moran, 'The United Nations and Transnational Corporations: a review and a perspective,' available at: http://citeseerx.ist.psu.edu/viewdoc/download?doi=10.1.1.538.3403&rep=rep1&type=pdf

Nadia Bernaz, 'Clearer, Stronger, Better? – Unpacking the 2019 Draft Business and Human Rights Treaty,' available at: http://rightsasusual.com/?p=1339

Nico Krisch and Benedict Kingsbury, 'Global Governance and Global Administrative Law in the International Legal Order,' *European Journal of International Law,* vol. 17, No. 1 (February, 2006)

Nicolas Bueno, 'The Swiss Popular Initiative on Responsible Business: From Responsibility to Liability,' available at:

Odile Roussel, 'Paving the Way: The Pioneering role of the French Duty of Vigilance Law and the Relevance for EU-Level Mandatory Due Diligence,' available at: https://www.business-humanrights.org/en/blog/paving-the-way-the-pioneering-role-of-the-french-duty-of-vigilance-law-and-its-relevance-for-eu-level-mandatory-due-diligence/

Olivier de Schutter, 'Toward a New Treaty on Business and Human Rights,' Business and Human Rights Journal, Vol. 1 (1)

P. Alston/G Quinn, 'The Nature and Scope of State Parties' Obligations under the International Covenant on Economic, Social and Cultural Rights,' Human Rights Quarterly (1987) Vol. 9,156 et seq.

Paula Alexander Becker, 'The Alien Tort Statute of 1789 and International Human Rights Violations: Kiobel v. Royal Dutch Petroleum Co.,' New England Journal of Entrepreneurship: Vol.17: No. 1, Article 6, available at: https://www.academia.edu/72112666/The_Alien_Tort_Statute_of_1789_and_International_Human_Rights_Violations_Kiobel_v_Royal_Dutch_Petroleum_Co

Peter T Muchlinski, 'Corporation sin International Law,' Max Planck Encyclopedia of Public International Law in R Wolfrum (ed.) (2010), available at: https://opil.ouplaw.com/display/10.1093/law:epil/9780199231690/law-9780199231690-e1513

Ralph G. Steinhardt, Special Edition Response, 'Losing the "Right" Way Preserves the Narrow Scope of the Alien Tort Statute: NESTLE USA, INC., v. John DOE,' Geo. Wash. L. Rev. (2021), available at: https://www.gwlr.org/losing-the-right-way-preserves-the-narrow-scope-of-the-ats/

Robledo, Le *jus cogens* international: sa génese, sa nature, ses fonctions, 172 *Hague Recuueil* 9, 167-187 (1981)

Rüdiger Wolfrum, 'General International Law, Principles, Rules, and Standards,' Max Planck Encyclopedia for Public International Law (2010)

Sanders, 'The Impact of the "Ruggie Framework" and the United Nations Guiding Principles on Business and Human Rights on Transnational Human Rights Litigation', LSE Law, Society and Economy Working Papers 18/2014 (2014)

Sarah Joseph, 'Liability of Multinational Corporations,' in *Social Rights Jurisprudence – Emerging Trends in International and Comparative Law* (Malcolm Langford ed.) (Cambridge University Press, 2011), 613-627

III. UNITED NATIONS MATERIALS

Alfred de Zayas, 'Statement of the Independent Expert on the promotion of a democratic and equitable international order at the Human Rights Council 33rd session,' (13 September 2016), available at: https://www.ohchr.org/en/2016/09/statement-mr-alfred-maurice-de-zayas-independent-expert-promotion-democratic-and-equitable

CCPR-Committee, General Comment No. 31 [80] *"The Nature of the General Legal*

Obligation Imposed on States Parties to the Covenant" UN DOC., CCPR/C/21/Rev.1/Add.13

CCPR-Committee, General Comment No. 3 *"Article 2 (Implementation at the national level)"* replaced by General Comment No. 31

CCPR-Committee, General Comment No. 5 *"Article 4 (Derogations)"* replaced by General Comment No. 29

CCPR-Committee, General Comment No. 7 *"Article 7 (Prohibition of torture or cruel, inhuman or degrading treatment or punishment)"* replaced by General Comment No. 20

CCPR-Committee, General Comment No. 18 *"Nondiscrimination"*

CCPR-Committee, General Comment No. 23 [50] *"Article 27"* (UN Doc., CCPR/C/21/Rev.1/Add.5)

CCPR-Committee, General Comment No. 31 UN Doc., HRI/GEN/1/Rev.9 (Vol 1) 243 (UN Doc., CCPR/C/21/Rev.1/Add. 13)

CCPR-Committee, *"Concluding Observations on Germany"* (UN Doc., CCPR/C/DEU/CO/7)

CCPR-Committee, *"Concluding Observations on the Republic of Korea"* (UN Doc., CCPR/C/KOR/CO/4)

CEDAW-Committee, General Recommendation No. 19

CEDAW-Committee, General Recommendation No. 24 (UN Doc., CEDAW/C/GC/24)

CEDAW-Committee, General Recommendation No. 28 (UN Doc., CEDAW/C/GC/28)

CEDAW-Committee, *"Concluding Observations for Ecuador"* UN Doc., A/58/38 (SUPP)

CERD-Committee, General Recommendation No. 23

CERD-Committee, General Recommendation No. 31 (2005) *"The prevention of racial discrimination in the administration and functioning of the criminal justice system"*

CERD-Committee, *"Concluding Observations for Guatemala"* (UN Doc., CERD/C/GTM/CO/11)

CERD-Committee, *"Concluding Observations for Guyana"* (UN Doc., CERD/C/GUY/CO/14)

CERD-Committee, *"Concluding Observations for Nigeria"* (UN Doc., CERD/C/NGA/CO/18)

CERD-Committee, *"Concluding Observations for Suriname"* (UN Doc., CERD/C/64/CO/9)

CESCR-Committee, *"Report on the forty-sixth and forty-seventh sessions,"* (UN Doc., E/C.12/2011/3)

CESCR-Committee General Comment No. 3 *on "The nature of States parties' obligations (art. 2, para. 1 of the Covenant),"* (UN Doc. E/1991/23– E/C.12/1990/8 and corr. 1, annex III)

CESCR-Committee, General Comment No. 4 *"The right to adequate housing (Article 11(1) of the Covenant)"* (UN Doc., E/1995/22)

CESCR-Committee, General Comment No.5 *"Persons with Disabilities"* (UN Doc., E/1995/22)

CESCR-Committee, General Comment No. 7 *"The right to adequate housing (Article 11(1) of the Covenant): Forced evictions"* UN (Doc., E/1995/22)

CESCR-Committee, General Comment No. 8 *"The relationship between economic sanctions and respect for economic, social and cultural rights"* (UN Doc., E/C.12/1997/8)

CESCR-Committee, General Comment No. 9 *"The domestic application of the Covenant"* (UN Doc., E/)

CESCR-Committee, General Comment No. 12 *"The right to adequate food"* (UN Doc., E/C.12/1999/5)

CESCR-Committee, General Comment No. 14 *"The right to the highest attainable standard of health"* (UN Doc., E/C.12/2000/4)

CESCR-Committee, General Comment No. 15 *"The right to water"* (UN Doc., E/C.12/GC/15)

CESCR-Committee, General Comment No. 16, *"The equal right of men and women to the enjoyment of all economic, social and cultural rights"* (UN Doc., E/C.12/GC/16)

CESCR-Committee, General Comment No. 17 *"The right of everyone to benefit from the protection of the moral and material interests resulting from any scientific, literary or artistic production of which he or she is the author"* (UN Doc., E/C.12/GC/17)

CESCR-Committee, General Comment No. 19 *"The right to social security"* (UN Doc., E/C.12/GC/19)

CESCR-Committee, Draft General Comment on *"State Obligations under the ICESCR in the Context of Business Activities"* (UN Doc., E/C.12/60/R.1)

CESCR-Committee, General Comment No. 24 (2017) *"State obligations under the International Covenant on Economic, Social and Cultural Rights in the context of business activities"* (UN Doc., E/C.12/GC/24)

CESCR-Committee, "*Statement on the obligations of States parties regarding the corporate sector and economic, social and cultural rights*" (UN Doc., E/C.12/2011/1)

CESCR-Committee, Communication No. 2 /2014, *I.D.G. v. Spain* (2015)

CESCR-Committee, *"Concluding Observations on the fourth periodic report of Argentina"* (UN Doc., E/C.12/ARG/CO/4)

CESCR-Committee, *"Concluding Observations on the fifth periodic report of Australia"* (UN Doc., E/C.12/AUS/CO/5)

CESCR-Committee, *"Concluding Observations on the fourth periodic report of Azerbaijan"* (UN Doc., E/C.12/AZE/CO/4)

CESCR-Committee, *"Concluding Observations on the fifth periodic report of Belgium"* (UN

Doc., E/C.12/BEL/CO/5)

CESCR-Committee, *"Concluding Observations for China"* (UN Doc., E/C.12/1/Add.107)

CESCR-Committee, *"Concluding Observations on the sixth periodic report of Colombia"* (UN Doc., E/C.12/COL/CO/6)

CESCR-Committee, *"Concluding Observations on sixth periodic report of Denmark"* (UN Doc., E/C.12/DNK/CO/6)

CESCR-Committee, *"Concluding Observations on the seventh periodic report of Finland"* (UN Doc., E/C.12/FIN/CO/7)

CESCR-Committee, *"Concluding Observations on the sixth periodic report of Germany"* (UN Doc., E/C.12/DEU/CO/6)

CESCR-Committee, *"Concluding Observations on the initial report of Guinea"* (UN Doc., E/C.12/GIN/CO/1)

CESCR-Committee, *"Concluding Observations on the third periodic report of Iceland"* (UN Doc., E/C.12/1/Add.89)

CESCR-Committee, *"Concluding Observations on the second periodic report of Kazakhstan"* (UN Doc., E/C.12/KAZ/CO/2)

CESCR-Committee, *"Concluding Observations on the third periodic report of Kuwait"* (UN Doc., E/C.12/KWT/CO/3)

CESCR-Committee, *"Concluding Observations on the initial report of Mali"* (UN Doc., E/C.12/MLI/1)

CESCR-Committee, *"Concluding Observations on the fifth periodic report of Mauritius"* (UN Doc., E/C.12/MUS/CO/5)

CESCR-Committee, *"Concluding Observations on the fourth periodic report of Mexico"* UN Doc. E/C.12/MEX/CO/4

CESCR-Committee, *"Concluding Observations on the combined fifth and sixth periodic reports of Mexico"* (UN Doc., E/C.12/MEX/CO/5-6)

CESCR-Committee, *"Concluding Observations on the initial report of Niger"* (UN Doc., E/C.12/NER/1)

CESCR-Committee, *"Concluding Observations on the sixth periodic report of Norway"* (UN Doc., E/C.12/NOR/CO/6)

CESCR-Committee, *"Concluding Observations on the fourth periodic report of the Republic of Korea"* (UN Doc., E/C.12/KOR/CO/4)

CESCR-Committee, *"Concluding Observations for the Russian Federation"* (UN Doc. E/C.12/1/Add.94)

CESCR-Committee, *"Concluding Observations on the sixth periodic report of the Russian Federation"* (UN Doc., E/C.12/RUS/CO/6)

CESCR-Committee, *"Concluding Observations on the initial report of South Africa"* (UN Doc., E/C.12/ZAF/CO/1)

CESCR-Committee, *"Concluding Observations on the fourth periodic report of Switzerland"* (UN Doc., E/C.12/CHE/CO/4)

CESCR-Committee, *"Concluding Observations on the sixth periodic report of the United Kingdom of Great Britain and Northern Ireland"* (UN Doc., E/C.12/GBR/CO/6)

CRC-Committee, General Comment No. 5 (UN Doc., CRC/GC/2003/5)

CRC-Committee, General Comment No. 7 (UN Doc., CRC/C/GC/7/Rev.1)

CRC-Committee, General Comment No. 16 *"State obligations regarding the impact of the business sector on children's rights"* (UN Doc., C/CRC/GC/16)

Eide Asbjørn, 'The Right to Food as a Human Right,' (UN Doc. E/CN.4/Sub.2/1987/23)

Gefion Schuler, 'Effective Governance through Decentralized Soft Implementation: The OECD Guidelines for Multinational Enterprises,' German Law Journal, vol. 9, Issue 11: Special issue – The exercise of Public Authority by International Institutions (2008), pp. 1753-1778;

John Ruggie, 'Business and human rights: mapping international standards of responsibility and accountability for corporate acts: Report of the Special Representative of the Secretary-General on the issue of human rights and transnational corporations and other business enterprises,' (UN Doc., A/HRC/4/35)

John Ruggie,'Report of the Special Representative of the Secretary-General on the issue of human rights and transnational corporations and other business enterprises, Addendum: State responsibilities to regulate and adjudicate corporate activities under the United Nations core human rights treaties: an overview of treaty body commentaries,' (UN Doc. A/HRC/4/35/Add.1)

John Ruggie, 'Report of the Special Representative of the Secretary-General on the issue of human rights and transnational corporations and other business enterprises, Addendum: Human Rights Policies and Management Practices: Results from questionnaire surveys of Governments and Fortune Global 500 firms,' (UN Doc., A/HRC/4/35/Add.3)

John Ruggie, 'Report of the Special Representative of the Secretary-General on the issue of human rights and transnational corporations and other business enterprises: Human rights impact assessments – resolving key methodological questions,' (UN Doc., A/HRC/4/74)

John Ruggie, 'Protect, Respect and Remedy: A Framework for Business and Human Rights: Report of the Special Representative of the Secretary-General on the issue of human rights and transnational corporations and other business enterprises,' (UN Doc., A/

HRC/8/5)

John Ruggie, 'Report of the Special Representative of the Secretary-General on the Issue of Human Rights and Transnational Corporations and other Business Enterprises: Clarifying the Concepts of "Sphere of influence" and "Complicity",' (UN Doc, A/HRC/8/16)

OHCHR Fact Sheet No. 2 (Rev.1) *The International Bill of Human Rights*

OHCHR Fact Sheet No. 3, *Frequently Asked Questions on Economic, Social and Cultural Rights*

OHCHR Fact Sheet No. 15 (Rev.1): *Civil and Political Rights: The Human Rights Committee*

OHCHR *"Report of the United Nations High Commissioner for Human Rights on the responsibilities of transnational corporations and related business enterprises with regard to human rights"* UN Doc., E/CN.4/2005/91

OHCHR, *Guiding Principles on Business and Human Rights: Implementing the United Nations Protect, Respect and Remedy Framework* UN Publication, HR/PUB/11/04

OHCHR, *"Improving accountability and access to remedy for victims of business-related human rights abuse: Report of the United Nations High Commissioner for Human Rights"* (UN Doc., A/HRC/32/19)

OHCHR, *"Guidance to improve corporate accountability and access to judicial remedy for business-related human rights abuse,"* (UN Doc., A/HRC/32/19, Annex)

OHCHR, 'Impact of new technologies on the promotion and protection of human rights in the context of assemblies, including peaceful protests: Report of the United Nations High Commissioner for Human Rights,' (UN Doc., A/HRC/44/24)

OHCHR, 'The right to privacy in the digital age: Report of the United Nations High Commissioner for Human Rights,' (UN Doc., A/HRC/48/31)

OHCHR, *National action plans on business and human rights* available at: https://www.ohchr.org/EN/Issues/Business/Pages/nationalactionplans.aspx

OHCHR, National Action Plan on Business and Human Rights (The United Kingdom) available at: https://assets.publishing.service.gov.uk/government/uploads/system/uploads/attachment_data/file/522805/Good_Business_Implementing_the_UN_Guiding_Principles_on_Business_and_Human_Rights_updated_May_2016.pdf

OHCHR, National Action Plan on Business and Human Rights (Germany) available at: https://www.ohchr.org/Documents/Issues/Business/NationalPlans/NAP_Germany.pdf

OHCHR, Universal Human Rights Index, available at: https://uhri.ohchr.org/en/search-human-rights-recommendations.

United Nations Sub-Commission on the Promotion and Protection of Human Rights, *"The relationship between the enjoyment of human rights, in particular, international labour and trade union rights, and the working methods and activities of transnational corporations"* (UN Doc., E/CN.4/Sub.2/1995/11)

United Nations Sub-Commission on the Promotion and Protection of Human Rights, *"Report of the Secretary-General: The impact of the activities and working methods of transnational corporations on the full enjoyment of all human rights, in particular economic, social and cultural rights and the right to development, bearing in mind existing international guidelines, rules and standards relating to the subject-matter,"* (UN Doc., E/CN.4/Sub.2/1996/12)

United Nations Sub-Commission on the Promotion and Protection of Human Rights, *"Working document on the impact of the activities of transnational corporations on the realization of economic, social and cultural rights, prepared by Mr. El Hadji Guissé, pursuant to Sub-Commission resolution 1997/11, "* (UN Doc., E/CN.4/Sub.2/1998/6)

United Nations Sub-Commission on the Promotion and Protection of Human Rights *"Report of the sessional Working Group on the Working Methods and Activities of Transnational Corporations on its 1st session"* (UN Doc., E/CN.4/Sub.2/1999/9)

United Nations Sub-Commission on the Promotion and Protection of Human Rights *"Draft Universal Human Rights Guidelines for Companies, Addendum 2,"* (UN Doc., E/CN.4/Sub.2/2002/WG.2/WP.1/Add.2)

United Nations Sub-Commission on the Promotion and Protection of Human Rights, *"Resolution on: The relationship between the enjoyment of economic, social and cultural rights and the right to development, and the working methods and activities of transnational corporations,"* (UN Doc., E/CN.4/Sub.2/RES/1998/8)

United Nations Sub-Commission on the Promotion and Protection of Human Rights, *"Resolution on: The effects of the working methods and activities of transnational corporations on the enjoyment of human rights,"* (UN Doc., E/CN.4/Sub.2/RES/2001/3)

United Nations Sub-Commission on the Promotion and Protection of Human Rights, *"Resolution on: The relationship between the enjoyment of economic, social and cultural rights and the right to development, and the working methods and activities of transnational corporations,"* (UN Doc., E/CN.4/Sub.2/RES/2002/8)

United Nations Sub-Commission on the Promotion and Protection of Human Rights, *"Resolution on: Responsibilities of transnational corporations and other business enterprises with regard to human rights,"* (UN Doc., E/CN.4/Sub.2/RES/2003/16)

United Nations Commission on Human Rights, *"Resolution adopted by the Commission on Human Rights: Human rights and transnational corporations and other business enterprises,"* (UN Doc., E/CN.4/RES/2005/69)

United Nations General Assembly, *"Report of the Special Rapporteur on the implications for human rights of the environmentally sound management and disposal of hazardous substances and wastes,"* (UN.Doc., A/75/290)

United Nations General Assembly, *"Resolution adopted by the General Assembly on Human Rights Council,"* (UN Doc., A/RES/60/251)

United Nations Human Rights Council, *"Summary of discussions of the Forum on Business and Human Rights, prepared by the Chairperson, John Ruggie,"* (UN Doc., A/HRC/FBHR/2012/4)

United Nations Human Rights Council, *"Summary of discussions of the Forum on Business and Human Rights, prepared by the Chairperson, Makarim Wibisono,"* (UN Doc., A/HRC/FBHR/2013/4)

United Nations Human Rights Council, *"Summary of discussions of the Forum on Business and Human Rights, prepared by the Chair, Mo Ibrahim,"* (UN Doc., A/HRC/FBHR/2014/3)

United Nations Human Rights Council, *"Fourth session of the Forum on Business and Human Rights: summary of discussions,"* (UN Doc., A/HRC/FBHR/2015/2)

United Nations Human Rights Council, *"Fifth session of the Forum on Business and Human Rights: summary of discussions,"* (UN Doc., A/HRC/FBHR/2016/2)

United Human Rights Council, "*Report of the Special Rapporteur on violence against women, its causes and consequences, Rashida Manjoo,*" (UN Doc., A/HRC/14/22)

United Nations Human Rights Council, "*Report on the first session of the open-ended intergovernmental working group on transnational corporations and other business enterprises with respect to human rights, with the mandate of elaborating an international legally binding instrument,*" (UN Doc., A/HRC/31/50)

United Nations Human Rights Council, "*Report on the second session of the open-ended intergovernmental working group on transnational corporations and other business enterprises with respect to human rights, with the mandate of elaborating an international legally binding instrument,*" (UN Doc., A/HRC/34/47)

United Nations Human Rights Council, "*Report on the third session of the open-ended intergovernmental working group on transnational corporations and other business enterprises with respect to human rights, with the mandate of elaborating an international legally binding instrument,*" (UN Doc., A/HRC/37/67)

United Nations Human Rights Council, *"Report of the Special Rapporteur on the rights of indigenous peoples,"* (UN Doc., A/HRC/39/17)

United Nations Human Rights Council, "*Report on the fourth session of the open-ended intergovernmental working group on transnational corporations and other business enterprises with respect to human rights, with the mandate of elaborating an international legally binding instrument,*" (UN Doc., A/HRC/40/48)

United Nations Human Rights Council, "*Report of the Special Rapporteur on the right to privacy,*" (UN Doc., A/HRC/43/52)

United Nations Human Rights Council, "*Summary report of the Special Rapporteur on the issue of human rights obligations relating to the enjoyment of a safe, clean, healthy and sustainable environment,*" (UN Doc., A/HRC/43/54)

United Nations Human Rights Council, "*Report on the fifth session of the open-ended intergovernmental working group on transnational corporations and other business enterprises with respect to human rights, with the mandate of elaborating an international legally binding instrument,*" (UN Doc., A/HRC/43/55)

United Nations Human Rights Council, "*Report on the sixth session of the open-ended intergovernmental working group on transnational corporations and other business enterprises with respect to human rights, with the mandate of elaborating an international legally binding instrument,*" (UN Doc., A/HRC/46/73)

United Nations Human Rights Council, "*Report on the seventh session of the open-ended intergovernmental working group on transnational corporations and other business enterprises with respect to human rights, with the mandate of elaborating an international legally binding instrument,*" (UN Doc., A/HRC/49/65)

United Nations Human Rights Council, "*Report on the eighth session of the open-ended intergovernmental working group on transnational corporations and other business enterprises with respect to human rights, with the mandate of elaborating an international legally binding instrument,*" (UN Doc., A/HRC/52/41)

United Nations Human Rights Council, "*Draft report on the ninth session of the open-ended intergovernmental working group on transnational corporations and other business enterprises with respect to human rights, with the mandate of elaborating an international legally binding instrument,*", available at: https://www.ohchr.org/sites/default/files/documents/hrbodies/hrcouncil/igwg-transcorp/session9/igwg-9th-report.pdf

United Nations Human Rights Council, "*Two draft treaty texts, the first one in the main treaty and the second one in the form of an optional protocol,*" available at: https://www.ohchr.org/Documents/HRBodies/HRCouncil/WGTransCorp/OEIGWG_RevisedDraft_LBI.pdf

United Nations Human Rights Council, the 2018 zero draft legally binding instrument, in international human rights law, to regulate the activities of transnational corporations and other business enterprises, available at: https://www.ohchr.org/Documents/HRBodies/HRCouncil/WGTransCorp/Session3/DraftLBI.pdf)

United Nations Human Rights Council, the revised draft legally binding instrument to regulate, in international human rights law, the activities of transnational corporations and other business enterprises in July 2019, available at: https://www.ohchr.org/Documents/HRBodies/HRCouncil/WGTransCorp/OEIGWG_RevisedDraft_LBI.pdf).

United Nations Human Rights Council, the 2019 revised draft legally binding instrument to regulate, in international human rights law, the activities of transnational corporations and other business enterprises, available at: https://www.ohchr.org/Documents/HRBodies/HRCouncil/WGTransCorp/OEIGWG_RevisedDraft_LBI.pdf)

United Nations Human Rights Council, the 3rd revised draft legally binding instrument to regulate, in international human rights law, the activities of transnational corporations and other business enterprises, available at: https://www.ohchr.org/Documents/HRBodies/HRCouncil/WGTransCorp/Session6/LBI3rdDRAFT.pdf)

United Nations Human Rights Council, the Updated draft legally binding instrument to regulate, in international human rights law, the activities of transnational corporations and other business enterprises, available at: https://www.ohchr.org/sites/default/files/documents/hrbodies/hrcouncil/igwg-transcorp/session9/igwg-9th-updated-draft-lbi-track-changes.pdf (Accessed as of 15 December 2023).

United Nations Human Rights Council, *"Resolution adopted by the Human Rights Council: Human rights and transnational corporations and other business enterprises,"* (UN Doc., A/HRC/RES/17/4)

United Nations Human Rights Council, *"Resolution adopted by the Human Rights Council: Elaboration of an international legally binding instrument on transnational corporations and other business enterprises with respect to human rights,"* (UN Doc., A/HRC/RES/26/9)

United Nations Human Rights Council, *"Resolution adopted by the Human Rights Council: Human rights and transnational corporations and other business enterprises,"* (UN Doc., A/HRC/RES/26/22)

United Nations Human Rights Council, *"Resolution adopted by the Human Rights Council: Business and human rights: mandate of the Working Group on the issue of human rights and transnational corporations and other business enterprises,"* (UN Doc., A/HRC/RES/35/7)

United Nations Human Rights Council, *"Resolution adopted by the Human Rights Council on 8 October 2021 (48/13): The human right to a clean, healthy and sustainable environment,*" (UN Doc., A/HRC/RES/48/13)

United Nations Working Group on Business and Human Rights, *"Report of the Working Group on the issue of human rights and transnational corporations and other business enterprises,"* (UN Doc., A/67/285)

United Nations Working Group on Business and Human Rights, *"Report of the Working Group on the issue of human rights and transnational corporations and other business enterprises,"* (UN Doc., A/68/279)

United Nations Working Group on Business and Human Rights, *"Report of the Working Group on the issue of human rights and transnational corporations and other business enterprises to the UN General Assembly,"* (UN Doc., A/73/163)

United Nations Working Group on Business and Human Rights, *"Report of the Working Group on the issue of human rights and transnational corporations and other business enterprises to the UN General Assembly,"* (UN Doc. A/73/163)

United Nations Working Group on Business and Human Rights, *"Report of the Working Group on the issue of human rights and transnational corporations and other business enterprises,"* (UN Doc., A/HRC/20/29)

United Nations Working Group on Business and Human Rights, "*Report of the Working Group on the issue of human rights and transnational corporations and other business enterprises,"* (UN Doc., A/HRC/38/48)

United Nations Working Group on Business and Human Rights, "*Report of the Working Group on the issue of human rights and transnational corporations and other business enterprises: Gender dimensions of the Guiding Principles on Business and Human Rights*," (UN Doc, A/HRC/41/43)

United Nations Working Group on Business and Human Rights, *"Report of the Working Group on the issue of human rights and transnational corporations and other business enterprises: Gender dimensions of the Guiding Principles on Business and Human Rights, Annex, – 'Gender Guidance for the Guiding Principles on Business and Human Rights,'"* (UN Doc, A/HRC/41/43, Annex)

United Nations Working Group on Business and Human Rights, *"Seventh session of the Forum on Business and Human Rights: Report of the Working Group on the issue of human rights and transnational corporations and other business enterprises,"* (UN Doc., A/HRC/41/49)

United Nations Working Group on Business and Human Rights, *"Eighth session of the Forum on Business and Human Rights: Report of the Working Group on the issue of human rights and transnational corporations and other business enterprises,"* (UN

Doc., A/HRC/44/56)

United Nations Working Group on Business and Human Rights, *"Ninth session of the Forum on Business and Human Rights: Report of the Working Group on the issue of human rights and transnational corporations and other business enterprises,"* (UN Doc., A/HRC/47/50)

United Nations Working Group on Business and Human Rights, *"Guidance on National Action Plans on Business and Human Rights,"* available: https://www.ohchr.org/Documents/Issues/Business/UNWG_NAPGuidance.pdf

Statement by the Permanent Mission of India to the United Nations Human Rights Council (2014)

Statement by the Permanent Mission of the U.S. to the United Nations Human Rights Council (2014)

Submission by BIAC, ICC, IOE and WBCSD to the Open-ended Working Group on Business and Human Rights, "UN Treaty Process on Business and Human Rights, Further considerations by the international business community on a way forward" dated 29 September 2016

IV. OTHER INTERNATIONAL ORGANIZATIONS MATERIALS

International Labour Organization (ILO), *Tripartite Declaration of Principles concerning Multinational Enterprise and Social Policy*

International Labour Organization (ILO), *ANNEX II to the ILO Tripartite Declaration of Principles concerning Multinational Enterprise and Social Policy*

Organization for Economic Cooperation and Development (OECD), *Guidelines for Multinational Enterprises*

Organization for Economic Cooperation and Development (OECD), *Guidelines for Multinational Enterprises (2011 Edition) Commentary on General Principles*

Organization for Economic Cooperation and Development (OECD), *Due Diligence Guidance for Responsible Business Conduct*

Organization for Economic Cooperation and Development (OECD), *Due Diligence for Responsible Business Conduct in General Corporate Lending and Securities Underwriting*

Organization for Economic Cooperation and Development (OECD), *Due Diligence Guidance for Responsible Supply Chains from Conflict-Affected and High-Risk Areas (Minerals Guidance)*

Organization for Economic Cooperation and Development (OECD), *Due Diligence Guidance for Responsible Supply Chains in the Garment and Footwear Sector*

Organization for Economic Cooperation and Development (OECD), *OECD-FAO Guidance for Responsible Agricultural Supply Chains*

Organization for Economic Cooperation and Development (OECD), *Recommendation of the Council on the OECD-FAO Guidance for Responsible Agriculture Supply Chains*

Organization for Economic Cooperation and Development (OECD), *Recommendation of the Council on the Due Diligence Guidance for Meaningful Stakeholder Engagement in the Extractive Sector*

Organization for Economic Cooperation and Development (OECD), *"Guidelines for Multination Enterprises: Responsible Business Conduct Matters"* available at: http://mneguidelines.oecd.org/MNEguidelines_RBCmatters.pdf (Accessed as of 06 June 2019)

Organization for Economic Cooperation and Development (OECD), *"Implementing OECD Guidelines for Multinational Enterprises: The National Contact Points from 2000 to 2015"* available at: http://mneguidelines.oecd.org/15-Years-of-the-National-Contact-Points-Highlights.pdf. (Accessed as of 25 May 2022)

Organization for Economic Cooperation and Development (OECD), *Annual Report on the OECD Guidelines for Multinational Enterprises 2018*

European Commission, *"Proposal for a Directive on corporate sustainability due diligence and annex,"* available at:https://commission.europa.eu/publications/proposal-directive-corporate-sustainability-due-diligence-and-annex_en

Members of European Parliament (MEP): "Adopt a negotiation mandate to participate in the UN negotiations for a binding treaty on business and human rights," available at: https://www.business-humanrights.org/sites/default/files/documents/2020-07-20%20-%20EU%20Parliament%20-%20Letter%20requesting%20a%20negociation%20mandate.pdf

V. TREATIES AND DECLARATIONS

The United Nations Charter

The Universal Declaration of Human Rights (UDHR), adopted and proclaimed by General Assembly resolution 217 A (III) of 10 December 1948

The International Convention on the Elimination of All Forms of Racial Discrimination (ICERD), adopted and opened for signature and ratification by General Assembly resolution 2106 (XX) of 21 December 1965

The International Covenant on Economic, Social and Cultural Rights (ICESCR), adopted and opened for signature, ratification and accession by General Assembly resolution 2200 A(XXI) of 16 December 1966

The Optional Protocol to the International Covenant on Economic, Social and Cultural Rights, adopted by General Assembly resolution 63/117 of 10 December 2008

The International Covenant on Civil and Political Rights (ICCPR), adopted and opened for signature, ratification and accession by General Assembly resolution 2200 A(XXI) of 16 December 1966

The Optional Protocol to the International Covenant on Civil and Political Rights (OP1-ICCPR), adopted and opened for signature, ratification and accession by General Assembly resolution 2200 A(XXI) of 16 December 1966

The Second Optional Protocol to the International Covenant on Civil and Political Rights (OP2-ICCPR), aiming at the abolition of the death penalty, adopted and proclaimed by General Assembly resolution 44/128 of 15 December 1989

The Convention on the Elimination of All Forms of Discrimination Against Women (CEDAW), adopted and opened for signature, ratification and accession by General Assembly resolution 34/180 of 18 December 1979

The Optional Protocol to the Convention on the Elimination of All Forms of Discrimination against Women, adopted by General Assembly resolution 54/4 of 6 October 1999

The Convention against Torture and Other Cruel, Inhuman or Degrading Treatment or Punishment (CAT), adopted and opened for signature, ratification and accession by General Assembly resolution 39/46 of 10 December 1984

The Optional Protocol to the Convention against Torture and Other Cruel, Inhuman or Degrading Treatment or Punishment (OP-CAT), adopted on 18 December 2002 at the fifty-seventh session of the General Assembly of the United Nations by resolution A/RES/57/199 and entered into force on 22 June 2006

The Convention on the Rights of the Child (CRC), adopted and opened for signature, ratification and accession by General Assembly resolution 44/25 of 20 November 1989

The Optional Protocol to the Convention on the Rights of the Child on the sale of children, child prostitution and child pornography, adopted and opened for signature, ratification and accession by General Assembly resolution 54/263 of 25 May 2000

The Optional Protocol to the Convention on the Rights of the Child on the involvement of children in armed conflict, adopted and opened for signature, ratification and accession by General Assembly resolution 54/263 of 25 May 2000

The Optional Protocol to the Convention on the Rights of the Child on a communications procedure, adopted by General Assembly resolution 66/138 of 19 December 2011

The International Convention on the Protection of the Rights of All Migrant Workers and Members of their Families (ICRMW), adopted by General Assembly resolution 45/158 of 18 December 1990

The Convention on the Rights of Persons with Disabilities (CRPD), adopted and opened for signature, ratification and accession by General Assembly resolution 61/106 of 13 December 2006

The Optional Protocol to the Convention on the Rights of Persons with Disabilities, adopted and opened for signature, ratification and accession by General Assembly resolution 61/106 of 13 December 2006

The International Convention on the Protection of All Persons from Enforced Disappearance (CED), adopted by General Assembly resolution 47/133 of 23 December 2010

United Nations, Human Rights: A Compilation of International Instruments (2002) (New York/Geneva)

ILO Indigenous and Tribal Peoples Convention (No. 169)

The United Nations Guiding Principles on Business and Human Rights: Implementing the United Nations Protect, Respect and Remedy Framework, Office of the United Nations High Commissioner for Human Rights, UN Publication, HR/PUB/11/04

The United Nations, *The Vienna Declaration and Programme of Action,* adopted by the World Conference on Human Rights in Vienna on 25 June 1993

The United Nations, General Assembly *"Resolution adopted on the Report of the Joint First and Third committee"* UN Doc., A/RES/43(I)

The United Nations General Assembly resolution 60/147, 'Basic Principles and Guidelines on the Right to a Remedy and Reparation for Victims of Gross Violations of International Human Rights Law and Serious Violations of International Humanitarian Law

The United Nations Sub-Commission on the Promotion and Protection of Human Rights *"Norms on the responsibilities of transnational corporations and other business enterprises with regard to human rights"* (UN Doc., E/CN.4/Sub.2/2003/12/Rev.2)

The Alma-Ata Declaration on primary health care

VI. CASES AND JUDGMENTS

International Court of Justice, *Military and Paramilitary Activities in and against Nicaragua*

(Nicaragua v United States of America), Merits (1986) ICJ Reports 14

International Court of Justice, *North Sea Continental Shelf Cases* (Federal Republic of Germany/Denmark; Federal Republic of Gernmany/Netherlands) ICJ Reports (1969) 3

International Centre for Settlement of Investment Disputes Case No. ARB/07/26, *Urbaser S.A. and others v. Argentina* (award of 8 December 2016)

VII. NATIONAL LEGISLATION

The Duty of Vigilance Act *(Loi de Vigilance)* (France)

The Act on Corporate Due Diligence Obligations in Supply Chains *(Lieferkettengesetz)* (Germany)

The US Alien Tort Claims Act (First Judiciary Act 1789 (ch. 20, §9(b)), 28 USC. § 1350)

The US Torture Victim Protection Act (U.S.C. ch.85 § 1350)

The US Trafficking Victims Reauthorization Act (U.S.C. ch.78)

VIII. MISCELLOUNOUS

Amnesty International *"Comment on the draft General Comment on State Obligations under the International Covenant on Economic, Social and Cultural Rights in the Context of Business Activities"* available at: https://www.ohchr.org/EN/HRBodies/CESCR/Pages/Submissions2017.aspx

American Law Institute, *2 Restatement of the Law Third. The Foreign Relations Law of the United States* (St Paul, Minn, American Law Institute, 1987) 161

Black's Law Dictionary, 8th edition (2006)

Business and Human Rights Resource Centre, http://business-humanrights.org/media/documents/statement-unhrc-legally-binding.pdf

Business and Human Rights Resource Centre, *"EU Parliament legal affairs committee adopts report requesting Commission to submit formal due diligence proposal,"* available at: https://www.business-humanrights.org/en/latest-news/eu-parliament-legal-affairs-committee-adopts-report-requesting-commission-to-submit-formal-due-diligence-proposal/

Business and Human Rights Resource Centre, National & regional movements for mandatory human rights & environmental due diligence in Europe – Business & Human Rights Resource Centre (business-humanrights.org)

Business and Human Rights Resource Centre, 'Responsibility from the top down: Why human rights due diligence must be a mandated concern of corporate boards' and: https://www.business-humanrights.org/en/blog/responsibility-from-the-top-down-why-human-rights-due-diligence-must-be-a-mnadated-concern-of -corporate-boards/?mc_cid=28a2442285&mc_eid=1de65b4c6f

Business and Human Rights Resource Centre, https://www.business-humanrights.org/en/latest-news/national-regional-movements-for-mandatory-human-rights-environmental-due-diligence-in-europe/

Business and Human Rights Resource Centre, https://www.business-humanrights.org/en/will-germany-become-a-leader-in-the-drive-for-corporate-due-diligence-on-human-rights?utm_source=Business+%26+Human+Rights+Resource+Centre+Updates&utm_campaign=199fcfe071-EMAIL_CAMPAIGN_2019_02_18_06_20&utm_medium=email&utm_term=0_c0049647eb-199fcfe071-182077453&mc_cid=199fcfe071&mc_eid=1de65b4c6f

Business and Human Rights Resource Centre, https://www.business-humanrights.org/en/german-development-ministry-drafts-law-on-mandatory-human-rights-due-diligence-for-german-companies

Business and Human Rights Resource Centre, https://www.business-humanrights.org/en/latest-news/germany-draft-key-points-of-a-mandatory-human-rights-due-diligence-law/

Business and Human Rights Resource Centre, National & regional movements for mandatory human rights & environmental due diligence in Europe – Business & Human Rights Resource Centre (business-humanrights.org)

Business and Human Rights Resource Centre, https://www.business-humanrights.org/en/netherlands-momentum-builds-towards-mandatory-due-diligence-regulation#c211314

Blog of Dr. Ekaterina Aristova, *"Call for EU Human Rights Due Diligence Legislation: What Can Be Learnt from France and the Netherlands?"*, available at: https://www.business-humanrights.org/en/call-for-eu-human-rights-due-diligence-legislation-what-can-be-learnt-from-france-and-the-netherlands

Letter by the Confederation of German Employers' Associations (BDA) to the State Secretary of the Germany Foreign Office Stephan Steinlein dated 19 June 2014, re-quoted from Martens and Seitz, *The Struggle for a UN Treaty: Towards global regulation on human rights and business, published by Global Policy Forum and Rosa Luxembourg Stiftung -New York Office,* available at: https://www.globalpolicy.org/home/270-general/52867-new-publication-the-struggle-for-a-un-treaty.html

CIDSE, *"Now more than ever, we need mandatory supply chain due diligence: to stop corporate abuse and guarantee global solidarity,"* available at: https://www.cidse.org/wp-content/uploads/2020/07/EN-Bishop-Statement-HRDD-6-July-2020-1.pdf

Columbia Center on Sustainable Investment, Danish Institute for Human Rights, and Sciences Po Law School Clinic, *A Collaborative Approach to Human Rights Impact Assessments*, (March 2017)

Corporate Justice, 'The Initiative Text with Explanations,' available at: https://corporatejustice.ch/wp-content/uploads/2018/06/KVI_Factsheet_5_E.pdf.

Corporate Justice, *"A Call for EU human rights environmental due diligence legislation,"* available at: https://corporatejustice.org/news/final_cso_eu_due_diligence_statement_2.12.19.pdf

FIAN, http//www.ohchr.org/Documents/HRBodies/HRCouncil/WGTransCorp/Session1/Panel3/Others/Food-First_InformationaandActionNetworkFIAN.pdf

Global Witness, *"Important step towards greater corporate accountability as European Commission commits to new EU rules to regulate supply chains,"* available at: https://www.globalwitness.org/en/press-releases/important-step-towards-greater-corporate-accountability-european-commission-commits-new-eu-rules-regulate-supply-chains/?utm_source=hootsuite&utm_medium=twitter_

ICJ, 'Needs and Options for a New International Instrument in the Field of Business and Human Rights,' accessed at: http://www.burmalibrary.org/docs19/ICJ-2012-06-Business&HR-Needs_and_Options_for_an_international_instrument.pdf

International Association for Impact Assessment (IAIA), *Social Impact Assessment: International principles* Special Publication Series No. 2 (May 2003)

International Association for Impact Assessment (IAIA), *Social Impact Assessment: Guidance for assessing and managing the social impacts of projects* (April, 2015)

International Federation of Human Rights (FIDH) *Corporate Accountability for Human Rights Abuses: A Guide for Victims and NGOs on Recourse Mechanisms* available at: https://corporateaccountability.fidh.org/the-guide/

Statements of US delegates during the 4th UN Forum on Business and Human Rights, Geneva (delivered during the session on: "The United Nations treaty process on business and human rights: business and other perspectives" and on side event "Connecting the Guiding Principles with the business and human rights treaty process"

Treaty Alliance Germany, *"Briefing Paper on the Zero Draft: Unpacking Arguments Against A Treaty,"* available at: https://www.business-humanrights.org/sites/default/files/documents/TreatyAllianceGermany_CounterArguments_Briefing_2-2019_en.pdf

Terre-Solidaire and Sherpa, « *Le radar du devoir de vigilance: Identifier les entreprises submises à la loi, 2020 edition*," available at: https://plan-vigilance.org/wp-content/uploads/2020/06/2020-06-25-Radar-DDV-Edition-2020.pdf

Responsible Business Initiative: https://corporatejustice.ch/about-the-initiative/ and https://www.arcinfo.ch/articles/suisse/votations-du-29-novembre-les-multinationales-responsables-et-le-materiel-de-guerre-au-menu-952299

White & Case, 'The German Parliament passed the "Act on Corporate Due Diligence in Supply Chains," available at: https://www.whitecase.com/publications/alert/german-parliament-passed-act-corporate-due-diligence-supply-chains-11-june-2021

Federal Ministry of Labour and Social Affairs and Federal Ministry for Economic Cooperation and Development of Germany, *"Draft key points of a Federal law on strengthening corporate due diligence to prevent human rights violations in global value chains (Due Diligence Act),"* available at: https://www.rph1.rw.fau.de/files/2020/06/key-points-german-due-diligence-law.pdf.

Initiative Lieferkettengesetz.de, *"Not there yet, but finally at the start: What the new Supply Chain Act delivers – and what it doesn't,"* https://lieferkettengesetz.de/wp-content/uploads/2021/06/Initiative-Lieferkettengesetz_Analysis_What-the-new-supply-chain-act-delivers.pdf

Letter by CSOs to Finland, the 2018 EU Presidency, available at: http://corporatejustice.org/news/12676-csos-call-for-an-ambitious-business-and-human-rights-agenda-during-the-finnish-eu-presidency

Index

R

S

T

U

[Cover Photo Description]

New York Cityscape